Lecture Notes in Artificial Intelligence 5042

Edited by R. Goebel, J. Siekmann, and W. Wahlster

Subseries of Lecture Notes in Computer Science

Anna Esposito   Nikolaos G. Bourbakis
Nikolaos Avouris   Ioannis Hatzilygeroudis (Eds.)

Verbal and Nonverbal Features of Human-Human and Human-Machine Interaction

COST Action 2102 International Conference
Patras, Greece, October 29-31, 2007
Revised Papers

Springer

Series Editors

Randy Goebel, University of Alberta, Edmonton, Canada
Jörg Siekmann, University of Saarland, Saarbrücken, Germany
Wolfgang Wahlster, DFKI and University of Saarland, Saarbrücken, Germany

Volume Editors

Anna Esposito
Department of Psychology, Second University of Naples,
and IIASS, Vietri sul Mare (SA), Italy
E-mail: iiass.annaesp@tin.it

Nikolaos G. Bourbakis
ATRC Center, Wright State University
Dayton, Ohio, USA
E-mail: nikolaos.bourbakis@wright.edu

Nikolaos Avouris
Electrical and Computer Engineering Department
University of Patras, Patras, Greece
E-mail: avouris@upatras.gr

Ioannis Hatzilygeroudis
Computer Engineering and Informatics Department
University of Patras, Patras, Greece
E-mail: ihatz@ceid.upatras.gr

Library of Congress Control Number: Applied for

CR Subject Classification (1998): I.5, I.4, I.2.10, I.2

LNCS Sublibrary: SL 7 – Artificial Intelligence

ISSN   0302-9743
ISBN-10   3-540-70871-5 Springer Berlin Heidelberg New York
ISBN-13   978-3-540-70871-1 Springer Berlin Heidelberg New York

Springer is a part of Springer Science+Business Media

springer.com

© Springer-Verlag Berlin Heidelberg 2008
Printed in Germany

Typesetting: Camera-ready by author, data conversion by Scientific Publishing Services, Chennai, India
Printed on acid-free paper   SPIN: 12443017   06/3180   5 4 3 2 1 0

Preface

This book is dedicated to the dreamers, their dreams, and their perseverance in research work.

This volume brings together the selected and peer–reviewed contributions of the participants at the COST 2102 International Conference on Verbal and Nonverbal Features of Human–Human and Human–Machine Interaction, held in Patras, Greece, October 29–31, 2007, hosted by the 19th IEEE International Conference on Tools with Artificial Intelligence (ICTAI 2008).

The conference was sponsored by COST (European Cooperation in the Field of Scientific and Technical Research, www.cost.esf.org) in the domain of Information and Communication Technologies (ICT) for disseminating the advances of the research activity developed within COST Action 2102: "Cross-Modal Analysis of Verbal and Nonverbal Communication"(www.cost2102.eu).

COST Action 2102 is a network of about 60 European and 6 overseas laboratories whose aim is to develop *"an advanced acoustical, perceptual and psychological analysis of verbal and non-verbal communication signals originating in spontaneous face-to-face interaction, in order to identify algorithms and automatic procedures capable of identifying the human emotional states. Particular care is devoted to the recognition of emotional states, gestures, speech and facial expressions, in anticipation of the implementation of intelligent avatars and interactive dialogue systems that could be exploited to improve user access to future telecommunication services"*(see COST 2102 Memorandum of Understanding (MoU) www.cost2102.eu).

The main theme of the conference was to foster existing and growing connections between the emerging field of technology devoted to the identification of individuals using biological traits and the fundamentals of verbal and nonverbal communication which include facial expressions, tones of voice, gestures, eye contact, spatial arrangements, patterns of touch, expressive movement, cultural differences, and other "nonverbal" acts.

The research topics proposed by the conference were particularly computer science oriented in order to be in theme with the call for features of human–computer interaction. The contributors to this volume are leading authorities in their respective fields. We are grateful to them for accepting our invitation and making (through their participation) the conference such a worthwhile event.

The book is broadly divided into two scientific areas according to a thematic classification, even though all the areas are closely connected and all provide fundamental insights for cross-fertilization of different disciplines.

The first area, "Static and Dynamic Processing of Faces, Facial Expressions, and Gaze," deals with the theoretical and computational issue of defining algorithms, programming languages, and determinist models for recognizing faces, emotions in faces, for synthesizing facial expressions and exploiting facial information during the interaction with interactive dialogue systems and intelligent avatars.

The second area, "Emotional Speech Synthesis and Recognition: Applications to Telecommunication Systems," underlines the importance of vocal emotional communication and reports on advanced experiments for the recognition and synthesis of emotional and non-emotional vocal expressions.

The editors would like to thank the COST- ICT Programme for its support in the realization and publication of this volume, and in particular the COST Science Officers Julia Stamm, and Sophie Beaubron for their constant help, guidance and encouragement. Great appreciation goes to Maria Marinaro, for her interest and support of the event.

Special appreciation goes to Tina Marcella Nappi of the International Institute for Advanced Scientific Studies, whose help in the organization of this volume was invaluable.

Finally, we are most grateful to all the contributors to this volume and all the participants in the COST 2102 International Conference for their cooperation, interest, enthusiasm and lively interactions, making it a scientifically stimulating gathering and a memorable personal experience.

Anna Esposito
Nikolaos G. Bourbakis
Nikolaos Avouris
Ioannis Hatzilygeroudis

Organization

International Advisory and Organizing Committee

Nikolaos Avouris	University of Patras, Greece
Nikolaos Bourbakis	Wright State University, USA
Anna Esposito	Second University of Naples, and IIASS, Italy
Nikos Fakotakis	University of Patras, Greece
Marcos Faundez-Zanuy	University of Mataro, Barcelona, Spain
Ioannis Hatzilygeroudis	University of Patras, Greece
Eric Keller	University of Lausanne, Switzerland

International Scientific Committee

Uwe Altmann	Technische Universität Dresden, Germany
Nikos Avouris	University of Patras, Greece
Ruth Bahr	University of South Florida, USA
Gérard Bailly ICP	Grenoble, France
Jean-Francois Bonastre	Universitè d'Avignon, France
Niels Ole Bernsen	University of Southern Denmark, Denmark
Jonas Beskow	Royal Institute of Technology, Sweden
Horst Bishof	Technical University Graz, Austria
Nikolaos Bourbakis	ITRI, Wright State University, Dayton, OH, USA
Maja Bratanić	University of Zagreb, Croatia
Antonio Calabrese	Istituto di Cibernetica – CNR, Naples, Italy
Paola Campadelli	Università di Milano, Italy
Nick Campbell	ATR Human Information Science Labs, Kyoto, Japan
Antonio Castro Fonseca	Universidade de Coimbra, Coimbra, Portugal
Aleksandra Cerekovic	Faculty of Electrical Engineering, Croatia
Mohamed Chetouani	Universitè Pierre et Marie Curie, France
Gerard Chollet	CNRS-LTCI, Paris, France
Muzeyyen Ciyiltepe	Gulhane Askeri Tip Academisi, Ankara, Turkey
Anton Čižmár	Technical University of Košice, Slovakia
Francesca D'Olimpio	Second University of Naples, Italy
Thierry Dutoit	Faculté Polytechnique de Mons, Belgium
Laila Dybkjær	University of Southern Denmark, Denmark
Matthias Eichner	Technische Universität Dresden, Germany
Aly El-Bahrawy	Faculty of Engineering, Cairo, Egypt
Engin Erzin	Koc University, Istanbul, Turkey
Anna Esposito	Second University of Naples, and IIASS, Italy
Sascha Fagel	Technische Universität Berlin, Germany
Nikos Fakotakis	University of Patras, Greece

Marcos Faundez-Zanuy	Escola Universitaria de Mataro, Spain
Dilek Fidan	Ankara Universitesi, Turkey
Carmen García-Mateo	University of Vigo, Spain
Björn Granström	Royal Institute of Technology, KTH, Sweden
Mohand-Said Hacid	Universitè Claude Bernard Lyon 1, France
Jaakko Hakulinen	University of Tampere, Finland
Ioannis Hatzilygeroudis	University of Patras, Greece
Immaculada Hernaez	University of the Basque Country, Spain
Javier Hernando	Technical University of Catalonia, Spain
Wolfgang Hess	Universität Bonn, Germany
Dirk Heylen	University of Twente, The Netherlands
Rüdiger Hoffmann	Technische Universität Dresden, Germany
David House	Royal Institute of Technology (KTH), Sweden
Amir Hussain	University of Stirling, UK
Ewa Jarmolowicz	Adam Mickiewicz University, Poznan, Poland
Jozef Juhár	Technical University Košice, Slovak Republic
Zdravko Kacic	University of Maribor, Slovenia
Maciej Karpinski	Adam Mickiewicz University, Poznan, Poland
Eric Keller	Université de Lausanne, Switzerland
Adam Kendon	University of Pennsylvania, USA
Stefan Kopp	University of Bielefeld, Germany
Jacques Koreman	University of Science and Technology, Norway
Robert Krauss	Columbia University New York, USA
Bernd Kröger	Aachen University, Germany
Gernot Kubin	Graz University of Technology, Austria
Alida Labella	Second University of Naples, Italy
Borge Lindberg	Aalborg University, Denmark
Wojciech Majewski	Wroclaw University of Technology, Poland
Pantelis Makris	Neuroscience and Technology Institute, Cyprus
Maria Marinaro	Salerno University and IIASS, Italy
Raffaele Martone	Second University of Naples, Italy
Dominic Massaro	University of California - Santa Cruz, USA
David McNeill	University of Chicago, USA
Nicola Melone	Second University of Naples, Italy
Peter Murphy	University of Limerick, Limerick, Ireland
Antonio Natale	Salerno University and IIASS, Italy
Eva Navas	Escuela Superior de Ingenieros, Bilbao, Spain
Géza Németh	Budapest University of Technology, Hungary
Friedrich Neubarth	Research Inst. Artificial Intelligence, Austria
Giovanna Nigro	Second University of Naples, Italy
Anton Nijholt	University of Twente, The Netherlands
Jan Nouza	Technical University of Liberec, Czech Republic
Igor Pandzic	Faculty of Electrical Engineering, Croatia
Harris Papageorgiou	Inst. for Language and Speech Processing, Greece
Ana Pavia	Spoken Language Systems Laboratory, Portugal
Catherine Pelachaud	Universite de Paris 8, France
Bojan Petek	University of Ljubljana, Slovenia

Harmut R. Pfitzinger	University of Munich, Germany
Francesco Piazza	Università Politecnica delle Marche, Italy
Neda Pintaric	University of Zagreb, Croatia
Isabella Poggi	Università di Roma 3, Italy
Jiří Přibil	Academy of Sciences, Czech Republic
Anna Přibilová	Slovak University of Technology, Slovakia
Michael Pucher	Telecommunications Research Center Vienna, Austria
Jurate Puniene	Kaunas University of Technology, Lithuania
Giuliana Ramella	Istituto di Cibernetica – CNR, Naples, Italy
Kari-Jouko Räihä	University of Tampere, Finland
José Rebelo	Universidade de Coimbra, Coimbra, Portugal
Luigi Maria Ricciardi	Università di Napoli "Federico II", Italy
Matej Rojc	University of Maribor, Slovenia
Algimantas Rudzionis	Kaunas University of Technology, Lithuania
Milan Rusko	Slovak Academy of Sciences, Slovak Republic
Zsófia Ruttkay	Pazmany Peter Catholic University, Hungary
Yoshinori Sagisaka	Waseda University, Tokyo, Japan
Silvia Scarpetta	Salerno University, Italy
Jean Schoentgen	Université Libre de Bruxelles, Belgium
Stefanie Shattuck-Hufnagel	MIT, Cambridge, MA, USA
Zdeněk Smékal	Brno University of Technology, Czech Republic
Stefano Squartini	Università Politecnica delle Marche, Italy
Piotr Staroniewicz	Wroclaw University of Technology, Poland
Vojtěch Stejskal	Brno University of Technology, Czech Republic
Marian Stewart-Bartlett	University of California, San Diego, USA
Jianhua Tao	Chinese Academy of Sciences, P. R. China
Jure F.Tasič	University of Ljubljana, Slovenia
Kristinn Thórisson	Reykjavík University, Iceland
Isabel Trancoso	Spoken Language Systems Laboratory, Portugal
Luigi Trojano	Second University of Naples, Italy
Wolfgang Tschacher	University of Bern, Switzerland
Markku Turunen	University of Tampere, Finland
Henk Van Den Heuvel	Radboud University Nijmegen, The Netherlands
Robert Vích	Academy of Sciences, Czech Republic
Klára Vicsi	Budapest University of Technology, Budapest, Hungary
Leticia Vicente-Rasoamalala	Alchi Prefectural University, Japan
Hannes Högni Vilhjálmsson	Reykjavík University, Iceland
Carl Vogel	University of Dublin, Ireland
Rosa Volpe	Université De Perpignan Via Domitia, France
Yorick Wilks	University of Sheffield, UK
Matthias Wimmer	Technische Universität Müchen, Germany
Matthias Wolf	Technische Universität Dresden, Germany

Bencie Woll	University College London, UK
Bayya Yegnanarayana	Institute of Information Technology, India
Jerneja Žganec Gros	Alpineon, Development and Research, Slovenia
Goranka Zoric	Faculty of Electrical Engineering, Croatia

Sponsors

The following organizations supported and sponsored COST Action 2102:

- European COST Action 2102 *"Cross Modal Analysis of Verbal and Nonverbal Communication"* www.cost2102.eu
- Second University of Naples, Faculty of Psychology (Italy)
- International Institute for Advanced Scientific Studies "E.R. Caianiello" (IIASS), Italy
- University of Patras, Greece, www.upatras.gr
- Regione Campania (Italy)
- Provincia di Salerno (Italy)

Table of Contents

Data Mining Spontaneous Facial Behavior with Automatic Expression Coding

Marian Bartlett[1], Gwen Littlewort[1], Esra Vural[1,3], Kang Lee[2],
Mujdat Cetin[3], Aytul Ercil[3], and Javier Movellan[1]

[1] Institute for Neural Computation, University of California,
San Diego, La Jolla, CA 92093-0445, USA
[2] Human Development and Applied Psychology, University of Toronto, Ontario, Canada
[3] Engineering and Natural Science, Sabanci University, Istanbul, Turkey
mbartlett@ucsd.edu, gwen@mpmlab.ucsd.edu,
movellan@mplab.ucsd.edu, vesra@ucsd.edu, kang.lee@utoronto.ca

Abstract. The computer vision field has advanced to the point that we are now able to begin to apply automatic facial expression recognition systems to important research questions in behavioral science. The machine perception lab at UC San Diego has developed a system based on machine learning for fully automated detection of 30 actions from the facial action coding system (FACS). The system, called Computer Expression Recognition Toolbox (CERT), operates in real-time and is robust to the video conditions in real applications. This paper describes two experiments which are the first applications of this system to analyzing spontaneous human behavior: Automated discrimination of posed from genuine expressions of pain, and automated detection of driver drowsiness. The analysis revealed information about facial behavior during these conditions that were previously unknown, including the coupling of movements. Automated classifiers were able to differentiate real from fake pain significantly better than naïve human subjects, and to detect critical drowsiness above 98% accuracy. Issues for application of machine learning systems to facial expression analysis are discussed.

Keywords: Facial expression recognition, machine learning.

Based on the following two conference papers:

(1) Littlewort, G., Bartlett, M.S. and Lee, K., (2007). Automated measurement of spontaneous facial expressions of genuine and posed pain. Proc. International Conference on Multimodal Interfaces, Nagoya, Japan. Copyright 2007 ACM 978-1-59593-817-6/07/0011.
(2) Vural, E., Cetin, M., Ercil, A., Littlewort, G., Bartlett, M., and Movellan, J. (2007). Machine learning systems for detecting driver drowsiness. Proc. Digital Signal Processing for in-Vehicle and mobile systems, Istanbul, Turkey. Copyright 2007 IEEE.

1 Introduction

The computer vision field has advanced to the point that we are now able to begin to apply automatic facial expression recognition systems to important research questions in behavioral science. This paper is among the first applications of fully automated

A. Esposito et al. (Eds.): HH and HM Interaction 2007, LNAI 5042, pp. 1–20, 2008.
© Springer-Verlag Berlin Heidelberg 2008

facial expression measurement to such research questions. It explores two applications of a machine learning system for automatic facial expression measurement to data mine spontaneous human behavior (1) differentiating fake from real expressions of pain, and (2) detecting driver drowsiness.

1.1 The Facial Action Coding System

The facial action coding system (FACS) (Ekman and Friesen, 1978) is arguably the most widely used method for coding facial expressions in the behavioral sciences. The system describes facial expressions in terms of 46 component movements, which roughly correspond to the individual facial muscle movements. An example is shown in Figure 1. FACS provides an objective and comprehensive way to analyze expressions into elementary components, analagous to decomposition of speech into phonemes. Because it is comprehensive, FACS has proven useful for discovering facial movements that are indicative of cognitive and affective states. See Ekman and Rosenberg (2005) for a review of facial expression studies using FACS. The primary limitation to the widespread use of FACS is the time required to code. FACS was developed for coding by hand, using human experts. It takes over 100 hours of training to become proficient in FACS, and it takes approximately 2 hours for human experts to code each minute of video. The authors have been developing methods for fully automating the facial action coding system (e.g. Donato et al., 1999; Bartlett et al., 2006). In this paper we apply a computer vision system trained to automatically detect FACS to data mine facial behavior under two conditions: (1) real versus fake pain, and (2) driver fatigue.

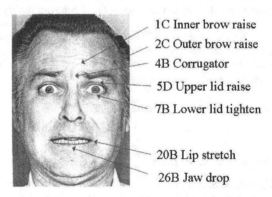

Fig. 1. Example facial action decomposition from the facial action coding system. A prototypical expression of fear is decomposed into 7 component movements. Letters indicate intensity. A fear brow (1+2+4) is illustrated here.

1.2 Spontaneous Expressions

The machine learning system presented here was trained on spontaneous facial expressions. The importance of using spontaneous behavior for developing and testing computer vision systems becomes apparent when we examine the neurological substrate for facial expression. There are two distinct neural pathways that mediate facial expressions, each one originating in a different area of the brain. Volitional facial movements originate in the cortical motor strip, whereas spontaneous facial expressions originate in the subcortical areas of the brain (see Rinn, 1984, for a review). These two pathways have different patterns of innervation on the face, with the cortical system tending to give stronger innervation to certain muscles primarily in the lower face, while the subcortical system tends to more strongly innervate certain muscles primarily in the upper face (e.g. Morecraft et al., 2001).

The facial expressions mediated by these two pathways have differences both in which facial muscles are moved and in their dynamics (Ekman, 2001; Ekman & Rosenberg, 2005). Subcortically initiated facial expressions (the spontaneous group) are characterized by synchronized, smooth, symmetrical, consistent, and reflex-like facial muscle movements whereas cortically initiated facial expressions (posed expressions) are subject to volitional real-time control and tend to be less smooth, with more variable dynamics (Rinn, 1984; Frank, Ekman, & Friesen, 1993; Schmidt, Cohn & Tian, 2003; Cohn & Schmidt, 2004).   Given the two different neural pathways for facial expressions, it is reasonable to expect to find differences between genuine and posed expressions of states such as pain or drowsiness. Moreover, it is crucial that the computer vision model for detecting states such as genuine pain or driver drowsiness is based on machine learning of expression samples when the subject is actually experiencing the state in question.

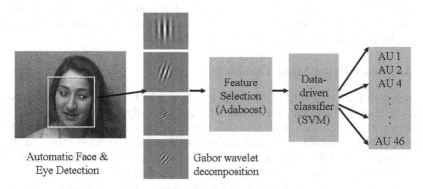

Fig. 2. Overview of the automated facial action recognition system

2 The Computer Expression Recognition Toolbox (CERT)

Here we extend a system for fully automated facial action coding developed previously by the authors (Bartlett et. Al, 2006; Littlewort et al., 2006). It is a user independent fully automatic system for real time recognition of facial actions from the Facial Action Coding System (FACS). The system automatically detects frontal faces in the video stream and codes each frame with respect to 20 Action units. In previous work, we conducted empirical investigations of machine learning methods applied to the related problem of classifying expressions of basic emotions. We compared image features (e.g. Donato et al., 1999), classifiers such as AdaBoost, support vector machines, and linear discriminant analysis, as well as feature selection techniques

(Littlewort et al., 2006). Best results were obtained by selecting a subset of Gabor filters using AdaBoost and then training Support Vector Machines on the outputs of the filters selected by AdaBoost. An overview of the system is shown in Figure 2.

2.1 Real Time Face and Feature Detection

We employed a real-time face detection system that uses boosting techniques in a generative framework (Fasel et al.) and extends work by Viola and Jones (2001). Enhancements to Viola and Jones include employing Gentleboost instead of AdaBoost, smart feature search, and a novel cascade training procedure, combined in a generative framework. Source code for the face detector is freely available at http://kolmogorov.sourceforge.net. Accuracy on the CMU-MIT dataset, a standard public data set for benchmarking frontal face detection systems (Schneiderman & Kanade, 1998), is 90% detections and 1/million false alarms, which is state-of-the-art accuracy. The CMU test set has unconstrained lighting and background. With controlled lighting and background, such as the facial expression data employed here, detection accuracy is much higher. All faces in the training datasets, for example, were successfully detected. The system presently operates at 24 frames/second on a 3 GHz Pentium IV for 320x240 images. The automatically located faces were rescaled to 96x96 pixels. The typical distance between the centers of the eyes was roughly 48 pixels. Automatic eye detection (Fasel et al., 2005) was employed to align the eyes in each image. The images were then passed through a bank of Gabor filters 8 orientations and 9 spatial frequencies (2:32 pixels per cycle at 1/2 octave steps). Output magnitudes were then passed to the action unit classifiers.

2.2 Automated Facial Action Classification

The approach presented here is a 2-stage system in which first an automated system CERT, is developed for detecting action units, and secondly CERT is applied to spontaneous examples of a state in question, and machine learning is applied to the CERT outputs. Here we describe the training of the facial action detectors in the first stage. The training data for the facial action classifiers came from three posed datasets and one dataset of spontaneous expressions. The facial expressions in each dataset were FACS coded by certified FACS coders. The first posed dataset was the Cohn-Kanade DFAT-504 dataset (Kanade, Cohn & Tian, 2000). This dataset consists of 100 university students who were instructed by an experimenter to perform a series of 23 facial displays, including expressions of seven basic emotions. The second posed dataset consisted of directed facial actions from 24 subjects collected by Ekman and Hager. Subjects were instructed by a FACS expert on the display of individual facial actions and action combinations, and they practiced with a mirror. The resulting video was verified for AU content by two certified FACS coders. The third posed dataset consisted of a subset of 50 videos from 20 subjects from the MMI database (Pantic et al., 2005). The spontaneous expression dataset consisted of the FACS-101 dataset collected by Mark Frank (Bartlett et al. 2006). 33 subjects underwent an interview about political opinions on which they felt strongly. Two minutes of each subject were FACS coded. The total training set consisted of 5500 examples, 2500 from posed databases and 3000 from the spontaneous set.

Twenty linear Support Vector Machines were trained for each of 20 facial actions. Separate binary classifiers, one for each action, were trained to detect the presence of the action in a one versus all manner. Positive examples consisted of the apex frame for the target AU. Negative examples consisted of all apex frames that did not contain

Table 1. (a) AU detection performance on posed and spontaneous facial actions. Values are Area under the roc (A') for generalization to novel subjects. (b) Additional 13 AU's trained for the driver fatigue study.

(a)

AU	Name	Posed	Spont
1	Inner brow raise	.90	.88
2	Outer brow raise	.94	.81
4	Brow Lower	.98	.73
5	Upper Lid Raise	.98	.80
6	Cheek Raise	.85	.89
7	Lids tight	.96	.77
9	Nose wrinkle	.99	.88
10	Upper lip raise	.98	.78
12	Lip corner pull	.97	.92
14	Dimpler	.90	.77
15	Lip corner Depress	.80	.83
17	Chin Raise	.92	.80
18	Lip Pucker	.87	.70
20	Lip stretch	.98	.60
23	Lip tighten	.89	.63
24	Lip press	.84	.80
25	Lips part	.98	.71
26	Jaw drop	.98	.71
1,1+4	Distress brow	.94	.70
1+2+4	Fear brow	.95	.63
Mean:		.93	.77

(b)

AU	Name
8	Lip Toward Each Other
11	Nasolabial Furrow Deepener
13	Sharp Lip Puller
16	Lower Lip Depress
19	Tongue Show
22	Lip Funneller
27	Mouth Stretch
28	Lips Suck
30	Jaw Sideways
32	Bite
38	Nostril Dilate
39	Nostril Compress
45	Blink

the target AU plus neutral images obtained from the first frame of each sequence. Eighteen of the detectors were for individual action units, and two of the detectors were for specific brow region combinations: fear brow (1+2+4) and distress brow (1 alone or 1+4). All other detectors were trained to detect the presence of the target action regardless of co-occurring actions. A list is shown in Table 1A. Thirteen additional AU's were trained for the Driver Fatigue Study. These are shown in Table 1B.

The output of the system was a real valued number indicating the distance to the separating hyperplane for each classifier. Previous work showed that the distance to the separating hyperplane (the margin) contained information about action unit intensity (e.g. Bartlett et al., 2006).

In this paper, area under the ROC (A') is used to assess performance rather than overall percent correct, since percent correct can be an unreliable measure of performance, as it depends on the proportion of targets to non-targets, and also on the decision threshold. Similarly, other statistics such as true positive and false positive rates depend on decision threshold, which can complicate comparisons across systems. A' is a measure is derived from signal detection theory and characterizes the discriminative capacity of the signal, independent of decision threshold. The ROC curve is obtained by plotting true positives against false positives as the decision threshold shifts from 0 to 100% detections. The area under the ROC (A') ranges from 0.5 (chance) to 1 (perfect discrimination). A' can also be interpreted in terms of percent correct. A' is equivalent to the theoretical maximum percent correct achievable with the information provided by the system when using a 2-Alternative Forced Choice testing paradigm.

Table 1 shows performance for detecting facial actions in posed and spontaneous facial actions. Generalization to novel subjects was tested using 3-fold cross-validation on the images in the training set. Performance was separated into the posed set, which was 2,500 images, and a spontaneous set, which was 1100 images from the FACS-101 database which includes speech.

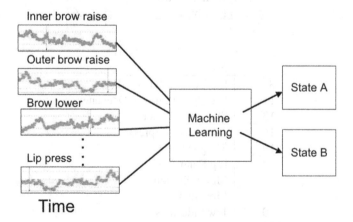

Fig. 3. Data mining human behavior. CERT is applied to face videos containing spontaneous expressions of states in question. Machine learning is applied to the outputs of CERT to learn a classifier to automatically discriminate state A from State B.

The overall CERT system gives a frame-by-frame output with N channels, consisting of N facial actions. This system can be applied to data mine human behavior. By applying CERT to face video while subjects experience spontaneous expressions of a given state, we can learn new things about the facial behaviors associated with that state. Also, by passing the N channel output to a machine learning system, we can directly train detectors for the specific state in question. (See Figure 3.) In Sections 3 and 4, two implementations of this idea are described.

3 Classification of Real Versus Faked Pain Expressions

An important issue in medicine is the ability to distinguish real pain from faked pain, (malingering). Some studies suggest that malingering rates are as high as 10% in chronic pain patients (Fishbain et a., 1999), and much higher in litigation contexts (Schmand et al., 1998). Even more important is to recognize when patients are experiencing genuine pain so that their pain is taken seriously. There is presently no reliable method for physicians to differentiate faked from real pain (Fishbain, 2006). Naïve human subjects are near chance for differentiating real from fake pain from observing facial expression (e.g. Hadjistavropoulos et al., 1996). In the absence of direct training in facial expressions, clinicians are also poor at assessing pain from the face (e.g. Prkachin et al. 2002; Grossman, 1991). However a number of studies using the Facial Action Coding System (FACS) (Ekman & Friesen, 1978) have shown that information exists in the face for differentiating real from posed pain (e.g. Hill and Craig, 2002; Craig et al., 1991; Prkachin 1992).

In previous studies using manual FACS coding by human experts, at least 12 facial actions showed significant relationships with pain across multiple studies and pain modalities. Of these, the ones specifically associated with cold pressor pain were 4, 6, 7, 9, 10, 12, 25, 26 (Craig & Patrick, 1985; Prkachin, 1992). See Table 1 and Figure 2 for names and examples of these AU's. A previous study compared faked to real pain, but in a different pain modality (lower back pain). This study found that when faking subjects tended to display the following AU's: 4, 6, 7, 10, 12, 25. When faked pain expressions were compared to real pain expressions, the faked pain expressions contained significantly more brow lower (AU 4), cheek raise (AU 6), and lip corner pull (AU 12) (Craig, Hyde & Patrick, 1991). These studies also reported substantial individual differences in the expressions of both real pain and faked pain.

Recent advances in automated facial expression measurement, such as the CERT system described above, open up the possibility of automatically differentiating posed from real pain using computer vision systems (e.g. Bartlett et al., 2006; Littlewort et al., 2006; Cohn & Schmidt, 2004; Pantic et al., 2006). This section explores the application of CERT to this problem.

3.1 Human Subject Methods

Video data was collected of 26 human subjects during real pain, faked pain, and baseline conditions. Human subjects were university students consisting of 6 men and 20 women. The pain condition consisted of cold pressor pain induced by immersing the arm in cold water at 5^0 Celsius. For the baseline and faked pain conditions, the water was 20^0 Celsius. Subjects were instructed to immerse their forearm into the water up to the elbow, and hold it there for 60 seconds in each of the three conditions. The order of the conditions was baseline, faked pain, and then real pain. For the faked pain condition, subjects were asked to manipulate their facial expressions so that an "expert would be convinced they were in actual pain." Participants facial expressions were recorded using a digital video camera during each condition. Examples are shown in Figure 4.

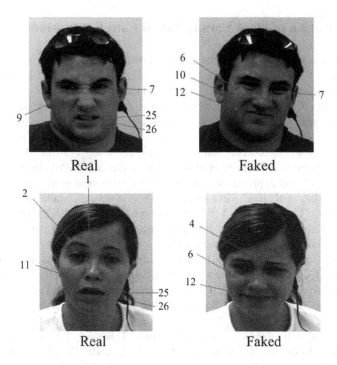

Fig. 4. Sample facial behavior and facial action codes from the real and faked pain conditions

A second subject group underwent the conditions in the counterbalanced order, with real pain followed by faked pain. This ordering involves immediate motor memory, which is a fundamentally different task. The present paper therefore analyzes only the first subject group. The second group will be analyzed separately in a future paper, and compared to the first group.

After the videos were collected, a set of 170 naïve observers were shown the videos and asked to guess whether each video contained faked or real pain. Subjects were undergraduates with no explicit training in facial expression measurement. They were primarily Introductory Psychology students at UCSD. Mean accuracy of naïve human subjects for discriminating fake from real pain in these videos was at chance at 49.1% (standard deviation 13.7%). These observers had no specific training in facial expression and were not clinicians. One might suppose that clinicians would be more accurate. However previous studies suggest that clinicians judgments of pain from the face are similarly unreliable (e.g. Grossman, 1991). Facial signals do appear to exist however (Hill & Craig, 2002, Craig et al., 1991; Prkachin 1992), and immediate corrective feedback has been shown to improve observer accuracy (Hill & Craig, 2004).

3.2 Human Expert FACS Coding

In order to assess the validity of the automated system, we first obtained FACS codes for a portion of the video from a human FACS expert certified in the Facial Action Coding System. For each subject, the last 500 frames of the fake pain and real pain conditions were FACS coded (about 15 seconds each). It took 60 man hours to collect the human codes, over the course of more than 3 months, since human coders can only code up to 2 hours per day before having negative repercussions in accuracy and coder burn-out.

The sum of the frames containing each action unit were collected for each subject condition, as well as a weighted sum, multiplied by the intensity of the action on a 1-5 scale. To investigate whether any action units successfully differentiated real from faked pain, paired t-tests were computed on each individual action unit. (Tests on specific brow region combinations 1+2+4 and 1,1+4 have not yet been conducted.) The one action unit that significantly differentiated the two conditions was AU 4, brow lower, (p<.01) for both the sum and weighted sum measures. This finding is consistent with the analysis of the automated system, which also found action unit 4 most discriminative.

3.3 Automated Coding

3.3.1 Characterizing the Differences between Real and Faked Pain

Applying CERT to the pain video data produced a 20 channel output stream, consisting of one real value for each learned AU, for each frame of the video. This data was further analyzed to predict the difference between baseline and pained faces, and the difference between expressions of real pain and fake pain.

We first examined which facial action detectors were elevated in real pain compared to the baseline condition. Z-scores for each subject and each AU detector were computed as $Z=(x-\mu)/\sigma$, where (μ,σ) are the mean and variance for the output of frames 100-1100 in the baseline condition (warm water, no faked expressions). The mean difference in Z-score between the baseline and pain conditions was computed across the 26 subjects. Table 2 shows the action detectors with the largest difference in Z-scores. We observed that the actions with the largest Z-scores for genuine pain were Mouth opening and jaw drop (25 and 26), lip corner puller by zygomatic (12), nose wrinkle (9), and to a lesser extent, lip raise (10) and cheek raise (6). These facial actions have been previously associated with cold pressor pain (e.g. Prkachin, 1992; Craig & Patrick 1985).

The Z-score analysis was next repeated for faked versus baseline. We observed that in faked pain there was relatively more facial activity than in real pain. The facial action outputs with the highest z-scores for faked pain relative to baseline were brow lower (4), distress brow (1 or 1+4), inner brow raise (1), mouth open and jaw drop (25 and 26), cheek raise (6), lip raise (10), fear brow (1+2+4), nose wrinkle (9), mouth stretch (20), and lower lid raise (7).

Table 2. Z-score differences of the three pain conditions, averaged across subjects. FB: Fear brow 1+2+4. DB: Distress brow (1,1+4).

A. Real Pain vs baseline:

Action Unit	25	12	9	26	10	6
Z-score	1.4	1.4	1.3	1.2	0.9	0.9

B. Faked Pain vs Baseline:

Action Unit	4	DB	1	25	12	6	26	10	FB	9	20	7
Z-score	2.7	2.1	1.7	1.5	1.4	1.4	1.3	1.3	1.2	1.1	1.0	0.9

C. Real Pain vs Faked Pain:

Action Unit	4	DB	1
Z-score difference	1.8	1.7	1.0

Table 3. Individual subject differences between faked and genuine pain. Differences greater than 2 standard deviations are shown. F>P: Number of subjects in which the output for the given AU was greater in faked than genuine pain. P>F: Number of subjects for which the output was greater in genuine than faked pain. FB: Fear brow 1+2+4. DB: Distress brow (1,1+4).

AU	1	2	4	5	6	7	9	10	12	14	15	17	18	20	23	24	25	26	FB	DB
F>P	6	4	9	1	7	4	3	6	5	3	5	5	1	4	3	4	4	4	6	5
P>F	3	3	0	0	4	0	4	4	4	2	3	1	3	1	1	1	2	4	2	0

Differences between real and faked pain were examined by computing the difference of the two z-scores. Differences were observed primarily in the outputs of action unit 4 (brow lower), as well as distress brow (1 or 1+4) and inner brow raise (1 in any combination).

Individual subject differences between faked and real pain are shown in Table 3. Difference-of-Z-scores between the genuine and faked pain conditions were computed for each subject and each AU. There was considerable variation among subjects in the difference between their faked and real pain expressions. However the most consistent finding is that 9 of the 26 subjects showed significantly more brow lowering activity (AU4) during the faked pain condition, whereas none of the subjects showed significantly more AU4 activity during the real pain condition. Also 7 subjects showed more cheek raise (AU6), and 6 subjects showed more inner brow raise (AU1), and the fear brow combination (1+2+4). The next most common differences were to show more 12, 15, 17, and distress brow (1 alone or 1+4) during faked pain.

Paired t-tests were conducted for each AU to assess whether it was a reliable indicator of genuine versus faked pain in a within-subjects design. Of the 20 actions tested, the difference was statistically significant for three actions. It was significant for AU 4 at $p < .001$, and marginally significant for AU 7 and distress brow at $p < .05$.

In order to characterize action unit combinations that relate to the difference between fake and real pain expressions, principal component analysis was conducted on the difference-of-Z-scores. The first eigenvector had the largest loading on distress brow and inner brow raise (AU 1). The second eigenvector had the largest loading on lip corner puller (12) and cheek raise (6) and was *lower* for fake pain expressions.

The third eigenvector had the largest loading on brow lower (AU 4). Thus when analyzed singly, the action unit channel with the most information for discriminating fake from real pain was brow lower (AU 4). However when correlations were assessed through PCA, the largest variance was attributed to two combinations, and AU 4 accounted for the third most variance.

Overall, the outputs of the automated system showed similar patterns to previous studies of real and faked pain using manual FACS coding by human experts. Exaggerated activity of the brow lower (AU 4) during faked pain is consistent with previous studies in which the real pain condition was exacerbated lower back pain (Craig et al. 1991, Hill & Craig, 2002). Another study performed a FACS analysis of fake and real pain expressions with cold pressor pain, but with children ages 8-12 (LaRochette et al., 2006). This study observed significant elevation in the following AUs for fake pain relative to baseline: 1 4 6 7 10 12 20 23 25 26. This closely matches the AUs with the highest z-scores in the automated system output of the present study (Table 2B). LaRochette et al. did not measure AU 9 or the brow combinations. When faked pain expressions were compared with real cold pressor pain in children, LaRochette et al found significant differences in AU's 1 4 7 10. Again the findings of the present study using the automated system are similar, as the AU channels with the highest z-scores were 1, 4, and 1+4 (Table 2C), and the t-tests were significant for 4, 1+4 and 7.

3.3.2 Automatic Discrimination of Real from Fake Pain

The above analysis examined which AU outputs contained information about genuine versus faked pain. We next turned to the problem of discriminating genuine from faked pain expressions in a subject-independent manner. If the task were to simply detect the presence of a red-flag set of facial actions, then differentiating fake from real pain expressions would be relatively simple. However, it should be noted that subjects display actions such as AU 4, for example, in both real and fake pain, and the distinction is in the quantity of AU 4. Also, there is inter-subject variation in expressions of both real and fake pain, there may be combinatorial differences in the sets of actions displayed during real and fake pain, and the subjects may cluster. We therefore applied machine learning to the task of discriminating real from faked pain expressions in a subject-independent manner.

A second-layer classifier was trained to discriminate genuine pain from faked pain based on the 20-channel output stream. For this second-layer classification step, we explored SVMs, Adaboost, and linear discriminant analysis. Nonlinear SVMs with radial basis function kernels gave the best performance. System performance for generalization to novel subjects was assessed using leave-one-out cross-validation, in which all the data from one subject was reserved for testing on each trial.

Prior to learning, the system performed an automatic reliability estimate based on the smoothness of the eye positions, and those frames with low reliability were automatically excluded from training and testing the real pain / fake pain classifier. Those frames with abrupt shifts of 2 or more pixels in the returned eye positions were automatically detected and labeled unreliable. This tends to occur during eyeblinks with the current eye detector. However future versions of the eye detector will correct that issue. The reliability filter had a relatively small effect on performance. The analysis of Table 2 was repeated under this criterion, and the Z-scores improved by about 0.1.

Note also that the reliability filter on the frames is not to be confused with dropping the difficult trials since a real pain / fake pain decision was always made for each subject.

The 60 second video from each condition was broken up into 6 overlapping segments of 500 frames. For each segment, the following 5 statistics were measured for each of the 20 AU's: median, maximum, range, first to third quartile difference, 90 to 100 percentile difference. Thus the input to the SVM for each segment contained 100 dimensions. Each cross-validation trial contained 300 training samples (25 subjects x 2 conditions x 6 segments).

A nonlinear SVM trained to discriminate posed from real facial expressions of pain obtained an area under the ROC of .72 for generalization to novel subjects. This was significantly higher than performance of naïve human subjects, who obtained a mean accuracy of 49% correct for discriminating faked from real pain on the same set of videos.

3.4 Discussion of Pain Study

The field of automatic facial expression analysis has advanced to the point that we can begin to apply it to address research questions in behavioral science. Here we describe a pioneering effort to apply fully automated facial action coding to the problem of differentiating fake from real expressions of pain. While naïve human subjects were only at 49% accuracy for distinguishing fake from real pain, the automated system obtained .72 area under the ROC, which is equivalent to 72% correct on a 2-alternative forced choice. Moreover, the pattern of results in terms of which facial actions may be involved in real pain, fake pain, and differentiating real from fake pain is similar to previous findings in the psychology literature using manual FACS coding.

Here we applied machine learning on a 20-channel output stream of facial action detectors. The machine learning was applied to samples of spontaneous expressions during the subject state in question. Here the state in question was fake versus real pain. The same approach can be applied to learn about other subject states, given a set of spontaneous expression samples. Section 4 develops another example in which this approach is applied to the detection of driver drowsiness from facial expression.

4 Automatic Detection of Driver Fatigue

The US National Highway Traffic Safety Administration estimates that in the US alone approximately 100,000 crashes each year are caused primarily by driver drowsiness or fatigue (Department of Transportation, 2001). Thus incorporating automatic driver fatigue detection mechanism into vehicles may help prevent many accidents.

One can use a number of different techniques for analyzing driver exhaustion. One set of techniques places sensors on standard vehicle components, e.g., steering wheel, gas pedal, and analyzes the signals sent by these sensors to detect drowsiness (Takei & Furukawa, 2005). It is important for such techniques to be adapted to the driver, since Abut and his colleagues note that there are noticeable differences among drivers in the way they use the gas pedal (Igarashi, et al., 2005).

A second set of techniques focuses on measurement of physiological signals such as heart rate, pulse rate, and Electroencephalography (EEG) (e.g. Cobb, 1983). It has been reported by re-searchers that as the alertness level decreases EEG power of the alpha and theta bands increases (Hung & Chung, 2005). Hence providing indicators of drowsiness. However this method has draw-backs in terms of practicality since it requires a person to wear an EEG cap while driving.

A third set of solutions focuses on computer vision systems that can detect and recognize the facial motion and appearance changes occurring during drowsiness (Gu & Ji, 2004; Zhang & Zhang, 2006).The advantage of computer vision techniques is that they are non-invasive, and thus are more amenable to use by the general public. There are some significant previous studies about drowsiness detection using computer vision techniques. Most of the published research on computer vision approaches to detection of fatigue has focused on the analysis of blinks and head movements. However the effect of drowsiness on other facial expressions have not been studied thoroughly. Recently Gu & Ji presented one of the first fatigue studies that incorporates certain facial expressions other than blinks. Their study feeds action unit information as an input to a dynamic Bayesian network. The network was trained on subjects posing a state of fatigue (Gu, Zhang & Ji, 2005). The video segments were classified into three stages: inattention, yawn, or falling asleep. For predicting falling asleep, head nods, blinks, nose wrinkles and eyelid tighteners were used.

Previous approaches to drowsiness detection primarily make pre-assumptions about the relevant behavior, focusing on blink rate, eye closure, and yawning. Here we employ machine learning methods to data mine actual human behavior during drowsiness episodes. The objective of this study is to discover what facial configurations are predictors of fatigue. In this study, facial motion was analyzed automatically from video using a fully automated facial expression analysis system based on the Facial Action Coding System (FACS) (Ekman & Friesen, 1978). In addition to the output of the automatic FACS recognition system we also collected head motion data using an accelerometer placed on the subject's head, as well as steering wheel data.

4.1 Driving Task

Subjects played a driving video game on a windows machine using a steering wheel [1]and an open source multi- platform video game[2] (See Figure 5). At random times, a wind effect was applied that dragged the car to the right or left, forcing the subject to correct the position of the car. This type of manipulation had been found in the past to increase fatigue (Orden, Jung & Makeig, 2000). Driving speed was held constant. Four subjects performed the driving task over a three hour period beginning at mid-night. During this time subjects fell asleep multiple times thus crashing their vehicles. Episodes in which the car left the road (crash) were recorded. Video of the subjects face was recorded using a DV camera for the entire 3 hour session.

In addition to measuring facial expressions with CERT, head movementwas meas-ured using an accelerometer that has 3 degrees of freedom. This three dimensional

---

[1] Thrustmaster[R]Ferrari Racing Wheel.

[2] The Open Racing Car Simulator (TORCS).

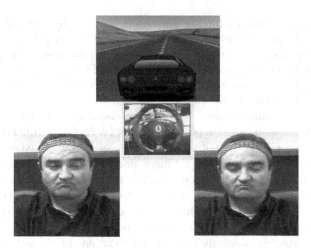

Fig. 5. Driving Simulation Task

accelerometer[3] has three one dimensional accelerometers mounted at right angles measuring accelerations in the range of 5g to +5g where g represents earth gravitational force.

4.2 Facial Actions Associated with Driver Fatigue

Subject data was partitioned into drowsy (non-alert) and alert states as follows. The one minute preceding a sleep episode or a crash was identified as a non-alert state. There was a mean of 24 non-alert episodes with a minimum of 9 and a maximum of 35. Fourteen alert segments for each subject were collected from the first 20 minutes of the driving task.

The output of the facial action detector consisted of a continuous value for each facial action and each video frame which was the distance to the separating hyperplane, i.e., the margin. Histograms for two of the action units in alert and non-alert states are shown in Figure 6. The area under the ROC (A') was computed for the outputs of each facial action detector to see to what degree the alert and non-alert output distributions were separated.

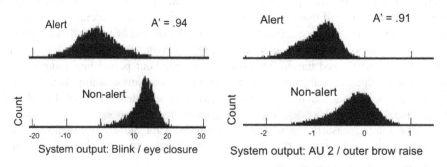

Fig. 6. Example histograms for blink and Action Unit 2 in alert and non-alert states for one subject. A' is area under the ROC.

In order to understand how each action unit is associated with drowsiness across different subjects, Multinomial Logistic Ridge Regression (MLR) was trained on each facial action individually. Examination of the A' for each action unit reveals the degree to which each facial movement was able to predict drowsiness in this study. The A's for the drowsy and alert states are shown in Table 4. The five facial actions that were the most predictive of drowsiness by increasing in drowsy states were 45, 2 (outer brow raise), 15 (frown), 17 (chin raise), and 9 (nose wrinkle). The five actions that were the most predictive of drowsiness by decreasing in drowsy states were 12 (smile), 7 (lid tighten), 39 (nostril compress), 4 (brow lower), and 26 (jaw drop). The high predictive ability of the blink/eye closure measure was expected. However the predictability of the outer brow raise (AU 2) was previously unknown.

We observed during this study that many subjects raised their eyebrows in an attempt to keep their eyes open, and the strong association of the AU 2 detector is consistent with that observation. Also of note is that action 26, jaw drop, which occurs during yawning, actually occurred less often in the critical 60 seconds prior to a crash. This is consistent with the prediction that yawning does not tend to occur in the final moments before falling asleep.

Table 4. MLR model for predicting drowsiness across subjects. Predictive performance of each facial action individually is shown.

More when critically drowsy

AU	Name	A'
45	Blink/Eye Closure	0.94
2	Outer Brow Raise	0.81
15	Lip Corner Depressor	0.80
17	Chin Raiser	0.79
9	Nose Wrinkle	0.78
30	Jaw Sideways	0.76
20	Lip stretch	0.74
11	Nasolabial Furrow	0.71
14	Dimpler	0.71
1	Inner Brow Raise	0.68
10	Upper Lip Raise	0.67
27	Mouth Stretch	0.66
18	Lip Pucker	0.66
22	Lip funneler	0.64
24	Lip presser	0.64
19	Tongue show	0.61

Less when critically drowsy

AU	Name	A'
12	Smile	0.87
7	Lid tighten	0.86
39	Nostril Compress	0.79
4	Brow lower	0.79
26	Jaw Drop	0.77
6	Cheek Raise	0.73
38	Nostril Dilate	0.72
23	Lip tighten	0.67
8	Lips toward	0.67
5	Upper lid raise	0.65
16	Upper lip depress	0.64
32	Bite	0.63

4.3 Automatic Detection of Driver Fatigue

The ability to predict drowsiness in novel subjects from the facial action code was then tested by running MLR on the full set of facial action outputs. Prediction performance was tested by using a leave-one-out cross validation procedure, in which one subjects' data was withheld from the MLR training and retained for testing, and the test was repeated for each subject. The data for each subject by facial action was first normalized to zero-mean and unit standard deviation. The MLR output for each AU feature was summed over a temporal window of 12 seconds (360 frames) before computing A'.

MLR trained on all AU features obtained an A' of .90 for predicting drowsiness in novel subjects. Because prediction accuracy may be enhanced by feature selection, in which only the AU's with the most information for discriminating drowsiness are included in the regression, a second MLR was trained by contingent feature selection, starting with the most discriminative feature (AU 45), and then iteratively adding the next most discriminative feature given the features already selected. These features are shown on Table 5. Best performance of .98 was obtained with five features: 45, 2, 19 (tongue show), 26 (jaw drop), and 15. This five feature model outperformed the MLR trained on all features.

Effect of Temporal Window Length. We next examined the effect of the size of the temporal window on performance. The five feature model was employed for this analysis. The performances shown in Table 5 employed a temporal window of 12 seconds. Here, the MLR output in the 5 feature model was summed over windows of N seconds, where N ranged from 0.5 to 60 seconds. Figure 7 shows the area under the ROC for drowsiness detection in novel subjects over time periods. Performance saturates at about 0.99 as the window size exceeds 30 seconds. In other words, given a 30 second video segment the system can discriminate sleepy versus non-sleepy segments with 0.99 accuracy across subjects.

Table 5. Drowsiness detection performance for novel subjects, using an MLR classifier with different feature combinations. The weighted features are summed over 12 seconds before computing A'.

Feature	A'
AU45,AU2,AU19,AU26,AU15	.9792
All AU features	.8954

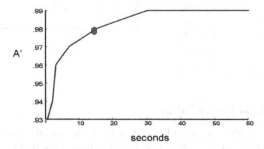

Fig. 7. Performance for drowsiness detection in novel subjects over temporal window sizes. Red point indicates the priorly obtained performace for a temporal window of 12 seconds.

4.4 Coupling of Behaviors

Coupling of steering and head motion. Observation of the subjects during drowsy and nondrowsy states indicated that the subjects head motion differed substantially when alert versus when the driver was about to fall asleep. Surprisingly, head motion increased as the driver became drowsy, with large roll motion coupled with the steering motion as the driver became drowsy. Just before falling asleep, the head would become still.

We also investigated the coupling of the head and arm motions. Correlations between head motion as measured by the roll dimension of the accelerometer output and the steering wheel motion are shown in Figure 8. For this subject (subject 2), the correlation between head motion and steering increased from 0.33 in the alert state to 0.71 in the non-alert state. For subject 1, the correlation between head motion and steering similarly increased from 0.24 in the alert state to 0.43 in the non-alert state.

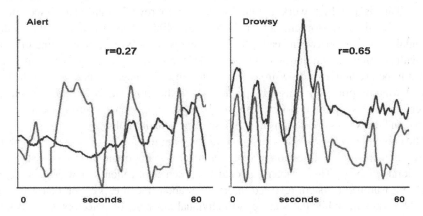

Fig. 8. Head motion (blue/gray) and steering position (red/black) for 60 seconds in an alert state (left) and 60 seconds prior to a crash (right). Head motion is the output of the roll dimension of the accelerometer.

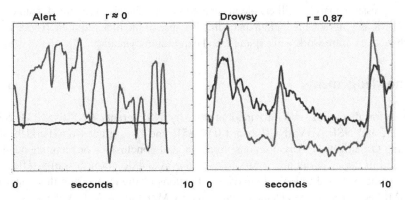

Fig. 9. Eye Openness (red/black) and Eye Brow Raises (AU2) (Blue/gray) for 10 seconds in an alert state (left) and 10 seconds prior to a crash (right)

The other two subjects showed a smaller coupling effect. Future work includes combining the head motion measures and steering correlations with the facial movement measures in the predictive model.

Coupling of eye openness and eyebrow raise. We observed that for some of the subjects coupling between eye brow up's and eye openness increased in the drowsy state. In other words subjects tried to open their eyes using their eyebrows in an attempt to keep awake. See Figure 9.

4.5   Conclusions of Driver Fatigue Study

This chapter presented a system for automatic detection of driver drowsiness from video. Previous approaches focused on assumptions about behaviors that might be predictive of drowsiness. Here, a system for automatically measuring facial expressions was employed to data mine spontaneous behavior during real drowsiness episodes. This is the first work to our knowledge to reveal significant associations between facial expression and fatigue beyond eyeblinks. The project also revealed a potential association between head roll and driver drowsiness, and the coupling of head roll with steering motion during drowsiness. Of note is that a behavior that is often assumed to be predictive of drowsiness, yawn, was in fact a negative predictor of the 60-second window prior to a crash. It appears that in the moments before falling asleep, drivers yawn less, not more, often. This highlights the importance of using examples of fatigue and drowsiness conditions in which subjects actually fall sleep.

The computer vision field has advanced to the point that we are now able to begin to apply automatic facial expression recognition systems to important research questions in behavioral science. This chapter explored two such applications, in which the automated measurement system revealed information about facial expression that was previously unknown. While the accuracy of individual facial action detectors is still below that of human experts, automated systems can be applied to large quantities of video data. Statistical pattern recognition on this large quantity of data can reveal emergent behavioral patterns that previously would have required hundreds of coding hours by human experts, and would be unattainable by the non-expert. Moreover, automated facial expression analysis will enable investigations into facial expression dynamics that were previously intractable by human coding because of the time required to code intensity changes. Future work will explore facial expression dynamics.

Acknowledgements

Support for this work was provided in part by NSF grants CNS-0454233, SBE-0542013, and NSF ADVANCE award 0340851, and by a grant from Turkish State Planning Organization. Any opinions, findings, and conclusions or recommendations expressed in this material are those of the author(s) and do not necessarily reflect the views of the National Science Foundation. Portions of the research in this paper use the MMI Facial Expression Database collected by M. Pantic & M.F. Valstar.

References

1. Bartlett, M.S., Littlewort, G.C., Frank, M.G., Lainscsek, C., Fasel, I., Movellan, J.R.: Automatic recognition of facial actions in spontaneous expressions. Journal of Multimedia 1(6), 22–35 (2006)

2. Cobb, W.: Recommendations for the practice of clinical neurophysiology. Elsevier, Amsterdam (1983)

3. Cohn, J.F., Schmidt, K.L.: The timing of facial motion in posed and spontaneous smiles. J. Wavelets, Multi-resolution & Information Processing 2(2), 121–132 (2004)

4. Craig, K.D., Hyde, S., Patrick, C.J.: Genuine, supressed, and faked facial behaviour during exacerbation of chronic low back pain. Pain 46, 161–172 (1991)

5. Craig, K.D., Patrick, C.J.: Facial expression during induced pain. J Pers Soc Psychol. 48(4), 1080–1091 (1985)

6. Donato, G., Bartlett, M.S., Hager, J.C., Ekman, P., Sejnowski, T.J.: Classifying facial actions. IEEE Trans. Pattern Analysis and Machine Intelligence 21(10), 974–989 (1999)

7. DOT, Saving lives through advanced vehicle safety technology. USA Department of Transportation. (2001), http://www.its.dot.gov/ivi/docs/AR2001.pdf

8. Ekman, P., Friesen, W.: Facial Action Coding System: A Technique for the Measurement of Facial Movement. Consulting Psychologists Press, Palo Alto (1978)

9. Ekman, P.: Telling Lies: Clues to Deceit in the Marketplace, Politics, and Marriage. W.W. Norton, New York (2001)

10. Ekman, P., Rosenberg, E.L. (eds.): What the face reveals: Basic and applied studies of spontaneous expression using the FACS. Oxford University Press, Oxford (2005)

11. Fasel, I., Fortenberry, B., Movellan, J.R.: A generative framework for real-time object detection and classification. Computer Vision and Image Understanding 98 (2005)

12. Fishbain, D.A., Cutler, R., Rosomoff, H.L., Rosomoff, R.S.: Chronic pain disability exaggeration/malingering and submaximal effort research. Clin J Pain 15(4), 244–274 (1999)

13. Fishbain, D.A., Cutler, R., Rosomoff, H.L., Rosomoff, R.S.: Accuracy of deception judgments. Pers Soc Psychol Rev. 10(3), 214–234 (2006)

14. Frank, M.G., Ekman, P., Friesen, W.V.: Behavioral markers and recognizability of the smile of enjoyment. J Pers Soc Psychol. 64(1), 83–93 (1993)

15. Grossman, S., Shielder, V., Swedeen, K., Mucenski, J.: Correlation of patient and caregiver ratings of cancer pain. Journal of Pain and Symptom Management 6(2), 53–57 (1991)

16. Gu, H., Ji, Q.: An automated face reader for fatigue detection. In: FGR, pp. 111–116 (2004)

17. Gu, H., Zhang, Y., Ji, Q.: Task oriented facial behavior recognition with selective sensing. Comput. Vis. Image Underst. 100(3), 385–415 (2005)

18. Hadjistavropoulos, H.D., Craig, K.D., Hadjistavropoulos, T., Poole, G.D.: Subjective judgments of deception in pain expression: accuracy and errors. Pain 65(2-3), 251–258 (1996)

19. Hill, M.L., Craig, K.D.: Detecting deception in pain expressions: the structure of genuine and deceptive facial displays. Pain 98(1-2), 135–144 (2002)

20. Hong, C.K.: Electroencephalographic study of drowsiness in simulated driving with sleep deprivation. International Journal of Industrial Ergonomics 35(4), 307–320 (2005)

21. Igarashi, K., Takeda, K., Itakura, F., Abut, H.: DSP for In-Vehicle and Mobile Systems. Springer, US (2005)

22. Kanade, T., Cohn, J.F., Tian, Y.: Comprehensive database for facial expression analysis. In: Proceedings of the fourth IEEE International conference on automatic face and gesture recognition (FG 2000), Grenoble, France, pp. 46–53 (2000)
23. Larochette, A.C., Chambers, C.T., Craig, K.D.: Genuine, suppressed and faked facial expressions of pain in children. Pain 126(1-3), 64–71 (2006)
24. Littlewort, G., Bartlett, M.S., Fasel, I., Susskind, J., Movellan, J.: Dynamics of facial expression extracted automatically from video. J. Image & Vision Computing 24(6), 615–625 (2006)
25. Morecraft, R.J., Louie, J.L., Herrick, J.L., Stilwell-Morecraft, K.S.: Cortical innervation of the facial nucleus in the non-human primate: a new interpretation of the effects of stroke and related subtotal brain trauma on the muscles of facial expression. Brain 124(Pt 1), 176–208 (2001)
26. Orden, K.F.V., Jung, T.P., Makeig, S.: Combined eye activity measures accurately estimate changes in sustained visual task performance. Biological Psychology 52(3), 221–240 (2000)
27. Pantic, M., Pentland, A., Nijholt, A., Huang, T.: Human Computing and machine understanding of human behaviour: A Survey. In: Proc. ACM Int'l Conf. Multimodal Interfaces, pp. 239–248 (2006)
28. Pantic, M.F.V., Rademaker, R., Maat, L.: Web- based Database for Facial Expression Analysis. In: Proc. IEEE Int'l Conf. Multmedia and Expo (ICME 2005), Amsterdam, The Netherlands (July 2005)
29. Prkachin, K.M.: The consistency of facial expressions of pain: a comparison across modalities. Pain 51(3), 297–306 (1992)
30. Prkachin, K.M., Schultz, I., Berkowitz, J., Hughes, E., Hunt, D.: Assessing pain behaviour of low-back pain patients in real time: concurrent validity and examiner sensitivity. Behav Res Ther. 40(5), 595–607
31. Rinn, W.E.: The neuropsyhology of facial expression: a review of the neurological and psychological mechanisms for producing facial expression. Psychol Bull 95, 52–77
32. Schmand, B., Lindeboom, J., Schagen, S., Heijt, R., Koene, T., Hamburger, H.L.: Cognitive complaints in patients after whiplash injury: the impact of malingering. J Neurol Neurosurg Psychiatry 64(3), 339–343
33. Schmidt, K.L., Cohn, J.F., Tian, Y.: Signal characteristics of spontaneous facial expressions: automatic movement in solitary and social smiles. Biol Psychol. 65(1), 49–66 (2003)
34. Schneiderman, H., Kanade, T.: Probabilistic Modeling of Local Appearance and Spatial Relationships for Object Recognition. In: Proceedings of the IEEE Conference on Computer Vision and Pattern Recognition, pp. 45–51 (1998)
35. Takei, Y., Furukawa, Y.: Estimate of driver's fatigue through steering motion. In: Man and Cybernetics, 2005 IEEE International Conference, vol. 2, pp. 1765–1770 (2005)
36. Viola, P., Jones, M.: Robust real-time face detection. J. Computer Vision 57(2), 137–154 (2004)
37. Vural, E., Ercil, A., Littlewort, G.C., Bartlett, M.S., Movellan, J.R.: Machine learning systems for detecting driver drowsiness. In: Proceedings of the Biennial Conference on Digital Signal Processing for in-Vehicle and Mobile Systems (2007)
38. Zhang, Z., Shu Zhang, J.: Driver fatigue detection based intelligent vehicle control. In: Proceedings of the 18th International Conference on Pattern Recognition, Washington, DC, USA, pp. 1262–1265. IEEE Computer Society, Los Alamitos (2006)

Ekfrasis: A Formal Language for Representing and Generating Sequences of Facial Patterns for Studying Emotional Behavior

Nikolaos Bourbakis[1], Anna Esposito[3], and Despina Kavraki[2]

[1] Wright State University, OH, USA
[2] AIIS Inc., OH, USA
[3] Second University of Naples, Department of Psychology, and IIASS, Italy
nikolaos.bourbakis@wright.edu, iiass.annaesp@tin.it

Abstract. Emotion is a topic that has received much attention during the last few years, both in the context of speech synthesis, image understanding as well as in automatic speech recognition, interactive dialogues systems and wearable computing. This paper presents a formal model of a language (called Ekfrasis) as a software methodology that synthesizes (or generates) automatically various facial expressions by appropriately combining facial features. The main objective here is to use this methodology to generate various combinations of facial expressions and study if these combinations efficiently represent emotional behavioral patterns.

Keywords: Model of emotional expressions, formal language, facial features.

1 Background

Emotion is a topic that has received much attention during the last few years, both in the context of speech synthesis, image understanding as well as in automatic speech recognition, interactive dialogues systems and wearable computing. The objective of this paper is to develop a software mechanism for automatic synthesis of facial features that contribute to the design of a system for learning, understanding and responding human emotional behavior. It is evident that the same words may be used as a joke, or as a genuine question seeking an answer, or as an aggressive challenge. Knowing what is an appropriate continuation of the interaction depends on detecting the register that the speaker is using, and a machine communicator that is unable to acknowledge the difference will have difficulty in managing a natural-like conversation. Thus, here the recognition of facial expressions is the main theme.

1.1 Recognizing Emotions in Faces [38-40]

The salient issues in emotion recognition from faces are parallel in some respects to the issues associated with voices, but divergent in others. As in speech, a long established tradition attempts to define the facial expression of emotion in terms of qualitative subjects - i.e. static positions capable of being displayed in a still photograph. The

A. Esposito et al. (Eds.): HH and HM Interaction 2007, LNAI 5042, pp. 21–31, 2008.

still image usually captures the apex of the expression, i.e. the instant at which the indicators of emotion are most marked, while the natural recognition of emotions is based on continuous variations of the facial expressions. The analysis of a human face emotional expression requires a number of pre-processing steps which attempt to detect or track the face, to locate characteristic facial regions such as eyes, mouth and forehead on it, to extract and follow the movement of facial features, such as characteristic points in these regions, and model facial gestures using anatomic information about the face. Most of the above techniques are based on a system for describing visually distinguishable facial movements, called Facial Action Coding System (FACS) [19, 34]. The FACS model has inspired the definition and derivation of facial animation parameters in the framework of the ISO MPEG-4 standard [27, 28]. In particular, the Facial Definition Parameters (FDPs) and the Facial Animation Parameters (FAPs) in the MPEG-4 standard have made possible the animation of synthetic faces reproducing emotional expressions through speech and faces [18, 20-26, 29, 36].

Most of the implemented automatic systems devoted to recognize emotional facial expressions attempt to recognize only expressions corresponding to six basic emotional states - *happiness, sadness, surprise, disgust, fear and anger* [32, 33] or to recognize the so called Action Units (AUs), i.e. visible movements of a single or a small group of facial muscles that are the basic units of the FACS [34] and that can be combined to define a mapping between changes in facial musculature and visible facial emotional expressions. There are 46 independent AUs that can be combined and 7000 distinct combinations of them have been observed in spontaneous interactions. In general, emotional facial expressions are recognized by tracking AUs and by measuring the intensity of their changes. Thus, approaches to classification of facial expressions can be divided into spatial and spatio-temporal. In spatial approaches, facial features obtained from still images are utilized for classifying emotional facial expressions. Artificial Neural Networks (ANNs), Support Vector Machines (SVMs) [35] and Linear Discriminant Analysis are the mathematical models exploited for such classifications. In spatio-temporal approaches also dynamic features extracted by video sequences are taken into account and therefore the mathematical tools most exploited are the Hidden Markov Models (HMMs) and Stochastic Petri-nets (SPNs) since they are able to consider also temporal variations.

2 Image Graph Description

2.1 The Local-Global (L-G) Graph

Graph theory is a very powerful methodology used on a great variety of computer science problems [8-14]. The graph's models are mostly used for the relational representation and recognition of images, objects, and their features [6-7] and attributes [10, 15]. In order to recognize patterns, or models in images, different graph techniques have been proposed. For example, the graph editing method is used to compute graph distance and, in turn, the graph distance becomes the measure of image similarity [8-9]. Sub-graph isomorphism techniques are deployed to perfect matching of part of one graph with another graph [11]. The L-G graph based method deploys region information in each graph node and interrelates the nodes with each other for expressing all possible relationships [4]. In particular, the *L-G* graph adds local information into graph making it more accurate for representing an object. By combining the Fuzzy-like Region Segmentation (FRS) method for describing image regions of certain RGB color and the *L-G* graph method, we can improve object recognition accuracy without increasing computation complexity. The main components of the L-G graph are: (i) the local graph that encodes size and shape information, and (ii) the skeleton graph that provides information about the internal shape of each segmented region [3, 5]. The global graph represents the relationships among the segmented regions for the entire image. The nodes P_i of the L-G graph ($GGA_{(Ni)}$) include the color, the texture and the skeleton graph of each segmented region. The local-global image graph components are briefly described in Figure 1.

Image regions and the GG graph

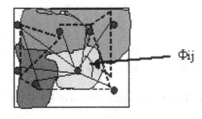

$$GGA_{(m)} = (P_1R_{12}P_2)\Phi_{23}(P_1R_{13}P_3)\Phi_{34}(P_1R_{14}P_4)....$$

Fig. 1. The L-G graph of a synthetic image consisted of 9 segmented regions

2.2 The Local-Global Graph for Representing Facial Expressions [3, 38-39]

For recognizing emotional facial expressions, the series of tasks to be performed are face detection, emotional facial feature recognition and then facial expression recognition. In the L-G graph method, after the face detection step, the various facial features from the image can be retrieved by the local-global graph node correspondences, as shown in Figure 2. The extra step needed for recognizing facial expressions is to compare the image LG graph with the existing Facial Expression LG graphs stored in the LG database. It should be noted that each facial expression is characterized by a specific configuration of the facial features. This particular configuration of each facial feature is represented by the Expression LG graph, similar to the Face LG graph defined in Figure 3.

The advantage of the proposed method over other existing methods is that each individual facial feature configuration is represented by a more detailed graph representation which allows us to represent even more subtle expressions. For recognizing expressions, each node in the LG graph is modified as shown below:

$$node = \{(x, y), color, texture, L, size, border, LG_{EXPR}, ..LG_{EXPRi}\}$$

Where LG_{EXPRi} represents an Expression LG graph. At the present stage, only five facial features are used to represent each expression. The features used are left and right eyebrows, eyes and mouth. Figure 3 shows the corresponding Expression LG graphs for neutral, happy, angry and scream expressions. The images used are taken from the AR face database [31].

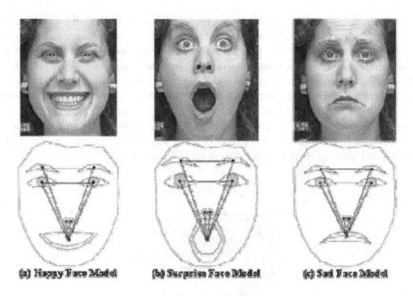

(a) Happy Face Model   (b) Surprise Face Model   (c) Sad Face Model

Fig. 2. The L-G graph representation of emotional facial expressions

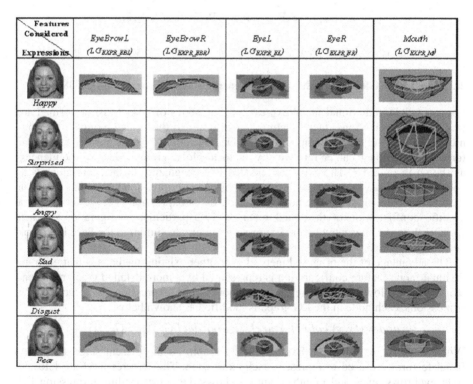

Fig. 3. The L-G graph representation of 6 facial expressions, using the AR Database

3 Ekfrasis: The Formal Language

In this section we present the formal definition of the language used to generate variation of facial expressions.

3.1 Formal Definitions

Definition: The Ekfrasis language is defined (or generated) by a grammar **G** $\{V_N,$
$V_T,$ PR, S$\}$, where V_N, is the set of non-terminal symbols and is defined as $V_N = \{S,$
T, k, L, X$\}$; V_T is the set of terminal symbols and is defined as $V_T = \sum U \{i/i\epsilon Z, \} U$
$\{\#\}$; S is the starting symbol of a sentence; T is the symbol for a terminal letter; L is
the symbol for the alphabet letters; $\sum$ is the alphabet; # is the synthesis symbol be-
tween letters of the alphabet; and PR is the set of production rules and is defined as:

$$PR=\{ S \rightarrow T; \quad S \rightarrow S \# T; T \rightarrow Lk; L \rightarrow L1/L2/L3/L4/L5/L6; k\epsilon Z, 1 \leq k \leq 6\}$$

Li $\epsilon \sum$, and

$$\sum = \{EBLi, EBRi, ELi, ERi, Ni, Mi (ULi, LLi)\}$$

where EBLi represents the L-G graph description of the left eyebrow; EBRi represents the L-G graph description of the right eyebrow; ELi represents the L-G graph
description of the left eye; ERi represents the L-G graph description of the right eye;
Ni represents the L-G graph description of the nose; Mi represents the L-G graph
description of the mouth (which consists of the upper ULi and lower LLi lips)
[3, 30];

Definition: The Ekfrasis language (L_{EF}) is defined over the G grammar as follows:

$$L_{EF} (G) = \{ Lei/Lei , V_T : S_G \rightarrow Lei \}$$

Proposition-1
A word of the Ekfrasis language represents a particular facial expression and is defined as:

a) Wn = Le1#Le2#Le3#Le4#Le5#Le6, where nϵ $\{1, ..., EF\}$, where EF is the max
number of all facial expressions;
b) The max length of each sentence (or word) is 6;
c) Li, ie $\{1,2,3,4,5,6\}$, represents a facial feature of the alphabet;

Proposition-2
a) The combination of the same letter twice (Lei#Lei) in a word is illegal;
b) The appearance of more than two letters Li (eyebrows) in a word, or more than two
letters Lj (eyes) in a word, or more than one letter Li (mouth) in a word, or more than
a letter Li (nose) in a word are considered illegal representations;

Proposition-3
The Abealian property Lei#Lej = Lej#Lei is true, where, i,je $\{1,2,3,4,5,6\}$, with i$\neq$j .

Example

For instance from the table displayed in Figure 3 the word W4 described by :

$$W4 = EBL4\#EBR4\#EL4\#ER4\#N4\#M4$$

represents the facial expression of sadness, where Le1=EBL4; Le2=EBR4; Le3=ER4;Le4=EL4;Le5=N4;Le6=M4. Note here that the letter N4 is not present in that table, but this does not diminish the idea of the example.

4   The Stochastic Petri-Net Graph Model

Here we briefly present the next steps to follow the generation of sequences of facial expressions in order to be used to represent emotional behavioral patterns. To accomplish this, we employ the Stochastic Petri-net (SPN) [1-2, 14, 16] in combination with the L-G graph.

A Petri-net model is a methodology with numerous variations and applications. Here we transform the SPN model in the form of a graph and we take the advantage of the SPN properties (timing, parallelism, concurrency, synchronization of events) for our synergistic methodology [1, 14]. The LG graph models described above have the capability of holding structural information about objects or subjects. The functional behavior of an object or subject is described by the states in which the particular subject could be changed to, after an appropriate trigger state is satisfied. A successful and powerful model capable of describing (or modeling) the functional behavior of a system is the SPN. Thus, in order to maintain the structural features of the graph model and the functional features of the SPN model, a mapping is presented here, where the SPN model is transformed into a SPN graph model by the following transformation: $m : LG \rightarrow SPN$, where, $N_i \rightarrow \{P_i\}$, a graph-node of the L-G graph corresponds into a number of SPN places, and the $\{a_{ij}\} \rightarrow \{t_{ij}\}$ relationships correspond into SPN transitions. In other words we transfer the structural properties of a graph node into a set of SPN places. This means that different states of the same object correspond to an equal number of different SPN places based on the SPN model definition. For instance, a SPN place P_k carries the structural properties of same object at the state k and all structural deformations of that object associated with the state k. There will be cases where the structural properties of an object are the same for all SPN places corresponding to this object. This means that the functional behavior of the object changes but the structural properties may remain the same. Thus, the relationships among graph nodes, which are represented by transitions on the SPN graph, will carry functional states (or behavioral states) that transfer the object from state j to state k, and structural transitions that carry structural relationships among the objects structural features. In this way, the SPN graph model carries not only the functional properties of the SPN graph but the structural properties of the L-G graph as well. The SPN graph is also successful for expressing body movements for the detection and recognition of emotions (see an example in a later section). Figure 4 illustrates the SPN graph of an object that has four different states (Places P_i, i=1,2,3,4). Each place P_i has its own structural features transferred from the corresponding graph node N_i. The transitions t_{14} and t_{43} represent relationships among the same parts of a subject and a stochastic distribution of time required to fire that transition. The t_{21} transition requires no time to fire.

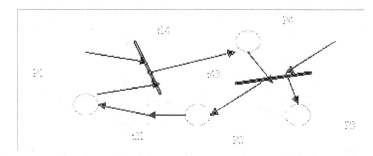

Fig. 4. A graphical example of an SPN model

4.1   Tracking and Associating Facial Emotion in Sequences of Images [17, 38]

In this section we provide an example where we present a sequence of three facial features extracted from different image frames and associated together to provide information related to the emotional behavior of a person (see Figures 5 and 6).

SPNG Associations [37]: Here we present the results of SPN graph associations for extracted facial features (mouth) from different image frames, (see Figure 6). More specifically, when the facial features are detected and tracked in different frames, the L-G graph method is used to establish a local graph for each region. These region-graphs are then associated to produce the global graph that connects all the region-graphs. Then each L-G graph is associated with other L-G Graphs (extracted from the next image frames) by producing a sequence of facial expressions related with a particular emotion. By tracking and associating these sequences (by using the SPN model) we create SPN-LG graph patterns that will allow us to analyze and better understand the emotions associated with human behavior that take place in sequences of frames. The SPN association of the L-G graph individual facial expressions is done by using an appropriate set of states (facial expressions) and their transitions from a certain state to the next appropriate one. The transition from one state (facial expression FEi) into the next state (facial expression FEj) is associated with "tokens". These

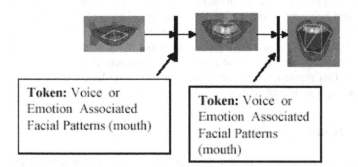

Fig. 5. A sequence of facial feature (mouth) L-G graphs represented by letters from the Ekfrasis language. Individual letters of the alphabet can be used to associate emotional patterns.

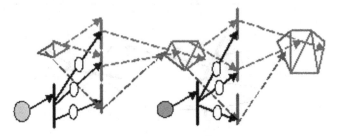

Fig. 6. The SPN association of the L-G graph of the facial features (mouth) extracted and represented from different image frames, and their activation via token (orange, and green for color image or filled circles for black and white image). The proposed example refers to a sequence of facial expressions related with happiness and laughter. The color token (filled circles in black and white) could be a joke or a happy thought or else.

tokens can be either thoughts of the individual or commands given by someone or other audio/visual stimulation. For instance, if someone takes a photo of you; he/she usually "commands" you to smile. This means that from an initial facial expression (FEi) you go through several intermediate facial stages (states, FEi+1, FEi+2, ...,) until to reach the final smiling facial expression (FEj). On the SPN graphical representations, colors are used to illustrate the transitions and flow using the token that represent the cause of these transitions, for instance token=voice or emotion. Note here that during a transition from one EFi state into FEj state, the token could be the same or different.

Figure 5 shows a sequence of mouth facial features from different image frames activated and associated with a voice (command) token or an emotional (thought) token. The SPN association of the L-G graph of the facial features (mouth) extracted and represented from different image frames, and their activation via token are displayed in Figure 6 (orange and green circles in color or filled circles in black and white). These mouth-L-G graphs represent letters from the Ekfrasis language. In this case, individual letters of the alphabet can be used to indicate facial expressions and their association (a language word) expresses an emotional pattern. In some cases there is no need for an entire set of facial expressions for a first stage understanding of the emotional behavior. This can be predicted by using the SPN patterns (that represent sequences of associated facial expressions). Note here that these sequences of individual letters of the formal language have to follow certain rules of state transitions. For instance, we cannot use a letter that represent a sad state and combine it with a letter that represents happiness without involving letters representing intermediate states, such as neutral or others.

5   Conclusions

In this paper we presented a formal methodology (a formal language called Ekfrasis) for generating and synthesizing facial expressions and a functional model (SPN) for associating facial expressions for representing and studying emotional behavior. The language and the SPN model have provided an efficient mechanism for studying facial expressions and then emotional behavior. The language based on the L-G graph (an existing method-tool in our lab) and the SPN model has provided an efficient mechanism for studying facial expressions and then emotional behavior. The method-ology-language has been used only in one case with limited clear facial expressions in the image frames (a case of a female individual with minor behavioral patterns), thus more research work must be done in order to assess its efficacy. We plan to improve the proposed language methodology applying it to different face views selected form the test case as well as from other cases in order to test the method on various real scenarios. The advantages of the proposed method-tool are that: (1) it is simple in use; (2) it provides near real-time responses; (3) it works on grey and color images; (4) it is compatible with our voice recognition method; (5) it works on sequences of image frames. The disadvantages are: (1) it does not provide very accurate results when the changes in the facial expression involve a limited number of pixels in the test image; (2) it is not real-time yet; (3) currently, it does not work on all face views. There is an on going research effort in order to overcome the listed drawbacks and improve the proposed methodology.

Acknowledgements. This work is partially supported by an AIIS Inc grant 2006-08, by COST 2102: Cross Modal Analysis of Verbal and Nonverbal Communication (www.cost2102.eu), and by Regione Campania, L.R. N.5 del 28.03.2002, Project ID N. BRC1293, Feb. 2006.

References

1. Bourbakis, N.: A Neural-based KB using SPNGs in Sequence of Images. AIRFORCE & SUNY-B-TR-1991, 1–45 (November 1991)
2. Bourbakis, N., Gattiker, J.: Representation of Structural and Functional Knowledge using SPN Graphs. In: Proc. IEEE Conf. on SEKE (1995)
3. Bourbakis, N.: Emulating Human Visual Perception for Measuring Differences in Images Using an SPN Graph Approach. IEEE T-SMC 32(2), 191–201 (2002)
4. Hilton, A., Illingworth, J., Li, Y.: A Relaxation Algorithm for Real-time Multiple View 3D-Tracking. Image and Vision Computing 20(12), 841–859 (2002)
5. Bourbakis, N.G., Moghaddamzadeh, A.: A Fuzzy Region Growing Approach for Segmen-tation of Color Images. PR Society Journal of Pattern Recognition 30(6), 867–881 (1997)
6. Ahuja, N., An, B., Schachter, B.: Image Representation Using Voronoi Tessellation. Com-puter Vision, Graphics and Image Processing 29, 286–295 (1985)
7. Ahuja, N.: Dot Pattern Processing Using Voronoi Neighborhoods. IEEE Trans. on Pattern Recognition and Machine Intelligence 4(3), 336–342 (1982)
8. Fu, K.S., Sanfeliu, A.: A Distance Measure Between Attributed Relational Graphs For Pat-tern Recognition. IEEE Trans. On Systems, Man, and Cybernetics 13(3), 353–362 (1983)
9. Kubicka, E., Kubicki, G., Vakalis, I.: Using Graph Distance in Object Recognition. In: ACM 18th Annual Computer Science Conference Proc., pp. 43–48. ACM, New York (1990)
10. Bourbakis, N.: A Rule-Based Scheme for Synthesis of Texture Images. In: Int. IEEE Conf. on Systems, Man and Cybernetics, Fairfax, VA, pp. 999–1003 (1987)
11. Currey, K.M., Jason, T.L., Shapiro, D.S., Wang, B.A., Zhang, K.: An Algorithm for Find-ing the Largest Approximately Common Substructures of Two Trees. IEEE T-PAMI 20(8), 889–895 (1998)

12. Amit, Y., Kong, A.: Graphical Templates for Model Registration. IEEE Trans. on Pattern Recognition and Machine Intelligence 18(3), 225–236 (1996)
13. Cross, A.D.J., Hancock, E.R.: Graph Matching with a Dual-Step EM Algorithm. IEEE T-PAMI 20(11), 1236–1253 (1998)
14. Bebis, G., Bourbakis, N., Gattiker, J.: Representing and Interpreting Human Activity and Events from Video. IJAIT 12(1) (2003)
15. Hu, M.K.: Visual Pattern Recognition by Moments Invariants. IRE Transaction of Information Theory 8, 179–187 (1962)
16. Murata, T.: Petri Nets: properties, Analysis and Applications. Proc. of the IEEE 7(4) (1989)
17. Bourbakis, N.: Motion Analysis of Multiple Humans for Guiding Visual Impaired. ITR-TR (2005)
18. Doyle, P.: When is a Communicative Agent a Good Idea? In: Proc. of Inter. Workshop on Communicative and Autonomous Agents, Seattle (1999)
19. Ekman, P.: Facial Expression of Emotion: New Findings. New Questions. Psychol. Science 3, 34–38 (1992)
20. Esposito, A., Garcia, O.N., Gutierrez-Osuna, R., Kakumanu, P.: Optimal Data Encoding for Speech Driven Facial Animation. Tech. Rep. N. CS-WSU-04-02, Wright State University, Dayton, Ohio, USA (2003)
21. Ezzat, T., Geiger, G., Poggio, T.: Trainable Video Realistic Speech Animation. In: Proc. of SIGGRAPH, San Antonio, TX, pp. 388–397 (2002)
22. Bojorquez, A., Castello, J., Esposito, A., Garcia, O.N., Kakumanu, P., Gutierrez-Osuna, R., Rudomin, I.: Speech-Driven facial Animation with Realistic Dynamic. Tech. Rep. N. CS-WSU-03-02, Wright State University, Dayton, Ohio, USA (2002)
23. Haber, J., Kähler, K., Seidel, H.: Geometry-Based Muscle Modeling for Facial Animation. In: Proc. Inter. Conf. on Graphics Interface, pp. 27–36 (2001)
24. Kakumanu, P., Gutierrez-Osuna, R., Esposito, A., Bryll, R., Goshtasby, A., Garcia, O.N.: Speech Driven Facial Animation. In: Proc. of ACM Workshop on Perceptive User Interfaces, Orlando, 15-16 November, pp. 1–4 (2001)
25. Morishima, S.: Face Analysis and Synthesis. IEEE Signal Processing Mag. 18(3), 26–34 (2001)
26. O'Reilly, W.S.N.: Believable Social and Emotional Agents. Ph.D. Thesis at the Carnegie Mellon University, Pittsburgh, PA (1996)
27. Ostermann, J.: Animation of Synthetic Face in MPEG-4. In: Proc. of Computer Animation, Philadelphia, June 8-10, pp. 49–51 (1998)
28. Overview of the MPEG-4 Standard, ISO/IEC JTC1/SC29/WG11 M2725, Seoul, South Korea (1999)
29. Rizzo, P.: Emotional Agents for User Entertainment: Discussing the Underlying Assumptions. In: Proc. of the Inter. Workshop on Affect in Interactions, the EC I3 Programme, Siena (1999)
30. Bourbakis, N.: Associating Facial Expressions for Identifying Individuals of Using Stochastic Petri-Nets for the Blind. In: IEEE Int. Conf. TAI-08, Dayton OH (November 2008)
31. AR Face Database, Purdue University, W-Lafayette, USA
32. Pantic, M., Patras, I., Rothkrantz, L.J.M.: Facial Action Recognition in Face Profile Image Sequences. In: Proceedings IEEE International Conference Multimedia and Expo, pp. 37–40 (2002), http://citeseer.ist.psu.edu/pantic02facial.html
33. Cohn, J., Kanade, T., Tian, Y.: Comprehensive Database for Facial Expression Analysis. In: Proc. of the 4th IEEE International Conference on Automatic Face and Gesture Recognition (FG 2000), pp. 46–53 (March 2000)

34. Ekman, P., Frisen, W.: Facial Action Coding System. Consulting Psychologists Press, Palo Alto (1978)
35. Bartlett, M.S., Fasel, I., Littlewort, G., Movellan, J.R., Susskind, J.: Dynamics of Facial Expression Extracted Automatically from Video. In: Proc. IEEE CVPR, Workshop on Face Processing in Video (2004),
    http://citeseer.ist.psu.edu/711804.html
36. Esposito, A., Bourbakis, N.: The Role of Timing on the Speech Perception and Production Processes and its Effects on Language Impaired Individuals. In: Proc. Int. IEEE Symposium on BIBE-2006, WDC, October 16-18, pp. 348–356 (2006)
37. Bebis, G., Bourbakis, N.: Associating Motion-Patterns of Events from Video. In: Proc. IEEE Conf. on TAI-2006, WDC (November 13–15, 2006)
38. Bourbakis, N., Kakumanu, P.: Recognizing Facial Expressions Using Local-Global Graphs for Blind. In: Proc. IEEE Int. Conf. on TAI-2006, WDC (November 13–15, 2006)
39. Bourbakis, N., Esposito, A., Kavraki, D.: Analysis of Invariant Meta-features for Learning and Understanding Disable People's Emotional Behavior Related to Their Health Conditions. In: IEEE Int. Symp. on BIBE-2006, WDC, pp. 357–369 (October 2006)
40. Esposito, A.: The Amount of Information on Emotional States Conveyed by the Verbal and Nonverbal Channels: Some Perceptual Data. In: Stylianou, Y., Faundez-Zanuy, M., Esposito, A. (eds.) COST 277. LNCS, vol. 4391, pp. 249–268. Springer, Heidelberg (2007)

On the Relevance of Facial Expressions for Biometric Recognition

Marcos Faundez-Zanuy and Joan Fabregas

Escola Universitària Politècnica de Mataró (Adscrita a la UPC)
08303 MATARO (BARCELONA), Spain
faundez@eupmt.es, fabregas@eupmt.es
http://www.eupmt.es/veu

Abstract. Biometric face recognition presents a wide range of variability sources, such as make up, illumination, pose, facial expression, etc. In this paper we use the Japanese Female Facial Expression Database (JAFFE) in order to evaluate the influence of facial expression in biometric recognition rates. In our experiments we used a nearest neighbor classifier with different number of training samples, different error criteria, and several feature extractions. Our experimental results reveal that some facial expressions produce a recognition rate drop, but the optimal length of the feature extracted vectors is the same with the presence of facial expressions than with neutral faces.

1 Introduction

According to a classical emotion theory, there are six or seven basic emotions, shared by all people regardless of their origin [1]. Such a conclusion has been supported by studies showing that people across the world from Westerners to members of isolated tribes are able to recognize these emotions readily from stereotypical facial displays (e.g. [2]). Facial expression analysis offers a good set of applications, such as human computer interaction to achieve user-friendly human-computer interaction. The face can be considered as a natural input "device" [5]. It is argued that for the computer to be able to interact with humans it must have the communication skills of humans, and one of these skills is the ability to understand the emotional state of the person. In fact, the most expressive way humans display emotions is through facial expressions [5]. However, for emotion analysis, higher level knowledge is required, and it goes one step further from facial expression analysis. Although facial expressions can convey emotion, they can also express intention, cognitive process, physical effort, or other intra or interpersonal meanings [5]. Facial analysis analyzes the facial actions regardless of context, culture, gender, etc.

In this paper, rather than trying to estimate the different facial expressions we will study a fully different problem: how affects the facial expression on the recognition rates of biometric systems [6] based on face images. This problem was also studied in [11] although with a database for biometric face recognition that contains a very small amount of expressions. The biometric recognition problem versus expression analysis goals can be summarized in the following way:

Biometric problem goal: a feature extraction insensitive to expression and highly discriminative among individuals.

A. Esposito et al. (Eds.): HH and HM Interaction 2007, LNAI 5042, pp. 32–43, 2008.

Expression analysis goal: a feature extraction insensitive to different individual's variation and highly discriminative among expressions.

Obviously these requirements are opposite, and a good parameterization for biometric systems should be bad for expression analysis. However, it is important to point out the situation that occurs with speech and speaker recognition problems, where the former tries to understand the message independently of the speaker and the latter tries to identify the speaker independently of the uttered message. In this case, the same kind of parameterization is suitable for both of them: the MEL-cepstrum. Thus, same situation could occur in face recognition. Although the classifier also plays an important role, this paper is focused on feature extraction.

2   Face Recognition

Usually, a pattern recognition system consists of two main blocks: feature extraction and classifier. Figure 1 summarizes this scheme. On the other hand, there are two main approaches for face recognition:

Statistical approaches consider the image as a high-dimension vector, where each pixel is mapped to a component of a vector. Due to the high dimensionality of vectors some vector-dimension reduction algorithm must be used. Typically the Karhunen Loeve transform (KLT) is applied with a simplified algorithm known as eigenfaces [10]. However, this algorithm is suboptimal.

Geometry-feature-based methods try to identify the position and relationship between face parts, such as eyes, nose, mouth, etc., and the extracted parameters are measures of textures, shapes, sizes, etc. of these regions.

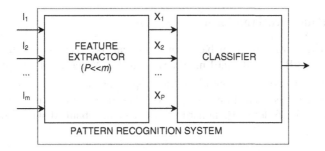

Fig. 1. General Pattern recognition system

In this paper, we mainly focus on the study of the feature extraction for the face recognition using statistical approaches. We will use the Discrete Cosine Transform (DCT) and Walsh Hadamard Transform (WHT).

2.1   The Discrete Cosine Transform

The DCT [9], which is at the base of coding image application as JPEG and MPEG, has been used with success also in face recognition [7], due to its capacities of fast computation, dimensionality reduction and robustness to illumination variations. The

DCT is a separable, linear transformation; this is, the two-dimensional transformation is equivalent to a one-dimensional DCT performed along a single dimension followed by a one-dimensional DCT on other side. The definition of a two-dimensional DCT for an input image A and a transformed image B is the following:

$$B_{pq} = \alpha_p \alpha_q \left\{ \sum_{m=0}^{M-1} \sum_{n=0}^{N-1} A_{mn} \cos\left(\frac{\pi(2m+1)p}{2M} \right) \cos\left(\frac{\pi(2n+1)q}{2N} \right) \right\}$$

Where:

$$0 \le p \le M-1 \text{ and } 0 \le q \le N-1$$

$$\alpha_p = \begin{cases} \dfrac{1}{\sqrt{M}}, & p = 0 \\ \sqrt{\dfrac{2}{M}}, & 1 \le p \le M-1 \end{cases} \qquad \alpha_q = \begin{cases} \dfrac{1}{\sqrt{N}}, & q = 0 \\ \sqrt{\dfrac{2}{N}}, & 1 \le q \le N-1 \end{cases}$$

M and N are respectively the row and column size of A.

The application of the DCT to an image (real data), produces a real result.

The DCT is used in many data compression applications in preference to the DFT (Discrete Fourier Transform) because of its property that is frequently referred to as "energy compactation". It's easy to observe that most of the energy is concentrated around the origin (low frequency components located on the upper left corner) [7]. In order to classify the image it is consequently possible to give just a portion of the transformed image to the classifier, considering just a square windows of N' x N' pixels, located in the upper left corner.

2.2 Walsh Hadamard Transform

The Walsh-Hadamard transform basis functions can be expressed in terms of Hadamard matrices [9]. A Hadamard matrix H_n is a $N \times N$ matrix of ±1 values, where $N = 2^n$. In contrast to error-control coding applications, in signal processing it is better to write the basis functions as rows of the matrix with increasing number of zero crossings. The ordered Hadamard matrix can be obtained with the following equations:

$$H(x,u) = \frac{1}{N}(-1)^{\sum_{i=0}^{n-1} b_i(x)p_i(u)}$$

Where:

$b_k(x)$ is the kth bit in the binary representation of x.

$$p_0(u) = b_{n-1}(u)$$
$$p_1(u) = b_{n-1}(u) + b_{n-2}(u)$$
$$p_2(u) = b_{n-2}(u) + b_{n-3}(u)$$
$$\vdots$$
$$p_{n-1}(u) = b_1(u) + b_0(u)$$

Where the sums are performed in modulo-2 arithmetic.

The two-dimensional Hadamard transform pair for an image U of $2^n \times 2^n$ pixels is obtained by the equation $T = H_n U H_n$. We have zero padded the 112×96 images to 256×256. Thus, in our experiments $n=8$.

[8] summarizes two measures that indicate the performance of transforms in terms of energy packing efficiency and decorrelation efficiency. It can be observed that the performance of the Walsh-Hadamard transform (WHT) is just a little bit worse than Discrete Cosine Transform (DCT) and Karhunen-Loeve Transform (KLT).

The WHT is a fast transform that does not require any multiplication in the transform calculations because it only contains ±1 values. This is very suitable for fixed point processors because no decimals are produced using additions and subtractions. Table 1 compares the computational burden of KLT, DCT and WHT [9]. It is interesting to observe that when dealing with DCT and WHT, basis functions are known in advance (they are not data dependent). In addition, it is important to emphasize that referent to performance gain, the transform choice is important if block size is small [9], say N<65. This is not our case, because we consider each image as a block of more than 10000 components. Table 2 provides execution times using a Pentium 4 processor at 3GHz.

Table 1. Computational burden of KLT, DCT and WHT for images of size $N \times N$

Transform	Basis function computation	Image transformation
KLT	$O(N^3)$ (to solve 2 $N \times N$ matrix eigen-value problems)	$2N^3$ multiplications
DCT	0	$N^2 \log_2(N)$ multiplications
WHT	0	$N^2 \log_2(N)$ additions or substractions

Table 2. Execution time for KLT, DCT and WHT

Transform	Basis function computation	Image transformation
KLT	347.78s	0.23s
DCT	0	0.0031s
WHT	0	0.0003s

We can define a rectangular mask [10]: it will be a square containing $N'\times N'$ pixels. This definition lets to easily obtain the coefficients. The dimension of the resulting vector is $N'\times N'$. It is interesting to observe that in image coding applications the image is split into blocks of smaller size, and the selected transformed coefficients of each block are encoded and used for the reconstruction of the decoded image. In face recognition all the operations are performed over the whole image (it is not split into blocks) and all the computations are done in the transformed domain. Thus, it is not necessary to perform any inverse transform. On the other hand in image coding the goal is to reduce the amount of bits without appreciably sacrificing the quality of the reconstructed image, and in image recognition the number of bits is not so important.

The goal is to reduce the dimensionality of the vectors in order to simplify the complexity of the classifier and to improve recognition accuracy.

3 Experimental Results

This section evaluates the results achieved using the WHT and DCT feature extraction methods using a Nearest Neighbor classifier [10].

3.1 Database

The JAFFE (Japanese Female Facial Expresion) database [3] contains posed emotional facial expression images of 10 Japanese female subjects (6 different emotion and neutral face displays), see Figure 2. The expressed emotions correspond to the 6 primary or basic emotions postulated by Ekman and Friesen [4] and possess each a distinctive content together with a unique facial expression. They seem to be universal across human ethnicities and cultures and comprise happiness, sadness, fear, disgust, surprise and anger. The images are in grayscale, tiff format at a size of 112×96.

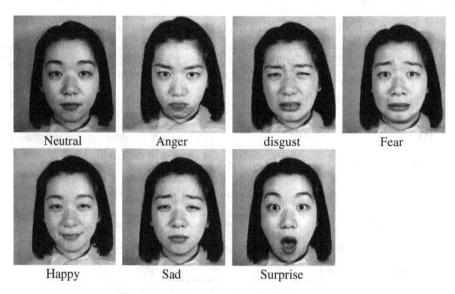

Neutral   Anger   disgust   Fear

Happy   Sad   Surprise

Fig. 2. Sample images of the JAFFE database

This database contains more samples for certain individuals and expressions. For this reason we have discarded some images in order to get the same number of images per person and emotion. Table 3 shows the number of experiments performed for each expression.

3.2 Conditions of the Experiments

Biometric identification rate and verification error has been obtained training with 1 neutral face per person (train 1) or 3 neutral faces per person (train 3), and testing

Table 3. Number of tests for training with 1 face image per person (train 1). For training with 3 images per person (train 3) we use the same number of tests except for the Neutral experiment, that cannot be done.

Expressions	Identification	Verification	
	Train 1	genuine	impostor
Angry	10×10×3	10×3	9×10×3
Disgust	10×10×2	10×2	9×10×2
Fear	10×10×3	10×3	9×10×3
Happiness	10×10×2	10×2	9×10×2
Neutral	10×10×2	10×2	9×10×2
Sadness	10×10×3	10×3	9×10×3
Surprise	10×10×3	10×3	9×10×3

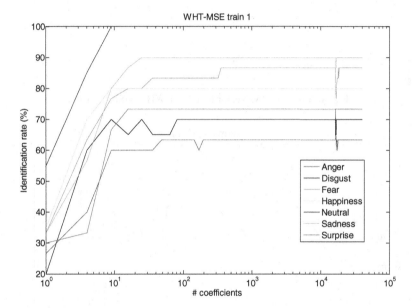

Fig. 3. Identification rate vs vector length for WHT-MSE train 1

with images with different expressions. Table 3 shows the number of training and testing samples in each case.

We used two different distance measures between training and testing vectors, Mean Squared Error (MSE) and the Mean Absolute Difference (MAD) defined as:

$$MSE(\vec{x}, \vec{y}) = \sum_{i=1}^{(N')^2} (x_i - y_i)^2 \qquad (1)$$

$$MAD(\vec{x}, \vec{y}) = \sum_{i=1}^{(N')^2} |x_i - y_i| \qquad (2)$$

Where $N' \times N'$ is the dimensionality of the vectors that represent faces.

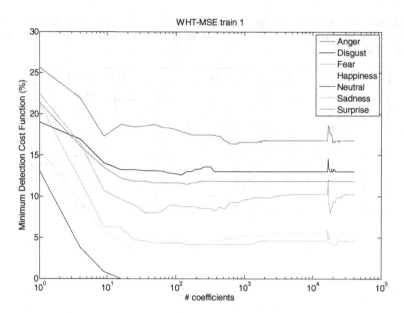

Fig. 4. Min (DCF) vs vector length for WHT-MSE train 1

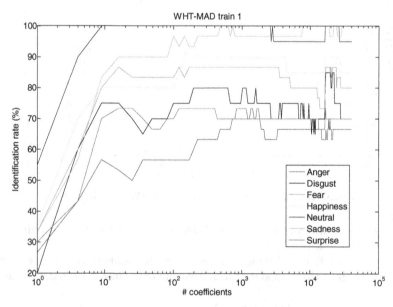

Fig. 5. Identification rate vs number of coefficients for WHT-MAD and 1 face for training

Figures 3, 4, 5, 6, 7, 8, 9 and 10 show the identification rates and verification errors for DCT and WHT versus the dimensionality of the vectors and for all the facial expressions. We can see that the optimal is around 100 components. This value is quite stable for different expressions.

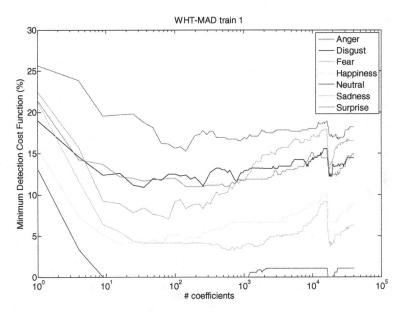

Fig. 6. Min(DCF) vs number of coefficients for WHT-MAD and 1 face for training

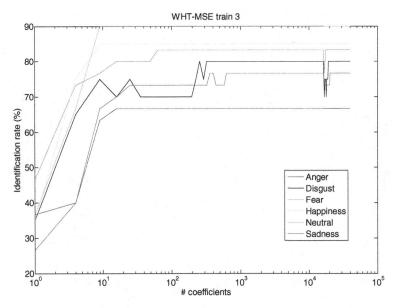

Fig. 7. Identification rate vs number of coefficients for WHT-MSE and 3 faces for training

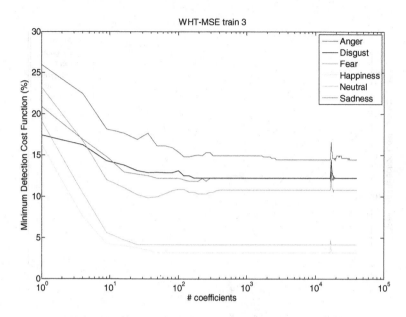

Fig. 8. Min(DCF) vs number of coefficients for WHT-MSE and 3 faces for training

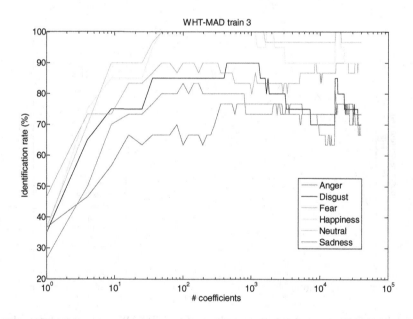

Fig. 9. Identification rate vs number of coefficients for WHT-MAD and 3 faces for training

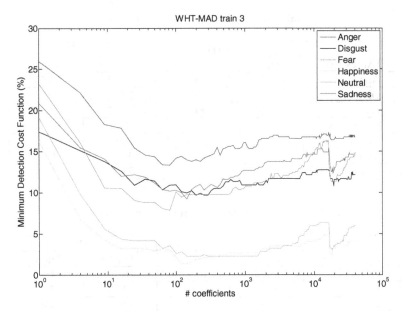

Fig. 10. Min(DCF) vs number of coefficients for WHT-MAD and 3 faces for training

Tables 4, 5, 6 and 7 represent the identification errors and min(DCF) obtained from previous plots for a number of 100 coefficients.

Table 4. Identification rates (%) for DCT

	MAD		MSE	
Expressions	Train 1	Train 3	Train 1	Train 3
Angry	70	83.33	66.67	73.33
Disgust	65	70	75	90
Fear	70	76.67	90	90
Happiness	80	90	95	100
Neutral	100		100	
Sadness	96.67	100	96.67	100
Surprise	96.67	100	90	100

Table 5. Minimum Detection Cost Function (%) for DCT

	MAD		MSE	
Expressions	Train 1	Train 3	Train 1	Train 3
Angry	13.91	10.46	14.7	11.32
Disgust	14.25	11.98	11.98	10.96
Fear	15.19	14.05	7.69	8.31
Happiness	9.85	4.63	3.75	2.73
Neutral	1.06		0	
Sadness	7.38	7.25	3.5	2.45
Surprise	8.54	7.92	4.91	3.5

Table 6. Identification rates (%) for WHT

Expressions	MAD		MSE	
	Train 1	Train 3	Train 1	Train 3
Angry	73.33	76.67	73.33	66.67
Disgust	85	90	70	80
Fear	86.67	90	86.67	83.33
Happiness	95	100	80	85
Neutral	100		100	
Sadness	100	100	90	90
Surprise	73.33	83.33	73.33	76.66

Table 7. Minimum Detection Cost Function (%) for WHT

Expressions	MAD		MSE	
	Train 1	Train 3	Train 1	Train 3
Angry	15.28	13.33	16.39	14.44
Disgust	10.92	9.67	12.58	12.26
Fear	7.06	7.87	7.99	9.84
Happiness	4.02	1.34	4.02	3.19
Neutral	0		0	
Sadness	3.31	2.27	4.17	4.17
Surprise	10.97	9.26	11.46	11.83

4 Conclusions

We have studied the relevance of facial expressions on biometric systems using two different feature extraction algorithms (DCT and WHT) and two different error criterion (MAD and MSE) with a Nearest Neighbor classifier. Main conclusions are the following:

a)   In our simulations, facial expression produces a drop on recognition rates (verification and identification applications).
b)   Optimal vector length for biometric recognition seems to be same value than in the absence of facial expression (100 components). This value is quite stable for all the studied scenarios (transform, error criterion and different facial expressions).

Acknowledgements

This work has been supported by FEDER, MEC, TEC2006-13141-C03-02/TCM and COST-2102.

References

1. Ekman, P., Friesen, W.V., Ellsworth, P.: What emotion categories or dimensions can observes judge from facial behavior? In: Ekman, P. (ed.) Emotions in the Human Face, pp. 39–55. Cambridge University Press, London (1982)
2. Ekman, P.: Cross-cultural studies of facial expression. In: Ekman, P. (ed.) Darwin and Facial Expression, pp. 169–222. Academic Press Inc., London (1973)
3. Lyons, M., Akamatsu, S., Kamachi, M., Gyoba, J.: Coding Facial Expressions with Gabor Wavelets. In: Third IEEE International Conference on Automatic Face and Gesture Recognition, pp. 200–205 (April 1998)
4. Ekman, P., Friesen, W.: Constants Across Cultures in the Face and Emotion. Journal of Personality and Social Psychology 17(2), 124–129 (1971)
5. Li, S.Z., Jain, A.K.: Handbook of face recognition. Springer, Heidelberg (2006)
6. Faundez-Zanuy, M.: Biometric security technology. IEEE Aerospace and Electronic Systems Magazine 21(6), 15–26 (2006)
7. Faundez-Zanuy, M.: Face Recognition in a Transformed Domain. In: IEEE Proceedings 37th Annual International Carnahan Conference On Security Tecnology, pp. 290–297 (2003)
8. Gibson, J.D.: Digital compression for multimedia, principles and standards. Morgan Kaufmann, San Francisco (1998)
9. Jain, A.K.: Fundamentals of digital image processing. Prentice Hall, Englewood Cliffs (1989)
10. Faundez-Zanuy, M., Roure, J., Espinosa-Duró, V., Ortega, J.A.: An efficient face verification method in a transform domain. Pattern recognition letters 28(7), 854–858 (2007)
11. Martinez, A.M.: Recognizing Imprecisely Localized, Partially Occluded, and Expres-sion Variant Faces from a Single Sample per Class. IEEE Transaction On Pattern Analysis and Machine Intelligence 24(6), 748–763 (2002)

Biometric Face Recognition with Different Training and Testing Databases

Joan Fabregas and Marcos Faundez-Zanuy

Escola Universitària Politècnica de Mataró (Adscrita a la UPC)
08303 MATARO (BARCELONA), Spain
fabregas@eupmt.es, faundez@eupmt.es
http://www.eupmt.es/veu

Abstract. Biometric face recognition presents a wide range of variability sources, such as make up, illumination, pose, facial expression, etc. Although some public available databases include these phenomena, it is a laboratory condition far away from real biometric system scenarios. In this paper we perform a set of experiments training and testing with different face databases in order to reduce the wide range of problems present in face images from different users (make up, facial expression, rotations, etc.). We use a novel dispersion matcher, which opposite to classical biometric systems, does not need to be trained with the whole set of users. It can recognize if two photos are of the same person, even if the photos of that person were not used in training the classifier.

1 Introduction

In this paper we extend our previous work [18] by means of a more sophisticated experimental section. So far most of literature present experiments based on a single public (or private) database. In the best case, experimental results are provide with two or three databases in order to demonstrate that the proposed algorithm can work fine in several scenarios and that it is not trimmed to only a single database. In this paper, thanks to a novel strategy for classification named dispersion matcher, we are able to train a classifier with users belonging to a given database and to test this system in a different one. This is due to the fact that we do not work out a specific model for each person. We just train a classifier to decide if two input samples (training and testing ones) belong to the same user or not. Thus, we only have two classes: genuine and impostor. Although this seems more focused to verification applications (1:1 comparisons) it is quite straight away to extend it to identification (1:N comparisons) by means of a set of verifications with all the existing users.

1.1 The Biometric Systems Problematic

Biometric security systems [1] offer a good set of advantages in front of classical systems (passwords, keys, etc.). Nevertheless a number of problems remain to be solved. In [2] we split these problems into four main categories (security, privacy,

A. Esposito et al. (Eds.): HH and HM Interaction 2007, LNAI 5042, pp. 44–55, 2008.

accuracy and scale). In this paper, a new mechanism that can alleviate two of these four problems is explained. Mainly they are:

a) Accuracy: How to accurately and efficiently represent and recognize biometric patterns.
b) Scale: How to acquire repeatable and distinctive patterns from a broad population.

Most of the current performed research on biometrics starts with the collection of a biometric database or the use of an available public/ private database, such as those previously described in [3]. This is a valid approach in an initial step. It alleviates the problem to have a large amount of volunteers available to test the system each time you modify some parameters of your algorithm, but it has some drawbacks. Some of them have been exposed in an ironic way, for instance, by Nagy in "Candide's practical principles of experimental pattern recognition" [4]. A rule, which certainly should not be stated by an honest researcher, is the following:

a) Theorem: there exists a set of data for which a candidate algorithm is superior to any given rival algorithm. This set may be constructed by omitting from the test set any pattern which is misclassified by the candidate algorithm.
b) Casey caution: do not ever make your experimental data available to others; someone may find an obvious solution that you missed.

Thus, database availability is important in order to validate a given algorithm, to make feasible a comparison between different algorithms, and also to develop an algorithm. This kind of evaluation is known as technology evaluation [16]. The goal of a technology evaluation is to compare competing algorithms from a single technology. Testing of all algorithms is carried out on a standardized database collected by a "universal" sensor. Nonetheless, performance with this database will depend upon both the environment and the population from which it is collected. Testing is carried out by using offline processing of the data. Because the database is fixed, the results of technology tests are repeatable.

Some important aspects of a given database are:

a) Number of users (a large number of users permits studying the discriminability capability of a given biometric trait).
b) Number of recording sessions (several sessions performed in different days permit to study the inter-session variability).
c) Number of different samples per session (several acquisitions per session permit to study the intra-session variability).

A major advantage of database availability is to set up the evaluation conditions that can avoid some common mistakes done in system designs [5]:

a) "Testing on the training set": the test scores are obtained using the training data, which is an optimal and unrealistic situation.
b) "Overtraining": The whole database is used too extensively in order to optimize the performance. This can be identified when a given algorithm gives exceptionally good performance on just one particular data set.

Databases include different material for training and testing in order to avoid the first problem. In addition, the availability of several databases helps to test the algorithms over new stuff and thus to check if the algorithms developed by a given laboratory can generalize their results (solving the second problem).

We can find an interesting observation in [13,page 161], in the context of on-line signature recognition [17]: "for any given database, perhaps a composite of multiple individual databases, we can always fine tune a signature verification system to provide the best overall error trade-off curve for that database –for the three databases here, I was able to bring my overall equal-error rate down to about 2.5%- but we must always ask ourselves, does this fine tune make common sense in the real world? If the fine tuning does not make common sense, it is in all likelihood exploiting a peculiarity of the database. Then, if we do plan to introduce the system into the market place, we are better off without the fine tuning." We have especially considered this smart observation and in order to fulfill this recommendation:

- We have not performed any fine tuning that although it would improve the results, it would yield no sense (unrealistic) error rates.
- We have gone one step further: we have trained and adjusted the system with one database and we have tested with two different ones that contain different users, zooms & pans, rotations, acquisition devices and in brief: different casuistic.

Usually in classical pattern recognition systems there are a limited number of classes and a great number of training samples. For example in the recognition of handwritten digits from U.S. postal envelopes described in [6] there are just ten classes (digits). This situation is clearly reversed in biometrics, where we normally take three to five measures per person during the enrollment (three to five samples per class for training) and the population enrolled in the database is large (much more classes than samples per class) [7]. In this situation there are not enough training samples for fitting a sophisticated model for each person.

In this paper, we will present:

a)   A new approach in order to manage the large number of classes and the limited number of samples per class.

b)   Some experiments on the face recognition case training with one database and testing with another one.

2   Training Strategy for Small Number of Training Samples

In general, pattern recognition can be approached from two distinct points of view [8]:

a)   Generative (also named Informative): The classifier learns the class densities, examines the likelihood of each class to produce the features measured and assigns to the most likely class. Because each class density is considered apart from the others, the model for each class is relatively easy to train. For biometrics, this corresponds to one model per person; just samples belonging to this user are used. In this case, the main problem is the small number of available samples per user. For instance, a value of 5 snapshots is typical for face recognition application. Examples include Linear Discriminant Analysis and Hidden Markov Models.

b) Discriminative: The classifier does not model the underlying class feature densities; it focuses on modeling the class boundaries or the class membership probabilities directly. For biometrics, this corresponds to training the classifier to differentiate one user from the others. This means that the algorithm requires samples from the given user but also samples belonging to the other ones. In this approach the number of samples is higher, but most of the samples are inhibitory (there is a small number of samples belonging to a given user, when compared with the number of samples belonging to the other users). These models are harder to train and often involve complex algorithms; examples include neural networks and support vector machines.

In the first case (generative model), when a new user must be added, a new model must be computed for this user. In the second case (discriminative), usually, the whole system must be retrained, which is time consuming and can be a drawback for a real operating system that must enroll new users quite frequently. Table 1 summarizes the main comparisons between the two approaches [8].

Table 1. Comparison between Generative and discriminative pattern recognition approaches

	Generative	Discriminative
Model assumptions	Class densities	Class boundaries (discriminant functions)
Parameter estimation	"Easy"	"Hard"
Advantages	More efficient if model correct.	More flexible, robust because fewer assumptions.
Disadvantages	Bias if model is incorrect.	May also be biased. Ignores information of the underlying distributions.

In order to avoid these disadvantages, we present an alternative method, which is called dispersion matcher, which is especially useful for biometric systems. We train a single classifier to solve the dichotomy: Are these two features vectors from the same person? In doing this, we solve the problem concerning the number of training samples per class. As we do not need to train the classifier with the people present in the operational database, it will be capable of classifying in an open world situation. As a matter of fact, the biometric system, in contrast with the classical discriminative and generative algorithms, does not learn any specific model for each user, and it has a larger generalization capability.

When a user wants to be authenticated by the system he/she presents his/her biometric sample, the dispersion matcher compares the biometric sample to authenticate with the samples used as references during the user enrollment. The user is accepted if the fusion of the scores [15] obtained with each comparison is larger than an established threshold. For example the mean of the scores as a fusion method can be used.

When we measure any physiological characteristic of a person, such as the length or width of a finger, the process is subject to errors and we do not always obtain the same result. Statistics points out that if we repeat the same measure many times, the values will be distributed according to the normal Gaussian distribution, $\mathcal{N}(x \mid \mu_i, \sigma_i^2)$ which is governed by the mean (μ_i) and the variance (σ_i^2) of the

measures. In many situations, the distribution of the mean of the physiological characteristic over the entire population becomes another normal distribution,
$\mathcal{N}(x \mid \mu_p, \sigma_p^2)$ governed by the mean (μ_p) and the variance (σ_p^2) over the population. The dispersion matcher is based on the fact that the variance σ_i^2 is always
smaller than σ_p^2. When stating the difference between two samples of this physiological measure, it will be normally smaller if they are from the same person than if they
come from different persons. This may be depicted, as in figure 1, with two Gaussians; one for differences corresponding to pairs of genuine samples and another that
corresponds to pairs of genuine and impostor samples.

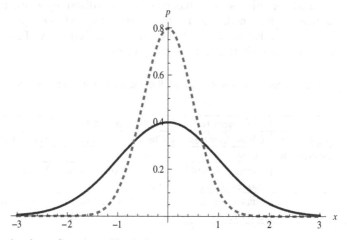

Fig. 1. Example of two Gaussians. The dashed one corresponds to differences between pairs of
genuine samples ($\mathcal{N}(x \mid 0, 0.25)$ in this example), and the continuous one to differences
between pairs of genuine and impostor samples ($\mathcal{N}(x \mid 0, 1)$ in this example).

A quadratic discriminant classifier [9] is an easy and good choice to solve the dichotomy, because in practice the distributions of each physiological characteristic are
bell-shaped and present linear correlations. Our results are obtained with one such
easy classifier to solve the dichotomy.

In order to understand the difference between our dispersion matcher and the other
classical pattern recognition approaches, we will analyze a simple example. The ORL
[10] database consists of 40 users, 10 different snapshots per user. A typical set parti-
tioning consists of five images per person for training and five different ones for testing. Table 2 summarizes the main available data for each kind of classifier in this
situation. It can be seen that the difference between strategies is in the number of
available samples for training, being the number of testing samples the same (thus, the
statistical significance of the experimental results is the same for all of them).

It is important to emphasize that generative and discriminative systems consider
each person as one class. On the other hand, dispersion matcher only has two classes:
genuine and impostors. For this reason we can get a higher number of samples per
class for the system training.

Table 2. Example of training and testing samples for one database with n individuals and s samples per individual, using half of the samples for training and half for testing

Strategy	Samples per class for training	Samples per person for testing	
		genuine	impostor
Generative	$\dfrac{s}{2}$ genuine samples	$\dfrac{s}{2}$	$(n-1)\dfrac{s}{2}$
Discriminative	$\dfrac{s}{2}$ genuine samples $(n-1)\dfrac{s}{2}$ impostors	$\dfrac{s}{2}$	$(n-1)\dfrac{s}{2}$
Dispersion matcher	$n\dfrac{s(s-1)}{2}$ pairs genuine-genuine $n(n-1)s^2$ pairs genuine-impostor	$\dfrac{s}{2}$	$(n-1)\dfrac{s}{2}$

3   Experimental Results for Face Recognition

One way to test a given face recognition algorithm in hard conditions far from a laboratory situation is to use several databases simultaneously. We train the system with one database and then we test the system with a different one, which has been acquired in a different environment and that contains a different set of users. We have trained the classifier to check if two input samples belong to the same class (genuine user) or not (impostor). Thus, when trying to verify a person whose data has not been used to train the system we just need to enter the following information into the classifier:

- The sample image acquired during enrollment that belongs to the claimed identity. This sample is stored in the database.
- The input test sample which has just been acquired.

It is irrelevant if a person has been used to train the classifier or not, because we are not fitting any model to each person. This is the core of the proposed algorithm that lets to obtain a major improvement when compared with the classical generative and discriminative systems.

3.1   Databases

We have used the ORL [10], AR [11] and JAFFE [12] databases.

Figures 2, 3 and 4 show the snapshots of one user belonging to each database, which has the following features:

a)   ORL: 10 different snapshots of 40 people. For some subjects, the images were taken at different times, varying the lighting, facial expressions (open/closed eyes, smiling / not smiling) and facial details (glasses / no glasses). See figure 2.

b) AR: 126 individuals, with 26 images for each, taken in two different sessions at a time distance of two weeks, varying the lighting and the facial expression. We have used 6 of the 26 images, excluding the ones overexposed and the ones in which the face was partially occluded by sunglasses or scarves. We perform our research focused on a collaborative scenario, where the user does not show any strange artefact, the illumination is controlled, etc. The study of the relevance of these phenomena, although challenging, are not our goal. Nine individuals were not complete or not available. Thus, we have only used 117. See figure 3.

c) JAFFE: It contains posed emotional facial expression images of 10 Japanese female subjects (6 different emotion and neutral face displays), see Figure 4. The expressed emotions correspond to the 6 primary or basic emotions. There are several snapshots for each person and emotion (2 or 3 images).

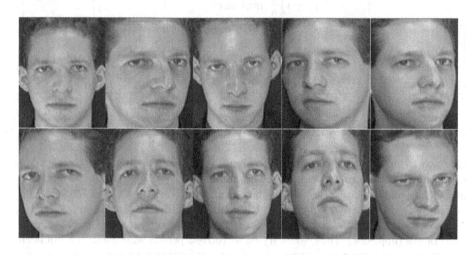

Fig. 2. Sample images of the first user of the ORL database

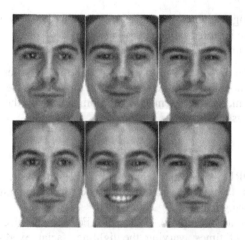

Fig. 3. Sample images of one persn from the AR database

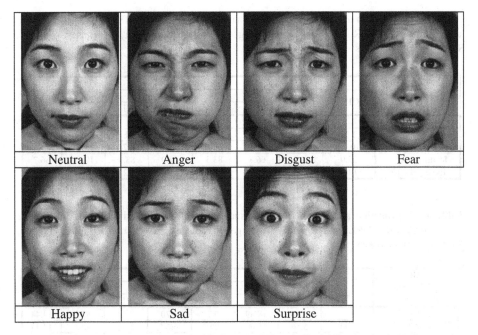

| Neutral | Anger | Disgust | Fear |

| Happy | Sad | Surprise |

Fig. 4. Sample images of the JAFFE (Japanese Female Facial Expression) database

3.2 Experiments

Feature extraction from face images is based on DCT and can be found in our previous work [14] and [18].

Table 3 and 4 present the experimental results with different training and testing conditions. We can see that although the best results are achieved when the whole experimentation is performed over the same database, we still get good enough results when trying to verify users from a different database. In addition, the experimental results are competitive with the state of the art face recognition systems. We have used three face reference samples per person and the max{·} fusion method [15]. For the JAFFE database we have chosen the three neutral snapshots as enrollment samples. We could improve the results mixing up the emotions for enrollment, but we feel that it is more challenging to discard the presence of emotions during enrollment and showing them to the classifier during testing phase.

For verification mode, the minimum detection cost function (DCF) [1] has been evaluated, which is an error measure close to the Equal Error Rate (EER). Thus, the smaller this value, the better the performance. DCF is the Detection Cost Function when the threshold is set up a priori, while min DCF is obtained with the threshold set up a posteriori (in the classical and unrealistic way). For identification mode we have measured the performance with the identification rate and the expected rank [7], defined as the expected position of the true identity in the list of enrolled candidates ordered according to their similarity with the presented biometric. Thus, the smaller this value, the better the performance. The minimum value is one and corresponds to

Table 3. Identification and verification performance training the classifier with ORL database and testing with AR and JAFFE (A=Anger, D=disgust, F=Fear, H=Happy, Sa=Sad, Su=Surprise) databases

ORL 19 features threshold = 10.73	Testing database							
	ORL	AR	JAFFE					
			A	D	F	H	Sa	Su
DCF (%)	-	7.74	23.52	15.74	18.89	10.19	6.48	20.37
min. DCF (%)	2.52	5.06	20.74	11.48	16.30	6.85	3.89	16.85
Threshold	10.73	6.38	4.66	14.01	9.38	8.74	15.14	4.05
Identi. rate (%)	95.0	80.6	66.7	83.3	70.0	83.3	100.0	66.7
Expected rank	1.06	1. 93	1.77	1.27	1.83	1.23	1.00	2.13

Table 4. Identification and verification performance training the classifier with AR database and testing with ORL and JAFFE (A=Anger, D=disgust, F=Fear, H=Happy, Sa=Sad, Su=Surprise) databases

AR 17 features threshold = 13.88	Testing database							
	AR	ORL	JAFFE					
			A	D	F	H	Sa	Su
DCF (%)	-	5.86	18.89	20.74	8.70	8.52	8.52	14.44
min. DCF (%)	3.11	5.56	15.00	10.93	6.67	2.04	4.81	14.44
Threshold	13.88	13.73	12.62	11.27	15.40	17.68	16.12	13.65
Identi. Rate (%)	93.0	87.1	73.3	73.3	83.3	96.7	100.0	80.0
Expected rank	1.12	1.43	1.5	1.47	1.17	1.03	1.00	1.30

100% identification rate. Figures 5, 6 and 7 show the performance of the system using the JAFFE database for testing.

For comparison, Table 5 shows the identification rate attained with the ORL database (training and testing with the same database) with other state of the art methods.

Table 5. Classification performance using the ORL database

Method	Eigenface [19]	Fisherface [20]	DLDA [21]	Waveletface [22]
Identification rate	90%	82.5%	89%	94.5%

It is important to emphasize that the proposed dichotomic classifier can manage an important set of situations where classical systems would fail or simply will not be able to manage. Mainly they are:

a)   It can decide if two snapshots (model and testing images) belong to the same person or not. It is not necessary that the information of this person took place for the system training.

b)   It is not necessary to re-train the system when new users are added in the system. This has been checked by the good performance in verifying people

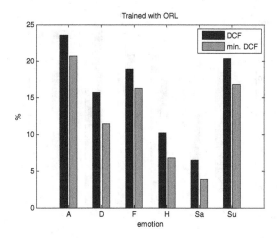

Fig. 5. Verification errors with threshold set up a priori (DCF) and a posteriori (min. DCF) training the classifier with the ORL database and testing with the JAFFE (Japanese Female Facial Expression) database. A=Anger, D=disgust, F=Fear, H=Happy, Sa=Sad, Su=Surprise.

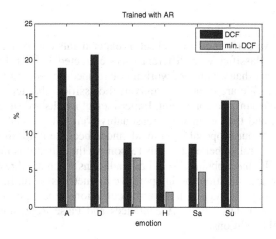

Fig. 6. Verification errors with threshold set up a priori (DCF) and a posteriori (min. DCF) training the classifier with the AR database and testing with the JAFFE (Japanese Female Facial Expression) database. A=Anger, D=disgust, F=Fear, H=Happy, Sa=Sad, Su=Surprise.

belonging to a database not used during classifier training. Just for some particular facial expressions there is an increment on error rates (mainly disgust and anger).

It is important to emphasize that an important property of the JAFFE database is that it contains faces which can be said to be distorted by emotional expression and as such present even more of a challenge to the method.

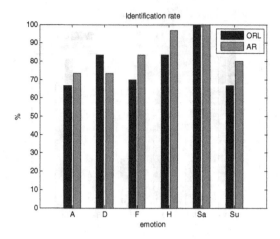

Fig. 7. Identification rates training the classifier with the AR and ORL databases and testing with the JAFFE (Japanese Female Facial Expression) database. A=Anger, D=disgust, F=Fear, H=Happy, Sa=Sad, Su=Surprise.

4 Conclusions

In this paper we have performed a novel set of experiments consisting of training and testing a biometric classifier with different users extracted from different databases. This is due to the fact that we are not working out a specific model for each user present in the database. We are training a "universal classifier" that tells us if two input images belong to the same person or not. Experimental results are similar to the state-of-the-art systems, and they even work reasonably well when facial expressions are present. Nevertheless our proposal is more advanced because it not fitted to a specific database and can generalize better. For this reason we think that it is more suitable for a real application. We have obtained small degradations when the threshold is set up a priori, which is the real situation for an operative biometric system. In fact, the classical EER measure corresponds to laboratory conditions (the threshold is set up a posteriori in order to balance False Acceptances and False Rejections) and is more optimistic than real conditions.

Acknowledgements

This work has been supported by COST2102, FEDER and MEC, TEC2006-13141-C03-02/TCM.

References

1. Faundez Zanuy, M.: Biometric security technology. IEEE Aerospace and Electronic Systems Magazine 21(6), 15–26 (2006)
2. Faundez-Zanuy, M.: Biometric recognition: why not massively adopted yet? IEEE Aerospace and Electronic Systems Magazine 20(8), 25–28 (2005)

3. Faundez-Zanuy, M., Fierrez-Aguilar, J., Ortega-Garcia, J., Gonzalez-Rodriguez, J.: Multimodal biometric databases: an overview. IEEE Aerospace and electronic systems magazine 21(9), 29–37 (2006)
4. Nagy, G.: Candide's practical principles of experimental pattern recognition. IEEE Trans. On Pattern Analysis and Machine Intelligence 5(2), 199–200 (1983)
5. Bolle, R.M., Ratha, N.K., Pankanti, S.: Performance evaluation in 1:1 Biometric engines. In: Li, S.Z., Lai, J.-H., Tan, T., Feng, G.-C., Wang, Y. (eds.) SINOBIOMETRICS 2004. LNCS, vol. 3338, pp. 27–46. Springer, Heidelberg (2004)
6. Hastie, T., Tibshirani, R., Friedman, J.: The Elements of Statistical Learning. In: Data Mining, Inference, and Prediction, Springer, Heidelberg (2001)
7. Bolle, R.M., Connell, J.H., Pankanti, S., Ratha, N.K., Senior, A.W.: Guide to Biometrics. Springer, Heidelberg (2004)
8. Rubinstein, Y.D., Hastie, T.: Discriminative vs Informative Learning, Knowledge Discovery and Data Mining, pp. 49–53 (1997)
9. Duda, R.O., Hart, P.E., Strork, D.G.: Pattern Classification, 2nd edn. Wiley-Interscience, Chichester (2001)
10. Samaria, F., Harter, A.: Parameterization of a stochastic model for human face identification. In: 2nd IEEE Workshop on Applications of Computer Vision, Sarasota (Florida) (December 1994)
11. Martinez, A.M.: Recognizing Imprecisely Localized, Partially Occluded, and Expression Variant Faces from a Single Sample per Class. IEEE Transaction On Pattern Analysis and Machine Intelligence 24(6), 748–763 (2002)
12. Lyons, M., Akamatsu, S., Kamachi, M., Gyoba, J.: Coding Facial Expressions with Gabor Wavelets. In: Third IEEE International Conference on Automatic Face and gesture
13. Jain, A.K., Bolle, R., Pankanti, S. (eds.): Biometrics, personal identification in networked society. Kluwer academic publishers, Dordrecht (1999)
14. Faundez-Zanuy, M., Roure-Alcobe, J., Espinosa-Duró, V., Ortega, J.A.: An efficient face verification method in a transformed domain. Pattern recognition letters 28(7), 854–858 (2007)
15. Faundez-Zanuy, M.: Data fusion in biometrics. IEEE Aerospace and Electronic Systems Magazine 20(1), 34–38 (2005)
16. Mansfield, A.J., Wayman, J.L.: Best Practices in Testing and Reporting Performance of Biometric Devices. Version 2.01. National Physical Laboratory Report CMSC 14/02 (August 2002)
17. Faundez-Zanuy, M.: Signature recognition state-of-the-art. IEEE Aerospace and Electronic Systems Magazine 20(7), 28–32 (2005)
18. Faundez-Zanuy, M., Fabregas, J.: On the relevance of facial expressions for biometric recognition. In: Esposito, A., et al. (eds.) Nonverbal Features of Human-Human and Human-Machine Interaction. LNCS. Springer, Heidelberg (submitted to, 2008) (to be published, 2008)
19. Turk, M., Pentland, A.: Eigenfaces for recognition. Int. J. Cog. Neurosci. 3(1), 71–86 (1991)
20. Belhumeur, P.N., Hespanha, J.P., Kriegman, D.J.: Eigenfaces vs. Fisherface: Recognition using class specific linear projection. IEEE Trans. Pattern Anal. Machine Intell. 19, 711–720 (1997)
21. Yu, H., Yang, J.: A direct LDA algorithm for high-dimensional data with applications to face recognition. Pattern Recognit 34(12), 2067–2070 (2001)
22. Chien, J.T., Wu, C.C.: Discriminant waveletfaces and nearest feature classifiers for face recognition. IEEE Trans. Pattern Anal. Machine Intell. 24, 1644–1649 (2002)

Combining Features for Recognizing Emotional Facial Expressions in Static Images

Jiří Přinosil[1], Zdeněk Smékal[1], and Anna Esposito[2]

[1] Brno University of Technology, Czech Republic
[2] Second University of Naples, Department of Psychology and IIASS, Italy
prinosil@feec.vutbr.cz, smekal@feec.vutbr.cz,
iiass.annaesp@tin.it

Abstract. This work approaches the problem of recognizing emotional facial expressions in static images focusing on three preprocessing techniques for feature extraction such as Principal Component Analysis (PCA), Linear Discriminant Analysis (LDA), and Gabor filters. These methods are commonly used for face recognition and the novelty consists in combining features provided by them in order to improve the performance of an automatic procedure for recognizing emotional facial expressions. Testing and recognition accuracy were performed on the Japanese Female Facial Expression (JAFFE) database using a Multi-Layer Perceptron (MLP) Neural Network as classifier. The best classification accuracy on variations of facial expressions included in the training set was obtained combining PCA and LDA features (93% of correct recognition rate), whereas, combining PCA, LDA and Gabor filter features the net gave 94% of correct classification on facial expressions of subjects not included in the training set.

Keywords: Principal Component Analysis, Linear Discriminant Analysis, Gabor filters, facial features, basic emotions.

1 Introduction

Over the last decades, a considerable part of the research in computer vision has been focused on the detection and recognition of particular objects in static images with complex background. Such objects include human faces. The detection and analysis of human faces is mainly exploited in biometric applications and security systems aimed at the verification and/or recognition of the subject's identity. Recently this area has received a lot of attention and, even though the problem of recognizing faces under gross environmental variations remains largely Unsolved. Several strategies have been proposed for the development of robust face recognition systems [47, 33]. Techniques for the recognition of emotional facial expressions have been directly borrowed from face recognition approaches with the difference that what is relevant here is the uniqueness of the facial expression instead of the uniqueness of the face.

Facial expressions as markers of emotions were first suggested by Darwin [5], who considered them as innate "ancient habits" that could partially be modified by learning and imitation processes. This idea was debated by several authors, among whom

A. Esposito et al. (Eds.): HH and HM Interaction 2007, LNAI 5042, pp. 56–69, 2008.

the most representative were Klineberg [21], La Barre [2], and Birdwhistell [3], and more recently White [45] and Fridlund [13], according to whom any behavior, and therefore also facial expressions of emotions, is learned.

Darwin's approach was recovered and reinforced about a century later by Tomkins [42], who posited the basis for the research on the instrumental role of facial movements and facial feedbacks in experiencing emotions. According to Tomkins, emotions are the driving forces of our primary motivational system acting as amplifiers of what we receive from the environment, and our face is the most important expression of these emotions. This is because facial expressions of emotions are universally shared. People from different cultures can easily recognize a happy or a sad face because of an "innate affective programme" for each of what is considered "a primary emotion" that acts on the facial musculature to produce emotional facial expressions. On this research line, Ekman [9, 10] and Izard [17] identified a small set of emotions (the primary ones: only six for Ekman - happiness, sadness, anger, fear, surprise, and disgust; to which Izard added contempt, guilt, interest, and shame) associated with a unique configuration of facial muscle movements, and both developed some anatomically based coding systems - the Facial Action Coding System, (FACS) [8], the Maximally Discriminative Facial Movement Coding System (MAX) and AFFEX [17] - for measuring facial behaviors and identifying emotional expressions. The categorization of emotions is, however, debated among researchers and different theories have been proposed for its conceptualization, among them dimensional models [35, 38]. Such models envisage a finite set of primary features (dimensions) into which emotions can be decomposed and suggest that different combinations of such features can arouse different affective states. Bringing the dimensional concept to an extreme, such theories suggest that, if the number of primary features extends along a continuum, it would be possible to generate an infinite number of affective states. This idea, even though intriguing, hurts with the principle of economy that seems to rule the dynamic of natural systems, since in this case, the evaluation of affective states may require an infinite computational time. Moreover, humans tend to categorize, since it allows making associations between multi-sensorial input and semantic content, enables rapid recovering of partially matched information and facilitates the handling of unexpected events, and therefore, categories may be favored in order to avoid excessive processing time.

Assuming, in the light of the above considerations, that there are some basic emotions from which other affective states can be derived, we will consider, in the following, the automatic classification of 4 basic emotional facial expressions exploiting methods derived from the face recognition area. These basic emotional expressions are: happiness, sadness, surprise, and anger.

The goal of this paper is to test the appropriateness of combining some feature extraction procedures for classifying facial expressions of the above mentioned basic emotions. To this aim, section 2 briefly reviews the procedure for an automatic analysis of facial expressions, and section 3 briefly describes the three feature extraction methods under examinations. Section 4 presents the classification results (benchmarked on the *Japanese Female Facial Expression* (JAFFE) database [20]) obtained using a Multi-layer Perceptron neural net that exploits either features provided by each method or their combinations. Section 5 is dedicated to the discussion and conclusions.

2 Automatic Facial Expression Analysis

As it has already been mentioned in the introduction, the approaches for extracting emotional facial features from facial expressions exploit similar principles used for face recognition. This means that similar pattern recognition paradigms on data reduction are employed, such as redundancy removal and dimensionality reduction with the aim to identify features describing the uniqueness of a facial expression with different faces instead of features describing the uniqueness of a face with different facial expressions.

The whole procedure for the automatic analysis of facial expressions requires the implementation of the following three consecutive stages, each of them being a research problem open to investigations into the identification of new methodologies and research ideas to advance in the field [11]:

* Face acquisition: this involves the detection, localization and normalization of the face and its facial features (eyes, mouth, nose, etc.) from an input image. Usually the image has the face in frontal view and some global information on the position of the face in the scene is known a priori. This is the case for the experiments reported in the present paper;
* Feature extraction: this involves the identification, selection, and extraction of appropriate facial features which are considered (according to a given criterion) to describe at the best the particular facial emotional features from the localized face;
* Classification of the emotional state: this involves the classification of a particular facial expression on the basis of the features extracted as belonging to an emotional category among a set of emotional states, generally established a priori.

In the present work, the first stage was implemented using a popular procedure proposed by Viola and Jones [44] for robust face detection, capable, at a very low computational cost, of processing images and detecting faces from them at a detection rate comparable to the best previous systems proposed in literature [41, 36, 38, 34]. The procedure consists of two phases. The first phase exploits a new image representation that the authors called "Integral Images", which uses simple rectangular features (of the kind of Haar Basis functions [30]) and filters instead of pixel intensities. In the second phase, simple classifiers select critical facial features from image regions, through a greedy feature selection process (the AdaBoost learning algorithm [16]) and then they are combined in a "cascade" in order to discard background regions.

3 Feature Extraction

The aim of this stage is to choose a small set of features that are unique for the specific facial expressions. It can be claimed that this is the most important part of the whole analysis, because only from properly selected features is it possible to correctly analyze and classify the corresponding emotional state expressed in the face. The selected features have to be invariant as regards the gender, age, race and appearance of the subject's face. Feature extraction methods can be divided into two major categories [28]:

- Holistic methods – the features are extracted from the whole face at once;
- Local-based methods – the features are extracted only from selected parts of the face (areas around eyes, mouth, etc.).

In this paper, two methods, *Principal Component Analysis* (PCA) and *Linear Discriminant Analysis* (LDA), are used for local feature extraction while one method, based on *Gabor filters*, is used as a holistic one.

3.1 Principal Component Analysis

The Principal Component Analysis (PCA) is a classical linear projection method for mapping described data from a higher dimensional space to a lower dimensional space [19]. The central idea behind PCA is to reduce the dimensionality on datasets containing a large number of interrelated variables, while retaining as much as possible the useful information for separating categories of unrelated data. This reduction is achieved by transforming the dataset at hand into a new set of variables, the Principal Components (PCs), which are supposed to be uncorrelated and are ordered such that the first few retain most of the variation present in the original data. For a given input vector Γ_i a PC is computed as a linear function of the elements of Γ_i which have the maximum variance. Any subsequent PC is then computed under the maximum variance assumption but also constrained in that it must not be correlated with the PCs previously computed. If the number of PCs is significantly lower than the number of the original variables and if these PC variables are interpretable, then an alternative and much simpler description of the data in a lower-dimensional space is obtained. PCA was first applied in the face recognition task by Turk and Pentland 1987 [43]. Since then, several modifications have been proposed aimed at improving the quality of processing in order to solve this task [22, 24, 27, 26, 32, 40, 25 and others].

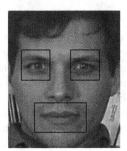

Fig. 1. Areas of interest

In the present work, following the procedure suggested in Padgett and Cottrell [1997], each input image was divided into three areas. The first two areas (35×40 pixels) are placed around the center of each eye and the third area (40×65 pixels) is placed around the center of the mouth, as displayed in Figure 1. Each area was again divided into three overlapping sub-areas, and each of these sub-areas was projected by PCA onto 15 principal components. The eigenvectors corresponding to the 1st, 5th and 10th highest eigenvalues of the right eye and mouth regions are displayed in Figure 2.

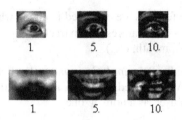

Fig. 2. Eigenvectors corresponding to the 1ˢᵗ, 5ᵗʰ and 10ᵗʰ highest eigenvalues of the right eye and mouth regions

3.2 Linear Discriminant Analysis

PCA has the drawback to determine the subspace with the largest variance among all the input images, even though the images under examination may represent the same emotional facial expression. LDA overcomes this limitation searching for a set of feature vectors obtained as a linear combination of features with the largest variance among classes and with the lowest variance within classes [38].

The goal is to maximize the between-class S_b while minimizing the within-class S_w variance, maximizing the ratio $det[S_b]/det[S_w]$, since it has been proven by Fisher 1938 [12] that if S_w is non-singular, this ratio is maximized when the column vectors of the projection matrix are the eigenvectors of $S_w^{-1}S_b$.

In our case, the same facial areas as for PCA were also processed through LDA. However, to guarantee the non-singularity of the matrix S_w, PCA was first applied to reduce the dimension of the input vectors, and successively LDA was used to select k linear discriminants ($k \leq M$) for feature description.

3.3 Gabor Filters

Both PCA and LDA perform a statistical evaluation of the pixel intensity of the input image areas, discarding any possible relationship between the remaining pixels in the image. To this aim they are local. Gabor filters instead consider the entire image which is filtered, in our case, through a set of 40 filters (8 different spatial orientations of the filter combined with 5 different filter lengths) [31] with an impulse response defined as a Gaussian function multiplied by a harmonic function.

In order to reduce the dimension of the set of feature vectors describing each image[1], the filtering is applied only to a set of 22 facial points (forming a facial mask) as illustrated in Figure 3a considering that neighboring coefficients can be assumed to be highly correlated and therefore can be discarded (as suggested by Lyons et al. [23]), and that the most visible changes in a given emotional face are produced around the eyes and mouth.

The 22-point facial mask is computed for each facial image in order to take into account different facial traits. This is done automatically (advance knowledge of eyes and mouth center positions are required). First, the mask is updated (expanded or compressed) in horizontal and vertical direction according to the distance between the

---

[1] Note that with 40 filters, any new processed image was described by a vector of 40× ($w \times h$) coefficients.

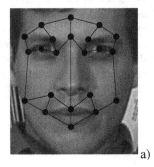 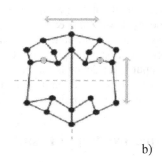

a)   b)

Fig. 3. Facial mask and its application

left and the right eye center positions (horizontal direction) and according to the distance between both eye center positions and mouth center position (vertical direction). The facial mask defined above was selected since the images to be processed are static and with a frontal facial view. In other cases it is suitable to use more complex techniques for placing/deforming the facial mask appropriately on the face as it is done with the *Active Appearance Models* (AAM) [1]). It should be noticed that AAMs require more processing steps and therefore more computational time in order to be implemented, and this is not a guarantee of improvement for the classification rate.

The facial mask is placed on each facial image such that the position of both the eye centers corresponds to the central eye points of the facial mask (as shown in Figure 3b).

According to the above procedure every emotional facial image is described using 880 features (40 filters × 22 points). This number is reduced by applying PCA and/or LDA.

4 Classification Methods

The classification of a particular emotional facial expression can be approached as a template-based, a rule-based or a neural-network-based classification method. Using a template-based classification method requires the definition of a set of templates for each facial expression category. The new facial expression is compared with the stored templates and is categorized under the class producing the best match (based on some distance measures). This approach was exploited by several authors [14, 15, and 24]. However, it was soon discarded since both the classification results were not very promising (the best accuracy was on the average 92% [24]) and the procedure of creating representative models of facial expression was quite time-consuming. Rule-based classification methods show similar drawbacks, i.e. poor accuracy recognition and quite time-consuming implementation procedures [29] since they rely on the implementation of complex expert systems. Neural-network-based classification approaches categorize facial expressions into multiple classes exploiting a categorization process learned through training examples. Even though the learning process remains a black-box procedure for the user, Neural Nets provide more effective results than the two previous discussed methods, as it can be seen from the papers published in literature [4], reaching in some cases a recognition accuracy of 100% (see the work of Zhao & Kearney [46]). The present work also exploits a neural-network-based classification approach that uses a three-layer feed-forward neural network and a back propagation learning algorithm. In our case the number of nodes in the input layer depends on the number of extracted features in input to the net, the hidden layer has 16 hidden node and the output layer 4 nodes, one for each emotional category under examination.

5   Experiments and Results

To validate both the analysis procedures and the classification task the *Japanese Female Facial Expression* (JAFFE, http://www.kasrl.org/jaffe.html) database was chosen, because the images included in the database are expression-labeled and a human viewer can identify emotional expression stimuli accurately enough. The database contains static images of ten young Japanese women expressing the six basic emotions of happiness, anger, fear, sadness, surprise and disgust, plus a neutral expression. Each basic facial emotional expression was expressed three times (allowing some variations) by the same subject, giving a total of 30 different emotional facial expressions of each basic emotion. The entire database contains 210 static images (30 different images for each basic emotion, plus 30 neutral expressions). The emotional value of the database was semantically rated by 60 Japanese female subjects on a 5 level scale (5-high, 1-low).

For the present experiments, only the four basic emotional expressions of happiness, anger, surprise and sadness were considered. Fear was excluded, due to some concerns expressed by Lyons (the author of the database) on the credibility of the fear facial expressions (http://www.kasrl.org/jaffe_info.txt) and disgust was not taken into account due to the debated position of this emotion [10]. The average rating score obtained was respectively 2.2 (SD= ±1.1) for happiness, 2.4 (SD= ±1.6) for surprise, 2.6 (SD= ±0.9) for sadness, 2.4 (SD= ±0.97) for anger.

For each of the four emotional categories, we used two images from seven subjects for a total of 56 images (7 subjects × 4 expressions × 2 images of each expression) for training of the neural net. The remaining images were used for testing and were

Table 1. Classification accuracy obtained on variations of facial emotional expressions produced by subjects included in the training set (task 1)

Facial Features	Anger	Happiness	Surprise	Sadness	Average Accuracy
PCA	93.8	93.8	100	81.3	92.2
LDA	100	87.5	100	75	90.6
PCA&LDA	**93.8**	**93.8**	**100**	**87.5**	**93.7**
Gabor(PCA)	100	87.5	100	75	90.6
Gabor(LDA)	100	87.5	100	75	90.6
Gabor(PCA&LDA)	**100**	**87.5**	**100**	**75**	**90.6**

divided into two sets, according to two different tasks proposed, one aimed at recognizing unseen emotional facial expressions of subjects included in the training set and one aimed at recognizing unseen facial expressions of subjects not included in the training set, i.e. never seen by the network.

A total of 48 (16 × 3) facial features were extracted from each image using either PCA or LDA or Gabor filters, and used as input to a three-layer feed-forward neural network, with 48 input, 16 hidden, and 4 output nodes was used for training. After PCA, LDA and Gabor facial features had been combined, the number of input nodes rose to 96. Table 1 and 2 report the classification accuracy obtained on separated and combined (in bold) facial features for the first and second task, respectively.

Table 2. Classification accuracy obtained on facial emotional expressions of new subjects (task 2)

Facial Features	Anger	Happiness	Surprise	Sadness	Average Accuracy
PCA	83.3	91.7	91.7	66.7	83.5
LDA	100	100	91.7	50	85.3
PCA&LDA	**91.7**	**100**	**91.7**	**83.3**	**91.7**
Gabor(PCA)	75	91.7	100	83.3	87.4
Gabor(LDA)	91.7	83.3	100	83.3	89.6
Gabor(PCA&LDA)	**91.7**	**83.3**	**100**	**100**	**93.8**

The average classification accuracy for each set of facial features and for both the tasks is displayed in Figure 4.

The results reported in Table 1 and 2 and in Figure 4 generate the following considerations:

- In general, the recognition accuracy of facial expressions of known subjects is higher than the recognition of facial expressions of unknown subjects (93.7% against 91.7% for PCA and LDA feature combination as the most representative method), with only one exception, namely when combined Gabor(PCA&LDA) features are used (93.75% against 90.65%);
- The recognition accuracy increases when facial features are combined but the rate of increase depends on both the facial features and the task. In recognizing variations of facial expressions of known subjects, combined LDA and PCA outperform combined Gabor(PCA&LDA) features, whereas the tendency is inverted when the task is to classify new facial emotional expressions;
- The recognition rate depends on the basic emotions to be recognized and on the task. For task 1, emotional facial expressions for surprise and anger are recognized with 100% accuracy by almost all the proposed coding procedures, whereas for sadness and happiness the accuracy rate depends on the coding (in particular combined PCA and LDA features increase the recognition accuracy of sad expressions). For task 2, anger and happiness are better recognized using LDA or combined PCA and LDA features, whereas surprise and sadness obtained an accuracy of 100% using Gabor or combined Gabor(PCA&LDA) features;
- The accuracy for PCA and LDA codings was 10% higher for task 1 than for task 2. These differences disappear when the features are combined.

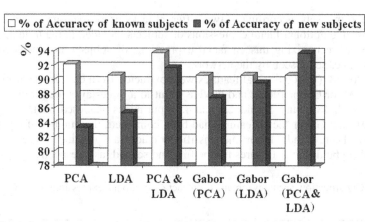

Fig. 4. Average accuracy for each set of facial features and for each proposed task

Table 3. Confusion matrix obtained by combining *PCA&LDA* facial features. Results are reported for both the proposed tasks.

	Anger		Happiness		Surprise		Sadness	
	Task1	Task2	Task1	Task2	Task1	Task2	Task1	Task2
Anger	93.8	91.7	0	0	0	8.3	6.2	0
Happiness	0	0	93.8	100	0	0	6.2	0
Surprise	0	8.3	0	0	100	91.7	0	0
Sadness	3.1	4.1	9.4	12.6	0	0	87.5	83.3

Table 3 and 4 display the confusion matrices for the results gathered by the most representative facial features (combined PCA&LDA and Gabor(PCA&LDA)).

As it could be noticed, there is a negligible percentage of false recognitions that does not depend on the facial feature extraction methods, i.e. some of the facial expressions are wrongly attributed to the same class independently of their facial feature coding.

The Gabor(PCA&LDA) facial coding for surprise and sadness gives significantly better classification accuracy than the PCA&LDA coding, but for happiness the trend is inverted.

Table 4. Confusion matrix obtained by combining *Gabor(PCA&LDA)* facial features. Results are reported for both the proposed tasks.

	Anger		Happiness		Surprise		Sadness	
	Task1	Task2	Task1	Task2	Task1	Task2	Task1	Task2
Anger	100	91.7	0	0	0	8.3	0	0
Happiness	0	0	87.5	83.3	3.1	12.6	9.4	4.1
Surprise	0	0	0	0	100	100	0	0
Sadness	3.1	0	18.8	0	3.1	0	75	100

The accuracy is differently affected by the coding according to the task. The task affects the correct identification of happiness and surprise when the PCA&LDA coding is used, whereas, for the Gabor(PCA&LDA) coding the task affects the correct identification of anger and sadness. The most confused facial expression in both the tasks and coding procedures is sadness.

Moreover, there is a relationship between false recognition and facial expressions. Happiness was largely confused with sadness and vice versa, and the same trend was observed for anger and surprise, suggesting that some facial expressions may share facial features and therefore are hard to discriminate.

To verify the robustness of the coding methods, they were tested using a different database. The reasoning behind this further set of experiment was to test if the features and the coding procedures assessed above are robust independently from the database. To this aim the ORL Database of Faces [37] was used. Such database contains ten different images of 40 distinct subjects. The images were taken at different times, varying the lighting, the facial expressions (open / closed eyes, smiling / not smiling) and the facial details (glasses / no glasses). All the images were taken against a dark homogeneous background with the subject in an upright, frontal position (with tolerance for some side movement). More details on the database are on the website http://www.cl.cam.ac.uk/research/dtg/attarchive/facedatabase.html.

The database includes a variety of smiling and not smiling human faces (different head poses, gender, age, and appearance) which were divided into a training and a testing set, in order to discriminate between these two different facial expressions (smiling and not smiling). The processing was focused only on the lip area (40x20 pixel area around the center of a mouth). Again, the benchmark consisted of two tasks; the first task used 40 images and the second task used only 20 images as training set, such that we first evaluated the coding procedures used for testing known features from the same subjects and then unknown features for new subject. For both tasks the number of tested images was 120 (60 smiling and 60 not smiling faces). The results are shown in Tables 5 and 6.

It is worth to notice that for both the tasks there is a decrease of the discrimination accuracy due to the great variety of noise in the images. Moreover, the accuracy did not increase combining coding features extracted from faces included in the training set, whereas, when this is not the case, as for the second task, combining PCA and LDA features produces a 3% of improvement.

The combination of Gabor filters and LDA processing does not seem to be suitable for the second task and in general using Gabor filters the accuracy is lower than that obtained for PCA and LDA.

Table 5. Results of smile/not smile recognition - task 1 (40 images in the training set)

Facial Features	Smile	Not smile	Average Accuracy
PCA	90%	73%	**82%**
LDA	93%	72%	**83%**
PCA&LDA	93%	73%	**84%**
Gabor(PCA)	80%	92%	**86%**
Gabor(LDA)	67%	73%	**70%**
Gabor(PCA&LDA)	80%	92%	**86%**

Table 6. Results of smile/not smile recognition – task 2 (20 images in the training set)

Facial Features	Smile	Not smile	Average Accuracy
PCA	85%	65%	**75%**
LDA	72%	63%	**68%**
PCA&LDA	87%	72%	**79%**
Gabor(PCA)	72%	82%	**77%**
Gabor(LDA)	65%	68%	**67%**
Gabor(PCA&LDA)	72%	82%	**77%**

The difference in accuracy among the proposed coding procedures can be attributed to the different sensitivity to noise. When LDA is used, the recognition accuracy greatly depends on the number of images included in the training and testing set. This means that a large number of highly variable images will increase the recognition accuracy. However, this is not true with Gabor filters due to their sensitivity to noise and orientation.

6 Conclusions

The present paper aims at assessing the effectiveness of Gabor filters, LDA, PCA and a combination of relevant features that these procedures extract from facial expressions. The processing methods were applied to two tasks that automatically classify variations of facial emotional expressions of subjects included in the training set, and facial emotional expressions of new subjects. Two different facial image databases (JAFFE and ORL) were used in order to test the robustness of the coding procedures. The results provide two sets of limitations, one depending on the general characteristics of the individual method and the second related to the task on which the method is applied.

Since PCA and LDA directly process the pixel intensity values of the input image, they are affected by changes in illumination. Gabor filters did not suffer this limitation since the intensity value is computed over a group of neighboring pixels. However, being sensible to orientation Gabor filters are affected (in the case of facial expression) by noise (variability present in the images) and head inclination.

When the task was to accurately classify variations of facial expressions on JAFFE combining PCA and LDA features the accuracy recognition was 93.7% against 90.6% obtained combining Gabor(PCA&LDA) features. However, for unseen faces Gabor(PCA&LDA) are better than PCA&LDA features (98.8% against 91.7% of correct recognition). The obtained recognition rates were better than those published in [1] where Adaptive Appearance Models were used, suggesting that the proposed coding procedures are preferable when static images are used. However, it must be said that this high accuracy was obtained on a (JAFFE) database with little noise (the subjects involved are of the same gender, age, race, etc.) and with particularly exaggerated expressions. In fact, when the ORL face database was used – where there are a great variety of subjects – the averaged recognition accuracy of only two facial expressions (smiling and not smiling) was around 80%. These concerns suggest that a more in dept investigation is necessary in order to assess the ability of the investigated coding procedures to extract features relevant for the recognition of facial expression from static images.

Acknowledgments

The paper has been supported partially by the National Research Project "Information Society" No 1ET301710509, by COST 2102: "Cross Modal Analysis of Verbal and Nonverbal Communication (www.cost2102.eu)", by the Ministry of Education, Youth and Sports OC-COST No OC08057, and by Regione Campania, L.R. N.5 del 28.03.2002, Project ID N. BRC1293, Feb. 2006.

References

1. Abbound, B., Davoine, F.: Facial Expression Recognition and Synthesis Based on an Appereance Model. Signal Processing: Image Communication 19, 723–740 (2004)
2. La Barre, W.: The Cultural basis of Emotions Gnd gestures. Journal of Personality 16, 49–68 (1947)
3. Birdwhistell, R.: Kinesies and Context. University of Pennsylvania Press, Philadelphia (1970)
4. Cohen, I., Cozman, F.G., Sebe, N., Cirelo, M.C., Huang, T.S.: Semisupervised Learning of Classifiers: Theory, Algorithms and their Application to Human-Computer Interaction. IEEE Transactions on PAMI 26, 1553–1567 (2004)
5. Darwin, C.: The Expression of the Emotions in Man and Animals. J. Murray, London (1872)
6. Ekman, P., Friesen, W.: Constants across Cultures in the Face and Emotion. Journal of Personality and Social Psychology (1971)
7. Ekman, P., Friesen, W.: Emotional Facial Action Coding System. Unpublished manual (1978)
8. Ekman, P., Friesen, W.V.: Facial Action Coding System: A Technique for the Measurement of Facial Movement. Consulting Psychologists Press, Palo Alto (1978)
9. Ekman, P.: The Argument and Evidence about Universals in Facial Expressions of Emotion. In: Wagner, H., Manstead, A. (eds.) Handbook of Social Psychophysiology, pp. 143–164. Wiley, Chichester (1989)
10. Ekman, P.: Facial Expression of Emotion: New Findings. New Questions. Psychological Science 3, 34–38 (1992)
11. Fasel, B., Luettin, J.: Automatic Facial Expression Analysis: A Survey. Pattern Recognition 36(1), 259–275 (2003)
12. Fisher, R.A.: The Statistical Utilization of Multiple Measurements. Annali of Eugenics 8, 376–386 (1938)
13. Fridlund, A.J.: The New Ethnology of Human Facial Expressions. In: Russell, J.A., Fernandez-Dols, J. (eds.) The Psychology of Facial Expressions, pp. 103–129. Cambridge University Press, Cambridge (1997)
14. Hong, H., Neven, H., von der Malsburg, C.: Online Facial Expression Recognition Based on Personalized Galleries. In: Proceedings of the International Conference on Automatic Face and Gesture Recognition, pp. 354–359 (1998)

15. Huang, C.L., Huang, Y.M.: Facial Expression Recognition Using Model-Based Feature Extraction and Action Parameters Classification. Journal of Visual Communication and Image Representation 8(3), 278–290 (1997)
16. Huang, S.H., Wu, Q.J., Lai, S.H.: Improved AdaBoost-based Image Retrieval with Relevance Feedback Via Paired Feature Learning. Multimedia Systems 12, 14–26 (2006)
17. Izard, C.E., Dougherty, L.M., Hembree, E.A.: A System for Identifying Affect Expressions by Holistic Judgments. Unpublished manuscript. Available from Instructional Resource Center, University of Delaware (1983)
18. Izard, C.E.: Innate and Universal Facial Expressions: Evidence from Developmental and Cross-Cultural Research. Psychological Bulletin 115, 288–299 (1994)
19. Jollife, I.T.: Principal Component Analysis, 2nd edn. Springer, New York (2002)
20. Kamachi, M., Lyons, M., Gyoba, J.: Japanese Female Facial Expression Database, Psychology Department in Kyushu University, http://www.kasrl.org/jaffe.html
21. Klinerberg, O.: Emotional Expression in Chinese Literature. Journal of Abnormal and Social Psychology 33, 517–520 (1938)
22. Lee, Y., Kim, I., Shim, J., Marshall, D.: 3D Facial Image Recognition Using a Nose Volume and Curvature Based Eigenface. In: Kim, M.-S., Shimada, K. (eds.) GMP 2006. LNCS, vol. 4077, pp. 616–622. Springer, Heidelberg (2006)
23. Lyons, M.J., Budynek, J., Akamatsu, S.: Automatic Classification of Single Facial Images. IEEE Transactions on Pattern Analysis and Machine Intelligence 21, 1357–1362 (1999)
24. Martýnez, A.M.: Recognition of Partially Occluded and/or Imprecisely Localized Faces Using a Probabilistic Approach. In: Proceeding of the International Conference on Computer Vision and Pattern Recognition, vol. 1, pp. 712–717 (2000)
25. Martýnez, A.M.: PCA versus LDA. IEEE Transactions on Pattern Analysis and Machine Intelligence 23(2), 228–233 (2001)
26. Moghaddam, B., Pentland, A.: Probabilistic Visual Learning for Object Representation. IEEE Transactions on Pattern Analysis and Machine Intelligence 19(7), 696–710 (1997)
27. Moon, H., Phillips, P.J.: Analysis of PCA-based Face Recognition Algorithms. In: Bowyer, K.J., Phillips, P.J. (eds.) Empirical Evaluation Techniques in Computer Vision. IEEE Computer Soceity, Los Alamitos (1998)
28. Pantic, M., Rothkrantz, J.M.: Automatic Analysis of Facial Expression: The State of the Art. IEEE Transactions on Pattern Analysis and Machine Intelligence 22(12), 1424–1445 (2000)
29. Pantic, M., Rothkrantz, J.M.: Expert System for Automatic Analysis of Facial Expression. Image and Vision Computing Journal 18(11), 881–905 (2000)
30. Papageorgiou, C., Oren, M., Poggio, T.: A General Framework for Object Detection. In: International Conference on Computer Vision, pp. 992–998 (1998)
31. Petkov, N., Wieling, M.B.: Gabor Filtering Augmented with Surround Inhibition for Improved Contour Detection by Texture Suppression. Perception 33, 68c (2004)
32. Phillips, P.J., Moon, H., Rauss, P., Rizvi, S.A.: The FERET Evaluation Methodology for Face-Recognition Algorithms. IEEE Transactions on Pattern Analysis and Machine Intelligence 22, 1090–1104 (2000)
33. Phillips, P.J., Flynn, P.J., Scruggs, T., Bowyer, K.W.: Overview of the Face Recognition Grand Challenge. In: Proc. IEEE Conf. Computer Vision and Pattern Recognition (2005)
34. Roth, D., Yang, M., Ahuja, N.: A SNoW-Based Face Detector. Advances in Neural Information Processing Systems, 855–861 (2000)
35. Russell, J.A.: A Circumplex Model of Affect. Journal of Personality and Social Psychology 39, 1161–1171 (1980)

36. Ryu, H., Chun, S.S., Sull, S.: Multiple Classifiers Approach for Computational Efficiency in Multi-scale Search Based Face Detection. In: Jiao, L., Wang, L., Gao, X.-b., Liu, J., Wu, F. (eds.) ICNC 2006. LNCS, vol. 4221. Springer, Heidelberg (2006)
37. Samaria, F., Harter, A.: The ORL Database of Faces, AT&T Laboratories Cambridge University,
    http://www.cl.cam.ac.uk/research/dtg/attarchive/facedatabase.html
38. Schneiderman, H., Kanade, T.: A Statistical Method for 3D Object Detection Applied to Faces and Cars. In: International Conference on Computer and Pattern Recognition, vol. 1, pp. 746–751 (2000)
39. Schlosberg, H.: Three Dimensions of Emotion. The Psychological Review 61(2), 81–88 (1953)
40. Simoncelli, E.P., Olshausen, B.A.: Natural Image Statistics and Neural Representation. Annual Review of Neuroscience 24, 1193–1216 (2001)
41. Sung, K., Poggio, T.: Example-Based Learning for View-Based Face Detection. IEEE Transaction on Pattern Analyses and Machine Intelligence 20, 39–51 (1998)
42. Tomkins, S.S.: Affect Theory. In: Scherer, K.R., Ekman, P. (eds.) Approaches to Emotion, pp. 163–196. Erlbaum, Hillsdale (1984)
43. Turk, M., Pentland, A.: Face Recognition Using Eigenfaces. In: Proceedings of IEEE Conference on Computer Vision and Pattern Recognition, pp. 586–591 (1991)
44. Viola, A.P., Jones, M.J.: Robust Real-Time Face Detection. International Journal of Computer Vision 57(2), 137–154 (2004)
45. White, G.M.: Emotion Inside Out the Anthropology of Affect. In: Haviland, M., Lewis, J.M. (eds.) Handbook of Emotion, pp. 29–40. Guilford Press, New York (1993)
46. Zhao, J., Kearney, G.: Classifying Facial Emotions by Backpropagation Neural Networks with Fuzzy Inputs. In: Proceedings of the International Conference on Neural Information Processing, vol. 1, pp. 454–457 (1996)
47. Zhao, W., Chellappa, R., Phillips, P.J., Rosenfeld, A.: Face Recognition: A Literature Survey. ACM, Computing Surveys 35(4), 399–458 (2003)

Mutually Coordinated Anticipatory Multimodal Interaction

Anton Nijholt, Dennis Reidsma, Herwin van Welbergen,
Rieks op den Akker, and Zsofia Ruttkay

Human Media Interaction Group (HMI)
Department of Computer Science, University of Twente
The Netherlands
{anijholt,dennisr,welberge,infrieks,zsofi}@cs.utwente.nl

Abstract. We introduce our research on anticipatory and coordinated interaction between a virtual human and a human partner. Rather than adhering to the turn taking paradigm, we choose to investigate interaction where there is simultaneous expressive behavior by the human interlocutor and a humanoid. Various applications in which we can study and specify such behavior, in particular behavior that requires synchronization based on predictions from performance and perception, are presented. Some observations concerning the role of predictions in conversations are presented and architectural consequences for the design of virtual humans are drawn.

1 Introduction

Virtual humans are based on implementations of models of human (expressive) behavior; models that are used to drive the interaction between a virtual human and human 'user'. Human behavior can not completely be understood as the execution of a preconceived program, a set of conditional rules, the application of which depends on the classification of observable events according to a number of preformatted classification schemes. These are the categories of the designer who has a complete specification of the motives that agents drive, the goals they have and the means they can use to realize these goals. On the contrary, the goal of a human activity is the realization of the person 'self'. How the actions become realized depends on the actions of other agents. Interaction is emergent, not the result of planned actions but something that simply shows up as a result of many synchronous activities as well as what has been established before. Thus there is a tension between the perspective of the designer of synthetic humanoid interactive characters and the creative emergent behavior in which humans realize themselves through interaction as social beings. A good example of this tension between emergent human conversational behavior and the design of interactive computers can be found in the discussions about the topic of turn-taking for virtual humans. People tend to talk 'in turns', but they do talk simultaneously as well. However, developers of virtual humans and conversational systems through the years have mostly turned to the turn-taking framework originally set out by Sacks et al. [38]. This work has been used as a normative description of

A. Esposito et al. (Eds.): HH and HM Interaction 2007, LNAI 5042, pp. 70–89, 2008.

coordination principles in conversation (even though it has been criticized as such by other theorists [12,29]): one speaker talks at a time, speakers take turns, a next speaker's turn commonly follows the previous turn with no gap and no overlap, etc. In dialogue systems this leads to a clear pipeline ordering of modules. First the interlocutor's utterance is perceived through the system's sensors (microphone, keyboard, etc), then the utterance is interpreted, next deliberation takes place in the system about the appropriate (re)action to be chosen, and finally the reaction of the system is produced. Although the framework has been criticized in many ways it is still the most used paradigm for conversational systems.

From the 'turn taking' theoretical viewpoint, feedback or backchannel [50] is seen as standing slightly outside the main conversation, helping regulate the turn taking process but not actually part of the main conversational exchange. Furthermore, since the turn taking paradigm privileges speech, the continuously ongoing non-verbal expressions of speakers and listeners cannot readily be given a place in turn taking patterns. It is therefore perhaps not surprising that the people building systems dealing with verbal and non-verbal feedback from listeners were the first to turn to other models of interaction, less embedded in the turn-taking framework. In the next section we will see how frequently speaker overlap occurs in four participant meetings.

In the research reported here we want to put aside the concept of prescriptive turn-taking models entirely. We envision conversational systems where two-way simultaneous interaction is not limited to a speaker speaking and a listener providing some feedback. Rather, we want to see perception and production occurring simultaneously on both sides of the conversation. A major theme then is that of alignment and synchronization. That is, simultaneous interaction (as opposed to sequential pipe-line interaction) needs a much tighter temporal coordination between the expressions of a virtual human on the one hand and the perception of the expressions of the human interlocutor on the other hand. We will discuss the need for anticipatory and predictive models and their place in the interaction. The generation of multi-modal expressions in virtual humans not only involves the planning of their content on a conceptual level, but also those expressions need to be executed using the appropriate modalities, in coordination with the conversational partner. Hence, we need to look at planning and re-planning problems and at the low level animation consequences for virtual humans on the production side, and at types of perception needed for turn-free two-way interaction.

Our research on simultaneous interaction is meant to become integrated in our Sensitive Artificial Listener (SAL) system [17]. Our inspiration comes also from related research on three applications where there is continuous interaction between user and system (virtual human): a dancer, a virtual music conductor and a physio-trainer. Each of those applications consists of an interactive virtual human capable of observing the user through sensors and expressing itself verbally and/or nonverbally. The applications investigate different aspects of simultaneous two-way interaction. The development as well as the evaluation of these applications leads to observations and questions about the design of more natural interaction with virtual humans and about the models needed for such. This paper presents different insights as well as open questions raised while working on the applications. Furthermore, our observations are confronted with related work in virtual human research as well as with relevant literature from linguistics and social psychology.

Section 2 of this paper is devoted to observations on synchronization in conversation. We discuss the useful and well-known turn taking model of Sacks et al. [38], but also comment on its shortcomings, in particular its lack of attention for the simultaneous expressive behavior of speaker and listener. In section 3 we discuss the aforementioned applications of an interactive dancer, an interactive conductor and an interactive trainer. In these applications we can speak of 'anticipatory synchronization' in the interaction, where behavioral timing is guided by music or a rhythm that has to be followed. In section 4 we present a preliminary investigation whether this view of anticipatory synchronization can also be recognized and explored in speech conversations. In section 5 we discuss the architectural consequences of anticipatory synchronization for virtual humans. Again, the initial ideas for an architecture that allows the generation of coordinated behavior started with the three applications mentioned earlier. In this section we discuss the Behavioral Markup Language (BML, [45]) for specifying synchronization of behaviors, including synchronization with external events. Some conclusions are drawn in the final section.

2 Synchronization and Interaction in Conversation

In games, formal social events, business meetings, in traffic, the notion of turn abounds and turns are pre-allocated, i.e. there is a protocol or system of rules that prescribes who may take turn when. In casual conversations speaker turns are not pre-allocated. Interactants "locally manage", that is on a turn by turn basis, who will be the next speaker. In their ground breaking paper Sacks, Schegloff and Jefferson (SSJ) propose a model that describes how turn taking is performed [38]. Such a model should clarify a number of phenomena that anyone can observe in casual conversations. Two of these observations are: 1) time between two adjacent speaker turns is usually small, and 2) speaker overlap is uncommon. According to the turn taking rules of the SSJ system the current speaker decides who will take turn, for example by addressing a question to a selected addressee, but if he doesn't listeners self-select to take turn. Important notion in SSJs system is *turn constructional unit* (TCU) and the related *transitional relevant place* (TRP). A listener will not take over turn at any arbitrary time; he will wait until a TCU has been completed by the speaker. A TCU is a semantical or informational complete phrase: a listener usually will not interrupt a speaker in the middle of such a TCU. TCUs are often prosodically marked phrases ending with a clear rising or lowering of pitch and energy. What is important in the light of the second observation (i.e. short time lags in between two speaker turns) is that TCU do project their ending: listeners recognize a TCU and are thereby often able to predict how long it takes before the TCU has been completely produced by the speaker. The attentive listener actively participates in formulating the ideas that he has recognized and that the speaker is uttering.

In her essay "The Paris Years" Carol Sanders discusses the way a listener identifies the relevant meaning of a word [39]. It both involves, according to Sanders, the concept of the listener as the mirror image of the speaker and as an active part of the 'circuit du langue'. She quotes the French linguist Michel Bréal (1897):

> "It is not even necessary to suppress the other meanings of the word: these meanings do not impinge on us ... for the association of ideas is based on the

sense of things, not on their sound. What we say about speakers is no less true about listeners. These are in the same situation: their thought run along with or precedes that of their interlocutor. They speak inwardly at the same time as we do: so they are no more likely than we are to be troubled by related meanings dormant in the depth of their minds."

The observation that listeners simultaneously with speakers 'speak', i.e. phrase the idea that is jointly worked out, is basic for understanding the shortness of response times and the shortness or even lack of gaps in turn transitions. Some people have understood SSJs theory to say that a conversation can only be successful if the participants obey the turn-taking rules as described by the model. Others have pointed at the fact that the participants themselves decide how a conversation enrolls. Both Cowley [12] and O'Connell et al. [29] criticize the turn-taking tradition for mistaking the *descriptive* paradigm for a *prescriptive* model. Coates suggests that in some contexts a 'free-for-all' metaphor, where everybody equally can contribute to the conversation at all times, is more appropriate. Then, overlapping speech is a signal of participant's active engagement rather than a signal of conversational malfunction [11]. Bavelas et al. [4] also give a more active role to the listener, extending beyond signaling attention and understanding over an underprivileged back channel to contributing pertinent content to a narrative through specific listener responses (other authors use the term content feedback).

Part of SSJs turn-taking systems concerns repair, describing how interlocutors operate together when they take turn simultaneously. We don't go into the details of this procedure, but note that simultaneous talk is not always considered problematic. Some people are able to listen and talk at the same time; or, for some people it sometimes doesn't matter what others have to say; why shouldn't they speak simultaneously? It is often hard to draw the line between interaction and parts in a conversation where there is no 'real' interaction, in particular because the refusal to interact (turning the back) is also a sign send out to be picked up by others in interaction. According to SSJ politeness, familiarity, and affect are important factors that determine how a conversation emerges. It will be clear that if participants build on the previous contribution they have to wait until the previous speaker is ready (you can't answer a question if you don't know the question). But if you already have understood the question before the speaker has finished the formulation waiting is more a matter of politeness, than a conceptual necessity.

Another comment on SSJ is that it restricts conversational actions to verbal communicative acts only. Some critics say that we should take non-verbal activities into account. If we do, we see that listeners are continuously and simultaneously active along with the speaker; they show behavior that communicates how they receive, and uptake the message being conveyed by the speaker. If for example someone is asking a question and sees during his speaking that the addressee looks puzzled, he will elaborate his question before yielding turn to the addressed person, while if the addressee looks eager to answer the question that he already grasped before the speaker finished his interrogative, the speaker will pass the turn and allow the addressed partner as soon as possible. This is not the place to discuss whether this is a valid critic on SSJs theory and model. What is important is that the notion of turn is highly problematic, in the sense that there is no computational model that for once and for all situations (even not for a restricted type of interactions, like casual conversations) tells us what is a turn and what is not.

Several systems have been implemented by different groups that incorporate different types of backchannelling behavior, which by definition involves simultaneous expressive behavior from a 'speaker' and a 'listener', often using non-verbal signals. In all of those systems, backchannel expressions given by the virtual human are defined and implemented in a 'reactive' way, i.e., upon perceiving certain features in the expressions of the speaker, the system will react directly with certain nonverbal feedback expressions [43,44,20,46,25,17].

Another way of looking at temporal aspects of coordination between humans in a conversation is by looking at a corpus of recordings of small group discussions. The fact that temporal coordination plays an important role in conversation can readily be seen by visualizing some aspects of the interaction, for example looking at the dynamics of the energy level in the sound produced by each of the speakers along the time axis.

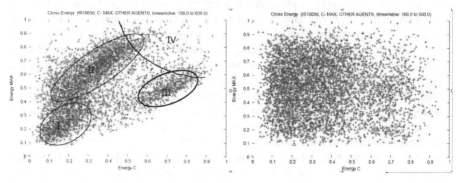

Fig. 1. Temporal coordination between one participant in a meeting and the others, visualized through the relation between energy levels in the audio channels

Figure 1 shows cross energy of audio channels in a four participant face-to-face meeting recorded in the AMI corpus [8]. Both graphs show the relation between the energy in the audio channel of participant C and the maximum energy in the other three audio channels. The energy levels on the X-axis and on the Y-axis in the leftmost graph are clearly correlated; every point in that graph is a point in time in the meeting. Area I is where both energy levels are low (no speech), area II is where C doesn't speak, but someone else speaks, area III is where C speaks and others don't, area IV is where C's talk overlaps with others' talk.

Thus, two things are clear from this graphical representation.

- There is overlap in talk (area IV)
- There are clear patterns of coordinated behavior shown in the energy levels of talk in interaction (see the clusters in areas I, II en III).

The rightmost graph was obtained by shifting all energy values in the audio channel of participant C a small amount in time. The result is a graph that shows no structure anymore.

To make the structure of the temporal coordination between participants in the meeting even clearer, Figure 2 shows a similar graph for two individual participants, namely participant C and D. The number of words spoken by each of the participants ranges from 400 to 450 in the recorded time frame of 400 sec. The dark cloud in the lower left corner (indicating low energy on both channels at the same time) of the graph in Figure 2 results from periods of no speech. Audio is recorded by means of lapel microphones.

If we look at the pictures in Figure 1 we see that the left one shows more structure than the other. This structure reflects the interaction between the participants in the meeting. The sounds produced by them are not completely independent, it shows some pattern, a pattern that recurs in different time frames, and also in different meetings, with different participants. It seems like a pattern that reveals something of the general idea of people having a conversation in a meeting.

As Basu [3] also shows, by making similar pictures of 'pseudo interactions' (similar as the one shown in right side of Figure 1), these patterns aren't a coincidence, but caused by the coordinated actions between different speakers in interaction. Basu uses this fact to find in a set of mixed audio streams those pairs of streams that form the two halves of one and the same conversation.

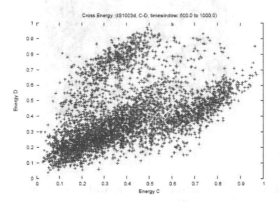

Fig. 2. Temporal coordination between two individual participants in a meeting, visualized through the relation between energy levels in the audio channels

An example of coordinated action is the correlation of gaze behavior and speaking behavior in backchannelling or in addressing. We may say that both 'behaviors', gaze and speech, are in fact part of the same activity; moreover they often go along with other 'behaviors', such as body movements towards the speaker or addressed person. Head and eye movements are highly dependent, because they participate in the same behavior.

An other illustration showing synchronization between nonverbal activities of participants having a conversation is based on the work of Ramseyer and Tschacher [31] (see also section 4).

Two video streams are recorded from the interaction between two persons: in our case both close-up videos showing head movements of the persons. In each of the video the amount of movements is measured as a function of time, by a simple *image difference* computation. The correlation between the functions is then computed. Since persons do not move their heads exactly at the same time, but with a short delay in response to each other, this computation is done by comparing each window of

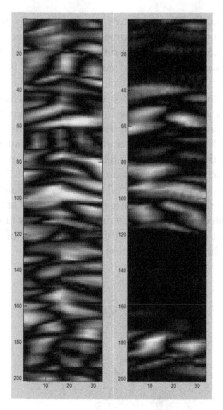

Fig. 3. Visualization of coordinated head-movements of two persons in interaction

person A with all windows of person B that are within a timeframe of -2 and +2 secs of the time of the window of A. We have generated these from data of a fragment of 200 windows (8 sec) in a conversation recorded in the SAL project [17].

In Figure 3 the vertical axis is the time axis and time runs from top to bottom, measured in window units. Each window is 4 secs; with 0.4 sec between two windows. The horizontal axis contains the 'time lag' between two windows (one of A, one of person B) for which the correlation has been computed, from -2 sec to +2 sec. The brighter the point, the stronger this correlation.

The left part of Figure 3 shows the graph for an interaction between persons A and B in the second part of a conversation. The right graphics is made up by cross-correlating two pieces of data of persons A and B from different parts of the conversation: data from A from 8 sec in the first part of a conversation is compared with data of person B from the second part of the conversation.

The conclusion that we can draw from these pictures is that on a local level there exists a meaningful temporal correlation between the movements made by the partners in interaction. Thus, these correlations can be used as cues for detecting interaction.

3   Mutually Coordinated Multi Modal Interaction: 3 Examples

We are building applications in which perception and production are parallel rather than sequential processes. As we have seen above, this needs a certain amount of coordination involving temporal aspects. The applications have all been described in more detail elsewhere - in this section we will shortly summarize them, stressing the aspects of mutual coordination between a virtual human and interlocutor.

3.1   Interactive Virtual Dancer

In a recent application built at HMI, a virtual dancer invites a real partner to dance with her [34]. The Virtual Dancer dances together with a human 'user', aligning its motion to the beat in the music input (see Figure 4). The system observes the movements of the human partner by using a dance pad to register feet activity and the computer vision system to gain information about arm and body movements. By responding to the way the human user is dancing, the virtual dancer implicitly invites the user to react to her as well. At any point in time, the virtual human in this application is both expressing herself (dancing to the beat), and perceiving the user's style of dancing. When the virtual dancer is in a 'following' mode she will break of dancing moves when they no longer fit with the user's style and continue with better fitting moves. When in 'leading' mode she may introduce dance moves with a completely new style in order to evoke reactions from the user.

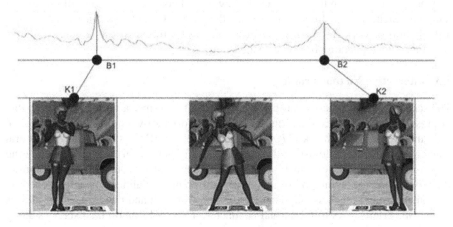

Fig. 4. An interactive virtual dancer dancing to the beat of the music

3.2   Interactive Virtual Conductor

We have designed and implemented a virtual conductor [6] that is capable of leading, and reacting to, live musicians in real time (see Figure 5). The conductor possesses knowledge of the music to be conducted, and it is able to translate this knowledge to gestures and to produce these gestures. The conductor extracts features through audio processing algorithms as the music is played and reacts to them, based on information of the knowledge of the score. The reactions are tailored to elicit the desired response from the musicians.

Fig. 5. An interactive virtual conductor conducting a human orchestra

Clearly, if an ensemble is playing too slow or too fast, a (human) conductor should lead them back to the correct tempo. He can choose to lead strictly or more leniently, but completely ignoring the musicians' tempo and conducting like a metronome set at the right tempo will not work. A conductor must incorporate some sense of the actual tempo at which the musicians play in his conducting, or else he will lose control. If the musicians play too slow, the virtual conductor will conduct a little bit faster than they are playing. When the musicians follow, it will conduct faster yet, till the correct tempo is reached again. In order to do this, the Virtual Conductor continuously makes a prediction of how the musicians will be playing in the next few beats, in order to coordinate its conducting behavior to their music.

3.3 Interactive Virtual Trainer

The scenario of the Reactive Virtual Trainer (RVT) describes a virtual human capable of presenting physical exercises that are to be performed by a human, monitoring the user and providing feedback [37]. The reactivity of the RVT is manifested in natural language comments, readjusting the tempo, pointing out mistakes or rescheduling the exercises. Such exercises can be performed at the beat of a user's favorite music. Exercises describe a mix of behaviors on different modalities, including exercise movement, sound (such as clapping, feet tapping), speech and music. This scenario is similar in certain ways to the virtual conductor. The RVT can do the exercises along with the user, adapting its tempo to the performance of the user, or attempting to lead the user when his/her tempo is lagging.

4 Mutual Coordination: Anticipatory Synchronization

In all three applications presented above, it turned out that behavior expressions had to be synchronized to predictions of perception of the environment (dancer and music) or the interlocutor's behavior (trainer, conductor). This is a type of behavior coordination that has hardly been addressed before. On first sight, it seems to be quite specific of the applications. In this section we survey some literature, and look at data in our corpora, to find out whether such 'anticipatory synchronization' only makes sense in the context of these specific applications, or whether there are underlying issues that make anticipatory synchronization a more generally applicable issue for virtual humans.

To start with, consider some literature about minimal reaction times for vocal responses for humans: Wilson and Wilson [49] say that vocal reaction time for highly primed subjects is 200 msec (citing Izdebski and Shipp [18], for a vocal 'react as fast as possible' task without any cognitive processing). Goodrich et al. [15] give minimal reaction times between 200 and 500 msec in a complex task with distraction. Slowiaczek [40] gives reaction times of 700-800 msec for a task that involves lexical lookup. To a certain extent, when more cognitive processing is required, minimal reaction times become larger.

Now consider some literature about the time scale on which certain communicative behaviors actually occur. For example, Nagaoka et al. [27] describe converging response latencies for some dyads in the 300-600 msec range; Jonsdottir et al. [20] show that content feedback comes within 500-1000 msec; Ward and Tsukahara [46] says that envelope feedback occurs in the range of 350 msec after an utterance; Cowley [12] describes some conversation timing effects within 300 msec and shorter range; Wilson and Wilson [49] present data on gaps between utterances where many are below 200 or even 100 msec, which is below the absolute physical reaction time for highly primed subjects.

Given such results it seems reasonable to suggest that the timing of some of the effects described above is in a range shorter than possible purely on reaction times. This observation also underlies the idea of, for example, projectability of utterances in the turn taking theory of Sacks et al. [38]. Humans anticipate the timing of expressions of their interlocutor in order to match their responses to it.

But what use is it to implement such effects of anticipatory synchronization in conversational virtual humans? Literature such as the work of Crown [13], Ramseyer and Tschacher [31] or Nagaoka et al. [27] on interactional synchrony or coordinated interpersonal timing in communication suggests that being able to coordinate one's actions in an anticipatory manner to those of one's interlocutor relates to a positive evaluation of the conversation partner and of the (effectiveness of) the interaction. Crown [13] for example relates interpersonal timing to affective relation in dyads, and concludes that a 'like/dislike/unacquainted' condition has a strong relation with interpersonal timing. Ramseyer and Tschacher [32] were the first to perform a large scale quantitative study of synchrony in a psychotherapeutic context; using the analysis developed by Boker et al. [5] they found a clear correlation between synchrony and certain positive therapy outcomes in a data set of 125 therapy sessions by 80 dyads. A good overview of themes and topics related to synchrony can be found in the survey of Nagaoka et al. [27]. Besides pointing the reader to a large amount of earlier work they discuss experiments with rhythmic entrainment (convergence of latencies between utterance and response, for speakerA/ListenerB and speakerB/listenerA transitions), showing how dynamics and alignment are an important elements of synchrony tendency. This in turn is important for conveying rapport and empathy, promotion of understanding emotion and making you assessed positively by the other. In summary, it appears that coordinated interpersonal timing can convey info about mental state and help influencing/persuading the other in some sense.

So far we have only discussed the precise timing in human-human interaction. But why do we need such precise timing relations in human-computer interaction? In other words, what happens if precise timing in an interaction is disrupted? Such a situation occurs frequently in video conferences, where speech and video is delayed by the transmission over a network. Such delays in transmission disrupt turn taking mechanisms [14]. This causes audio collisions and a reduction of interactivity: the turns are longer and backchannel feedback occurs less. Even when a timing disruption goes unnoticed it can have social impact. In [33], it is shown that a delay between audio and video causes users to evaluate a speaker as less interesting, less pleasant, less influential, more agitated and less successful in their delivery, even if they did not notice the asynchrony itself.

More specifically in the context of human computer interaction, we do know that at least to a certain extent interactional synchrony also works for human-VH interaction. For example, Suzuki et al. [41], working on prosody, say that echoic humming mimicry has a positive influence on affective perception of the conversational partner, even if that partner is a computer. Bailenson and Yee [2] also specifically addresses the dynamics of the movement: interactional synchrony, in the form of mimicry (repeat head movements of partner after 4 secs) is effective for VHs to be more persuasive and effective. This is all not very surprising, as Reeves and Nass [33] already showed that this type of aspects in human-human communication transfer to human media communication.

More on the topic of timing, Robins et al. [36], working with robots rather than virtual humans, conclude qualitatively from an exploratory study about "Rhythm, kinesics, body motion and timing" that "[...] responding with appropriate timing so as to mesh with the timing of human actions encourages sustained interaction" and "Robot-human temporal interaction kinesics will eventually need to be studied deeply in order to put this dimension within the purview of HRI designers".

However, modeling and implementing anticipatory synchronization in conversational virtual humans is easier said than done. In the applications presented above the music, or the fitness exercise, defines a rhythmic structure that can be taken as starting point for the prediction of the behavioral timing of the interlocutor. But in normal conversation one does not match ones behavior to that of the interlocutor through the mediation of music or another externally defined rhythm. When we want to extend these concepts to conversations with a virtual human we should explore the vast amount of literature on investigations into the rhythmic nature of speech. Although it is not trivial to find a rhythmic organization that can be used for predicting e.g. turn endings [7] or other practical uses [21]. So, if we want to have anticipatory synchronization in conversation, we should spend effort finding ways to model in a sense the rhythm of the speaker in order to predict a timing to which the interlocutor can synchronize. This model needs not necessarily be in terms of a rhythm or beat pulse, but can possibly also be in terms such as turn shift latencies (investigated by Nagaoka et al. [27]) or the oscillators of Wilson and Wilson [49]. The quote from Bréal in Section 2, about listeners who in a sense 'speak along' with the speaker, could form a metaphor for a way of modeling speaker behavior that includes anticipation as a core element.

5 Architectural Consequences

In the preceding sections we discussed some aspects of coordination apparent in human-human conversation and three of our applications in which coordination between a virtual human and the human user is a central theme. After coming to the conclusion that it is worthwhile to pursue a way of designing anticipatory synchronization for virtual humans, we now turn to our work on the development of an architecture for flexible generation of coordinated multimodal behavior. We have worked on this architecture in the context of many different applications where the expressive behavior of virtual humans needed to be specified and executed. Initially it was mostly concerned with coordination between the different modalities within the behavior expressions [47]. Over time, coordination with the behavior of a virtual human's interlocutor came to play a greater role. In this section we review our current architecture and foreseen developments with a special focus on coordination and anticipatory synchronization.

5.1 The Behavior Markup Language

Currently, our architecture for specifying and executing expressive behavior for a virtual human is based on the Behavior Markup Language (BML) [45]. In BML, multimodal expressions are composed of *behaviors*: instances of a certain 'action' by a virtual human on a single modality (for example a single pointing gesture, or a spoken sentence). Behaviors contain different *phases. Synchronization points* are defined at the bounds of the behavior phases. Figure 6 shows the mandatory phases and synchronization points of a BML behavior, but specific behaviors can also be defined with custom synchronization points, and thus custom phases. The duration of a phase can be 0. Coordination is achieved simply by specifying the alignment of synchronization points in gestures, speech and possibly other 'behaviors' in other modalities. A *sequence* of behaviors can be specified using 'before' and 'after' constraints. An 'after' constraint e.g. specifies that a synchronization point of one behavior should occur after a synchronization point in another behavior. The BML specification leaves it up to the modules

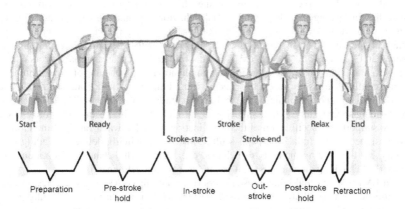

Fig. 6. Mandatory gesture phases and synchronization points in BML, picture modified from Kopp et al. [23]

that actually generate the animations (the BML realizer) to determine how long after the synchronization point that is. Other such constraints can specify that synchronization points of behaviors should occur at a certain absolute time or that two or more synchronization points of different behaviors should occur at the same time. A leading modality is not required, complex coordination is achieved at generation time (see also the inset "Multimodal Coordination in Virtual Humans: A Brief History").

5.2 External Synchronization

Synchronization can also align behavior with events occurring in the world 'outside' the virtual human. The exact form that such alignment takes depends on the type of event, and its predictability. For some events, one can 'predict' that they might occur, but not when (e.g., another person entering the room, or suddenly offering to shake your hand). Currently BML can specify synchronization to such events in a reactive way: if the designer included the appropriate reactions to somebody offering to shake hands, BML allows one to plan that reaction using an event/wait system described below. For other events, it might be possible to predict the timing with which they occur, such as for some pauses in speech. Below, we introduce the synchronization of behaviors to timing-predictable events in the outside world using the BML^T 'observer' extension. (As a third case, there are of course also events outside the domain modeled by the system, such as an escaped tiger entering the office. Clearly, most virtual humans will not be able to sensible coordinate their behavior with tigers entering the office).

Multimodal Coordination in Virtual Humans: A Brief History

In classic multimodal systems [9,10,42,28], speech and gesture are coordinated by timing the gestures to speech generated by a speech synthesizer. Speech then guides the timing of the gestures; speech is the leading modality [47]. However, speech/gesture timing in humans shows more complex coordination. For example: speech output can be delayed so that a complex gesture can be finished or a gesture's hold phase can be used to correct the timing of a gesture that was started too early [24].

MURML [22] is the first gesture and speech synthesis system that does not require speech as a leading modality. Multimodal behavior is planned as a concatenation of chunks, based on McNeill's [26] segmentation hypothesis. The chunks contain a segment of speech and/or one gesture, which are timed at their synchronization points. If only hand gestures and speech are to be coordinated, such an approach works fine. However, in many multimodal generation applications the behavior of virtual humans is not confined to just gesture and speech: virtual humans could operate and discus the working of complex machinery [19], behave naturally in a war zone [35], comment on an ongoing soccer match [1], or simply walk through an environment while conversing.

To support the specification of the coordination of such a wider range of modalities, we designed MultiModalSync [47]. MultiModalSync implicitly defines a leading modality, but this leading modality can change over time. Such a change does not emerge from the behavior generation itself, it has to be specified beforehand.

In BML [45], virtual human researchers (including those who designed the systems mentioned above), collaborate to provide a framework in which multimodal alignment to both internal modalities and external events can be specified in a flexible way.

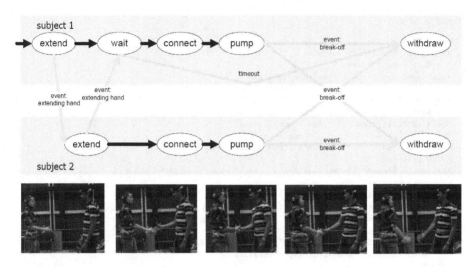

Fig. 7. Two agents that run a BML script shaking hands. Synchronization between scripts is achieved using the BML event/wait system.

Reactive coordination. Using an event/wait system, BML can be used to specify a script segment that handles a specific event that might occur during a specified time period in the scripts execution. Such events come from the outside, and possibly from other agents (executing their own BML scripts).

Figure 7 shows how the event/wait system can be used to model a handshake between two agents, independently running their own BML script. Possible scripts for the handshake are shown in Figure 8. Although these scripts form a good starting point for reactive coordination with an interlocutor, they suffer from the fact that there is no monitoring feedback loop that allows one agent to use predictions of the behavior of the other to coordinate his behavior. In the example script, one of them extends his hand, and then waits for the other to grasp that hand. Normally when two people shake hands, they will coordinate the timing of their behavior in such a way that they together arrive at the 'connect' point.

Observing and predicting. Currently we are collaborating on extending BML with possibilities to align multimodal behavior to predicted timing of external events. Predictions can concern physical events (predict where the ball will be in order to be able to catch it, or predict the beat in music) as well as social events (predict behavior of conversational partner in order to plan and synchronise contingent behavior). Such synchronization can not be achieved by the event/wait system described in core BML since BML events are, by design, non-repeatable and unpredictable. Therefore, the BML^T 'observer' extension is developed to provide coordination with outside world events. An 'observer' is a module that provides predictions of the timing of events in the form of synchronisation points, the exact time stamp of which can dynamically be modified with updated predictions. In the dancer for example, such synchronisation points are made available for predictions of the beat of the music. The dance movements can be specified as being aligned to those predictions (cf. Figure 4).

Script for agent 1

```
<bml>
  <handshake:extend id="extend1"/>
  <!--Emit extend event-->
  <emit id="emit_extend1" start="extend:end">
      <event id="extend_p1" type="behavior"/>
  </emit>
  <!--Wait for p2 to extend, stop script if no extend in 10 seconds-->
  <wait id="wait_connect2" start="extend1:end"
               event="extend_p2" duration="10"
               no-event="FAIL: not connecting"/>
  <!--Connect-->
  <handshake:connect id="connect1" start="wait_connect:end"/>
  <!--Shake hands-->
  <handshake:pump id="pump1" start="connect1:end"/>
  <!--Wait for p2 to disconnect, active while we pump ourselves-->
  <wait id="wait_disconnect1" start="pump1:start" end="pump1:end" event="disconnect_p2" />
   <!--Emit disconnect event-->
  <emit id="emit_disconnect1" start="wait_disconnect1:end">
      <event id="disconnect_p1" type="behavior"/>
  </emit>
  <handshake:withdraw id="withdraw1" start="wait_disconnect1:end"/>
</bml>
```

Script for agent 2

```
<bml>
  <!--Wait for p1 to extend-->
  <wait id="wait_extend_p1" event="extend_p1"/>
  <handshake:extend id="extend2" start="wait_extend_p1:end"/>
  <!--Emit extend event-->
  <emit id="emit_extend2" start="extend2:end">
      <event id="extend_p2" type="behavior"/>
  </emit>
  <handshake:connect id="connect2" start="extend2:end"/>
  <handshake:pump id="pump2" start="connect2:end"/>
  <!--Wait for p1 to disconnect, active while we pump ourselves-->
  <wait id="wait_disconnect2" start="pump2:start" end="pump2:end" event="disconnect_p1" />
  <!--Emit disconnect event-->
  <emit id="emitter2" start="wait_disconnect2:end">
      <event id="disconnect_p2" type="behavior"/>
  </emit>
  <handshake:withdraw id="withdraw2" start="wait_disconnect2:end"/>
</bml>
```

Fig. 8. The handshake BML script for agent 1 and agent 2

5.3 An Architecture That Supports Anticipatory Coordinated Multimodal Interaction

Figure 9 summarizes the overall architecture of our system. The scheduler is responsible for the alignment of the behaviors on different modalities. It generates an execution plan, based on the provided BML script. The execution of a BML^T script requires dynamic (re)-planning capabilities, since the predicted times are not fully known beforehand and can and will be updated during the execution of the script. For example, in the dancer the timing of dance moves is adapted so that it is aligned to changing predictions of the beat of the music, while the dance animation is being executed. Replanning can involve

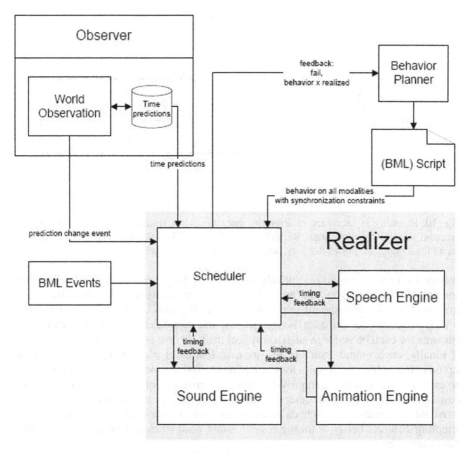

Fig. 9. Architecture

1. translating the start time of behaviors
2. stretching or skewing behaviors to fit timing constraints
3. skip behaviors that have low priority (as indicated by the BML script)
4. or, if the methods above fail, inform the behavior planner that generated the BML script, which in turn can provide an alternative script

Figure 10 shows some of the strategies that can be used to retime behaviors so that timing constraints are met. Many more retiming strategies are possible. Retiming by stretching and/or skewing behaviors raises two issues:

1. How can a behavior be stretched/skewed?
2. Which of the behaviors have to be stretched/skewed by how much?

Different modalities stretch and skew in different ways. Our previous research explored the stretching and skewing of exercise motion [48]. While a timing constraint specifies the timing of only one behavior phase, a stretch/skew operation possibly influences the timing of all phases in the behavior.

The alignment of behaviors is specified using time constraints. To satisfy these constraints, one or more of the behaviors that are to be aligned have to be stretched or

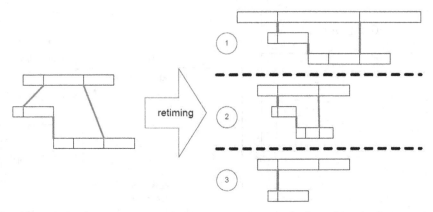

Fig. 10. Retiming is necessary to align the three behaviors (indicated by the 3 rectangles), executed at different modalities. Retiming strategy 1 stretches the first behavior. Strategy 2 skews the second and third behaviors. Strategy 3 omits the third behavior.

skewed by a certain amount. Typically, an infinitely large set of different stretch/skew amounts on the behaviors that are to be aligned can satisfy the alignment time constraints. The scheduler should select one of these. If a cost can be calculated for each stretch/skew amount on each behavior, then the scheduler can select stretch/skew amounts for each behavior in such a way that the total cost is minimized.

Finally, each output modality has its own low-level planner. Given timing constraints on a behavior, the previous behavior(s) on this modality and the behavior to be executed, the planners can provide timing information for each behavior phase, the cost of the behavior and whether or not the behavior can be executed satisfying the provided constraints. The scheduler can query the planners for this information, attempting different behavior timing combinations, until an execution plan is found that has minimal cost.

6 Conclusions

In this paper we reported about our research in progress on mutually coordinated anticipatory multimodal interaction. We looked at three applications of this research: an interactive virtual dancer, an interactive virtual conductor, and an interactive virtual trainer. In these applications expressive behavior of a virtual human has to be synchronized with external events and predictions that are related to the performance of the virtual human or its perception of the environment. We discussed anticipation in conversations and continuous synchronizing expressive behavior in conversations based on expectations. Specification of synchronization is investigated with the Behavioral Markup Language (BML) and extensions of this language that are introduced to accommodate synchronization required for our applications. Architectural consequences for a virtual human that has to act human-like have been discussed. In particular the issue of replanning and retiming of actions to be performed by a virtual human need to be addressed.

In our future research we will investigate more examples of natural continuous multimodal interaction that appear in real-life situations. That is, interactions in 'ambient intelligence' environments, where the environments or their virtual inhabitants have to deal with human partners in charge of multiple related and unrelated tasks (e.g., in a smart home office environment) or where the virtual humans have to take into account that their human partners are also involved in family related activities (e.g., in a smart home environment) that have impact on the planning and timing of their expressive behavior in their interaction with virtual partners.

Acknowledgements. This work has been supported by funding from the European IST Programme Project FP6-033812 (Augmented Multi-party Interaction, publication AMIDA-82), the COST Action 2102 (Cross-Modal Analysis of Verbal and Non-verbal Communication), and the GATE project, funded by the Netherlands Organization for Scientific Research (NWO) and the Netherlands ICT Research and Innovation Authority (ICT Regie). This paper only reflects the authors' views and funding agencies are not liable for any use that may be made of the information contained herein.

References

1. André, E., Rist, T., van Mulken, S., Klesen, M., Baldes, S.: The automated design of believable dialogues for animated presentation teams. In: Cassell, J., Prevost, S., Sullivan, J., Churchill, E. (eds.) Embodied Conversational Agents, pp. 220–255. MIT Press, Cambridge (2000)
2. Bailenson, J.N., Yee, N.: Digital chameleons: Automatic assimilation of nonverbal gestures in immersive virtual environments. Psychological Science 16(1), 814–819 (2005)
3. Basu, S.: Conversational scene analysis. MIT Press, Cambridge (2002)
4. Bavelas, J.B., Coates, L., Johnson, T.: Listeners as co-narrators. Journal of Personality and Social Psychology 79(6), 941–952 (2000)
5. Boker, S.M., Xu, M., Rotondo, J.L., King, K.: Windowed cross-correlation and peak picking for the analysis of variability in the association between behavioral time series. Psychological Methods 7(3), 338–355 (2002)
6. Bos, P., Reidsma, D., Ruttkay, Z.M., Nijholt, A.: Interacting with a virtual conductor. In: [16], pp. 25–30
7. Bull, M.: An analysis of between-speaker intervals. In: Proceedings 1996 of the Edinburgh Postgraduate Conference in Linguistics and Applied Linguistics, pp. 18–27 (1996)
8. Carletta, J.C., Ashby, S., Bourban, S., Flynn, M., Guillemot, M., Hain, T., Kadlec, J., Karaiskos, V., Kraaij, W., Kronenthal, M., Lathoud, M., Lincoln, M., Lisowska, A., McCowan, I., Post, W.M., Reidsma, D., Wellner, P.: The AMI meeting corpus: A preannouncement. In: Renals, S., Bengio, S. (eds.) MLMI 2005. LNCS, vol. 3869, pp. 28–39. Springer, Heidelberg (2006)
9. Cassell, J., Pelachaud, C., Badler, N., Steedman, M., Achorn, B., Becket, T., Douville, B., Prevost, S., Stone, M.: Animated conversation: rule-based generation of facial expression, gesture & spoken intonation for multiple conversational agents. In: SIGGRAPH 1994: Proceedings of the 21st annual conference on Computer Graphics and Interactive Techniques, pp. 413–420. ACM Press, New York (1994)
10. Cassell, J., Vilhjálmsson, H.H., Bickmore, T.: BEAT: The behavior expression animation toolkit. In: Fiume, E. (ed.) SIGGRAPH 2001, Computer Graphics Proceedings, pp. 477–486. ACM Press, New York (2001)
11. Coates, J.: No gap, lots of overlap: turn-taking patterns in the talk of women friends. Multilingual Matters, 177–192 (1994)
12. Cowley, S.J.: Of timing, turn-taking, and conversations. Journal of Psycholinguistic Research 27(5), 541–571 (1998)

13. Crown, C.L.: Coordinated Interpersonal Timing of Vision and Voice as a Function of interpersonal Attraction. Journal of Language and Social Psychology 10(1), 29–46 (1991)
14. Emmott, S.J., Travis, D.: Information superhighways: multimedia users and futures. Academic Press, Inc., Duluth (2005)
15. Goodrich, S., Henderson, L., Allchin, N., Jeevaratnam, A.: On the peculiarity of simple reaction time. The Quarterly Journal of Experimental Psychology Section A 42(4), 763–775 (1990)
16. Harper, R., Rauterberg, M., Combetto, M. (eds.): 5th International Conference on Entertainment Computing. LNCS, vol. 4161. Springer, Heidelberg (2006)
17. Heylen, D., Nijholt, A., Poel, M.: Generating nonverbal signals for a sensitive artificial listener. In: Esposito, A., Faundez-Zanuy, M., Keller, E., Marinaro, M. (eds.) COST Action 2102. LNCS (LNAI), vol. 4775, pp. 264–274. Springer, Heidelberg (2007)
18. Izdebski, K., Shipp, T.: Minimal reaction times for phonatory initiation. Journal of Speech and Hearing Research 21(4), 638–651 (1978)
19. Johnson, L.L., Rickel, J.W., Lester, J.: Animated pedagogical agents: Face-to-face interaction in interactive learning environments. International Journal of Artificial Intelligence in Education 11, 47–78 (2000)
20. Jonsdottir, G.R., Gratch, J., Fast, E., Thórisson, K.R.: Fluid semantic back-channel feedback in dialogue: Challenges and progress. In: [27], pp. 154–160
21. Keller, E.: Beats for individual timing variation. In: Esposito, A., Keller, E., Marinaro, M., Bratanic, M. (eds.) The Fundamentals of Verbal and Non-verbal Communication and the Biometrical Issue. NATO Security through Science: Human and Societal Dynamics, vol. 18, pp. 115–128. IOS Press, Amsterdam (2007)
22. Kopp, S.: Surface realization of multimodal output from xml representations in MURML. In: Invited Workshop on Representations for Multimodal Generation (2005)
23. Kopp, S., Krenn, B., Marsella, S., Marshall, A.N., Pelachaud, C., Pirker, H., Thórisson, K.R., Vilhjálmsson, H.H.: Towards a common framework for multimodal generation: The behavior markup language. In: Gratch, J., Young, M.R., Aylett, R., Ballin, D., Olivier, P. (eds.) IVA 2006. LNCS (LNAI), vol. 4133, pp. 205–217. Springer, Heidelberg (2006)
24. Kopp, S., Wachsmuth, I.: Model-based animation of co-verbal gesture. In: CA 2002: Proceedings of the Computer Animation Conference, p. 252. IEEE Computer Society, Washington (2002)
25. Maatman, R.M., Gratch, J., Marsella, S.: Natural behavior of a listening agent. In: Panayiotopoulos, T., Gratch, J., Aylett, R., Ballin, D., Olivier, P., Rist, T. (eds.) Intelligent Virtual Agents. Lecture Notes in Computer Science, vol. 3661, pp. 25–36. Springer, Berlin (2005)
26. McNeill, D.: Hand and Mind: What Gestures Reveal about Thought. University of Chicago Press, Chicago (1995)
27. Nagaoka, C., Komori, M., Yoshikawa, S.: Synchrony tendency: interactional synchrony and congruence of nonverbal behavior in social interaction. In: Proceedings International Conference on Active Media Technology, pp. 529–534 (2005)
28. Noot, H., Ruttkay, Z.: The Gestyle language. In: International workshop on gesture and sign language based human-computer interaction (2003)
29. O'Connell, D.C., Kowal, S., Kaltenbacher, E.: Turn-taking: A critical analysis of the research tradition. Journal of Psycholinguistic Research 19(6), 345–373 (1990)
30. Pelachaud, C., Martin, J.-C., André, E., Chollet, G., Karpouzis, K., Pelé, D. (eds.): Intelligent Virtual Agents, 7th International Conference. LNCS, vol. 4722. Springer, Heidelberg (2007)
31. Ramseyer, F., Tschacher, W.: Synchrony: A Core Concept for a Constructivist Approach to Psychotherapy. Constructivism in the Human Sciences 11(1), 150–171 (2006)

32. Ramseyer, F., Tschacher, W.: Synchrony in dyadic psychotherapy sessions. In: Simultaneity: Temporal Structures and Observer Perspectives, ch. 18. World Scientific, Singapore (to appear, 2008)
33. Reeves, B., Nass, C.: The media equation: how people treat computers, television, and new media like real people and places. Cambridge University Press, New York (1996)
34. Reidsma, D., Welbergen, H., van Poppe, R., Bos, P., Nijholt, A.: Towards bidirectional dancing interaction. In: [16], pp. 1–12
35. Rickel, J.W., Gratch, J., Marsella, S., Swartout, W.: Steve goes to Bosnia: Towards a new generation of virtual humans for interactive experiences. In: AAAI Spring Symposium of Artificial Intelligence and Interactive Entertainment (2001)
36. Robins, B., Dautenhahn, K., Nehaniv, C.L., Mirza, N.A., Francois, D., Olsson, L.: Sustaining interaction dynamics and engagement in dyadic child-robot interaction kinesics: Lessons learnt from an exploratory study. In: Proc. of the 14th IEEE International Workshop on Robot and Human Interactive Communication, RO-MAN 2005 (2005)
37. Ruttkay, Z.M., Zwiers, J., Welbergen, H., van Reidsma, D.: Towards a reactive virtual trainer. In: Gratch, J., Young, M., Aylett, R.S., Ballin, D., Olivier, P. (eds.) IVA 2006. LNCS (LNAI), vol. 4133, pp. 292–303. Springer, Heidelberg (2006)
38. Sacks, H., Schegloff, E.A., Jefferson, G.: A simplest systematics for the organization of turn-taking for conversation. Language 50(4), 696–735 (1974)
39. Sanders, C.: The Paris years. In: Sanders, C. (ed.) The Cambridge Companion to Saussure, Ch. 2., pp. 30–46. Cambridge University Press, Cambridge (2005)
40. Slowiaczek, L.M.: Semantic priming in a single-word shadowing task. The American Journal of Psychology 107(2), 245–260 (1994)
41. Suzuki, N., Takeuchi, Y., Ishii, K., Okada, M.: Effects of echoic mimicry using hummed sounds on human-computer interaction. Speech Communication 40(4), 559–573 (2003)
42. Theune, M., Heylen, D., Nijholt, A.: Generating Embodied Information Presentations. In: Stock, O., Zancanaro, M. (eds.) Multimodal Intelligent Information Presentation, Ch. 3. Kluwer Series on Text, Speech and Language Technology, vol. 27, pp. 47–70. Kluwer Academic Publishers, Dordrecht (2005)
43. Thórisson, K.R.: Communicative humanoids: a computational model of psychosocial dialogue skills. PhD thesis, MIT Media Laboratory (1996)
44. Thórisson, K.R.: Natural Turn-Taking Needs No Manual: Computational Theory and Model, from Perception to Action. In: Multimodality in Language and Speech Systems, pp. 173–207. Kluwer Academic Publishers, Dordrecht (2002)
45. Vilhjálmsson, H.H., Cantelmo, N., Cassell, J., Chafai, N.E., Kipp, M., Kopp, S., Mancini, M., Marsella, S., Marshall, A.N., Pelachaud, C., Ruttkay, Z.M., Thórisson, K.R., van Welbergen, H., van der Werf, R.J.: The behavior markup language: Recent developments and challenges. In: [30], pp. 99–111
46. Ward, N., Tsukahara, W.: A Responsive Dialog System. In: Wilks, Y. (ed.) Machine Conversations, pp. 169–174. Kluwer Academic Publishers, Dordrecht (1999)
47. Welbergen, H., van, N.A., Reidsma, D., Zwiers, J.: Presenting in virtual worlds: Towards an architecture for a 3D presenter explaining 2D-presented information. IEEE Intelligent Systems 21(5), 47–53 (2006)
48. Welbergen, H., van Ruttkay, Z.: On the parameterization of clapping. In: Proc. 7th International Workshop on Gesture in Human-Computer Interaction and Simulation (to appear, 2007)
49. Wilson, M., Wilson, T.P.: An oscillator model of the timing of turn-taking. Psychonomic Bulletin & Review 12(6), 957–968 (2005)
50. Yngve, V.H.: On getting a word in edgewise. In: Papers from the 6th Regional Meeting of the Chicago Linguistics Society, pp. 567–577. University of Chicago (1970)

Affordances and Cognitive Walkthrough for Analyzing Human-Virtual Human Interaction

Zsófia Ruttkay[1,2] and Rieks op den Akker[1]

[1] HMI, University of Twente, The Netherlands
[2] ITK, Pázmány Péter Catholic University, Hungary
zsofi@cs.utwente.nl

Abstract. This study investigates how the psychological notion of affordance, known from human computer interface design, can be adopted for the analysis and design of communication of a user with a Virtual Human (VH), as a novel interface. We take as starting point the original notion of affordance, used to describe the function of objects for humans. Then, we dwell on the human-computer interaction case when the object used by the human is (a piece of software in) the computer. In the next step, we look at human-human communication and identify actual and perceived affordances of the human body and mind. Then using the generic framework of affordances, we explain certain essential phenomena of human-human multimodal communication. Finally, we show how they carry over to the case of communicating with a 'designed human', that is an VH, whose human-like communication means may be augmented with ones reminiscent of the computer and fictive worlds. In the closing section we discuss and reformulate the method of cognitive walkthrough to make it applicable for evaluating the design of verbal and non-verbal interactive behaviour of VHs.

Keywords: Affordance theory, virtual humans, embodied conversational agents, cognitive walkthrough, HCI.

1 Introduction

James J. Gibson coined the term *affordance* [8] in order to describe the relationship between animals and their environment. Donald Norman introduced the new term *perceived affordance* to represent the relationship between users and artificial designed products [11].

Recently this notion, which has been in use as crucial concept to evaluate the design of technological products (including computer programs), has been used in a much broader sense in the community of researchers developing computer systems where the user communicates with virtual humans. Virtual humans (VHs) are synthetic characters produced by computational means, which are intended to look like and communicate as real people do [1]. The design and evaluation of VHs, as new generation in user interfaces, is a hot topic [13]. Cassell talked already years ago about the "affordances of the human body" [1], Marsella raised the issue whether nonverbal signals can be understood as (perceived) affordances [9], which idea was

A. Esposito et al. (Eds.): HH and HM Interaction 2007, LNAI 5042, pp. 90–106, 2008.

explored further by Ruttkay and Ten Hagen [16]. These initial and incomplete examples ask for a thorough analysis of this notion and its benefits for human-virtual human interaction (HVHI). The question is if we gain new insight by adopting the notion of affordance in the broader sense, as a useful novel reference framework to analyse HVHI. Or, are notions we are already familiar with, like non-verbal signals with meaning, equally suitable for the same analysis of phenomena and properties of this new type of user interface?

We claim for the first, affirmative answer: the concept of affordance, if taken in a broad sense, not only lends itself as a good frame of reference for human-VH communication, but makes its design and analysis transparent. It enables the researcher to treat human- and computer-related communications in the same way, and to use the traditional method of cognitive walkthrough of HCI for the novel case of HVHI.

Affordance theory has been used primarily in connection with the new, mediated communication means of computer technology. Whittaker [18] used the concept to confront the communication by mediated technologies, that is, the traditional means of HCI, and face to face communication. He did not extend the concept for phenomena in human-human interaction. Gaver [7] investigated the affordances of the physical environment, such as new technologies, for social interaction and emerging new behaviours. In robotics, learning affordances was addressed [11]. Affordance theory has been used as the basis for rapid generation and reusability of synthetic agents and objects [3]. The authors borrowed affordance theory to solve the AI problem of multiple representation of views of the same world in different agents' mind. They found the concept very useful, both for design and engineering multi-agent systems: "We conclude that Affordance Theory is an elegant solution to the problem of providing both rapid scenario development and the simulation of individual differences in perception, culture, and emotionality within the same agent architecture." They restricted the usage of the concept for describing the utilities of the (virtual and real) world for agents with different background. What they exploited from the theory is that the same object may offer different usage for different agents.

In [10] the authors compare Gibson's original definition with the use of the term by Norman. They also present a survey of the use of the concept in the HCI literature, more specifically in the annual CHI conference proceedings. Their conclusion is just the opposite of ours: "As the concept of affordances is used currently, it has marginal value because it lacks specific meaning."

In our paper we set out to grasp the meaning of affordance in human-computer interaction (HCI) and in particular, in HVHI. In the rest of the paper we will argue step by step. We take as starting point the original notion of affordance, used to describe the usage of objects by humans. Then, we dwell on the human-computer interaction case when the object used by the human is a (piece of software in) the computer. In the next chapter, we look at human-human communication and identify actual and perceived affordances of the human body and mind. Then using the generic framework of affordances, we explain certain essential phenomena of human-human multimodal communication. Finally, we show how they carry over to the case of communicating with a 'designed human', that is a VH, whose human-like communication means may be augmented with ones reminiscent of the computer and fictive worlds. We give an illustrative example from the case of conversation with an VH assistant for money retrieval. In the closing section we discuss and reformulate the method of cognitive walkthrough so as to make it applicable for evaluating the design of verbal and non-verbal interactive behaviour of VHs.

2 The Notion of Affordance in HCI

2.1 The Original Concept of Affordance

Originally, affordance was invented to describe how animals make use of objects in their environments [8, p. 127.]:

> "The affordances of the environment are what it offers the animal, what it provides or furnishes, either for good or ill. The verb to afford is found in the dictionary, but the noun affordance is not. I have made it up. I mean by it something that refers to both the environment and the animal in a way that no existing term does. It implies the complementarity of the animal and the environment. If a terrestrial surface is nearly horizontal (instead of slanted), nearly flat (instead of convex or concave), and sufficiently extended (relative to the size of the animal) and if its substance is rigid (relative to the weight of the animal), then the surface affords support... Note that the four properties listed - horizontal, flat, extended, and rigid - would be physical properties of a surface if they were measured with the scales and standard units used in physics. As an affordance of support for a species of animal, however, they have to be measured relative to the animal. They are unique for that animal. They are not just abstract physical properties. "

Note how in its original, most limited meaning affordance is relative to the 'user' of an object. This characteristic will be crucial in the subsequent generalizations too.

2.2 Perceived and Actual Affordance

What is the meaning of affordance in HCI? The notion of affordance was introduced in HCI by D. Norman [12]:

> "... the term affordance refers to the perceived and actual properties of the thing, primarily those fundamental properties that determine just how the thing could be used. A chair affords ('is for') support and, therefore, affords sitting."

In their widely used course book "Human Computer Interaction", Alan Dix and others defines the concept in the following way [6, p. 135.]:

> "The psychological notion of affordance says that things may suggest by their shape and other attributes what you can do to them: a handle affords pulling or lifting, a button affords pushing. These affordances can be used when designing novel interaction elements. (...) Affordances are not intrinsic, but depend on the background and culture of users. Most computer scientists will click on an icon. This is not because they go around pushing pictures in art galleries, but because they have learned that this is an affordance of such objects in a computer domain...."

Some psychologists argue that there are intrinsic properties, or affordances, of any visual object that suggest to us how they can be manipulated. The appearance of the object stimulates a familiarity with its behaviour. For example, the shape of a door handle can suggest how it should be manipulated to open a door, and a key on a keyboard suggests to us that it can be pushed. In the design of a graphical user interface, it is implied that a soft button used in a form's interface suggests it should be pushed (though it does not suggest how it is to be pushed via the mouse). Effective use of the affordances which exist for interface objects can enhance the familiarity of the interactive system. "

The above definitions adapt the original affordance concept by putting the human in the actor role, and the (designed) artefacts, especially computer systems in place of the objects of the natural environments. Moreover, the single notion is split into two related, but different notions of affordance (see also [16]):

- *perceived affordance*: what the object or system suggest the user can do or use it for;
- *actual affordance*: what the object or system can actually do/be used for.

The perceived affordance depends on two factors. First of all, on the appearance of the object or system. This is usually a visual appearance, but acoustic signals may also be used. E.g. the affordance "to read a message" may be indicated by an icon, and/or by an earcon, on the mobile phone or a computer screen. The appearance may be that of the object itself (e.g. the example of chair above), or may be a separate, designed signal (e.g. the exit signal above a door). Second, the mapping of the visual signal to the assumed function is done by the receiver, and is a result of learning. Things are in order if the perceived and actual affordances coincide. This requires, basically, that the user associates the perceived signal with the actual affordance. Such an association is often the result of learning. There are established, though may be in different ethnic or professional groups different, signals for certain actual affordances.

In HCI, the user interface designer is the one to care for a match between the perceived and the actual affordance. In general the appearance of the user interface should make clear to the user the 'tools' available in each situation, and these tools should be suited to perform each of the acts the user could possibly intend to do in a given situation. This could be considered as an important design principle for human-computer interfaces; a principle that we will call the *Affordance Requirement:*

For every item, visible on the user interface at any time during the interaction with the user, it's perceived performance should match it's actual performance.

There is a strong relation between the above formulated notion of affordance with the requirements mentioned and Cognitive Walkthrough, a well-known method for evaluation of user interfaces. The very sense of a the Cognitive Walkthrough method for evaluating a computer system is to check whether the user interface satisfies the design principles, one of these is the Affordance Requirement. We come back to this later.

2.3 Devices and Functions in HCI

What kind of affordances are common in HCI? For a careful analysis of devices and their function in HCI, we look at them from different aspects.

Realization: Physical versus abstract. In case of a computer, we must differentiate between physical input and periphery devices as physical affordances, and abstract 'devices' which form part of the software, and are to perform specific tasks. Examples of physical devices: the keyboard, the mouse, a printer attached to the pc, ... Examples of abstract devices (all depicted on the display): a trash-bin, a screen-locker, a mailbox.

In the first case, using/manipulating the physical device results in some action by the device, like entering a character, locating a point on the screen. (We'll return to the printer later.) In the second case, there are conventional ways to activate the abstract devices, either by dragging and dropping some 'object' the device has to operate on (e.g. dragging a file to the dustbin, to be thrown away), or to click the device to activate the function (e.g. locking the screen by clicking the lock-screen icon). In case of abstract devices thus, one uses simple physical devices (most often, the mouse, or a specific key combination of the keyboard) to activate them.

Range of functions: Simple (or basic) versus complex. The printer and the mailbox are complex devices in the sense that they make possible a set of functions, each to be activated by some sub-part of the entire complex device. E.g. on the printer, the printing options can be specified, a page can be printed, or a new paper can be fed. A mailbox usually stands for a mail program, allowing to send/receive/store and sort mails.

Range of objects/targets they (may) act on: Given versus to be chosen. The target of activation may be specified too (the file to be selected which needs to be deleted, printed, ...). This is not unlike with the affordances in the real world. While a lamp switch will always act on a single lamp, a knife as an affordance to cut must be applied to some object. The range of possible targets is, however, constrained: one should not try to cut a piece of metal or stone with a knife. This analogy also applies for HCI, where the parameters of files may be decisive if it is a proper object for an affordance, e.g. printing can be applied only to specific types of 'printable' documents.

There may be other side-conditions to activate some abstract devices, like time, availability of certain resources. So some abstract devices are applicable in certain contexts only. The context can be that a proper target has been selected (in an implicit way). Hence an abstract device may be context dependent or independent. A complex physical device may have some context dependent behaviour: the print function may be active only if there is printing paper available.

Another observation is that an abstract device may be linked directly or indirectly to a physical device, think of the example of a printer drive as abstract device and a printer as a physical device.

3 Affordances in Human-Human Interaction

3.1 Affordances of the Speaker and the Listener

The original context of affordances was the utility of objects for humans (and animals). In HCI, the 'objects of the world' was replaced by physical and abstract devices of computers. In both cases, the intelligent human is the one to act and use the affordances of the (unintelligent, non-reactive) world. In case of computer affordances, the 'dead objects' though may show some reactive and dynamic behaviour, limited to indicating applicability in a given context.

Now let's have a look how affordances are attributed to the human body by J. Cassell [1]: "Only humans can communicate using language and carry on conversations with one another. And skills of conversation have developed in humans in such a way as to exploit all of the unique *affordances of the human body*." Affordances seem to be essential for human language usage, and in more general, to interactive behaviour. Examples are multimodal gestures, like an open hand, or looking at the partner, which signal that one has given turn, and thus is can be talked to now.

At a first glance it seems that in the conversational context the term 'affordance' is used in a different sense. What is to be achieved is certain *behaviour* of the conversant, who isn't an object that a user is supposed to do something with. But the behaviour of the other is a necessary condition for the user to perform some action: one speaks only if there is a listener around. And the listener does signal that he is not a deaf person being present, but one listening to and understanding what the other is saying. Hence there is signalling of a *function* the speaker may exploit, albeit this function is different from that of using an object as a tool: it is to manage communication.

When talking about affordances in human-human interaction, there are major differences, with respect to human-world or human-computer interaction:

- It takes place between two (or more), in facilities and capabilities (by and large) *equal parties*.
- For a successful conversation, constant *co-operation by the speaker and listener* is needed.
- A human person has an *arsenal of physical and mental affordances* (see below) to be used for communication, and they adapt to the situation and partner in using the most appropriate one.
- The correspondence between perceived and actual physical and mental affordances is more intricate, as the *mapping is many to many*, and it highly *depends on culture and other factors*.

3.2 Comparison of Affordances in Human-Object, Human-Computer and Human-Human Interaction

The perception and usage of affordances was a relatively simple task in the previous two cases: the human had to recognize an affordance and make use of its unique function. (He had to discover the switch next to the door, and use it if he wanted to have the light on.) In human-human communication, one of the parties, the speaker does take the initiative with addressing the other, the listener, assuming that the partner is a receiver of what he is to say. However, it highly depends on the partner if he will actually function as a receiver of the words uttered by the speaker. Problems may arise at different levels: it is not sure if the partner hears him, understands him, is interested in what he is saying. In affordance terminology, the listener may not have (permanently or temporarily) all the physical and mental affordances needed altogether to function as a listener. In human-human communication, it is thus common to give feedback on the availability of simple or complex, mental and physical affordances.

In concrete, talking to somebody may invoke very different reactions from him/her, such as:

- No sign from the listener, as if deaf, or not noticing that he is talked to;
- Some sign (e.g. puzzled facial expression) from the listener indicating that he has not understood what the speaker was telling.
- Answer or action according to what the speaker has told.

When a speaker (S) is talking, it is assumed that the listener (L) can hear and understand S, and that L is interested and listening to S. Thus for a successful conversation one has to take into account the affordances used by S (English speech) and the affordances available at the moment for L (hearing, understanding English, etc.). The multitude of affordances, their temporal availability and the symmetrical role of the communicating partners are the major differences and cause of complexity of the affordance concept in human-human interaction. In Table 1, we give a comparison of the concept in the three domains.

Below we look at the different aspects in detail.

Physical vs mental affordance. *A physical affordance* is some low-level functionality of a part or organ of the body, e.g. the ability to move limbs, to make facial expressions, to articulate voices, to sense sound or to see. A *mental affordance* is a capability of interpreting signals produced by a physical affordance, e.g. talking and understanding a language, interpreting facial expressions. Note that mental affordances assume the existence of certain physical affordances: to be able to interpret facial expressions, the vision system must be functioning. (We will not deviate here to a discussion of the extent to which a mental affordance is the sum of low-level physical affordances, if one allows that all low-level bodily functions are physical affordances.) Moreover, it is a widely shared opinion that most of the mental affordances are learnt, and are culture-specific. In the VH community J. Cassell talks about the 'affordances of the human body' in the sense of physical affordances, as 'faculties' or 'devices' for (multimodal) communication [1].

Role of affordances in human-human communication. In the physical world, or in traditional HCI, the affordance was always associated with an object, from the point of view of the human user. Hence there the role is asymmetric. In human-human communication, the communicating partners play, in principle, a symmetrical role. A person's affordance of hearing and English language understanding are valuable for somebody else who has the matching affordances of the ability to talk and speak English. One may speak several languages, thus having a multitude of affordances, each valuable only for certain people, namely those speaking a given language. Hence

Table 1. Comparison of aspects of the concept affordance in human-object, human-computer and human-human interaction. In the last columns, the affordance is discussed from the speaker's (S) point of view. Note however, that S has own physical and mental affordances essential to initiate communication.

Aspect\Type of interaction	Human-object	Human-computer	Human-human
The 'user' of the affordance	A human	A human	Human speaker (S) or listener (L)
The affordance	The non-responsive object	The static physical or abstract device, may be with a few and well-understood possible states (e.g. with a printer: paper jam, ink problem, or ready to print)	An active human (L), responsive, with a wide range of possible states related to availability of actual physical and mental resources, but also individual deviations
Actual affordance	Physical, one per object	Physical or abstract, few per object	Physical or mental, several per human
Perceived affordance (signal)	The object itself, or a static designed visual/acoustic sign to indicate function	The object itself, or a designed visual/acoustic sign, with a few parameters to indicate context	Multimodal signals produces by L in a non-deterministic way during the conversation as feedback.
Signalling lack of actual affordance	Rarely (e.g. red light indicating problem with device)	Sometimes (e.g. broken connection)	Often signalled
Decoding the actual affordance from perceived one	Based on learning, experience and agreed design protocols	Abstract affordances are not always easy to decode, due to lack of or misuse of design protocols. Mapping is one to one, though.	Coding (by L) decoding (by S) protocols are complex, may differ, and many to many mappings often exist between signal and function

affordances of a speaker and a listener complement each other. Note that this relative nature of the affordance concept was present in how Gibson used the term, then for animals exploiting objects of the environment: a flat surface may be a suitable seat for one animal, and not so for another one. But the difference is that in the animal-object relationship Gibson talked about different species of animals with very different physical and physiological characteristics, while in the case of human-human communication the relativity of an affordance is caused by the diversity in learnt, mental affordances over the (reatively-speaking) physically uniform humans.

We can talk about symmetry in an another sense too, namely that two conversing humans posses, by and large, an identical set of physical and mental affordances, and they use different – but not disjoint – subsets depending on who is the speaker and who is the listener.

Perceiving affordances of a human. How to find out if a person has the affordance of understanding spoken English? A straightforward way is to ask - but if the person is deaf, or does not understand English, he or she will not be able to answer. On the other hand, in real life communication, the person spoken to does in general signal back if they have heard and grasped what he was told, also stating in an indirect way that he can hear and understand English [13]. In human-human communication there are two layers, both of which may make use of verbal and/or nonverbal modalities [17]:

- the transfer of some information content;
- a meta-level signalling, which provides feedback (among other things) about the availability and proper functioning of the devices needed to organize the conversation and decode the message.

Affordances for dialogue control. A conversation requires the coordination of the division of floor: who is the speaker and who is listening in each moment. The low-level bodily affordances (eye gaze, posture, speech characteristics) are used to signal such information as turn to be given, turn asked for, turn taken and kept, or listening to the speaker. Hence the multi-modal signals can be seen as visualizations of some 'state' the human is in a given moment: listening, talking to the partner, finishing his/her speech, recalling data while talking. In these states, one utilizes different sets of affordances. The different states can be thus associated with the affordances available for the conversants. E.g. if someone is in 'talking' state, the partner should not interrupt, which would be appropriate only if the speaker stops talking and indicates that now the 'listening' affordances are available. As well as signalling one's own affordances being active, one may also signal to the partner a particular affordance they are required to use. E.g. gazing at the partner signals that one has finished talking and can be talked to from now on. Further on, after some time if the partner has not started talking, pointing at him with open palms upwards as a sign that he should take the turn, that is, use the relevant physical and mental affordances. So in human-human communication we can identify affordances and differentiate the two types introduced by Norman, as follows: Actual affordances are the arsenal of physical and mental faculties of a human to communicate. In order to perceive an affordance, some speech and/or nonverbal signals may be produced that the human has some actual affordances operating, or just about to use, or not using, or having problems with using it. Note that in the extreme, one may not produce any signal to indicate the existence of an affordance, e.g. listening to somebody without any feedback, with a poker face.

As we see, the affordance concept becomes more complex because of the huge set of potential affordances, of which only some are available at each moment. Also a further feature is that verbal and nonverbal signaling is used to indicate not only (in the original view, static) availability of an affordance, but also temporary problems with (or lack of) an affordance.

The decoding of the signal by the partner as intended by the signaling person. While in case of objects and computers as affordances, there may be some culture-dependent protocol for the design of the visualization of the affordance (e.g. design style of the 60-ies, or Swedish design for lamp switches), in case of human-human communication the mapping between affordances and signals is far more complicated. The cultural and social background of the listener plays a role in how he decodes signals, that is, what affordance he perceives. Moreover, there is a variety from time to time how a signals is (not) used, according to the static or dynamic characteristics of the speaker. E.g. an introverted person may use fewer and less articulate facial expressions for back-channelling a conversation; a certain eyebrow movement may be the idiosyncratic signal in case of a given person of boredom, sadness may alter the signaling of back-channeling, etc.

Separation of signal, affordance and target of action. If we look at affordances of the real world, there we find two kinds: ones where the target of operation is unique, the object having the affordance itself (e.g. to open a door, the handle needs to be pushed – the affordance has a single function, to open the given door), and ones which may be applied to achieve certain goals (e.g. an iron bar may be used to break in all kinds of doors, windows, using the affordance of the iron bar 'breaking firm objects'.) In the designed world we already stated that the signal may be separate form the object itself (e.g. sign of exit). In human-human interaction (HHI), the discourse regulation affordances are signaled by some organs and body parts, which are not the target of the action (the hand signals but is not the object the partner is expected to operate on). If we think of the analogy of opening a door, then the task can be the collaborative interaction of two communicating partners. But on the interaction level, they use the communicational affordances which make the information exchange possible (by speech, or other means) which may lead to solving the problem. Hence affordances in HHI are on a meta-level, to assure successful communication, and not on the level of solving some concrete task. In this respect the function of affordances of HHI is similar to the function of some of the affordances in HCI, namely those which indicate for the user to 'take a step' from the allowed ones, e.g. by typing in a command, or confirming an action to be performed by the system.

4   Affordances for Human-Virtual Human Interaction

4.1   Virtual Humans as Design Products

With human-virtual human interaction, we arrive back to a special type of human-computer interaction, that is, to a domain where everything offered for the user is the result of conscious design decisions (or unconscious mistakes). In order to explore the merit of the affordance concept for H-VH communication, we first turn to Daniel C. Dennett's theory about how people try to explain why things and phenomena are the way they experience them. He distinguished three stances that we can take towards these phenomena.

Physical stance. Clarification is based on laws of nature, e. g. this stone falls because of its mass and the law of attraction. Causes are physical causes.

Design stance. Clarification is based on the function it has obtained by the technical designer. All arts and technology, handcraft as well as machines work because of their design by humans. They use laws of physics and express new combinations of natural laws and qualities in order to make something happen that suits humans goals.

Intentional stance. Clarification based on motives or intention or goals that the system or thing itself has. Some people say that computers or robots have intentions (as humans have).

Note that often it depends on the person how he/she looks at a phenomenon: from a physical,. design or intentional stance. For instance, a mechanical clock works by exploiting physical laws, and the motion of its parts can be explained as a physical process. However, the clock, as a device is a designed artifact. As such it can be (and most naturally it is) looked at from a design stance. A person who has never seen a clock, may take an intentional stance and say that "the big hand chases the small hand", or that a bird flies out every now and then to look around.

Then, there is the important distinction between spontaneous, immediate reaction versus using something as a tool. The fact that my behaviour has some particular effect on someone else, because he interprets this behaviour in a certain way, doesn't imply that I use this behaviour deliberately to bring about this responsive behaviour. Natural (and non-verbal) language use is different in this respect from the use of a tool as a means to reach some goal.

People usually indicate in one way or another their feelings or mood, unless they make efforts to hide them, due to social 'display rules' or personal reasons. Others thus usually can notice - from the way how someone looks, stands or walks – one's emotion, mood and physical state. These are spontaneous expressions, not signals deliberately produced in order to express these feelings.

In a computer application with a VH, human behaviour is used in a consciously designed way, in order to reach some effects on the user. What was natural behaviour in the first place now, from the system designer's point of view, becomes a 'tool' to bring about desired effects in interaction with the human user of a system. E.g. in order to make the user answer, the VH should turn towards the user at the end of his speech, and keep gazing at the user. Looking at this from the user's point of view, he takes the intentional stance, and attributes intention of 'waiting for an answer' to the VH. The VHs are 'good' if they fool the user to believe that the VH acts and behaves intentionally, and really understands what the user is saying.

The above mentioned usage of 'natural' signaling by VHs, however, can be seen just as signals in HCI to inform the user what may or may not be allowed in a given situation.

It is the perspective of the design stance by Dennett which links the (spontaneous) natural human behaviour and the consciously chosen communicational protocol of HCI, the signals used among humans and the specific ones used in HCI. It's not uncommon nowadays to talk about 'facial display' the way people show for an outside observer how they want to be seen. From this stance we see verbal and non-verbal behaviour as presenting signs in order to signal what the subject self is doing or what the subject self expects the observer to do. The use of the notion of affordance for discourse functions in natural behaviour thus gives us a more clear picture of the meaning it already had in classical HCI literature.

Further on, in H-VH communication, the 'natural' affordances and their signaling protocols may be used interwoven with the unnatural, designed protocols of HCI. In other words, there may be unrealistic capabilities and signalling mechanisms of VH, which can be more efficient than the natural ones. Such an example is when, in a scene where multiple VHs are present, the one to be addressed (the listener in a given moment) is indicated by a red arrow above the head, instead of or in addition to the normal natural signaling which may be difficult to produce or notice from a distance, or due to limitations in animation and rendering. But one may think of a richer repertoire of bodily affordances. E.g. if speech not understood properly, the VH's ears could grow big, indicating the problem with catching words. This is similar to what people do when they enlarge the ears by putting the two open palms behind. While such a non-realistic capability is accepted in animation films, mixing of real and fictional, or human and computer interaction protocols is yet an unexplored field for VHs. The question, basically, reduces to "what extent is a virtual human looked upon as a real one?" The answer surely depends on the application domain.

4.2 An Example

Below we illustrate the discussed aspects of affordances in HVHI. The example assumes an internet banking site which is supervised by a VH as assistant. In our example we assume that the interaction takes place by the traditional question-answer protocol. Only if problems arise, or the user has not taken action for a long time or asked for help explicitly, the VH intervenes, as in the example. The human user (U) has reached the point where his account number is to be given. For the first time in the interaction, there is no input from him for 10 seconds. Then the VH appears:

VH: "Give your bank account number!"
U: No reaction for another 10 seconds.

Let's have a careful look at the possible causes of the silence:

1. Listener is deaf.
2. L does not speak English.
3. L did not catch the words.
4. L did not realize he was addressed.
5. L expects more polite treatment.
6. L does not know how to give the required number.
7. L does not have a bank account
8. L cannot answer now, as he is busy with talking to somebody.
9. L has his right hand in cast, is busy with figuring out the numbers with a left finger,
10. The user told his bank account, as an answer for the speech of the VH.
11. L had left earlier.
...

The nature of the cause of the user not answering is different in the above cases, related to problem with

- the physical affordance as hearing, needed to be addressed (1, 3),
- the mental affordance of understanding English (2)

- mental processing capacity (8),
- bodily affordance (9)
- perceiving an affordance (4, 6)
- the perceived and actual affordance of the VH (10),

So in such a simple case there can be at least 6 kinds of problems with affordances. (Of course, the cause of delay or no reaction can be other than problems with affordances, like lacking the information required for the reaction (7), not trusting the VH because of the ordering tone (5), or not being present at all (11).) Note that the problem with 3 may be attributed also to VH (e.g. speaking in a robot-like synthetic voice, difficult to understand), not only to H (not hearing well, or not mastering English). But in this case it may be the context (e.g. noisy street scene) which made speech as an affordance inappropriate. In case of 4. and 6. there is a problem with associating a signaled affordance (talking to somebody, indicating on a screen that digits are to be typed in) and the actual affordance. It may be the user who did not do the right mapping of the signaled and actual affordance, but it may also be that the signaled affordance was poor: the VH who did not signal clearly enough that he was addressing the user or it is not indicated at all on the screen that some digits are to be typed in by the user. If the latter, it is clearly a design mistake.

When designing the dialogue with the VH, it should be investigated how the above cases need to be dealt with. First of all, the design of the VH and the system should be such that many of the possible causes get eliminated. E.g. the VH should address the U in a noticeable way, by turning towards him, changing posture. The voice quality, loudness, speech tempo should be chosen such that it is easy to catch the words, the noise level of the environment should be considered.

Some other causes (8, 9, 11) can be excluded if the VH has visual perception capabilities, but this is usually not the case. A common, related problem with VH is that more is expected from the VH than it is capable of, in terms of natural communication. In our case, it is assumed that the speaking VH can also hear and understand language, which may not be true. Such false expectations can be countered by telling explicitly at the beginning, or in the commands, what input modalities are to be used. That is, in our case "Type in your bank account number."

So the dialogue should be designed in such a way that no possible cause of miscommunication remains ignored. Which is a challenging task, as in a given situation it is only one of the 10 possible problems which causes no answer by the user. There can be different AI techniques exploited to make the best guess, like single user modeling, tuning probabilistic transitions based on statistical analysis of performance. Another, complementary approach could be to use more modalities for signaling affordances (e.g. blinking space where the numbers need to be typed in, or the VH pointing at the screen location while asking for the input).

5 Cognitive Walk through to Analyse HVHI

Cognitive walkthrough was introduced to underpin the informal and subjective walkthrough technique with psychological theory. We present the revised version of this method for evaluating the design of the human computer interface as it has been developed more recently to make it accessible for system designers [6]. We will discuss here the relevance of this method for evaluating interactive behaviour, especially with respect to possible communication failures. Can these failures be avoided by a cognitive walkthrough of the interactive behaviour of the VH? Cognitive walkthrough is presented as an evaluation method to check whether the design of the interactive behaviour satisfies the Affordance Requirement. In the above example, this was happening in an unsystematic way already.

We first give the formulation of the method in terms of 'classical' interface design.

Before you can start a cognitive walkthrough evaluation you need:

1. A detailed description of the system (prototype)
2. A description of the task the user is to perform with the help of the system
3. A complete, written list of the actions needed to complete the task with the system.
4. An indication of who the users are and what kind of experience and knowledge the evaluators can assume about them.

As you see it is rather indicative and not very precisely specified. And it is clear that the method doesn't apply without any modifications to the analysis of affordance issues in interactive behaviour using VHs. Cognitive walkthrough is the method in which the evaluator goes through the action sequence mentioned in item 3 above to "critique the system and tell a believable story about its usability" [6]. This is done by systematically trying to answer the sets of questions below in each situation. We, again, first, follow the formulation in terms of classical human computer interface elements.

1. Will users be trying to produce whatever effect an action has? Are the assumptions about what task the action is supporting correct, given the users' experience and knowledge up to this point in the interaction?
2. Will users be able to notice that the correct action is available? Will users see the button or menu item, for example, by which the next action is actually achieved by the system?
3. Once users find the correct action at the interface, will they know that it is the right one for the effect they are trying to produce? This complements the previous question. It is one thing for a button or item to be visible, but will the users know that if it is the one they are looking for to complete their task?
4. After the action is taken, will users understand the feedback they get? Assuming the users did the correct action, will they notice that?

The group 2 and 4 of the above questions can be reformulated such that they are appropriate for a system where the interface is a VH, and where the traditional interactio means of HCI, like buttons and menus are replaced by natural human interaction facilities, i.e. using natural language supported by non-verbal conversational gestures. Actually, this was the approach taken to trace places and causes of problems occurring with two implemented prototype systems at the VH Workshop [9]. Below are the questions adapted to test the design of the communication with a VH:

1R Will the user be aware of what they can do to achieve a certain task: to talk to several (all) VHs on the screen, to use gestures, gaze and head movement as those are perceived by the VHs?

2R   Will users notice (when) they need to give an answer? Will they notice whom they may   address (who is listening)?

4R   Will there be a feedback to acknowledge the (natural, may be multi-modal) answer given by the user? Does the feedback indicate for the user if his/her action was correct? (In case of natural communication, this distinction means if something 'syntactically correct' was said and thus properly parsed, or something was said which is (one of the) expected answers in such a situation.)

Note that nothing prevents us from analysing systems with the method of cognitive walkthrough where natural communication takes place with a VH, interwoven with communication using elements of traditional HCI techniques. One has to keep in mind that 'signal' may be a natural communicational signal as well as a signal used in traditional HCI methods. Even more, the two types of signaling may be mixed. E.g. in a scene where several VHs are present, the one to be addressed may be indicated by an arrow, or blinking appearance.

Finally we mention that cognitive walkthrough is not the method to evaluate how efficient the user or the system is to solve some task. Think of two systems, one which allows to delete files one by one only, the other which allows to delete a selected set at once. Both can be well or badly designed, from a HCI point of view. Which has nothing to do with the fact that the 2nd system per se offers more functionality. What interface problem is, to be spotted by cognitive walkthrough, if a user in the 2nd case remains deleting a big number of files one by one, taking no notice of a functionality. Such problems as not using all the functionality of a system, or not using it efficiently could be also spotted by automatic methods, similar to ones used in the analysis of complex systems.

6   Conclusion

We have extended the use of the term affordance for the context of interaction with real and virtual humans, based on some abstract correspondence with the situation where the use of the word was already established and obtained a meaning: in traditional technology of designed objects (tools, devices and computer). From the design stance we can see that there is an aspect in human communicative behaviour - verbal as well as non-verbal - that structurally resembles certain communication means and their functions of traditional HCI. Based on the ideas of intentional and design stance we tried to unravel this deeper understanding. We identified the Affordance Requirement and reformulated the evaluation strategy known as cognitive walkthrough so as to make it applicable as an evaluation strategy for the design of the interactive behaviour of VHs. The proposed evaluation method seems particularly suitable for discovering potential flaws in this behaviour that may lead to communication failures. This aspects motivated S. Marsella to raise the issue, and later on, make empirical evaluations of different ECA systems on a 'cognitive walkthrough' basis [9].

We believe that a common terminology of systems with traditional and human-like interfaces gives a new insight to the latter systems, which have been compared to real human performance and evaluated from the point of their (subjective and objective) effect on the user. In our opinion, the generalization of affordances for human-human communication helps to look at h-h (and thus, h-virtual human) communication from an objective, design and performance perspective; makes the effect of the characteristics of the user, the computer and operational environment explicit, and helps to bridge the gap between human-computer and human-virtual human interaction. This new point of view allows the adaptation of evaluation techniques well-known in traditional HCI and system evaluation, such as cognitive walkthrough or automatic run-time evaluation.

Future work, based on the clarified concept of affordances in human-virtual human interaction, could be a formal framework where design principles are formulated and can be checked systematically. Also alternative perceived affordances for a single actual affordance, both in the design stage and as choices available could be handled, depending on the physical environment (level of noise) , the implementation constraints (speech input available or not) and last but not least, the user group. In [16] we made a first step in this direction.

We finally come back to a basic principle of interface design, that we encountered earlier. "What you must not do is depict a real-world object in a context where its normal affordances do not work!" ([6] p. 217) Does this imply that we *must not* make computer interfaces that give the user the impression that our computer systems with a virtual human as interface understand 'natural' language when they actually do not? This question would lead us to the polemy of how appropriate it is to use virtual humans, which may get attributed with all the mental affordances of humans.

Acknowledgements

We are grateful to Herman Koppelman for pointing at the literature on design and evaluation, and for Paul ten Hagen and Dirk Heylen for discussing ideas and commenting on earlier versions of the paper. We are indebted for comments from the anonymous reviewers. This work was partially carried out in the framework of the COST2102 action. This research has been supported by the GATE project, funded by the Netherlands Organization for Scientific Research (NWO) and the Netherlands ICT Research and Innovation Authority (ICT Regie).

References

1. Cassell, J., Sullivan, J., Prevost, S., Churchill, E. (eds.): Embodied Conversational Agents. MIT Press, Cambridge (2000)
2. Cassell, J., Bickmore, T.W., Vilhjálmsson, H.H., Yan, H.: More than just a pretty face: affordances of embodiment. In: Proc. of Intelligent User Interfaces, pp. 52–59 (2000)
3. Cornwell, J., O'Brien, K., Silverman, B.G., Toth, J.: Affordance theory for improving the rapid generation, composability, and reusability of synthetic agents and objects. In: Proc. of 12th Conf. on Behavior Representation in Modeling and Simulation (2003)
4. Dennett, D.C.: True believers: The intentional strategy and why it works. In: Heath, A.F. (ed.) Scientific Explanations: Papers based on Herbert Spencer Lectures Given in the University of Oxford, Reprinted in The Nature of Consciousness (David Rosenthal, ed.) (1981)
5. Dennett, D.C.: The Intentional Stance. MIT Press, Cambridge (1987)

6. Dix, A., Finlay, J., Abowd, G., Beale, R.: Human Computer Interaction. Prentice Hall, Englewood Cliffs (2004)
7. Gaver, W.: Affordances for interaction: The social is material for design. Ecological Psychology 8(2), 112–129 (1996)
8. Gibson, J.J.: The ecological approach to visual perception. Houghton, Mifflin, Boston (1979), http://www.alamut.com/notebooks/a/affordances.html
9. Personal communication at the AAMAS 2004 ws 'Balanced Perception and Action in ECAs' (2004)
10. McGrenere, J., Ho, W.: Affordance: Clarifying and Evolving a Concept. In: Proceedings of Graphics Interface, Montreal, Canada, pp. 179–186 (2000)
11. Murphy, R.R.: Case studies of applying Gibson's ecological approach to mobile robots. IEEE Transactions on Systems, Man, and Cybernetics, Part A 29(1), 105–111 (1999)
12. Norman, D.: The psychology of everyday things, Basic Books, New York(1988), http://www.jnd.org/dn.mss/affordances_and_desi.html
13. Peters, C., Pelachaud, C., Bevacqua, E., Mancini, M.: Engagement Capabilities of ECAs. In: AAMAS 2005 Ws on Creating Bonds with ECAs, Utrecht (2005)
14. Ruttkay, Zs., Pelachaud, C. (eds.): From Brows to Trust: Evaluating Embodied Conversational Agents. Kluwer, Dordrecht (2004)
15. Reeves, B., Nass, C.: The Media Equation. How People Treat Computers, Television and New Media Like Real People and Places. CSLI Publication Cambridge University Press, Cambridge (1998)
16. Ruttkay, Zs., Ten Hagen, P.: Reactive Monologues Modeling Refinement and Variations of Interaction Protocols of ECAs. In: Proc. of AAMAS 2004, Workshop on Balanced Perception and Action in ECAs, New York (2004)
17. Thórisson, K.R.: Natural Turn-Taking Needs No Manual. In: Granström, B., House, D., Karlsson, I. (eds.) Multimodality in Language and Speech Systems, pp. 173–207. Kluwer Academic Publishers, Dordrecht (2002)
18. Whittaker, S.: Theories and Methods in Mediated Communication. In: Graesser, A., Gernsbacher, M., Goldman, S. (eds.) The Handbook of Discourse Processes, pp. 243–286. Erlbaum, NJ (2002)

Individual Traits of Speaking Style and Speech Rhythm in a Spoken Discourse

Nick Campbell

National Institute of Information and Communications Technology
& ATR Spoken Language Communication Research Laboratory,
Keihanna Science City, Kyoto 619-0288, Japan
nick@nict.go.jp

Abstract. This paper describes an analysis of the verbal and nonverbal speaking characteristics of six speakers of Japanese when talking over the telephone to partners whose degrees of familiarity change over time. The speech data from 100 30-minute conversations between them was transcribed and the acoustic characteristics of each utterance subjected to an analysis of timing characteristics to determine individuality with respect to duration of utterance, degree of overlap, pauses, and other aspects of speech and discourse rhythm. The speakers showed many common traits, but noticeable differences were found to correlate well with degree of familiarity with the interlocutor. Several different styles of interaction can be automatically distinguished in the conversational speech data from their timing patterns.

Keywords: Interactive speech, social interaction, nonverbal behaviour, natural data, statistical modelling, real-world applications.

1 Introduction

This paper shows that conversational interaction is very much a two-way process, that involves not just the transfer of information related to meaningful content, but also affective displays of attention, involvement, interest, and concern, as well as discourse-level management of the turn-taking and joint processing of the emergent conversational flow. It presents a balanced left-brain/right-brain view of the processing of conversational speech [1] wherein not just linguistic verbal information but also affective paralinguistic and nonverbal information is exchanged by means of frequent back-channels and other short non-lexical utterances used to mark discourse events.

One of the basic and frequently repeated assumptions of conversation analysis is that people talk in turns, and that usually only one person talks at a time [2]. Levinson has defined conversational speech as "a kind of talk in which two or more participants freely alternate in speaking" [3]. This alternation accords well with our sense of the rhythm of a conversation, but it is not well supported by a quantitative analysis of a large number of telephone conversations where people were paid "just to talk" to each other [4]. Goffman [5] differentiates unfocussed

A. Esposito et al. (Eds.): HH and HM Interaction 2007, LNAI 5042, pp. 107–120, 2008.

interaction, where participants are simply concerned with the "management of sheer and mere copresence", from focussed interaction where persons "openly cooperate to sustain a single focus of attention". The present study examines data wherein people pass the time by chatting with each other about a variety of topics. Timing details derived from time-aligned manual transcriptions of these recordings reveal considerable overlapping speech in the discourse. The paper shows that discourse engagement and participation style can be inferred from the structure of these patterns in interactive conversations.

2   A Corpus of Telephone Conversations

The data underlying this study come from a corpus of recorded telephone conversations. One hundred thirty-minute telephone conversations were recorded over a period of several months, with paid volunteers coming to an office building in a large city in Western Japan once a week to talk with specific partners in a separate part of the same building over an office telephone. While talking, they wore a head-mounted Sennheiser HMD-410 close-talking dynamic microphone and recorded their speech directly to DAT (digital audio tape) at a sampling rate of 48kHz. They did not see their partners or socialise with them outside of the recording sessions. Partner combinations were controlled for sex, age, and familiarity, and all recordings were transcribed and time-aligned for subsequent analysis.

In all, ten people took part as speakers in these recordings, five male and five female. Six were Japanese, two Chinese, and two native speakers of American or Australian English. All conversations were held in Japanese. The non-native speakers were living and working in Japan, competent in Japanese, but not at a level approaching native-speaker fluency. Partners were initially strangers to each other, but became friends over the period of the recordings. There were no constraints on the content of the conversations other than that they should occupy the full thirty-minute time slot. Recordings continued for a maximum of ten sessions between each pair, or five for the non-native speakers.

The speech data were transferred to a computer and transcribed manually using Wavesurfer public-domain speech transcription software [6] to provide a time-aligned record of what was spoken when, by who and to whom. The transcribed speech was aligned at the 'utterance' level to acoustic events in the speech waveform.

The definition of an 'utterance' in conversational speech is problematic. A common practice is to use e.g., any pause in the speech of greater than 200 milliseconds as an objective delimiting boundary, but it was noticed that even many single words contained pauses of more than 300 milliseconds in these conversational data.

It was therefore proposed that our transcribers should use a perception-based "one-yen-per-line" criterion for segmenting the speech, whereby they would increase their payment for more lines produced by cutting the speech into shorter utterances, but would be penalised for breaking up a single utterance into too small or "unnatural" units.

The segmentation was thus largely performed at the level of the phrase, or 'minor intonation unit', i.e., an utterance being a word or group of words demarcated by a single intonation contour. However, in many cases the transcribers actually produced longer and more complex utterance units, with some including punctuation marks such as commas, perhaps because of uncertainty about whether a clearly distinguishing intonational break could be heard or not.

3   Analysis of the Patterns of Speech Activity

A computer program was written to combine and align the separate transcriptions of each speaker's conversations and to calculate the amount of time each person spent silent or talking during the 30-minute sessions.

Four classes of conversational speech activity were thus distinguished from the on/off nature of the speech: (a) both partners silent, (b) both partners talking at the same time, and (c, & d) one or the other partner talking while the other was silent, presumably listening.

Annotations of these speech-activity types were stored in a file along with a record of the length in milliseconds of each utterance, the duration of the pause preceding it, the duration of the previous utterance, and the duration of the pause preceding that. Similar durations were stored for the conversation partner, to facilitate an analysis of the speech activity in general as part of a computer speech processing system for the detection of nonverbal behavior and human participation styles from conversational speech.

The hundred conversations provided 98,698 utterances of between one and fifty syllables in length. 25% of these utterances were less than 500 milliseconds and another 25% longer than 1.5 seconds, with the longest being 11.5 seconds. Median duration of all utterances was 0.9 seconds. Figures 1 to 5 show example sequences. It is clear from the figures that there is often considerable overlap in the conversational speech, and that the definition of a "turn" in such data can be even more problematic than that of an utterance. This point will be addressed further in a subsequent section.

Using the definition of an utterance given above, several utterances can be combined to form a speaker turn. In this implementation, the program counted through each, incrementing if another utterance from the same speaker followed, but resetting the counters whenever the conversation partner started speaking, storing the number of uninterrupted utterances as a parameter in the data table, independently of the duration of any gap between them. A variable indicating whether or not the partner was speaking at the time of onset of the speaker's new utterance was also stored. Table 1 gives details of (a) the number of utterances, and (b) the number of utterances per turn (and total turn counts) thus derived for the six native-speakers of Japanese in the corpus. By the above criteria, it is clear that by far the majority of turns consist of a single utterance.

The transcribed utterances were then classified into 5 types: (i) 'frequent utterances', i.e., those special speech patterns which appeared more that 25 times each in the transcriptions, (ii) 'Talk', or infrequent content-bearing utterances appearing less than 25 times each, assumed to be more propositional than phatic in content, (iii) laughs, which were subdivided into longer more expressive variants and (iv) shorter more common simple laughs of up to three syllables, and (v) other non-speech noises (grunts) such as sniffs, sharp intake of breath, or coughs which might be used for discoursal purposes. Table 2 shows the distributions of these according to number of utterances in the turn. The table shows a clear difference between distributions for turn-initial speech when the partner is silent at onset of talking (shown in the left part) as against overlapping speech (shown in the right part). It also shows a tendency to avoid longer utterances when the partner is talking, but confirms that many more utterances are initiated while the partner is still speaking.

Table 1. Showing the total number of utterances per speaker in the top part and the number of utterances per turn (indicating complexity of turn) and total turn counts in the bottom part for the six Japanese speakers of the corpus. JFB and JMB spoke only to Japanese partners and so took part in more conversations.

JFA	JFB	JFC	JMA	JMB	JMC
15,543	21,624	13,038	13,122	20,841	11,530

	1	2	3	4+	total
JFA	5,349	2,384	932	721	9,386
JFB	6,724	3,068	1,254	1,488	12,534
JFC	5,394	2,013	694	408	8,509
JMA	6,868	1,807	531	286	9,492
JMB	8,428	3,049	1,117	814	13,408
JMC	4,711	1,718	595	416	7,440

Table 2. Showing distributions of utterance types factored according to whether the partner is silent at the onset of speech (left) or still talking (right). A clear tendency can be seen for shorter turns (i.e., fewer utterances) when the partner is talking. The numbers in the first column show number of utterances per turn. Note how short utterances are significantly more frequent when the partner is still talking at onset of speech. Overlaps are common.

len	partner silent					partner talking				
	freq	talk	laugh	freq-l	grunt	freq	talk	laugh	freq-l	grunt
1	9,988	11,550	1,065	378	285	16,590	15,588	2,298	1082	954
2	6,773	9,698	900	373	304	1,966	1,731	307	133	119
3	3,120	3,908	413	179	158	226	184	49	14	14
4	1,246	1,514	150	93	81	27	25	4	1	1
5	1,063	865	123	77	69	6	4	2	0	0

4   Patterns of Speech and Silence

As Figures 1 to 5 show, there is no clear on/off switching between speech turns and silence as might be found if both speakers were using a half-duplex communications channel (as with a 'walkie-talkie' for example), nor is it clear at exactly which point the turn dominance shifts from one speaker to the other. There are clear periods when one partner appears to dominate, but the listener is usually far from passive during these periods. The figures suggest that constant feedback is essential to a conversation and that the nature or style of the conversations can perhaps be characterised by these patterns of speech activity.

4.1   Patterns of Overlapping Speech

In this section we examine in more detail the patterns of overlapping speech of one female speaker from the corpus. Table 3 (from [7]) shows summary durations

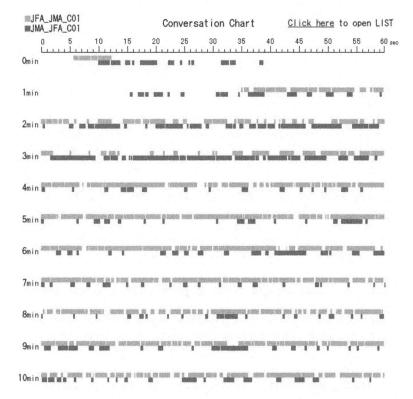

Fig. 1. A speech activity plot for the first thirteen minutes of the first conversation between Japanese female JFA (pink upper bars in the plot) and her male partner JMA (blue lower bars in the plot). She is considerably older than him and tends to dominate the conversation after the first few minutes. This dominance is clear from the patterns of interaction of speech and non-speech activity. Note how much overlap takes place in their speech from his backchannel activity.

in minutes for overlapping speech, solo speech, silence, and total talking time for speaker JFA and her various partners, averaged across thirty conversations. The table differentiates between solo talking, when only one partner is active, overlapping speech, when both are simultaneously active, and silence. Talk time shown is the sum of solo and overlapping speech times. Silence is similarly split between times when one partner is talking (and the other is presumably listening) and those when neither is active. Similar data has been produced for all speakers of the corpus and is summarised in Table 4.

On average she spends 22.7 minutes (sd=2.11) talking during each 30-minute session. Her partners spend on average 17.5 minutes talking with her (sd=2.6). These times sum to more than the total time of each conversation and there is on average 8.6 minutes (sd=2.3) of overlapping speech, with an average of 14.2 minutes of solo speech for JFA with an average of 8.9 minutes of solo speech per partner. We find not only that her partners spend the same amount of time in overlapping speech as they do in solo speech but also that the duration of her

Fig. 2. A speech activity plot for the first thirteen minutes of the second conversation between Japanese female JFA (pink) and her male partner JMA (blue). Note that now the balance is more or less equal between the two partners although there is still considerable overlapping speech. Note too how the relative dominance shifts from one speaker to the other throughout this typical conversation fragment.

Fig. 3. A speech activity plot for the first thirteen minutes of the last conversation between Japanese female JFA and male partner JMA. Note that by the final conversation the male clearly dominates throughout the first part of the conversation but there is no evidence of a ping-pong-like exchange of turns.

overlapped speech is equivalent to almost 60% of the duration of her solo talking time. Table 4 (also from [7]) confirms that she is not exceptional. Across the whole range of quartiles for similar data for all speakers, comparing solo talking time to overlapping talking time reveals that all partners spend more than half of their total talking time speaking while the other is also speaking.

4.2   Patterns of Interaction

Taking into account the large amount of speech overlap, this section proposes a measure for categorising the different types of speaker and listener interaction in a dialogue for use in the automatic processing of participant involvement.

A computer program was written to process the raw transcription files which contain speaker, partner, conversation number, start-time, duration and utterance transcription for each utterance of the corpus. The program calculated for a sliding window of three consecutive utterances the average amount of time spent speaking (from three values) and the average amount of time spent silent (from four values) and produced a ratio of the speech time divided by the time not speaking, that was scaled by the duration of the centre utterance, as shown in Equation 1.

$$flow = sd_t * (sd_{t-1} + sd_t + sd_{t+1}/3)/(nsd_{t-1} + nsd_t + nsd_{t+1} + nsd_{t+2}/4) \quad (1)$$

where sd_t represents the duration of utterance at time t, and nsd_t represents the pause duration preceding the utterance at time t.

This measure is high when the speech-to-silence ratio is high, and low when the pauses surrounding an utterance tend to be long. It thus provided a measure

Table 3. Showing mean durations in minutes for overlapping speech, solo speech, silence, and total talking time for speaker JFA and her four partners for their total of 30 30-minute conversations (10 each with the Japanese partners JFA & JFB, and 5-each with the non-native-speakers CFA & EMA). Silence is recorded when neither partner is speaking, overlap when both are speaking at the same time. 'Silent' shows the total time each speaker individually was quiet throughout the conversation, presumably while listening. 'Solo' shows the total duration of non-overlapping speech per speaker, and 'talk' the total overall speech time including overlaps. All times are shown in minutes.

	JMA	JFB	CFA	EMA
silent	2.72	1.84	2.42	3.66
overlap	8.64	10.93	7.15	5.12
solo JFA	14.94	12.31	15.6	15.01
solo other	8.24	8.96	8.63	10.31
silent JFA	10.96	10.81	11.06	13.96
silent other	17.67	14.13	18.01	18.65
talk JFA	23.59	23.23	22.75	20.13
talk other	16.88	19.91	15.79	15.42

Table 4. Showing quantiles summarising speech activity durations for the one-hundred conversations in the corpus. Durations are calculated from the manually time-aligned transcriptions of all 30-minute conversations. 'Total' shows duration quantiles for the entire set of conversations (assumed to be 30 minutes by default).

	min	25%	median	75%	max
silent	0.99	2.08	2.85	3.81	7.03
overlap	2.66	5.53	7.01	9.04	12.80
solo self	4.14	9.51	11.66	14.68	18.17
solo other	4.55	8.39	10.64	13.32	18.90
silent self	6.73	10.68	14.02	16.91	22.46
silent other	5.72	13.09	14.68	17.68	21.58
talk self	10.80	16.04	18.75	22.44	28.52
talk other	12.20	15.66	17.93	20.15	27.15
total	28.57	32.00	32.93	33.96	37.98

Fig. 4. A speech activity plot for the first thirteen minutes of the last conversation between Japanese male JMA (pink, upper bars) and female English-native-speaker partner EFA (blue, lower bars). Note how evenly-balanced their interactions have become by the final conversation. Neither dominates, and their conversation appears much more fragmented than the previous examples, perhaps because of her limited command of the Japanese language.

of local 'density' of speech activity, or 'flow' of the dialogue. High values occur at times of high information content, and low values at times of backchannel or 'active-listening' activity.

Figure 6 plots histograms of the averaged speech (sp) and silence (gp) durations in the log domain. Original times are in seconds, so for example a value of 0 represents a second, 1 represents 2.718 seconds, and -2 135 milliseconds. The values, being durations, plot close to normal on a log scale, but the difference between the upper plot (speech) and the lower plot (silence) shows the tendency for fewer long pauses with a clear skew to the left for the pause durations.

Figure 7 shows boxplots of the average *flow* values for the ten conversations of speaker JFB talking to JFA. A clear trend can be seen for increasing values between the first and fourth conversation, then a reset (for some reason perhaps explained by her catching a cold during the winter break) before another clear and progressive increase from the fifth to the tenth conversation. These trends can be interpreted as representing a shift from more passive interaction in the early stages, to a more active role in the conversations with the progression of time and the increase in familiarity between the two conversants.

Figure 8 plots similar boxplots showing the mutual interactions between JMC talking with JFB (top left), JMC talking with JMB (top right), JFB talking with JMC (bottom left), and JMB talking with JMC (bottom right). A tendency towards reciprocity can be seen in many cases between upper and lower pairs as one partner relatively dominates each conversation to a different extent.

Table 5 shows the correlations measured between flow measures averaged across all conversations between each pair of speakers in the Japanese native-speaker dialogues. If the 'ping-pong' model of conversational turn-taking is correct, with one partner remaining quiet while the other is speaking, then we would expect all pairs to show similar correlations to that found between male JMB

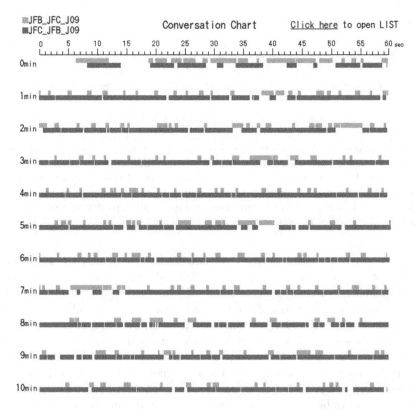

Fig. 5. A speech activity plot for the first thirteen minutes of the last conversation between Japanese female JFB (pink, upper bars) and Japanese female partner JFC (blue, lower bars). Note how JFC totally dominates the conversation, and how often JFB briefly joins in with her own short contributions.

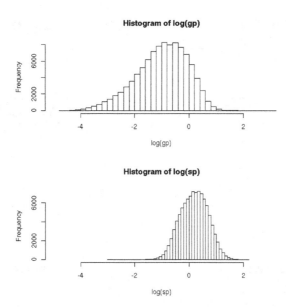

Fig. 6. Histograms of log pause (upper part, gp) and speech (lower part, sp) durations, showing a distribution close to normal for the speech segments (mean 0.53 secs, sd: 0.51), but a distinct skew indicating more short and fewer long pauses (mean 1.35 secs, sd: 0.69)

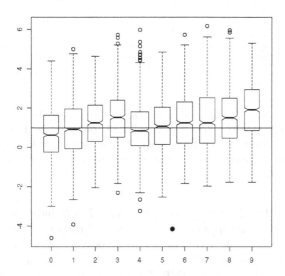

Fig. 7. A boxplot of the flow values for speaker JFB talking with JFA across a series of ten conversations. We can see a clear increase of dominance across the first four conversations, then a reset, then a continued increase with time as they become more familiar.

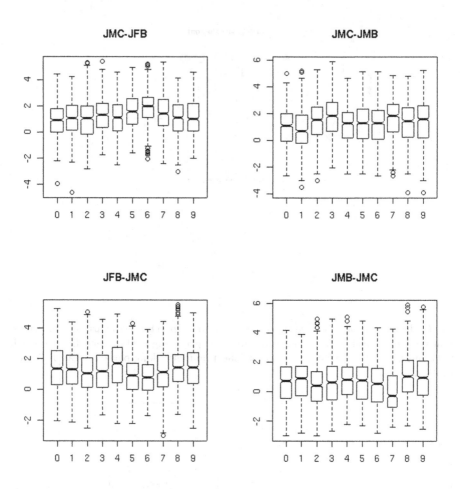

Fig. 8. 4 boxplots showing the mutual interactions between JMC talking with JFB (top left), JMC talking with JMB (top right), JFB talking with JMC (bottom left), and JMB talking with JMC (bottom right). A tendency towards reciprocity can be seen in both upper-lower pairs as one partner relatively dominates each conversation to a different extent.

and female JFC. Their high negative correlation of -0.75 indicates that he tends to listen quietly when she speaks, and vice versa. However, of the five remaining pairs of speakers, the table shows only two weak correlations of $r = -0.3$ and three very weak correlations of less than $r = -0.1$, being in fact weakly *positive* for the two male speakers JMC JMB. This indicates that these two men each showed a tendency to speak when the other was speaking and to be quiet when the other was quiet. They bonded well. Much the same can be said for all other pairs except JFB and JMC.

Table 5. Correlations between measures of discourse flow for each pair of conversants. The measures show surprisingly little reciprocity.

speakers	correlation
JFB JMC	r= -0.749
JFC JFB	r= -0.314
JMA JMB	r= -0.306
JFB JFA	r= -0.070
JFC JMB	r= -0.010
JMC JMB	r= 0.068

5   Discussion

It appears from this data that a naturally interactive dialogue is not like a tennis match, where there is only one ball that can only be in one half of the court at any given time. Rather it is like a volley of balls being thrown in several directions at once. The speaker does not usually wait silently while the listener parses and reacts to an utterance; there is a constant exchange of speech and gesture, resulting in a gradual process of mutual understanding wherein a consensual 'meeting of the minds' can take place [8].

There is not room in the present paper to discuss the local variations of the flow measure throughout a given dialogue, but this analysis is part of present and future work to automatically determine the level of rapport between participants in a dialogue and to measure on an utterance-by-utterance basis the degree to which they can be said to be involved in the conversation.

6   Conclusion

This paper has presented some results of an analysis of a large body of conversational speech recordings. It has shown that contrary to naive assumptions of dialogue as a tennis-like exchange of question and answer or topic and comment, it actually presents a complex pattern of simultaneous talking as partners take turns to dominate in the interaction. There appear to be no clear boundaries between one turn and the next, and the shift from backchannel feedback to conversational dominance appears to be more subtle.

A measure was proposed that quantifies the degree of participant interaction in a dialogue by estimating the ratio of speech to non-speech and length of utterance versus length of surrounding pauses. This measure can be used to chracterise a conversation in terms of joint activity of the partners, and it was shown that in the majority of partner pairs, both tended to speak simultaneously in many cases.

Acknowledgement

This work is partly supported by the National Institute of Information and Communications Technology (NiCT), and includes contributions from the Japan

Science & Technology Corporation (JST), and the Ministry of Public Management, Home Affairs, Posts and Telecommunications, Japan (SCOPE). The author is especially grateful to the management of Spoken Language Communication Research Labs at ATR for their continuing encouragement and support.

References

1. Springer, S.P., Deutch, G.: Left brain, right brain: perspectives from cognitive neuroscience, 5th edn. W.H. Freeman, N.Y (1998)
2. Sacks, H., Schegloff, E.A., Jefferson, G.: A simplest systematics for the organization of turn taking for conversation. In: Schenkein (1978)
3. Levinson, S.C.: Pragmatics. Cambridge University Press, Cambridge (1983)
4. Campbell, N.: Databases of Expressive Speech. Journal of Chinese Language and Computing 14(4), 295–304 (2004)
5. Goffman, E.: Behaviour in public places: Notes on the social organisation of gatherings. Free Press of Glencoe, New York (1963)
6. Wavesurfer, Open Source tool for sound visualization and manipulation, http://www.speech.kth.se/wavesurfer/
7. Campbell, N.: Approaches to Conversational Speech Rhythm: Speech Activity in Two-Person Telephone Dialogues. In: Proc XVIth International Congress of the Phonetic Sciences, Saarbrucken, Germany, pp. 343–348 (2007)
8. McNeill, D., Quek, F., McCullough, K.-E., Duncan, S., Furuyama, N., Bryll, R., Ma, X.-F., Ansari, R.: Catchments, Prosody, and Discourse. Gesture 1, 9–33 (2001)

The Organization of a Neurocomputational Control Model for Articulatory Speech Synthesis

Bernd J. Kröger[1], Anja Lowit[2], and Ralph Schnitker[3]

[1] Department of Phoniatrics, Pedaudiology, and Communication Disorders,
University Hospital Aachen and Aachen University, Aachen, Germany
bkroeger@ukaachen.de
[2] Speech and Language Therapy Division,
Department of Educational and Professional Studies, University of Stratclyde, UK
a.lowit@strath.ac.uk
[3] Central Service Facility "Functional Imaging" at the ICCR-BioMat,
University Hospital Aachen and Aachen University, Aachen, Germany
ralph@izkf.rwth-aachen.de

Abstract. The organization of a computational control model of articulatory speech synthesis is outlined in this paper. The model is based on general principles of neurophysiology and cognitive psychology. Thus it is based on such neural control circuits, neural maps and mappings as are hypothesized to exist in the human brain, and the model is based on learning or training mechanisms similar to those occurring during the human process of speech acquisition. The task of the control module is to generate articulatory data for controlling an articulatory-acoustic speech synthesizer. Thus a complete "BIONIC" (i.e. BIOlogically motivated and techNICally realized) speech synthesizer is described, capable of generating linguistic, sensory, and motor neural representations of sounds, syllables, and words, capable of generating articulatory speech movements from neuromuscular activation, and subsequently capable of generating acoustic speech signals by controlling an articulatory-acoustic vocal tract model. The module developed thus far is capable of producing single sounds (vowels and consonants), simple CV- and VC-syllables, and first sample words. In addition, processes of human-human interaction occurring during speech acquisition (mother-child or carer-child interactions) are briefly discussed in this paper.

Keywords: Computational model, neural model, speech production, articulatory speech synthesis, speech acquisition, self-organizing maps.

1 Introduction

While a lot of knowledge has been collected over the last decades concerning articulatory-acoustic models, i.e. front-end components for articulatory speech synthesis, which convert articulatory information into acoustic speech signals using an artificial vocal tract (Badin et al. 2002, Beautemps et al. 2001, Birkholz et al. 2006, Birkholz et al. 2007a, Engwall 2003, Kröger and Birkholz 2007), a remaining goal is the

A. Esposito et al. (Eds.): HH and HM Interaction 2007, LNAI 5042, pp. 121–135, 2008.

development of a human-like control component to generate articulatory, including phonatory, speech information. A comprehensive gestural control concept for articulatory speech synthesis has been introduced by Kröger and Birkholz (2007), but the best way of collecting realistic gestural speech data for generating high-quality segmental and prosodic control information for controlling the articulatory-acoustic front-end system, i.e. the artificial vocal tract model, remains an open question.

One possible solution is to employ *articulatory data* from a test subject with the objective of reproducing or mimicking the articulatory strategies of this speaker (e.g. Birkholz et al. 2007b). However, it is not trivial to extract the underlying data for controlling the movements of model articulators from articulatory flesh-point movement data in the form in which they are currently available, for instance from widely used tracking devices like EMA systems (Perkell et al. 1992, Stone 1997). A different approach is the direct use of *acoustic data*, since toddlers are extremely successful at learning to speak just by listening to persons without knowing their implicit articulatory strategies.

In this paper a neuro-computational control concept for articulatory speech synthesis is introduced, which is capable of mimicking important aspects of the natural process of speech acquisition like babbling and imitation. During the natural process of speech acquisition the toddler starts to explore his own vocal tract just by producing speech-like phonation while the vocal tract is not constricted. This enables the toddler to learn the acoustic-auditory consequences of different articulatory vowel-like states. Later on the toddler produces random vocal tract closing and opening movements and in addition learns the acoustic-auditory consequences of different articulatory consonant-like states. Both processes take place within the *babbling phase of speech acquisition* (Oller et al. 1999). Then the toddler is ready for imitating syllables or words produced by external speakers. This second phase is called the *imitation phase of speech acquisition* (Oller et al. 1999). During this phase the basis for the development of the mental syllabary and the mental lexicon is established for the target language (Levelt et al. 1999, Levelt and Wheeldon 1994, Indefrey and Levelt 2004).

A consideration of these natural processes of speech acquisition suggests that a successful strategy to develop high-quality articulatory speech synthesis could be to mimic these processes, i.e. to allow the model to explore its sensorimotor mappings during an artificial babbling phase, and to explore the production of syllables, words and utterances by imitating given acoustic speech items. Using this approach the organization of the computational control model should be designed in a similar way to the presumed *organization of speech production paths in the human brain* and the *learning strategies for acquiring phonetic and linguistic knowledge* should be similar to those processes which take place during natural speech acquisition. The organization of our computational control module with respect to neurophysiologic and neuropsychological knowledge as well as an outline of the learning processes for acquiring general phonetic and language specific speech knowledge are described in this paper.

2   The Computational Control Model

The control model is implemented quantitatively (computer-implemented) using artificial neural network algorithms (feed-forward networks and self organizing networks, cf. Kohonen 2001, Zell 2003) but the overall organization of the model (Fig. 1) mainly

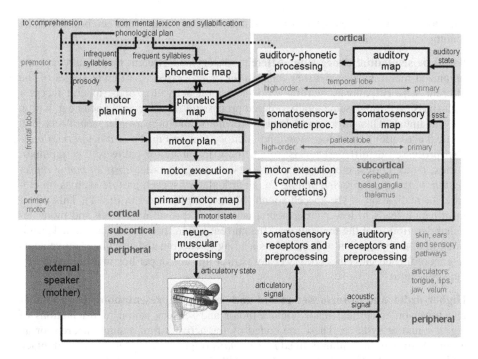

Fig. 1. Computational neural model of speech production. Boxes with black outlines represent neural maps, arrows indicate processing paths or neural mappings. Boxes without black outline indicate processing modules.

refers to basic neurophysiologic and neuropsychological principles (cf. Kandel et al. 2000, Frackowiak et al. 2004, Fadiga and Craighero 2004) given below.

Parallel processing: Primary somatosensory and primary motor cerebral cortical maps are topographically organized (somatotopy). The articulators (lips, tongue tip, tongue body, tongue root, velum, larynx) are controlled by parallel neural projections from the cerebral motor cortex (from the primary motor map, Fig. 1) to the peripheral motor units controlling different effectors (efferent pathways for lips, tongue, jaw, velum, larynx). *Motor information* is forwarded in parallel for different articulators. Furthermore motor information is forwarded in parallel by using two different main processing routes. A *direct route* forwards motor information from the primary cortical motor map to the motor units via the pyramidal tract. An *indirect route* is a mediated forwarding of motor information from the primary cortical motor map to motor units via basal ganglia and cerebellum. *Somatosensory information* is forwarded by parallel neural projections from the somatosensory receptor cells to the somatosensory cerebral cortex (afferent pathways for auditory and somatosensory information, Fig. 1). Somatosensory information from different articulators and vocal tract walls (e.g. hard and soft palate, pharynx wall) is also forwarded by parallel neural projections. *Auditory information* in different frequency regions (i.e. from different regions of the basilar membrane) is forwarded by parallel neural projections from the auditory receptor cells within the cochlea to the primary auditory map of the cerebral cortex by tonotopical projections.

Serial or sequential processing: Afferent sensory and efferent motor pathways are organized hierarchically. *Sensory information* is processed at different stages of the afferent sensory pathway starting with the neural activation of peripheral receptor cells, passing through sequentially ordered processing stages (neural nuclei e.g. within the thalamus). This information leads to primary and higher-order neural cerebral cortical activations (somatosensory and auditory map in Fig. 1). *Motor information* is also processed at different levels within the efferent motor pathway (i.e. premotor cortex, motor cortex, motor units), starting with a higher-order *abstract motor representation of a goal-directed action,* i.e. an articulatory speech gesture such as lip closure for realization of the speech sound [b] (*motor plan level* in Fig. 1). This motor information leads to lower-order neural activations, providing a more and more detailed description of the realization of the current action. It ends with a detailed specification of the activation of motor units leading to coordinated articulator movements (e.g. coordinated movement of lower jaw, lower lips and upper lips in the case of a lip closure action).

Higher-order and lower-order motor and sensory representations: Higher-order and lower-order cortical maps contain motor and sensory neural representations of e.g. a sound or syllable. These are coded by the activation of a single neuron, or an ensemble of neurons within defined *neural maps* (represented by the boxes with black outlines in Fig. 1). Neural maps are found within the primary cortical sensory or motor areas, within unimodal association areas, and within hetero- or multimodal association areas of the cerebral cortex. Unimodal association areas process information coming from one single sense (e.g. auditory or somatosensory); hetero- or multimodal association areas process information coming from more than one sense. *Neural interactions, associations or mappings* connect neural maps (represented by the arrows between the boxes with black outlines in Fig. 1). These cortico-cortical mappings are complex: Parallel and sequential processing, known to operate in lower-order motor and sensory pathways, also occur for cortico-cortical sensory associations from the primary, via the uni-modal sensory to the multimodal sensory maps. In addition, complex mappings occur for cortico-cortical motor associations from the prefrontal cortex via the premotor cortex to the motor cortex. Furthermore, multimodal cortico-cortical associations (mirror neuron circuits, Fadiga et al. 2002 and Kohler et al. 2002) connect cortical maps and lead to a hypermodal co-activation of sensory, motor, and abstract linguistic (phonological) states for speech items. A hypermodal neural map or state is a neural map or state collecting information from all other maps. This map or state itself can not be attributed to a single (auditory or somatosensory) modality. It is beyond any modality. In the case of our approach, a hypermodal *phonetic map* is defined (see below).

Sensory neural processing leads to *integration* of information: Speech items are handled in parallel by different sensory systems (auditory and somatosensory) and are then integrated into a *hetero-, multi-, or hypermodal abstract percept* (e.g. a percept of a syllable or word). This integration is represented by the *phonetic map* in our model (Fig. 1). Here, auditory, somatosensory, phonemic, and motor planning information is brought together in one map.

Motor neural processing: planning and execution. Motor neural processing can be subdivided into planning (selection and preparation) and execution (see Fig. 1). The *selection phase of planning* leads to a temporally coordinated plan of abstract internal representation of goal-directed actions (motor plan of speech gestures, Fig. 2). On this level gestures are defined just by their goal. An example is presented in Figure 2., where three gestures are shown, namely (i) labial closing (clla): closing the lips; (ii) vocal tract formation: shaping the vocal tract – mainly tongue and lower jaw – into a specific form, e.g. into the form of an [a]-vowel (aavt); (iii) glottal opening (opgl): opening the glottal slit with the goal of ceasing vocal fold vibration. In addition, at this level the duration of each gesture (boxes with black outlines in Fig. 2) and their temporal coordination are defined. The duration of a gesture is the sum of the time required for the movement quantified as gestural rapidity or gestural onset (first light portion within the outlined box, representing each gesture in Fig. 2) and the following target portion (following dark portion within the outlined box representing each gesture in Fig 2; A more complete survey on the concept of gesture and gestural organization of speech is given in Kröger and Birkholz 2007).

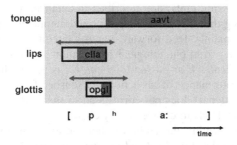

Fig. 2. Gestural organization (motor plan) of the syllable /pa/. Outlined boxes indicate gestural duration; aavt = [a]-forming vocal tract gesture, clla = labial closing gesture; opgl = glottal opening gesture. The arrows indicate the fact that temporal coordination of gestures (i.e. degree of temporal overlap of gestures) may vary.

The *preparation phase of planning* leads to a context-dependent higher-order specification of each gesture, e.g. specification of amplitude, temporal duration and temporal coordination of the gestures before they are performed. The planned (i.e. selected and prepared) gestures are then held in *working memory* for execution. *Execution* is the concrete lower-order realization of the gestures with respect to all of the articulators involved (i.e. lips and lower jaw in the case of a labial closing gesture). The earliest possible starting time for execution of an utterance is the completion of planning, at least for the first syllable of an utterance. The preparation and execution of a plan of speech gestures always takes place within a specific speaking context and is always modified within respect to this specific speaking context, e.g. whether the speaker is talking casually in a quiet environment, whether the speaker is speaking aloud in a noisy environment, or whether the speaker is presenting to a large audience.

Motor equivalence: A distinct gesture can be executed with a high degree of flexibility at the primary motor and at the articulatory level. If more than one articulator is involved in gesture-execution, these articulators contribute to the execution with different strengths: in the case of a labial closing gesture, the jaw, the lower and upper lips are involved. The articulators produce larger movement amplitudes in [aba] than in [ibi] since overall jaw lowering is higher in the [a]- than the [i]-environment. Furthermore, depending on the context, one distinct gesture may start from different initial positions of the gesture executing vocal tract organ, and may exhibit different gestural duration and amplitude. Motor equivalence is mainly handled by the motor execution module (Fig. 1).

Control circuits: Speech motor control is based on the principles of *feed-forward (or anticipatory) control* and *feedback control* which underlie the performance of *skilled actions,* in a similar way to the motor control of other voluntary motor actions such as grasping. Speech movements are skilled actions and thus can be learned from "novel" or "untrained" to "automatic", "trained" or "overlearned". Learning of actions is described as *implicit learning.* Thus, at the beginning of training, a person uses feedback control circuits to monitor movements (see feedback loops for auditory and somatosensory signals in Fig. 1, starting with auditory and somatosensory preprocessing and leading to possible corrections of the motor plan via the auditory-phonetic and somatosensory-phonetic processing units, not described in detail in this paper), but at the end of successful training the action will be performed automatically "without thinking about it" by using mainly feed-forward control circuits (see the feed-forward pathway in Fig. 1, starting from phonological information and going down to neuromuscular processing). *Feedback or closed loop control* is accomplished by continuously monitoring the performance of an action via sensory feedback. If the desired state (reference sensory signal) does not correspond to the feedback signal, an error signal is produced, which leads to compensatory changes to the motor execution (error signals are calculated within the auditory-phonetic and somatosensory-phonetic processing units in our model, Fig. 1). *Feed-forward, or open loop control* is the direct motor execution of pre-learned skilled actions. The actual programming of these actions also needs sensory information about the state of the vocal organs of the speaker and about the environmental state (see above), but this is solely sensory information which is available *before* the action is performed. No sensory information controlling the accomplishment of the goal-directed movement, i.e. sensory information gained *during* the performance of the action is necessary. This is realized in our model by using the neural path starting with a phonological representation of a speech item (sound, syllable, word, or utterance) and generating its motor representation via the phonetic map (Fig. 1). In this case sensory states of the speech item may be co-activated as well via the phonetic-sensory mappings (Fig. 1), but that is not mandatory for the feed-forward execution of a speech item.

Learning and storing (acquiring) speech items: Two basic learning paradigms can be differentiated for the acquisition of speech gestures. *Babbling* is learning to associate the auditive and the somatosensory (tactile and proprioceptive) outcome of (random or semi-random) vocal tract motor activity with a (higher-order) representation of this motor activity. Learning during babbling mainly forms the sensorimotor mappings via the phonetic map (Fig. 1). *Imitation* means the active repeating and rehearsing of a perceived speech item stimulated by human-human interaction (i.e. between toddler and carer). Imitation needs basic sensorimotor knowledge already gained during babbling. On the one hand, learning or training of motor skills can be described as *implicit learning* and thus leads to implicit knowledge stored in implicit memory (information on *how* a gesture is performed; involving the parietal hetero-modal association cortex, cerebellum, and supplementary motor cortex, see Fracko-wiak et al. 2004, p. 25). Implicit training needs a high degree of repetition and the skill increases slowly until the task or gesture is overlearned and the action can be performed automatically and without attention. On the other hand, an action is de-fined on an abstract level mainly by the goal with which it is associated, and corre-sponds to sensory (visual, auditory, and/or somatosensory) cues. Thus a motor action can be linked to its sensory goal by *explicit learning,* leading to explicit knowledge (information on *what* gesture has to be executed; involving the prefrontal cortex and basal ganglia system, see Frackowiak et al. 2004, ibid.).

Integrative vs. cellular paradigm: Our control model in its current state is based on the neurophysiologic and neuropsychological principles given above and thus incor-porates the *integrative neural paradigm.* However, it is also necessary to take into consideration the *detailed cellular paradigm* in order to understand the neurophysiol-ogy of speech production satisfactorily. The integrative approach only stipulates *where* neural processing occurs (i.e. which brain region is activated) and *what* is proc-essed, but not *how* it is processed by an ensemble of or by single nerve cells (neu-rons). This detailed quantitative neural processing is achieved in the current model by using artificial neural networks. The architecture and function of these networks is based on general or basic neurophysiologic assumptions (e.g. Kohonen 2001, Zell 2003) as follows:

Neural maps (on a cortical level): Actions, percepts, or abstract representations of e.g. a speech item, also called *neural states* or *neural representations,* are represented on the detailed cellular neural level by *specific activation patterns* within distinct cellular collectives, i.e. in distinct neural maps (e.g. sensory maps, motor maps, pho-netic, or phonological maps, Fig. 1).

Neural mappings are capable of linking two or more neural maps (arrows in Fig. 1). Two kinds of networks are used within our approach: *One-layer feed-forward networks* are capable of projecting states of one map (input map) on neural states of a second map (output map), e.g. from a lower-order auditory representation to a higher-order auditory representation or from a higher-order motor representation to a lower-order motor representation (Fig. 1). In addition, *self-organizing maps (SOMs)* and their mappings to related maps are capable of projecting states of one related map to states of one or more other related maps, e.g. from a higher-order sensory repre-sentation to a higher-order motor representation or to a symbolic linguistic (i.e. pho-nemic) representation. The central SOM itself is represented as *phonetic map* in our model and the related maps are the phonemic, auditory, somatosensory, and motor plan map (Fig. 1). The organization of these mappings may lead to co-activation (par-allel activation) of phonemic, sensory and motor states (mirror neuron assumption, Fadiga et al. 2002, Kohler et al. 2002). In both types of networks (feed-forward and SOM), a vast number of neural connections (dendrites and axons) connect each neu-ron of one map with each neuron of another (associated) map. And in both types of neural networks, neurons fire if their activation threshold value is exceeded. Firing leads to positive or negative activation (exhibition or inhibition) of associated cells in associated maps. The sign and degree of activation of the associated cells is determined by the *synaptic link weight* between two associated cells.

Neural learning or training: Synaptic link weights of all neural connections within a neural mapping are adjusted by exposing the network to a defined set of external stimuli. This procedure can be called training or learning. Standard learning or training algorithms (cf. Kohonen 2001, Zell 2003) are used for learning or training in both types of networks in our approach.

Overall organization of the control model: On the basis of the neurophysiologic and neuropsychological principles given above, a concrete organization of a neural model of speech production can be proposed (Fig. 1). The model comprises peripheral, subcortical, and cortical modules. Peripherally a 3-dimensional articulatory-acoustic model (also called "artificial vocal tract") provides the front-end device for producing articulatory and acoustic signals (cf. Kröger and Birkholz 2007). At the subcortical and peripheral level the motor signals control neuromuscular units and subsequently the vocal tract organs or articulators of the articulatory-acoustic model. The articulatory and acoustic signals subsequently generated by the articulatory-acoustic model are processed by somatosensory and auditory peripheral and subcortical preprocessing instances and are forwarded to the primary cortical auditory and a primary cortical somatosenory (tactile and proprioceptive) level (i.e. current sensory state related to a produced speech item). On the cortical level definite motor, sensory, phonemic, or phonetic states within neural maps (outlined boxes in Fig. 1) are activated via neural mappings (arrows in Fig. 1; neural processing units comprising maps and mappings are indicated by non-outlined boxes in Fig. 1). Cortico-cortical sensorimotor mappings are trained mainly during the babbling phase of speech acquisition using self-organizing maps (SOMs) for different types of motor states (see below). Self-organizing maps for different types of sounds (vowels, plosives, fricatives etc.) and for different types of syllables (CV, VC, CVC, ...) are outlined as phonetic map. In addition a phonemic-phonetic mapping is trained during the imitation phase of speech acquisition, storing the relations between phonemic speech items and sensory states (i.e. how a speech sound, syllable, or word should sound and should feel like; i.e. the internal sensory representation of a speech item) and storing the relations between phonemic speech items and motor states (i.e. how a speech item has to be produced). Thus after imitation training the model is capable of (i) executing automated or highly overlearned speech items without extensively using feedback control (i.e. using previously stored or pre-learned motor plans as occurs for frequent syllables) directly by activating the appropriate stored motor state and (ii) of calculating and executing motor plans for infrequent syllables by using the motor planning module (via motor planning module, Fig. 1; the motor planning module and its mappings are not described in detail in this paper). The training of concrete phonetic submaps e.g. for proto-vocalic states during babbling and of vocalic states during the imitation phase of speech production is briefly described in Kröger et al. (2007).

Important features of the neural speech production model outlined above are (i) the differentiation of feed-forward and feedback control (cf. Guenther et al. 2006 and Guenther 2006), (ii) the separation of production paths for frequent syllables (via phonetic map) and infrequent syllables (via motor planning module) and (iii) the differentiation between a higher level motor representation of speech items (motor plan level, Fig. 1) and a lower level motor representation (primary motor representation). While on the motor plan level all speech gestures forming the speech item, their intragestural parameters (gestural target values, gestural rapidity and gestural duration), and the temporal coordination between speech these gestures is defined (Fig. 2), the concrete execution of the gestural plan by concrete articulator movements is defined at the primary motor level (see also neurophysiologic and neuronpsychological principles given above).

3 Babbling and Imitation Phase of Speech Acquisition

Following Oller et al. (1999) the prelinguistic phase of speech acquisition or *babbling phase* can be subdivided into a phonation phase, a primitive articulation phase, an expansion phase, and a canonical phase. In the phonation phase speech-like proto-vocalic articulation occurs while during the later phases the toddler starts to produce sounds which include primitive vocal tract closing and opening movements for building up and releasing vocal tract constrictions or vocal tract closures. In our approach two cases of proto-articulation (or prelinguistic articulation) are modelled, i.e. the production of proto-vocalic and simple proto-consonantal closing gestures (cf. Kröger et al. 2007). During this phase of speech acquisition the model learns to relate sensory states to motor states for these proto-speech gestures. Thus with increasing babbling training, the model is capable of predicting motor states from sensory states. For example the model is then capable of predicting the articulatory target positions of a proto-vocalic gesture from a definite static F1-F2-F3 formant pattern or is capable of predicting the place of articulation of a proto-consonantal gesture from the temporal F1-F2-F3 transition pattern. In terms of the gestural concept (Kröger und Birkholz 2007) the model is capable of predicting *intra*gestural parameters from auditory states, i.e. gestural parameters defining the gestural target, the speed at which the target is reached (rapidity), and the overall duration of a gesture (cf. Fig. 2). Since all types of gesture are learned separately, they constitute different phonetic (sub-) maps for describing the sensorimotor relations for proto-vocalic and different proto-consonantal speech gestures. Motor plan and auditory link weight values are visualized in Fig. 3 for the vocalic phonetic map after babbling training. The training items comprise 540 proto-vocalic self-productions, covering the whole proto-vocalic articulator space between a cardinal [i], [a], and [u] (cf. Kröger et al. 2007). Standard training procedures were used (Kohonen 2001). Due to the knowledge stored within this vocalic map, proto-vocalic motor states can be predicted with high accuracy from their auditory states (prediction error below 1%). Furthermore it can be seen, that the vocalic states are ordered within this vocalic map with respect to the motor and auditory link weight values; link weight values change smoothly from neuron to neuron.

Since babbling training enables the model to predict motor states from sensory states, the *sensorimotor knowledge* stored within the phonetic map serves as a helpful basis for imitation of acoustic speech items produced by external speakers (mother or carer) during the imitation phase of speech acquisition.

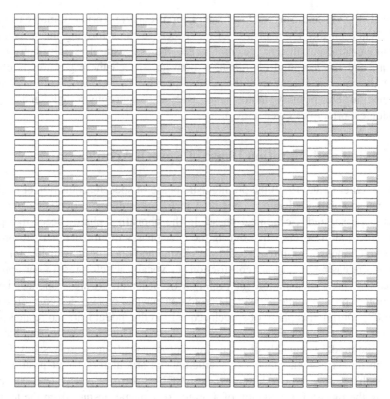

Fig. 3. Diagram of motor plan and auditory link weight values after proto-vocalic babbling training for each neuron within the vocalic phonetic map (15x15 neurons). Link weight values are given for two motor plan parameters within each neuron box: back-front (left bar) and low-high (right bar). Link weight values are given for three auditory parameters: bark scaled F1, F2, and F3 (horizontal lines within each neuron box).

In contrast to with babbling, during the *imitation training* of language specific vowels, consonants, syllables, or words, knowledge concerning phonological categories of sounds and concerning meaning of words is needed. For this imitation training a training set is used in our approach that comprises knowledge concerning the phonological category together with the knowledge concerning the auditory state of a speech item. The model starts training the phonological-auditory mapping via the phonetic map, i.e. enforces the neural connections between the phonological and auditory representation of this speech item (cf. Fig. 1). But how does a model get the knowledge concerning phonological categories and concerning the meaning of a word? This knowledge results from complex processes of human-human interaction: The toddler develops the neural connections between the acoustic form of a spoken object word and its meaning for example by pointing at an object (table, chair, door etc.) and by looking simultaneously at the carer, enforcing her/him to name the object. In the case of abstract words the learning process for combining auditory form and word meaning is even more complex. Currently this complex human-human interaction is not included in our modeling process. In our model this knowledge is directly incorporated in the training sets for imitation training. The training set is organized as a heap of N acoustic realizations for each phonemic speech item (N=100 for different vowel phonemes and for consonant phonemes in different vocalic contexts, cf. Kröger et al. 2007) for training the phonological-auditory mapping followed by one imitation of each realization for training the phonological-motor mapping. For the vocalic phonetic map the motor plan and auditory link weight values are visualized in Fig. 4 after an imitation training of 500 vocalic productions which represent a 5 phoneme system /i/, /e/, /a/, /o/, and /u/ (cf. Kröger et al. 2007). This imitation training was performed after the vocalic babbling training described above. It is obvious that the vocalic states are ordered within this map in the same way as after babbling training. In addition five regions can be found within this vocalic phonetic map, which label high phonemic link weights and therefore potential realiations of the five vocalic phonemes defined in the training set.

Furthermore motor plan and auditory link weight values are visualized in Fig. 5 for the VC phonetic map for consonantal closing gestures after babbling training of three labial, apical, and dorsal closing gestures starting from 25 different proto-vocalic

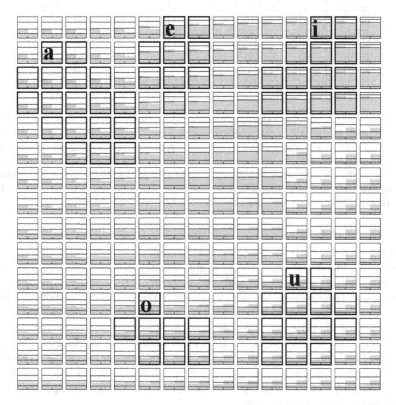

Fig. 4. Diagram of motor plan and auditory link weight values after vocalic imitation training for each neuron within the vocalic phonetic map (15x15 neurons; cf. Fig. 3). In addition the outlined boxes mark neurons within the vocalic phonetic map, which represent phoneme realizations.

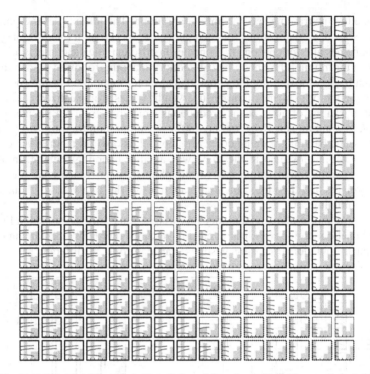

Fig. 5. Diagram of motor plan and auditory link weight values after proto-consonantal babbling training for each neuron within the vocalic phonetic map (15x15 neurons). Link weight values are given for five motor plan parameters within each neuron box. First three columns: vocal tract organ which performs the closing gesture (labial, apical, dorsal); two last columns: back-front value (forth column) and low-high value (fifth column) of the starting vowel within the VC-sequence. Link weight values are given for three auditory parameters: bark scaled F1, F2, and F3 (formant transitions within each neuron box). Outlined boxes: see text.

states each (i.e. set of 225 training items). Phonemic identification as /b/, /d/, or /g/ is obtained here by identifying all neurons by means of a dominant motor parameter "labial" as /b/, of a dominant motor parameter "apical" as /d/ and of a dominant motor parameters "dorsal" as /g/ ("dominant" means neural activation above .8 or 80% for the articulator motor neuron; see outlined boxes in Fig. 5: full outline bottom left: /d/, full outline top right: /g/; dashed outline: /b/). Also it can be seen that the VC states in this consonantal phonetic map are ordered within this map with respect to the motor and auditory link weight values. Three distinct regions can be detected within this consonantal phonetic map, which represent potential realizations of the three consonant phonemes. Standard training algorithms (Kohonen 2001) are used for the training of this VC-SOM resulting in a rate below 5% for the correct detection of a VC-syllable from the auditory state.

On the level of the mental lexicon (not displayed in our model), single neurons are defined for each word, leading to sub-activations of the phonological forms of the syllables and sounds, which make up the word on the level of the phonological map (Fig. 1). Also on the level of the phonological map, one single neuron represents a definite syllable or speech sound. Phonological-auditory neural connections are built syllable by syllable between the phonological form of syllables and the appropriate auditory form via the phonetic map by (passive) listening. The following step of imitation training is necessary to learn the appropriate production, i.e. the appropriate motor plan for each phonological speech item. Starting with auditory states of simple gestures realizing vocalic sounds or simple syllables (CV and VC) composed of closing or opening gestures, the appropriate intragestural parameter values can be estimated by using the sensorimotor knowledge gained during the babbling phase (see above). In addition these intragestural parameter values are fine-tuned with respect to the language-specific auditory sound representations just learned for different phonological items. This results in language-specific gesture representations for all phonemes and simple syllables of a language.

In a further step this training is expanded to more complex speech items, i.e. to complex syllables and to words. Since the intragestural parameters are already trained for the language specific gestures, only learning of *inter*gestural timing of gestures within syllables and words remains. This training or learning procedure is performed by generating different motor plans of a syllable or word with differing intergestural timing. During the learning procedure the optimal intergestural timing values are estimated by minimizing the distance between the auditory representation for each motor plan and the already stored target auditory representation for the speech item. While successful training or fine-tuning of vocalic and consonantal gestures is obtained using self-organizing maps, our first modeling results suggest that this later training of intergestural timing can be performed successfully using simple one-layer feed-forward networks, connecting the phonological representation of the speech item directly with a quantitative description of gestural timing on the motor plan level.

4 Results and Discussion

The problem of developing high-quality articulatory speech synthesis by using "natural" control rules has not yet been solved, but this paper gives an outline for a "BIONIC" (biologically motivated technical) control concept for articulatory speech synthesis. The organization of this neurocomputational control concept for speech synthesis, or more generally for speech production, is described in this paper and is discussed with respect to general and basic principles of neurophysiology and neuropsychology. Based on this approach, structure and knowledge can easily be separated within the neural speech production system. The structure is given by the organization of the control model into neural maps (cf. Fig. 1), while the knowledge of speech production is stored within the neural link weights of the mappings connecting different maps. This knowledge is gathered during learning or training procedures (speech acquisition). In its current state the neurocomputational model was trained to produce static vowels and simple CV- and VC-syllables, i.e. simple opening and closing gestures producing voiced plosives.

An important feature of this neurocomputational control concept is the *separation of motor planning and motor execution* by using the gestural concept for describing articulatory speech movements and their control. First experiments for learning complex speech items composed of more than one gesture and especially for training the intergestural timing have been carried out.

One feature, which is beyond the scope of the actual model, but whose inclusion is an important aspect of the future development of this neurocomputational model is the modeling of *human-human interaction*. As has been discussed above, the toddler uses human-human interaction (toddler-carer interaction) for gaining the phonetics-phonology relations (i.e. for being able to associate meaning and phonetic word forms) and furthermore the toddler needs toddler-carer interactions in order to judge the quality of his productions during the imitation phase of speech acquisition: E.g. on the one hand no or negative reaction of the caretaker if a word is produced falsely, and on the other hand strong or positive reaction of the caretaker if a word is produced correctly the first time gives a strong support for learning word motor plans. Currently, the learning results of these human-human interactions, i.e. this knowledge is directly included in the training data used. It is beyond the scope of our current model to include strategies for gaining this knowledge.

Finally it should be mentioned that the control concept developed thus far focuses on the production path for *frequent syllables* via phonemic map, phonetic map to motor plan. In this pathway of the production model a phonemic-sensory and phonemic-motor mapping exists for each frequent syllable. An important question is how the toddler is able to generalize phonetic knowledge for sounds, syllabic subunits like onset and rhyme and for different types of syllables like CV, VC, CCV, CVC, etc. from the phonetic knowledge stored for each (frequent) syllable. This generalized phonological-phonetic knowledge could be used as basic knowledge for processing infrequent syllables, i.e. for computing motor plans for infrequent syllables from the appropriate phonological plans.

In summary the suggested modeling framework can serve as a basis for future models incorporating more explicit solutions for human-human interaction during speech acquisition. It should be used for modeling the vocabulary spurt, i.e. for modeling the development of the mental lexicon, not explicitly focused on in this paper. Furthermore the neural control model introduced here can be seen as a concrete neurophysiological and neuropsychological concept for the generation of speech movements starting from linguistic or phonological brain activations, and thus can be seen as a useful extension for more linguistically oriented word or utterance production models (cf. Levelt et al. 1999, Dell et al. 1999) generating the phonological form from a concrete communicative intention.

Acknowledgments. This work was supported in part by the German Research Council DFG grant Kr 1439/13-1. Acknowledgments go to the anonymous reviewers for giving helpful corrections and suggestions and to Jane F. Utting PhD for correcting the English.

References

Badin, P., Bailly, G., Revéret, L., Baciu, M., Segebarth, C., Savariaux, C.: Three-dimensional articulatory modeling of tongue, lips and face, based on MRI and video images. Journal of Phonetics 30, 533–553 (2002)

Beautemps, D., Badin, P., Bailly, G.: Linear degrees of freedom in speech production: Analysis of cineradio- and labio-film data and articulatory-acoustic modeling. Journal of the Acoustical Society of America 109, 2165–2180 (2001)

Birkholz, P., Jackèl, D., Kröger, B.J.: Construction and control of a three-dimensional vocal tract model. In: Proceedings of the International Conference on Acoustics, Speech, and Signal Processing (ICASSP 2006), Toulouse, France, pp. 873–876 (2006)

Birkholz, P., Jackèl, D., Kröger, B.J.: Simulation of losses due to turbulence in the time-varying vocal system. IEEE Transactions on Audio, Speech, and Language Processing 15, 1218–1225 (2007a)

Birkholz, P., Steiner, I., Breuer, S.: Control Concepts for Articulatory Speech Synthesis. In: Proceedings of the 6th ISCA Workshop on Speech Synthesis, Bonn, Germany, pp. 5–10 (2007b)

Dell, G.S., Chang, F., Griffin, Z.M.: Connectionist models of language production: lexical access and grammatical encoding. Cognitive Science 23, 517–541 (1999)

Engwall, O.: Combining MRI, EMA and EPG measurements in a three-dimensional tongue model. Speech Communication 41, 303–329 (2003)

Fadiga, L., Craighero, L.: Electrophysiology of action representation. Journal of Clinical Neurophysiology 21, 157–168 (2004)

Fadiga, L., Craighero, L., Buccino, G., Rizzolatti, G.: Speech listening specifically modulates the excitability of tongue muscles: a TMS study. European Journal of Neuroscience 15, 399–402 (2002)

Frackowiak, R.S.J., Friston, K.J., Frith, C.D., Dolan, R.J., Price, C.J., Zeki, S., Ashburner, J., Penny, W.: Human Brain Function, 2nd edn. Elsevier Academic Press, Amsterdam (2004)

Guenther, F.H.: Cortical interactions underlying the production of speech sounds. Journal of Communication Disorders 39, 350–365 (2006)

Guenther, F.H., Ghosh, S.S., Tourville, J.A.: Neural modeling and imaging of the cortical interactions underlying syllable production. Brain and Language 96, 280–301 (2006)

Indefrey, P., Levelt, W.J.M.: The spatial and temporal signatures of word production components. Cognition 92, 101–144 (2004)

Kandel, E.R., Schwartz, J.H., Jessell, T.M.: Principles of Neural Science, 4th edn. MacGraw-Hill, New York (2000)

Kohonen, T.: Self-organizing maps. Springer, Berlin (2001)

Kohler, E., Keysers, C., Umilta, M.A., Fogassi, L., Gallese, V., Rizzolatti, G.: Hearing sounds, understanding actions: action representation in mirror neurons. Science 297, 846–848 (2002)

Kröger, B.J., Birkholz, P.: A gesture-based concept for speech movement control in articulatory speech synthesis. In: Esposito, A., Faundez-Zanuy, M., Keller, E., Marinaro, M. (eds.) COST Action 2102. LNCS (LNAI), vol. 4775, pp. 174–189. Springer, Heidelberg (2007)

Kröger, B.J., Birkholz, P., Kannampuzha, J., Neuschaefer-Rube, C.: Modeling the perceptual magnet effect and categorical perception using self-organizing neural networks. In: Proceedings of the 16th International Congress of Phonetic Sciences, Saarbrücken, Germany, pp. 789–792 (2007)

Levelt, W.J.M., Wheeldon, L.: Do speakers have access to a mental syllabary? Cognition 50, 239–269 (1994)

Levelt, W.J.M., Roelofs, A., Meyer, A.: A theory of lexical access in speech production. Behavioral and Brain Sciences 22, 1–75 (1999)

Oller, D.K., Eilers, R.E., Neal, A.R., Schwartz, H.K.: Precursors to speech in infancy: the prediction of speech and language disorders. Journal of Communication Disorders 32, 223–245 (1999)

Perkell, J., Cohen, M., Svirsky, M., Matthies, M., Garabieta, I., Jackson, M.: Electronetic midsaggital articulometer (EMMA) systems for transducing speech articulatory movements. Journal of the Acoustical Society of America 92, 3078–3096 (1992)

Stone, M.: Laboratory techniques for investigating speech articulation. In: Hardcastle, J., Laver, J. (eds.) The Handbook of Phonetic Sciences, pp. 11–32. Blackwell, Oxford (1997)

Zell, A.: Simulation neuronaler Netze. Oldenbourg Verlag, München Wien (2003)

Automatic Speech Recognition Used for Intelligibility Assessment of Text-to-Speech Systems

Robert Vích[1], Jan Nouza[2], and Martin Vondra[1]

[1] Institute of Photonics and Electronics, Academy of Sciences of the Czech Republic
Chaberská 57, CZ 18251 Prague 8, Czech Republic
[2] Institute of Information Technology and Electronics, Technical University of Liberec
Hálkova 6, CZ 46117 Liberec, Czech Republic
{vich,vondra}@ufe.cz, jan.nouza@tul.cz

Abstract. Speech intelligibility is the most important parameter in evaluation of speech quality. In the contribution, a new objective intelligibility assessment of general speech processing algorithms is proposed. It is based on automatic recognition methods developed for discrete and fluent speech processing. The idea is illustrated on two case studies: a) comparison of listening evaluation of Czech rhyme tests with automatic discrete speech recognition and b) automatic continuous speech recognition of general topic Czech texts read by professional and nonprofessional speakers vs. the same texts generated by several Czech Text-to-Speech systems. The aim of the proposed approach is fast and objective intelligibility assessment of Czech Text-to-Speech systems, which include male and female voices and a voice conversion module.

Keywords: Speech recognition, speech synthesis, speech assessment.

1 Introduction

There are two speech processing areas where speech intelligibility assessment is of primary interest:

- speech coding and speech synthesis;
- speech enhancement.

For comparison of speech processing algorithms and for evaluation of their implementation in communication systems and different applications, a large number of speech and voice quality assessment techniques have been formulated [1], [2], [3] and [4]. In Fig. 1 the common principle of voice quality measurement approaches is illustrated. The left side block represents, e.g., speech coding, speech synthesis, speech degradation, speech enhancement, speech conversion, etc.

Speech quality measures can be generally classified into two classes according to the measurement approach:

- objective quality measures;
- subjective quality measures.

A. Esposito et al. (Eds.): HH and HM Interaction 2007, LNAI 5042, pp. 136–148, 2008.

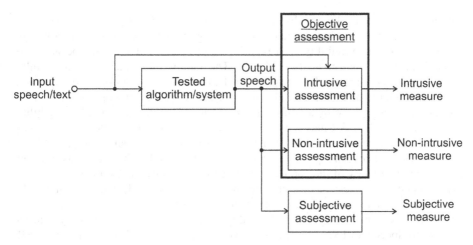

Fig. 1. Speech quality measurement

Objective speech quality measures are based on mathematical distances between the original and processed speech signals, e.g., on spectral distances, signal-to-noise ratio, etc. They can be categorized into two types:

- intrusive speech measures;
- non-intrusive speech measures.

Intrusive measures are based on computation of the distance between the original input speech signal and the processed/degraded output speech signal. *Non-intrusive measures* use only the degraded speech signal without comparison with the original input speech signal.

Subjective speech quality measures are based on comparison of the original and processed speech by a group of listeners, who adjudge the acoustically perceived speech to a given scale. Subjective measures can be further divided into those using word, rhyme or logatom tests and subjective quality measures using, e.g., the *Mean Opinion Score* (MOS), see Table 1.

In this contribution we shall not discuss the classical speech quality measures that are specific for different telecommunication systems and are standardized and recommended by the International Telecommunication Union-Telecommunication Standardization Sector (ITU-T). We try to propose and develop a new *objective intelligibility measure* based on reading Czech rhyme tests and general topic texts, but

Table 1. ITU 5-point MOS listening quality scale

MOS score	Speech quality
5	Excellent
4	Good
3	Fair
2	Poor
1	Bad

without subjective evaluation by a group of listeners [5], [6]. The evaluation is performed using a Czech automatic speech recognition (ASR) system described in Chapter 3. This intelligibility measurement is *objective* and *intrusive* because the input – the text – is known (see Fig. 1). The intelligibility measurement is fully *reproducible*. This approach is also justified in man-machine information systems, where the human voice may be coded, synthesized, degraded by noise and enhanced and has to be interpreted by an information system. The objective voice intelligibility metrics provided by ASR may replace the human panel. It can be called *document-to-speech functionality test*. Because the input to this intrusive assessment is text, *no time synchronization* between input and output is needed. The reliability of this assessment is given by the quality of the applied speech recognition system. For the intelligibility assessment of rhyme tests, a discrete-utterance (or isolated-word) ASR system is fully appropriate, because there are no syntactical or grammatical relations between words used in the test. On contrary, for intelligibility evaluation of sentences read by humans or Text-to-Speech (TTS) systems, we have to employ complete continuous ASR systems developed for the given language.

2 Automatic Speech Recognition

Recently, the performance of many ASR systems have achieved the level that allows them to be employed in many practical tasks such as dictation, broadcast news transcription or voice operated information services. When used under normal (non-noisy) conditions and by a cooperative user, they are able to transform spoken utterances into text with fairly high precision above 90 %. ASR systems have become available also for Czech language, though some of them still remain prototypes whose development is under development.

In this contribution we will focus on those ASR systems that have been developed by the research team at the Technical University of Liberec during the last 3 years. The systems employ two types of ASR engines: one for *Discrete-Utterance Recognition* (DUR) and the other for *Continuous Speech Recognition* (CSR). The former has been used in systems like voice control of a PC, or isolated-word dictation [7]. The main advantage of the DUR system is that it can be very robust and it can work fast even for very large vocabularies needed for Czech (at least half a million of words and more). The CSR system is more natural for use, namely in the dictation task, and it is the only one that can be applied for transcribing fluent speech, like it is described in [8]. Unfortunately, the performance of the CSR system is limited as to the vocabulary size, which currently is about 300 thousand words. In principle, both DUR and CSR systems are insensitive to speech prosody and may be therefore used only for speech intelligibility assessment.

2.1 Discrete Speech Recognition

For the purpose of the proposed rhyme-test experiments we have utilized the ASR engine developed for discrete-speech recognition in Czech. The engine designed at the Technical University in Liberec in late 1990s has been recently employed in two products aimed as voice-controlled aids for motor-handicapped people. One of them is

MyVoice, a voice-operated replacement of keyboard and mouse, the other is MyDictate, which allows completely hands-free dictation and editing of Czech texts [7].

It was shown that the former achieves above 97 % *Word Recognition Rate* (WRR) for typical command lists containing of properly chosen (i.e. easily pronounceable and acoustically distant) command words. The latter has to solve a much more difficult task: to distinguish between more than 500.000 Czech words included in the dictionary. The average recognition score achieved when dictating normal Czech texts is about 65 % when no language model is applied and about 92 % if prior word probability is taken into account in the recognition process. These figures are mentioned here to compare the ASR performance in common tasks with those described later, when acoustically very confusable short utterances are recognized.

The acoustic front-end operates as follows: the speech signal is sampled at 8 kHz sampling frequency and further processed in 25 ms frames shifted every 10 ms. Each signal frame is parameterized to get 13 mel-frequency cepstral coefficients (MFCC) and their 1st and 2nd derivatives. Hence, a feature vector is composed of 39 parameters. Speech start and end points are searched by evaluating log signal energy and detecting points, where its value crosses a set of adaptively set levels. Word models are composed of phoneme models of HMM (hidden Markov model) type. A set of 41 Czech phoneme models and 7 noise models has been trained on a database containing about 40 hours of annotated speech of some 500 speakers. A major part of this training database was made of recorded words spoken in isolated way, i.e. in the same way as the ASR system is used in practice. All the HMMs have three states, each represented by an output probability density function in form of a mixture of 64 Gaussians. The recognition procedure is based on the classical Viterbi beam search.

2.2 Continuous Speech Recognition

The CSR system was developed also at the TU of Liberec [8] and it is able to transcribe any Czech utterance (up to 5 minute long) and compare its output with the reference text. The system's evaluation module computes the word recognition rate for that sentence in usual way as *Accuracy = (N − S − D − I)/N*, where S is the number of wrongly recognized words (Substitutions), D is the number of omitted words (Deletions), I is the number of inserted words (Insertions) and N is the total number of words in the reference transcription.

Some facts about the employed ASR engine: the CSR engine operates with 16 kHz sampled data, uses the standard 39 MFCC feature set, its acoustic (gender-dependent) model is based on 3-state 100-mixture HMMs of 41 Czech phonemes and 7 noises (trained on approximately 50 hours of speech provided by almost 800 different speakers) and the language model uses smoothed bigrams computed from a large amount (more than 3 GB) of Czech (mainly newspaper) text.

3 Experiments

The idea of evaluating speech intelligibility by means of ASR systems consists in the fact that if we know what has been said and how it was recognized, we can compute a recognition accuracy score. We believe that the score can be used as a *relative measure* of the intelligibility of the speech input. The adjective *relative* is important here, because we know that the ASR system itself introduces some recognition errors which are caused, e.g. by words missing in the vocabulary.

Our initial experiments in this area tried to imitate the subjective intelligibility evaluation method known as *rhyme tests*. They consist in recording groups of words that sound very similar (usually they differ only in one phoneme) and replaying them to a panel of listeners, who should decide which word they heard. In our automatic approach the listeners are replaced by a DUR system.

In all the other experiments we worked with recordings of *continuous speech*. Therefore, we used the latest version of the CSR system that works with the vocabulary containing 312 thousand most frequent Czech words. For this type of experiments we collected two text databases read by humans and by TTS systems.

3.1 Czech Rhyme Test

Czech rhyme tests were developed in Tesla Electronics Research Institute in cooperation with the Institute of Czech Language of the Czechoslovak Academy of Sciences. They were developed and used in the 80th for intelligibility measurement of Czech communication systems in parallel with word and logatom tests. Intelligibility measurement using rhyme tests differ from the other two mentioned in that the listener knows several variants of the read word and marks the one, which he suppose to hear. The rhyme test words differ only in one consonant. In this case we call the test *closed or constrained choice* in contrary to the others where the choice is *free*, the

Table 2. Czech rhyme test

1	pes	nes	mez	ves	rez
2	ten	den	ven	len	jen
3	kát	dát	vát	lát	rád
4	důl	hůl	vůl	kůl	sůl
5	pás	pád	pán	pár	pák
6	mop	sob	cop	top	lob
7	šít	výt	být	pít	mít
8	šeď	teď	veď	meť	leť
9	brát	drát	prát	zrát	hrát
10	disk	zisk	tisk	pysk	risk
11	klec	klej	klen	klel	kles
12	trn	trs	trp	trh	trk
13	lej	led	lev	len	les
14	taje	saje	čaje	kaje	laje
15	lil	byl	šil	vyl	myl
16	koří	hoří	moří	noří	choří
17	její	jedí	ječí	ježí	jetí
18	vonný	vosí	voní	vozí	volí
19	míjí	mýlí	míní	míří	mísí
20	ryčí	fičí	tyčí	řičí	ničí

listener can write an arbitrary word or logatom. The results of measured intelligibility using rhyme tests lie between the intelligibility of word tests and intelligibility of logatom tests.

The first used Czech rhyme test contained 250 words in 50 rows. Each row contained 5 similar words with one or two syllables that differ only in their leading consonantal phonemes. For efficient and fast evaluation of different speech processing systems the rhyme test has been modified and shortened. This new shortened Czech rhyme test is given in Table 2. It contains 100 words in which the occurrence of consonants approximates the occurrence of consonants in the Czech language shown in Fig. 2. The shortened rhyme test is simple; it has proved its efficiency and reliability and the results were reproducible. Since each individual experiment consisted of recognizing a set of 100 words, its WRR was computed as the number of correctly recognized words, which is exactly the recognition rate expressed on the per cent scale. They were systematically used for speech synthesis intelligibility measurement.

3.2 Rhyme Test Intelligibility

The ASR experiments were prepared in the following way: to simplify the experiment organization and at the same time to make the recognition harder (to avoid scores approaching 100 %), each of the 100 test words was matched to all 100 candidates (models of all the rhyme test words). It can be stated that the proposed approach is much harder than the corresponding subjective listening test. Thus it could happen (and sometimes it really did) that a word was recognized as one from another rhyme test group. It was caused by various reasons, e.g. by not very clear pronunciation, or on the contrary by so called hyper-correct (non-natural) pronunciation, or because of

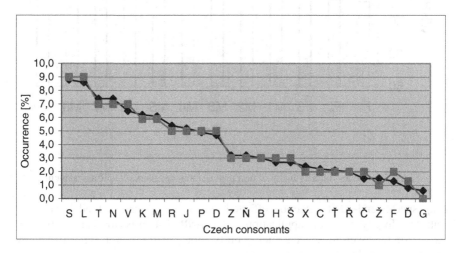

Fig. 2. Occurrence of consonants in the Czech language. The curve with black squares corresponds to the occurrence of consonants in the Czech rhyme test.

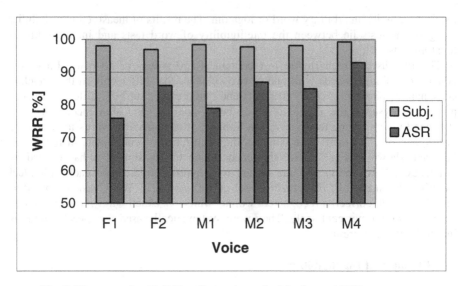

Fig. 3. Rhyme test intelligibility. Comparison of subjective and DUR assessment.

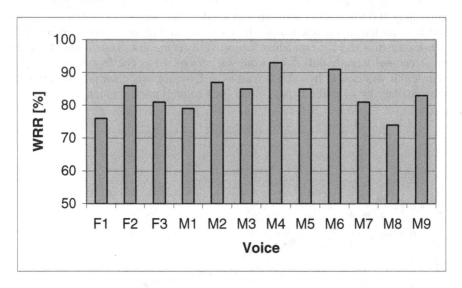

Fig. 4. Rhyme test intelligibility of non professional speakers – DUR assessment

wrong speech end-point detection effected, e.g. by a lip-smack, loud breath-in or breath-out. In any case, this application of the ASR system performance reflected a measure of the over-all speech intelligibility, not just the confusion between two similar phonemes in the rhyme test groups.

In Fig. 3 we can see the intelligibility results obtained by subjective listening tests of Czech rhyme test by a panel of 12 listeners for 2 females (F), 4 males (M) with the WRR of the DUR system. All experiments were performed for the sampling frequency $F_S = 8$ kHz. It is interesting to note that the subjective intelligibility of analog rhyme test realization (not band pass filtered) for speaker M1 is WRR = 99.7% in comparison to WRR = 98.5% for 8 kHz sampling frequency.

For comparison of the WRR of a broader test sample six new speakers have been included into the test. The results for altogether 3 female and 9 male speakers are shown in Fig. 4. The mean WRR of the DUR system for all speakers is WRR = 85%.

In Fig. 5 the DUR intelligibility of two Czech TTS systems is shown. The male voice M10 is a TTS voice of a diphone based system with hand labeled 441 diphones and sub phonemes and cepstral speech synthesis [9] and was constructed by labeling of the male voice M1. The male voice M11 (higher fundamental frequency corresponding to a young male voice) and the female voice F4 were obtained by voice conversion from the male voice M10 [10]. It is interesting to note that the recognition rate of the synthesized voice M10 is higher by 7% than that of the original voice M1, which can be explained by reduction of the "infinite" sound production of the natural voice M1 into the restricted unit inventory of the Czech TTS system and by careful labeling in diphone inventory construction. The two other TTS voices have lower intelligibility than the original voice M1. The male voice M12 is also a TTS voice, but of a Czech triphone based PSOLA system [11], [12], [13] with hand labeled 1840 triphones from the male voice M8. The female voice F5 is the output of the same Czech triphone based system.

In Fig. 6 the word recognition rates of pure voice conversion of the male voice M1 into female voice F2 and vice versa realized by nonlinear frequency warping and synthesized using a cepstral vocoder are given [14]. It is interesting that cepstral resynthesis of the male voice has lower recognition rate than the original male voice M1 by 2 %, the conversion of the male voice M1 into the female voice is lower by 25% than F2. The resynthesis of the female voice F2 is lower by 10%, but the female voice conversion into the male voice is higher by 1% than M1.

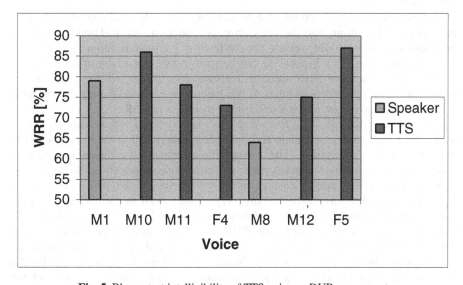

Fig. 5. Rhyme test intelligibility of TTS voices – DUR assessment

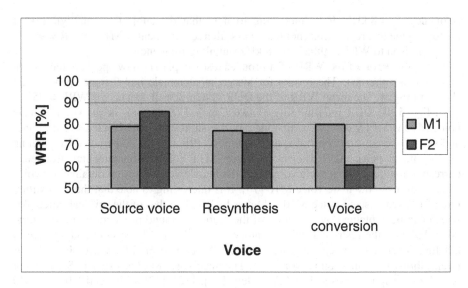

Fig. 6. Rhyme test intelligibility of voice conversion – DUR assessment

3.3 Continuous Speech Databases

To test the application of the CSR engine for intelligibility assessment of fluent speech we started to collect a special speech database that is made of the same text spoken by multiple subjects. The unique property of this database, i.e. the fact that several speakers recorded the same text, makes it very suitable for initial experiments focused on evaluating the intelligibility of speech produced by different subjects and TTS systems.

Our hypothesis was: if several speech recordings have identical text content and if the recording conditions and the ASR setup are the same, the difference in speech recognition results should reflect the difference in pronunciation between the individual speakers. This hypothesis can be proved by comparison of the achieved ASR results with those from subjective evaluations, which will be organized in collaboration with phoneticians later. At this moment we focused mainly on preparing the tests and on investigating the intelligibility by means of ASR.

The speech part of the *first database* is collected of recordings of 8 *nonprofessional speakers* – 5 male and 3 female speakers. All of them were asked to read the same 45 utterances. The text of the utterances was taken from Czech newspapers and contained selected parts of 3 articles dealing with 3 different topics (learning foreign languages, Czech economy, and modern architecture). The text of the selected articles was modified only very slightly with the aim to avoid some unusual foreign proper names. Most utterances were quite long and consisted of 3 to 5 sentences. The whole set contained 2040 words, i.e. in average 46 words per utterance. Eight of these 2040 words were not present in the 312K-word lexicon, so the *out-of-vocabulary rate* was 0.39 %. None of the test speakers occurred in the list of persons who provided the data for the acoustic model training and none of the utterances was used in the language model training. The speakers were asked to read the articles in a *natural* way as they usually do it. The same text was synthesized using six TTS systems and evaluated by CSR engine described in Section 2.2.

The above mentioned database was collected from utterances of nonprofessional speakers. For comparison of voices of nonprofessional and professional speakers a smaller *second database* composed of utterances of *professional speakers* at the Czech public TV station, one male and one female, was created. The two recordings contain 40 sentences with about 500 words. The same texts were also synthesized using two TTS systems and evaluated by the CSR engine.

3.4 Continuous Speech Intelligibility

In the initial experiment, we simply let the CSR engine transcribe the utterances of these 8 speakers and 6 TTS voices (3 diphone and 3 triphone based) and compared the obtained WRR results. They are shown in Fig. 7. It is evident that there are big differences between the speakers (more than 14 % between the best and the worst one) and between the TTS voices (about 8 %). This clearly corresponded to the subjectively perceived pronunciation quality of the individual voices. It is interesting to see that in general the TTS-generated speech was recognized better than the same text read by non-professional speakers. We explain this rather surprising fact by a hypothesis that the regularity of artificial speech fits well with the probabilistic speech model. Also we should note that the best TTS voice M10 is male diphone based cepstral synthesis [10], the next best F5 is female triphone based PSOLA synthesis [12]. The voices M12 and M13 are also PSOLA with triphones, M14 and M15 are again diphone based voices.

To estimate the influence of fundamental frequency modification on TTS voice intelligibility we changed in the PSOLA triphone TTS system the fundamental frequency for the male voice M12 in steps 90, 95 (basic fundamental frequency), 100 and 110 Hz and for the female voice F5 in steps 185, (basic fundamental frequency),

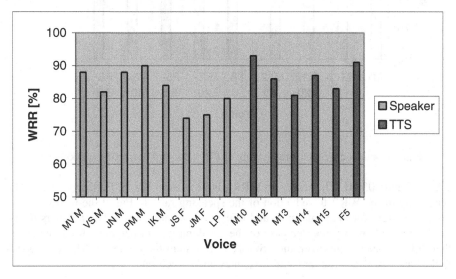

Fig. 7. Continuous speech intelligibility of natural and TTS voices

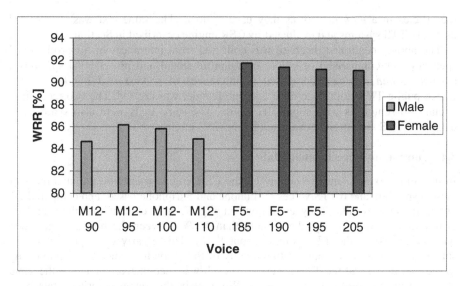

Fig. 8. Continuous speech intelligibility of TTS voices for several fundamental frequencies

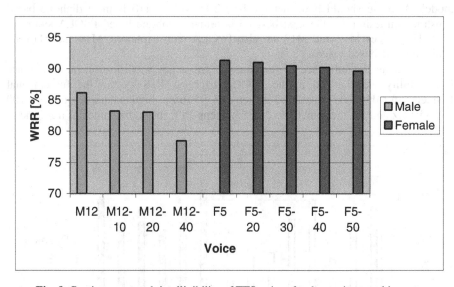

Fig. 9. Continuous speech intelligibility of TTS voices for decreasing speaking rate

190, 195 and 205 Hz. The results in WRR can be seen in Fig. 8. Further we tested the sensitivity of the WRR to reduction of the speaking rate. In Fig. 9 the results for the PSOLA system for the same male and female voices are shown. The numbers below the voice label specify the decrease of the speaking rate in percents. It can be stated that in both experiments with the PSOLA TTS system the highest WRR corresponds to the basic speaker's fundamental frequency and speech rate.

In the last series of experiments we compared the intelligibility of texts read by professional TV speakers with the same texts synthesized by parametric diphone based (M10, F4) and PSOLA triphone based TTS systems (M12, F5). The results are shown in Fig. 10. It can be stated that the intelligibility of the TTS systems measured by WRR is, with exception of the voice M12, approximately equal to the intelligibility of the professional speakers, which were again surprising findings.

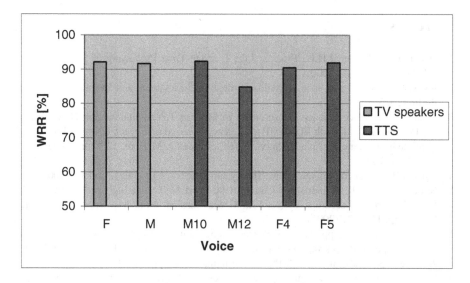

Fig. 10. Continuous speech intelligibility of professional speakers und TTS voices (M-male, F-female voices)

4 Conclusion

An attempt to investigate an automatic approach to intelligibility measurement of speech is presented in this contribution. It is based on the application ASR methods that try to replace human listeners in evaluating either classical rhyme tests or the intelligibility of fluent speech read by human speakers and TTS systems. These intelligibility measurements are intrusive, reproducible and do not require time synchronization between input and output. The proposed method is fast and not as expensive and time consuming as subjective listening tests. It can be used, together with other intrusive measures, for comparison of various algorithms prior to its application in practice. This application of rhyme tests and DUR enables also the detection of segmental imperfections in phoneme realization in the tested algorithms. The proposed approach was applied to intelligibility assessment of several TTS tasks, like comparison of different TTS systems, voice conversion, modification of fundamental frequency and speech rate, etc.

On the other hand, the result of this intelligibility measurement does not give an answer to overall quality, e.g., by means of MOS scale, acceptability measure, etc. Therefore this intelligibility assessment must be combined with further speech quality evaluation. In the future work, we want to focus on measuring the correlation of this proposed approach with other speech and voice quality assessments.

Acknowledgments. This work was supported within the framework of the National Research Programs of the Academy of Sciences of the Czech Republic *Information Society* No 1ET301710509 and *Targeted Research* 1QS108040569.

References

1. Deller, J.R., Hansen, J.H.L., Proakis, J.G.: Discrete-Time Processing of Speech Signals. IEEE Press, N. York (2000)
2. Jekosch, U.: Voice and Speech Quality Perception, Assessment and Evaluation. Springer, Berlin (2005)
3. Mahdi, A.E.: Voice Quality Measurement in Modern Telecommunication Networks. In: CD Proceedings of the 6th EURASIP Conference Focused on Speech & Image Processing, Multimedia Communications & Services (EC-SIPMCS), Maribor, Slovenia, June 27-30, pp. 29–36 (2007)
4. Loizou, P.: C. Speech Enhancement. Theory and Practice. CRC Press, London (2007)
5. Nouza, J., Vích, R., Vondra, M.: Can ASR be Used for Evaluating Speech Quality? In: Vích, R. (ed.) Proceedings of the 17th Czech-German Workshop Speech Processing, Prague, pp. 115–121 (2007)
6. Vích, R., Nouza, J.: Application of Speech Recognition and Rhyme Tests for Assessement of Czech Speech Processing Systems. In: Duběda, T., Vlčková, J. (eds.) Proceedings of the 2nd Czech-Slovak Conference ISPhS, Karolinum, Prague, pp. 141–151 (2007)
7. Červa, P., Nouza, J.: Design and Development of Voice Controlled Aids for Motor-Handicapped Persons. In: Proceedings of Interspeech, pp. 2521–2524. Antwerp (2007)
8. Nouza, J., Žďánský, J., Červa, P., Kolorenč, J.: A System for Information Retrieval from Large Records of Broadcast Programs. In: Text, Speech and Dialogue. Lecture Notes in Artificial Intelligence, LNAI, vol. 4188, pp. 401–408. Springer, Berlin (2006)
9. Přibil, J., Přibilová, A.: Czech TTS Engine for BraillePen Device Based on Pocket PC Platform. In: Vích, R. (ed.) Proceedings of the 16th Conference Electronic Speech Signal Processing joined with the 15th Czech-German Workshop Speech Processing, Prague, pp. 402–408 (2005)
10. Přibilová, A., Přibil, J.: Nonlinear Frequency Scale Mapping for Voice Conversion in Text-to-Speech System with Cepstral Description. Speech Communication 48, 1691–1703 (2006)
11. Hanika, J., Horák, P.: Epos – A New Approach to Speech Synthesis. In: Proceedings of the First Workshop on Text, Speech and Dialogue – TSD 1998, Brno, pp. 51–54 (1998)
12. Horák, P., Hesounová, A.: Czech Triphone Synthesis of Female Voice. In: Vích, R. (ed.) Proceedings of the 11th Czech-German Workshop Speech Processing, Prague, pp. 32–33 (2001)
13. Horák, P., Hanika, J.: Epos Text-to-Speech System (2007), http://epos.ufe.cz/
14. Vondra, M., Vích, R.: Speech Identity Conversion. In: Chollet, G., Esposito, A., Faúndez-Zanuy, M., Marinaro, M. (eds.) Nonlinear Speech Modeling and Applications. LNCS (LNAI), vol. 3445, pp. 421–426. Springer, Heidelberg (2005)

ECESS Platform for Web Based TTS Modules and Systems Evaluation

Matej Rojc[1], Harald Höge[2], and Zdravko Kačič[1]

[1] University of Maribor, Faculty of Electrical Engineering and Computer Science,
Maribor, Slovenia
[2] Siemens AG, Corporate Technology, Germany
{matej.rojc,kacic}@uni-mb.si, harald.hoege@t-online.de

Abstract. The paper presents platform for web based TTS modules and systems evaluation named RES (Remote Evaluation System). It is being developed within the European Centre of Excellence for Speech Synthesis (ECESS, www.ecess.eu). The presented platform will be used for web based online evaluation of various text-to-speech (TTS) modules, and even complete TTS systems, presently running at different Institutes and Universities worldwide. Each ECESS partner has to install the RES module server locally and connect it with its TTS modules. Using the RES client, partners will be able to perform different evaluation tasks for their modules using any necessary additional modules and/or language resources of their other partners, installed locally at the other partners' sites. Additionally, they will be able to integrate their own modules into the complete web-based TTS system in conjunction with the necessary modules of other partners. By using the RES client they could also build-up a complete TTS system via web, without using any of their own modules. Several partners can contribute their modules, even with the same functionality, and it is easy to add a new module to the whole web-based distributed system. The user will decide which partner's module to use in his own configuration or for a particular evaluation task. Evaluation can be done by any institution, able to access modules for evaluation without the need to install these modules locally. The platform will be used within the evaluation campaigns of different TTS modules and complete TTS systems carried-out by the ECESS consortium. The first remote-based evaluation campaign of text processing modules using the developed platform is foreseen for January 2008.

Keywords: ECESS consortium, text-to-speech synthesis, remote evaluation.

1 Introduction

The main goal of ECESS (European Centre of Excellence on Speech Synthesis) is to push TTS technology and at the same time, speeding up the process from basic research to product. In order to achieve this goal, clearly defined procedures for evaluating different TTS components and assessment of complete TTS systems have to be defined (Perez et al., 2006). In order to establish a so-called common test-bed for development and evaluation purposes, a web-based distributed system has been

A. Esposito et al. (Eds.): HH and HM Interaction 2007, LNAI 5042, pp. 149–157, 2008.

developed and named RES (Remote Evaluation System). The idea is that each ECESS partner would be able to place locally one or even more TTS components on the web, or that each partner would be able to access various TTS components from different partners available via the web. Consequently, evaluation can be done remotely by any Institution able to access modules for evaluation without the need to install these modules locally.

All modules included in the RES platform are accessible via TCP/IP. MRCP protocol is used for data exchange. The platform integrates a RES server with one or more RES module servers, and RES clients. Each of these modules performs a specific sequence of actions, as defined by XML- based protocol descriptions and their implementation as finite-state machines. The proprietary RES protocol composed of requests and responses is implemented between RES server and RES module servers. The TC-STAR XML format is used as protocol data format.

Within TC-STAR project a complete TTS system was constructed by adaptation of the UIMA system from IBM (UIMA, 2007). Nevertheless, ECESS idea about splitting TTS system in more specified modules is new and also the related evaluation of modules. This allows to test in more detail the different algorithms within a TTS system.

The remainder of this paper is organized as follows. Section 2 describes the basic architecture of the RES TTS system. Section 3 describes protocols used in the RES system. Following chapters describe RES system modules from user perspective. Therefore, section 4 presents RES client, section 5 RES server, and section 6 RES module server. RES tools are presented in section 7. The last section draws the conclusions.

2   Distributed Architecture for the Development of an RES TTS System

The basic architecture of the RES system is shown in Figure 1. It consists of an RES client, RES server, and one or more RES module servers. The RES client and RES module servers are located by different partners worldwide. All modules are connected to the internet using TCP/IP and UDP connections. Using such architecture, partners are able to place their modules locally (tools) on the web. Via a remote-access mechanism, each partner can then access any of these modules.

The RES server can interact with arbitrary RES clients and can communicate with several clients at the same time. Furthermore, RES module servers can also communicate with several clients at the same time. The whole RES system is organized as complex client/server architecture. Firstly, an RES client establishes connection with the RES server and then the RES server further establishes client/server connection with the RES module server on the web. Inside ECESS there are partners who have only installed RES clients and also partners who have installed one or even more RES module servers. Each partner wanting to evaluate their module must also install a dedicated RES module server.

The RES system is dedicated to distributing web-based online evaluation of various ECESS TTS components running at different Institutes and Universities worldwide. By using it, it is possible to run partial or complete TTS system, composed of selectable ECESS TTS components, on the web. An evaluation institution is able to perform different evaluation tasks by sending test data from the RES client and by

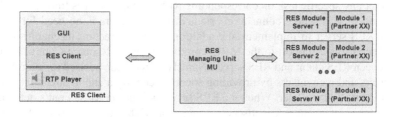

Fig. 1. RES system architecture

receiving results from the selected RES module servers running corresponding partners' TTS components. The RES system can be used by partners needing to use the ECESS TTS modules or TTS components of other partners to test and improve the performances of their own modules or tools. Partners are able to perform different evaluation tasks of their modules using those necessary additional modules and/or language resources of other partners installed locally at the other partners' sites. Partners are able to integrate their own modules into a complete web-based TTS system using any necessary remaining modules of other partners. By using RES system, the partners can also build-up a complete TTS system via web, without using any of their own modules. How is it used? Partners have to use RES client in order to put input data to the RES system. Then they have to select one of the available XML scenarios for performing specific evaluation task. Selected scenarios are automatically transferred to RES server and RES module server(s). They define the behaviour of the RES system, which is strongly connected with the desired evaluation task. In agreement with the selected scenario, the users can then select the desired TTS component(s) available on the web, and run the RES system. Next, input data from the RES client are transferred to the RES server (main managing unit). The RES server establishes connection(s) with selected RES module server(s) and sends received data. The RES module server accepts data sent from the user and runs the partners' tool. The generated output is sent back to the RES server and further to the RES client of the user, where it is automatically shown in the GUI interface. In order to make TTS component available to other partners, the partner needs to install the RES module server. He has to configure the RES module server with proper IP/port settings, specify the command-line syntax used for running his TTS component, and finally run the RES module server. After this is performed, all ECESS partners are able to run, test or evaluate his TTS component. Information which TTS components are available on the web is specified at the RES server. Every time an RES client establishes connection with the RES server, a list of available partners' TTS components is automatically sent to the users, before selection of the desired TTS component is possible. In contrast to the TC-STAR, no manual effort is necessary for the developers of a TTS component to take part in the evaluation.

3 Protocols

Figure 2 shows the detailed distributed architecture of the RES system. The RES clients open real time streaming protocol (RTSP) sessions using an RES server, which then closes after any specific task on corresponding RES module server is finished. As RTSP is based on TCP, a secure connection-oriented protocol, there is no need for the RES client or RES server to implement any additional error-correction mechanisms. RTSP protocol serves as a support to the MRCP protocol (Media Resource Control Protocol) used between RES client and RES server. Namely, MRCP can be used to control speech synthesizers and recognizers by providing speech recognition and to stream audio from a common location to a user. When the RES server accepts an RES client's demand in a specific thread, it opens a client/server connection with those specified RES module servers in which the specific task is performed, and the results are obtained. Results (output) are then sent back to the RES client. Only proprietary XML-based protocol is used between RES server and RES module servers, for exchanging input/output data with the ECESS modules on the web. There are slight differences between some TTS components regarding output. E.g. text processing, prosody processing TTS components use only text I/O data, but acoustic TTS components use text/audio I/O data. Therefore, RTP protocol is used for transmitting audio data. Audio data are transferred in this way from the corresponding RES module server through the RES server to the RES client, where the RTP player must also be activated. The data used in the RES system are in TC-STAR data format (Bonafonte et al., 2006).

Evaluation tasks can result in several different possible scenarios. Hard-coded protocol implementation, in this case, seems to be an inflexible and inefficient solution. Therefore, all RES modules are implemented as finite-state engines (Copeland, 2007, Shalyto, 2001). Actions (functions) applied for specified scenarios and RES modules, are then defined according to the specified protocols described as graphs. The graph is written already off-line and added to the RES modules as XML description. The transitions in the graph are triggered by series of event instances during running RES modules. This approach enables flexible and fast configuration of all RES modules' and protocols' logic, and module behaviour is not hard-coded.

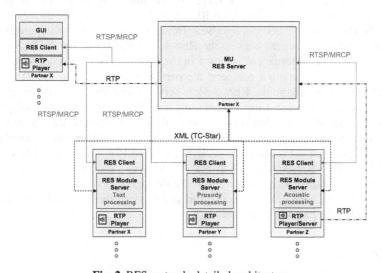

Fig. 2. RES system's detailed architecture

4 RES Client

An RES client facilitates development by providing support for the key functionality required for developing an MRCP-based application. It can be used with or without an RTP player. This is specified by XML configuration and protocol description files. An RTP player is only needed when acoustic TTS components or the whole TTS systems are tested and evaluated. Therefore, in order to start using the RES client, each partner has to configure the IP/port information for the RES server located at the University of Maribor and specify the desired XML scenario for the module. The selected scenario then defines the behaviour of the RES client – what the RES client will actually do. E.g. run a text-processing server, prosody-processing server, acoustic-processing server, or several other possible combinations of these servers etc. It is important that users are able to select any module on the web they wish to test. In order to do this, they have to know what is actually available. This information is served to the RES client and user at the start of the RES client's. After that the user is able to select a desired module and proceed with running the test as shown in Figure 3.

In Figure 3, a text-processing TTS component from Siemens was selected, as an example. The user has then to copy the desired input text into the 'Input' panel as

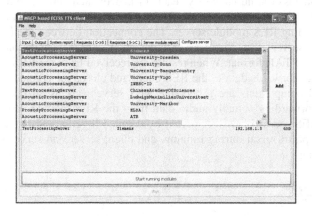

Fig. 3. RES client – selection of ECESS modules available on the web

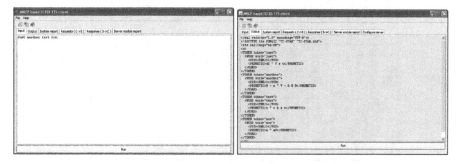

Fig. 4. RES client – Running text-processing servers

shown in Figure 4 left, and press the 'Start running modules' button in the 'Configure server' panel. The result from the Siemens module is shown immediately in the 'Output' panel, in TC-STAR data format as shown in Figure 4 right. When it is finished, the user can repeat the process in the same way, and as many times as he wants. The RES client is also supported by detailed logging and report information, in regard to graph traversal during running and client/server packet exchange.

5   RES Server

This module provides support for the key functionality required when developing an MRCP-based application. As can be seen in Figure 5, it contains more panels that are all used for monitoring working of the server. When there is a call from the RES client, the special thread is picked from the pool of threads and a specific MRCP session is established with the client. When no more threads are available, the server just rejects calls from the RES clients. The default number of threads is currently 200, but can be changed in the configuration file. Each RES client actually sends an XML scenario description on the RES server, which specifies what and how an RES server should perform. Therefore, it is possible that for example, 200 clients perform different evaluation tasks simultaneously, each in a dedicated thread. When connection with the RES client is established, the RES server transfers input data from the client to a corresponding RES module server. The connection between the RES server and RES module server is a client/server connection. These connection data are exchanged in TC-STAR format. When results are received from the RES module server, the RES server forwards data to the RES client and closes the connections. When the acoustic TTS components are tested, the RES server acts as an RTP receiver and transmitter, forwarding actually audio data from the RES module server to the RES client. The RES server is also supported by detailed logging and report information, regarding graph traversal during running, and client/server and server/server module packet exchange.

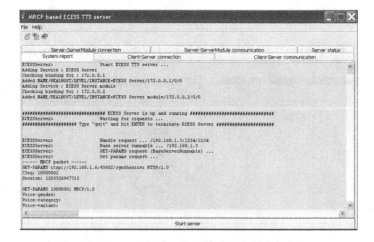

Fig. 5. RES server GUI

6 RES Module Server

Partners who want to 'integrate' their modules into the RES system must also use one RES module server for each additional ECESS module (Figure 6). The GUI contains more panels that are all used for monitoring working of the server. The RES module server is rather differently organized than the RES client or RES server. Nevertheless, it also contains a pool of threads, and dedicates threads for each call from the RES client. The default number of threads is 200, but can be changed in the configuration file.

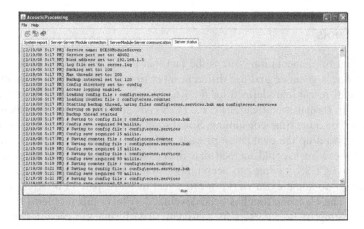

Fig. 6. RES module server GUI

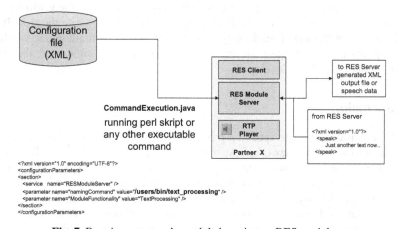

Fig. 7. Running a partner's module by using an RES module server

When the acoustic TTS component is run by an RES module server, the RTP transmission transfers generated audio data to the RES server. In order for the RES module server to run a partner's ECESS module, the specific 'CommandExecution' module server class has to be used. This object is used for running tools, commands or event scripts on the partner's site. The user has just to configure the RES module server regarding IP/port setting and define it in the configuration file about how to run their module. The process running the partner's module is shown in Figure 7.

Therefore, partners do not need to change, in any way, their modules in order to integrate them into the RES system. The RES module server is totally separate from the partner's module and will remain active even when the partner's modules have problems with a given input. An error handling mechanism will report any error to the RES server and RES client. The RES module server is supported by detailed logging and report information, in regard to graph traversal during running and server/module server packet exchanges.

7 RES Tools

An important implementation issue is the fact that the ECESS modules developed by ECESS partners generate and use different input/output data formats. Usually, this is much more different than defined for the RES system. Adaptation of these formats to the RES data format specifications (i.e., TC-STAR specifications), can take-up a lot of effort and be quite time-consuming. Some solution has to be found for this problem in order to speed-up the evaluation process and other actions inside the ECESS consortium. Otherwise it could happen that many partners will not be able to provide resources or ECESS modules to accomplish some evaluation task or even find the motivation to do some extra work, in order just to participate in different evaluation campaigns. The *Unforma* tool has been developed to solve this problem. This tool enables the writing of Java parsers for automatic data format conversion from proprietary formats into TC-STAR formats, and vice versa.

The other implementation issue is that all RES modules should run several different scenarios. Namely, ECESS activities will be very colourful and there will be many various scenarios in the form of XML descriptions. In order to write these XML descriptions in flexible and efficient ways, and be able to perform automatic validation and compilation of the finite-state machine description at the same time, the *ProtocolGen* tool has also been developed.

8 Conclusion

ECESS organisation aims to speed-up progress in speech synthesis technology by providing an appropriate framework. Test simulations performed by ELDA, Siemens and University of Maribor showed flexibility of the RES system and practically real-time transfer of input/output data within RES system. Currently, RES software is not open source software. Yet the evaluation campaigns are open to externals (e.g. observers). Two areas for evaluation campaigns have been established: evaluation of ECESS speech synthesis modules (text-processing, prosody, acoustic synthesis) and evaluation of ECESS tools (pitch extraction, voice activity detection, phonetic segmentation). The functionalities and interfaces of the ECESS modules and procedures for evaluation have been developed through a joint effort between ECESS and the EC-funded project TC-STAR. The next ECESS evaluation campaign for modules will focus on UK English module evaluation. This will also be the first evaluation campaign totally based on a remote-evaluation procedure, and is scheduled for December 07/January 08.

References

1. Perez, J., Bonafonte, A., Hain, H.-U., Keller, E., Breuer, S., Tian, J.: ECESS Inter-Module Interface Specification for Speech Synthesis. In: Proc. LREC 2006 (2006)
2. Bonafonte, A., Höge, H., Kiss, I., Moreno, A., Ziegenhain, U., Van den Heuvel, H., Hain, H.-U., Wang, X.S., Garcia, M.N.: TC-STAR: Specifications of Language Resources and Evaluation for Speech Synthesis. In: Proc. LREC 2006 (2006)
3. Copeland, T.: Generating Parsers with JavaCC, Centennial Books, Alexandria (2007)
4. Shalyto, A.A.: Logic Control and "Reactive" Systems: Algorithmization and Programming. Automation and Remote Control 62(1), 1–29 (2001); Translated from Avtomatika i Telemekhanika, 1, 3–39 (2001)
5. UIMA Overview & SDK Setup,2007. Written and maintained by the Apache UIMA Development Community (2007), http://incubator.apache.org/uima/downloads/releaseDocs/2.2.0incubaing/docs/html/overview_and_setup/overview_and_setup.html

Towards Slovak Broadcast News Automatic Recording and Transcribing Service

Matúš Pleva, Anton Čižmár, Jozef Juhár, Stanislav Ondáš,
and Michal Mirilovič

Department of Electronics and Multimedia Communications,
Technical University of Košice, Letná 9, 042 00 Košice, Slovak Republic
{Matus.Pleva,Anton.Cizmar,Jozef.Juhar,
Stanislav.Ondas,Michal.Mirilovic}@tuke.sk

Abstract. The information is one of the most valuable commodities nowadays. The information retrieval mechanisms from broadcast news recordings is then becoming the one of the most requested services from the end-users. The planned Slovak automatic broadcast news (BN) processing service provides automatic transcribing and metadata extracting abilities, enabling users to obtain information from the processed recordings using a web interface and the search engine. The resulted information is then provided trough multimodal interface, which allows users to see not only recorded audio-visual material, but also all automatically extracted metadata (verbal and nonverbal), and also to select incorrectly automatically identified data. The architecture of the present system is linear, which means every module starts after the previous has finished the data processing.

Keywords: Broadcast news, automatic continuous speech recognition, human computer interaction, metadata collection, information retrieval.

1 Introduction

The broadcast news recordings automatically stored everyday only as audio-video materials, make these multimedia collections unusable for searching. The biggest challenge in this information retrieval area is to automatically retrieve as many metadata from the recordings as it is possible now. For example the speaker name, transcribed text of the speech, speaker's gender, speaker's emotions, topic of the speech and many others are one of the most useful information, which are needed for the BN databases, and also very reliable for hearing impaired users of the database.

Slovak Broadcast News Automatic Recording and Transcribing Service (Slovak BN-ATRS) enables automatic metadata retrieval from automated recorded BN news and stores them in the metadata BN database.

The Slovak language belongs to a family of Slavic languages that are known to have a very high degree of inflection [1]. A similar automatic metadata retrieval system of Czech language (which is very close to Slovak) was presented years ago with 21% WER, and our goal is to bring our system to this degree of functionality [2]. Automatic Broadcast News annotation systems exists years ago also for major

A. Esposito et al. (Eds.): HH and HM Interaction 2007, LNAI 5042, pp. 158–168, 2008.

European languages as English [3], French [4, 5], German [6], Spanish [7], Portuguese [8], Greek [9], Italian [10, 11] and others.

The goal of the project is then also to realize a presentation web server, which will allow the users to search among the BN recordings database, see the recording with synchronized transcriptions (as subtitles), and all the stored metadata, including detected emotions of the speech segments.

In this contribution the architecture of the Slovak BN-ATRS solution and used combination of algorithms are described. And finally the future work and new ideas, on which the speech processing team on our department is working now, are listed.

2 BN-ATRS Architecture

The Broadcast News Automatic Transcribing and Recording (BN-ATRS) service consists of servers with linear architecture, which means every module loads all the data and then stores the results, then the next module is launched (see Fig. 1). Now the audio processing side is in the evaluation period. So for now, the parallel processing is not necessary. In the future it will be useful to have real-time metadata producing engine, and then the architecture will be changed. All the processes are controlled with Perl scripts which are very easy to read and modify, also for new developers.

All modules could run on another platform or PC device because all data between modules goes trough files stored on specified available storage location.

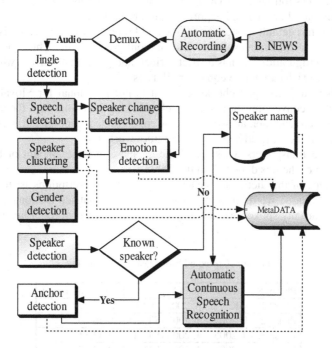

Fig. 1. Complete system architecture

3 Corpuses Used for the Service Development

3.1 Slovak KEMT-BN Database Collection

For development of the previously mentioned modules the KEMT-BN broadcast news corpus was used, which contains 52 hours (3-hours is a copy from BN-COST278 SK national part of the database) of broadcast news recordings annotated with 6 annotators (Hub4 transcription standard [12]). The annotation (except the COST278 part [13]) was not corrected, so the database could not be used as a reference at this time, but the corrections will be done soon [14].

The database was recorded from Slovak Television channel "Jednotka" using DVB-T Technisat Airstar PCI card from terrestrial broadcast on channel 44 in Košice region. The MPEG2 Transport stream is then truncated using Mpeg2Cut freeware, which removes the recording parts before and after the broadcast news jingles. This part was done manually, but we are working on jingle recognition module, which will automatically mark the beginning and the end of the TV show. Then the audio channel is de-multiplexed from the stream using MPEG Tools from "TMPGEnc" software resulting .mp2 file (48 kHz stereo 224 kbps CBR). According to compatibility with the COST278-BN database the audio is then resampled to 16 kHz (original: 48kHz stereo) and one channel using "sox" audio tool. Also the recording is recoded to "real media" format with 352x288 resolution for smaller file size.

Transcription process consists of manual orthographic transcriptions of the whole audio recording using resampled audio file and Transcriber freeware tool [15]. The annotation process follows the LDC transcription conventions for HUB4 [12]. Resulting file is xml based .trs file and exported .stm format, too.

Transcriber has default western encoding and French noise labels, so it is important for transcribers to load our evaluated Slovak configuration file. This was a problem because the configuration file has a strict format, and gives many errors when loading an edited one, which can not be equal for all users.

Transcriber supports spell checking, but it is not functional for Slovak language due to encoding conversions problems. Spell checking was done with the text in spell checking software and then all word errors were corrected again in Transcriber. Solve this problem will be a big advantage in the future work, too.

There was 5 transcribers working on the database and the amount of transcribed data from each of them is depicted on the Table 1 below.

The statistics of the dictionary generated from the transcriptions is: total 371636 words; 47050 unique words in dictionary; 8239 words outside dictionary (not complete words, partially spoken words, ungrammatical terms or foreign language words or indexes).

Table 1. Collected broadcast news materials

Phase: Recording time (TV)	Duration [h:m:s]
COST278-SK: 5., 6. 2003 (TA3)	03:10:37
Phase 2: 11. 2004 – 3. 2005 (STV1)	10:26:00
Phase 3: 10. 2005 – 4. 2006 (STV1)	05:42:11
Phase 4: 8. 2006 – 4. 2007 (STV1)	32:23:17
Summary	51:42:06

The KEMT-BN database contains 21 hours (1-hour is a copy from BN-COST278 SK) of clean speech (F0 – prepared speech in studio environment [16]). Also the transcription of the next BN shows for KEMT-BN database is always in progress. The database includes audio, video, and manually annotated metadata (except emotional states now).

3.2 Slovak Textual Database Collection for Slovak Language Model Training

The language database necessary for Slovak automatic continuous speech recognition engine is partly the Slovak language corpus. The Slovak language corpus contains whole books and other Slovak texts (copyrighted) so we can use only extracted statistical information from the Slovak sentences in the corpus. Our additionally collected language corpus contains 400MB of corrected newspapers texts (using RSS feeds). We collected Slovak National Corpus statistical data of the words in sentences using our inspected scripts (certified for collecting only the statistics) running on the corpus with cooperation with the corpus administrators. The corrected newspapers texts database collecting is in progress on every day basis.

The correction of the texts means mainly converting the numbers to the specified written form in correct case and type (date, time, quantity, etc.), and elimination of the tables or picture captions from the texts.

Also the corrected and converted annotations from KEMT-BN database will be added to the language corpus automatically in the future. Now we are testing the recognition engine on the whole KEMT-BN database, so adding the texts to the language model training database will lead to inaccurate results.

4 Modules of the System

There are 6 functional audio processing modules, which extract the metadata from the audio materials recorder from the TV news broadcasters: speech segment detection, speaker change detection, gender detection, speaker clustering, speaker detection and finally the Slovak automatic continuous speech recognition module. The emotion detection and anchor verification modules are in development phase now; the jingle detection module is in the research phase.

4.1 Speech Segment Detection

To avoid detecting the speaker name or any other metadata for segments without a speech, the speech detection module performs speech-nonspeech segmentation. The input for the speech-nonspeech detection is the whole (approximately 20 minutes) audio recording, which is segmented during the process of speech detection.

The speech segment detection was done using the HTK tools [17]. From 1 to 64 mixtures (12 MFCC) HMM models was trained on 2 hours of training Slovak BN database using 3, 5 and 7 - state ergodic/left-right models for speech and non-speech and the results was compared. The tests for special acoustic models for all focus (background F0 - FX) conditions (12 models = 6 for speech + 6 for non-speech) were also made, but the results were comparable as for 2 models (speech/non-speech).

Results from the best acoustic models (7state ergodic) trained on BN database was finally: Speech 98.3%, Non-speech 59.2% of correct classification.

The speech segments results were not used for next module of speaker change detection, but it will be used and the results will be compared, and then the value of our speech detection module will be clarified.

4.2 Speaker Change Detection

For speaker change detection, the 2-pass DISTBIC algorithm was used. In the first pass of the algorithm the symmetric Kullback-Liebler deviation (KL2) [18] was computed from 12 MFCC coefficients (the same coefficients as in the previous module). In the second pass the Bayesian information criteria (BIC) helps to identify the borders of one speaker segment. The algorithm was tested in Matlab and then rewritten to C++ and compiled for universal use in the system.

The results for the best evaluated parameters from all tests were: Recall: 71.3%, Precision: 64%, F measure: 68% (see Fig. 2). As it was mentioned before, the speech detection results (using only speech segments) may increase these values, and the speaker change detection results will be then compared and finally the process will be also revised.

4.3 Speaker Clustering

The speaker clustering module is responsible for joining together in one set, all segments originating in one speaker. The inputs for this module are the speaker segments from speaker change detection module. The 5 state ergodic HMM models were used to model every speaker segment and then to identify which segments belong to one speaker, which name is not known at this time. The classification of different speaker modules is done using 12 MFCC coefficients, which are again the same as in all previous modules.

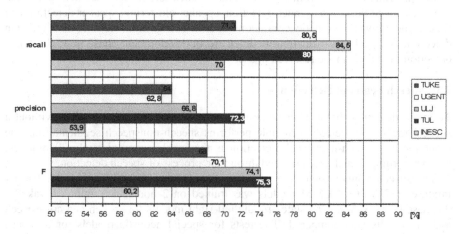

Fig. 2. Speaker change detection (2-pass DISTBIC algorithm) performance using Precision, Recall and F measures comparing to other institutions from COST-278 project (University Ghent, Ljubljana, Liberec and INESC Lisabon)

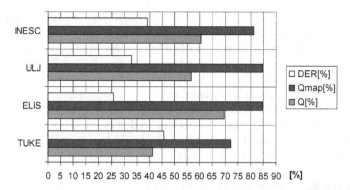

Fig. 3. Speaker clustering performance using DER, Q and Qmap measures comparing to other institutions from COST-278 project (INESC Lisabon, University Ljubljana and ELIS – Ghent University)

The results for the best evaluated parameters of the recognition module using hierarchical aglometative clustering method were: Q measure was 41.3%, Q-map was 72.3% and DER (diarization error rate) was 45.6% (see Fig. 3). The algorithm needs to be tuned for better results, changing the decision parameters and also the method of identifying the same speaker segments.

4.4 Gender Detection

For gender detection algorithm the HMM models for *male, female* and *other* was trained on 2 hours of BN Slovak data. The 7-state ergodic models contain 12 MFCC coefficients and 64 PDF mixtures.

The results for model trained on 2 hours data were: Male 98.2% of correct identification, Female 98.7% and the accuracy was 98.4.

As we mentioned before these results were made from detecting the models on the whole recording, not only on speech segments or only on one speaker segment. The next steps will be testing the gender detection on clustered speaker sets and testing the detection on speaker change detection results (one speaker segments). Then the results will be compared, and the process will be also evaluated and tuned.

4.5 Speaker Detection

The speaker detection algorithm was tested using GMM models and MFCC coefficients (from 128 to 1024 mixtures). During the evaluation also RASTA classifiers was tested, but the results was not satisfactory.

The GMM models were trained on SPEECH-DAT (E)-SK database [19] (telephone speech) using 50 speakers and a small recorded database of 30 speakers. Testing was realized on SPEECH-DAT database (on other 50 speakers) and the result was 98% accuracy, and testing on a new recorded database of 30 speakers was about 96% accuracy. In the new recorded database was only a small amount of speakers and every speaker has about 3 minutes of training speech and a minute of testing speech. The small database was recorded for department testing purposes.

In the next steps the BN speaker database will be built and the testing on the BN database segments, clustered with speaker clustering module, will be used for testing the speaker detection robustness. The BN database also needs to be corrected, because some speaker names were differently annotated during the manual transcribing process of the KEMT-BN database [16] (in annotations there are for example: M. Pleva, Matúš Pleva, Matus Pleva, Pleva Matus, etc.).

In the next phase the "Anchor verification" module will be built, to verify the anchor speech segments, and than the personalized acoustic models could be used for speech recognition engine, for example. This should lead to increasing of the Slovak continuous automatic language transcriptions accuracy for the anchor [2].

4.6 Automatic Continuous Speech Recognition

The module of Slovak automatic continuous speech recognition engine was built in conjunction with spoken language dialogue system development [20] based on SpeechDat [19] and MobilDat [20] triphone acoustic models. We tested HMM triphone acoustic models trained on SpeechDat [19] (telephone speech from PSTN line) and models trained on KEMT-BN database will be also tested in the next step.

The continuous speech recognition also needs the language model. There was unigram, bigram and trigram language models trained using the statistical information from Slovak National Corpus (SNC) [22] and 400MB of corrected newspapers texts (using RSS feeds). The unigram, bigram & trigram language models were trained on Slovak national corpus only and then also on combined language database (SNC & RSS) and the results were compared. The decrease of the WER (Word Error Rate) for the combined database (SNC & RSS) was caused by the domain specific newspapers texts, too. The language models were trained on most frequently used words in the corpus from 60k to 240k and the results and RTx (real-time) factor were compared.

Firstly, the testing was done using the special recorded testing database (approximately 100 minutes) 750 sentences database recorded by one speaker from PSTN line (according to training model type), reading newspapers texts, which were not the same texts as in the text corpus for the used language model.

Next, also the testing on the whole KEMT-BN database were done. The transcribed texts from the KEMT-BN database were not in the training corpus for the Slovak language model.

The recognition engine [23] has no morphological data, which are very important for inflective languages as Slovak language is. In the future the Slovak morphological database will be prepared and used for the Slovak recognition engine [24]. The Slovak morphological database building will accelerate the automatic morphology annotator for Slovak language [25], on which the language processing team is working now.

The best result for the special recorded testing database was reached using bigram language model (built on combined language database SNC & RSS with 240k most frequently used words) where WER was: 26.6% (see Fig. 4).

The model with the best results from special recorded testing database was used for testing on the 52 hours KEMT-BN database, too. The results were worse, also because the BN database has not corrected transcriptions, so they are also errors where recognized word does not match because of the bad transcription. Even though, the result for the whole 52 hours of KEMT-BN recordings was 49.9% WER. And the result for clean prepared studio speech (F0 acoustic condition) was 39.9% WER.

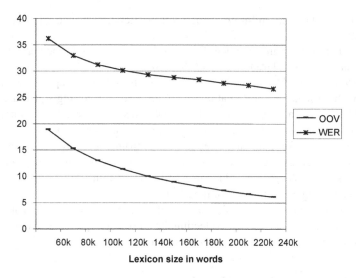

Fig. 4. Slovak continuous speech recognition performance when testing on the special recorded testing database (using bigram language & triphones acoustical models) using WER (Word Error Rate) and OOV (Out of Vocabulary words) measures

There were also comparative tests made for grapheme and phoneme language models [26] and the result is that the WER value for grapheme model was better for bigram but worse for unigram and trigram models. We are working on mixed grapheme and phoneme model optimized for Slovak language.

4.7 Emotion Detection

The emotion detection module development is in progress. The recording of posed emotions in 16 neutral sentences was done for only 30 speakers for now (male/female, different ages, accents), using 4 emotional states (angry, neutral, happiness, sad) and 4 background conditions (home, quiet, public place, office). Only a short-time analysis [28] using the 5-state ergodic HMM models was done with 49% accuracy. This module is in the development phase and will be trained on a big spontaneous emotional database after the annotation will be done from the live TV discussions.

The non-verbal information about the emotion of the spoken speech segment could give the hearing impaired users of the BN database a better understanding of the automatic transcribed texts, which could lead to better information efficiency.

5 Management of the Database

The BN database should be a living base of everyday updated audio visual materials with automatically generated metadata. A part of the database is also a corrected training set for building the acoustic and language models. Secondly a part of the corrected database is also a testing set for evaluation of the system. Of course all data needs to be available to end-users trough a user friendly interface, for example as a web portal.

All this data needs a management for presentation, managing the corrected set and recording and automated transcribing of the new BN shows.

Presentation module – could be a website with searching capabilities and video preview with all metadata presentation, including a section for registered users, where they could also assign a wrong data, which could be sent to error correction module.

Error correction module – saves information about all wrong segments assigned during the process for manual correction (also from registered users on website), manage the manual corrections of not corrected metadata set, manage manually corrected data set, which could be added to KEMT-BN training database set, manage the training and testing corrected part of the database.

Recording module – responsible for everyday recording and segmentation for the automatic annotation service, and collecting the shows and the metadata to the presentation part of the database (not manually corrected data set).

6 Conclusion and Future Work

There is a lot of work that needs to be done before the service will be started as a website for end-users. First of all, the emotion detection, speaker identification and anchor verification modules need to be finished to the final state and precisely serialized using a script language or any other development tool. Also modules for using personalized acoustic models (speakers' database with trained acoustic models) for continuous speech recognition should increase the functionality of the service. After correcting the KEMT-BN database also the BN acoustic models for speaker and speech recognition modules will be trained and tested.

The speech processing team is working also on collecting manually corrected logs (audio logs and corresponding ASR recognized texts) from IRKR Automatic Interactive Voice Response (IVR) server [20] and then they could be used for re-training of ASR server's acoustic models with real spontaneous IVR telephone user recordings.

For acceleration of the acoustic models generating, using BN shows recordings (for example personalized models for the anchors); the Transcriptor tool development is in progress. This tool will provide automatic Slovak phonetic transcription and phonetic dictionary generation or optimized Slovak mixed phoneme/grapheme dictionary for best recognition results (according to similar phoneme to grapheme recognition performance for Slovak language [29]).

The final project activities will be oriented to tune the tested system. We will try to select the best available solution and increase the robustness of the solution, according to the first users' feedback, and publish all the results on the project website.

Acknowledgements

Research described in the paper was supported by the Slovak Ministry of Education under research projects AV 4/0006/07, VEGA 1/4054/07 and MVTS COST2102/07.

References

1. Nouza, J., Nejedlova, D., Zdansky, J., Kolorenc, J.: Very Large Vocabulary Speech Recognition System for Automatic Transcription of Czech Broadcast. In: Proceedings of ICSLP 2004, Jeju Island, Korea, October 2004, pp. 409–412 (2004) ISSN 1225-441x
2. Nouza, J., Zdansky, J., Cerva, P., Kolorenc, J.: Continual on-line monitoring of Czech spoken broadcast programs. In: INTERSPEECH-2006, paper 1478-Wed1CaP.13 (2006)
3. Seymore, K., Chen, S., Doh, S.J., Eskenazi, M., Gouvea, E., Raj, B., Ravishankar, M., Rosenfeld, R., Siegler, M., Stern, R., Thayer, E.: The 1997 CMU Sphinx-3 English Broadcast News transcription system. In: Proceedings of the DARPA Speech Recognition Workshop (1998)
4. Gauvain, J.-L.: The LIMSI 1999 Hub-4E Transcription System. In: Proceedings of DARPA Speech Transcription Workshop 2000 (2000)
5. Gauvain, J.L., Lamel, L., Adda, G.: The LIMSI Broadcast News Transcription System. In: Speech Communication (2002),
   http://citeseer.ist.psu.edu/gauvain02limsi.html
6. McTait, K., Adda-Decker, M.: The 300k LIMSI German Broadcast News Transcription System. In: Eurospeech 2003, Genova,
7. Huerta, J.M., Thayer, E., Ravishankar, M., Stern, R.M.: The Development of the 1997 CMU Spanish Broadcast News Transcription System. In: Proceedings of the DARPA Broadcast News Transcription and Understanding Workshop, Landsdowne, Virginia (February 1998)
8. Meinedo, H., Caseiro, D., Neto, J., Trancoso, I.: AUDIMUS.media: a broadcast news speech recognition system for the European Portuguese language. In: Mamede, N.J., Baptista, J., Trancoso, I., Nunes, M.d.G.V. (eds.) PROPOR 2003. LNCS, vol. 2721, pp. 9–17. Springer, Heidelberg (2003)
9. Riedler, J., Katsikas, S.: Development of a Modern Greek Broadcast-News Corpus and Speech Recognition System. In: Nivre, J., Kaalep, H.-J., Muischnek, K., Koit, M. (eds.) Proceedings of the 16th Nordic Conference of Computational Linguistics NODALIDA 2007, pp. 380–383. University of Tartu, Tartu (2007)
10. Marcello, F.: A System for the Retrieval of Italian Broadcast News. Speech Communication 33(1-2) (2000)
11. Brugnara, F., Cettolo, M., Federico, M., Giuliani, D.: Advances in automatic transcription of Italian broadcast news. In: Proceedings of ICSLP, Beijing, China, vol. II, pp. 660–663 (2000)
12. Che, C., Yuk, D., Chennoukh, S., Flanagan, J.: Development of the RU Hub4 system. In: Proceedings of DARPA Speech Recognition Workshop (1997)
13. Zibert, J., Mihelic, F., Martens, J.-P., Meinedo, H., Neto, J., Docio, L., Garcia-Mateo, C., David, P., Zdansky, J., Pleva, M., Cizmar, A., Zgank, A., Kacic, Z., Teleki, C., Vicsi, K.: COST278 broadcast news segmentation and speaker clustering evaluation. In: Interspeech 2005 Proceedings of the 9th European Conference on Speech Communication and Technology, Lisboa, pp. 629–632. Universität Bonn, Bonn (2005)
14. Pitz, M., Molau, S., Schluter, R., Ney, H.: Automatic transcription verification of broadcast news and similar speech corpora. In: Proceedings of the DARPA Broadcast News Workshop (March 1999)
15. Manta, M., Antoine, F., Galliano, S., Barras, C., Geoffrois, E., Liberman, M., Wu, Z.: Transcriber tool website,
   http://trans.sourceforge.net/en/presentation.php

16. Pleva, M., Juhár, J., Čižmár, A.: Slovak broadcast news speech corpus for automatic speech recognition. In: RTT 2007: Research in Telecommunication Technology: 8th international conference: Žilina - Liptovský Ján, Slovak Republic, September 10-12, 2007, pp. 334–337 (2007) ISBN 978-80-8070-735-4

17. Young, S.: ATK: An application Toolkit for HTK, version 1.3. Cambridge University, Cambridge (2004)

18. Žibert, J., Mihelič, F.: Development, Evaluation and Automatic Segmentation of Slovenian Broadcast News Speech Database. In: Proceedings of the 7th International Multi-Conference Information Society IS 2004, Jozef Stefan Institute, Ljubljana, Slovenia, October 13th - 14th 2004, vol. B, pp. 72–78 (2004) ISBN 961-6303-64-3

19. Pollak, P., Černocký, J., Boudy, J., Choukri, K., Rusko, M., Trnka, M.: SpeechDat(E) „Eastern European Telephone Speech Databases. In: Proceedings of LREC 2000 Satellite workshop XLDB - Very large Telephone Speech Databases, Athens, Greece, pp. 20–25 (May 2000)

20. Juhár, J., Ondáš, S., Čižmár, A., Rusko, M., Rozinaj, G., Jarina, R.: Development of Slovak GALAXY/VoiceXML based spoken language dialogue system to retrieve information from the Internet. In: Interspeech 2006 - ICSLP, Pittsburgh, Pennsylvania, USA, September 17-21, pp. 485–488. Universität Bonn, Bonn (2006) ISSN 1990-9772

21. Rusko, M., Trnka, M., Darjaa, S.: MobilDat-SK - A Mobile Telephone Extension to the SpeechDat-E SK Telephone Speech Database in Slovak. In: SPEECOM 2006, Sankt Petersburg, Russia (July 2006) (accepted)

22. Simkova, M.: Slovak National Corpus – history and current situation. In: Insight into Slovak and Czech Corpus Linguistics, Bratislava: Veda, pp. 152–159 (2005)

23. Mirilovič, M., Lihan, S., Juhár, J., Čižmár, A.: Slovak speech recognition based on Sphinx-4 and SpeechDat-SK. In: Proceedings of DSP-MCOM 2005 international conference, Košice, Slovakia, pp. 76–79 (Septembert 2005)

24. Mirilovič, M., Juhár, J., Čižmár, A.: Steps towards the stochastic language modeling in Slovak. In: Proceedings of ECMS 2007: 8th International Workshop on Electronics, Control, Modeling, Measurement and Signals, May 21-23, 2007, p. 19. Technical University of Liberec, Liberec (2007) ISBN 978-80-7372-202-9

25. Mirilovič, M., Juhár, J., Čižmár, A.: Automatic segmentation of Slovak words into morphemes. In: Proceedings of RTT 2007: Research in Telecommunication Technology: 8th international conference, Žilina - Liptovský Ján, Slovak Republic, September 10-12, 2007, pp. 259–263 (2007) ISBN 978-80-8070-735-4

26. Zgank, A., Kacic, Z., Diehl, F., Juhar, J., Lihan, S., Vicsi, K., Szaszak, G.: Graphemes as basic units for crosslingual speech recognition. In: Proceedings of ASIDE 2005: ISCA Tutorial and Research Workshop (ITRW), 10th and 11th November 2005, pp. 23–27. Aalborg University, Aalborg (2005)

27. Hain, T., Woodland, P.C.: Segmentation and Classification of Broadcast News Audio. In: Proceedings of ICSLP 1998 - 5th International Conference on Spoken Language Processing, Sydney, Australia, November 30 - December 4 (1998)

28. Navas, E., Hernaéz, I., Luengo, I., Sainz, I., Saraxaga, I., Sanchez, J.: Meaningful Parameters in Emotion Characterisation. In: Esposito, A., Faundez-Zanuy, M., Keller, E., Marinaro, M. (eds.) COST Action 2102. LNCS (LNAI), vol. 4775, pp. 74–84. Springer, Heidelberg (2007)

29. Lihan, S., Juhár, J., Čižmár, A.: Comparison of Slovak and Czech speech recognition based on grapheme and phoneme acoustic models. In: Proceedings of Interspeech 2006 ICSLP: Proceedings of the Ninth International Conference on Spoken Language Processing, Pittsburgh, Pensylvania, USA, September 17-21, 2006, pp. 149–152. Universität Bonn, Bonn (2006)

Computational Stylometry:
Who's in a Play?

Carl Vogel and Gerard Lynch

Centre for Computing and Language Studies,
School of Computer Science and Statistics,
Trinity College Dublin, Dublin 2 Ireland
{vogel,gplynch}@tcd.ie

Abstract. Automatic text classification techniques are applied to the problem of quantifying strength of characterization within plays, using a case study of the works of four sample playwrights that are freely available in machine-readable form. Strong characters are those whose speeches constitute homogeneous categories in comparison with other characters—their speeches are more attributable to themselves than to their play or their author.

Keywords: Computational stylistics, text classification, forensic linguistics.

1 Introduction

We report on experiments in text classification for computational stylistics. Automatic text classification techniques are fervently under research, development and exploitation, widely used in their current state for a wide range of tasks: authorship attribution, lexicography, news analysis, spam filtering, sentiment analysis, ontology extraction, social network analysis. The tasks, whatever similarity metric is employed, in general have common features: assessment of similarity of a text to a category of texts with a quantifiable degree of certainty, assessment of homogeneity of categories. In our work, we have been extending methods from the literature in assessing the former, and have adopted a common-sense approach to the latter, with respect to both the *a priori* category appropriate to a category, and the categories that are appropriate *post hoc* by virtue of clustering under the objective similarity metrics. Interestingly, many of the successful similarity metrics are based on comparisons of distributions of sub-lexical features— letter n-gram distributions and not directly lexical or part of speech distributions.

The work described here uses computational stylometry to assess the homogeneity of individual textual contributions of characters in dramatic works, and hence the heterogeneity of characters and plays constructed by authors, thus contributing a new kind of analysis to computational stylistics. Moreover, the techniques discussed here have applications outside dramatic or other literary works. We have, for example, applied them to measuring a spectrum of non-governmental political parties on the basis of their election manifestos, for example [23], within a robust area of research in contemporary political science [13,12]. The methods are related to those explored in work on forensic linguistics for authorship attribution [2,3]. They have further potential application in the domain of human-computer interaction in assessing intelligent avatars.

A. Esposito et al. (Eds.): HH and HM Interaction 2007, LNAI 5042, pp. 169–186, 2008.

Recent work in this area focuses on alignment of behavior (verbal and nonverbal) of artificial agents interacting with humans [17], as humans experience some degree of conversational alignment in human-human interactions. Just as these techniques have been applied to measuring the degree of alignment in such human interactions [8], they can also be used to evaluate the levels of realism in alignment in human-machine interactions. Presumably one would like to parameterize the functionality of avatars' adaptive verbal behaviors so that some may become indistinguishable from those of their interlocutor, and others may retain their designed distinctive style of communication.

Here we examine these techniques as applied to questions of stylistics. This follows on from recent work in classifying poems within a single author's writings in terms of the poetic persona constructed within and across poems [26]. There it was found using directly comparable techniques that distinctive persona could be individuated within and across poems in the canon of Brendan Kennelly, clustering in positive correlation with subjective reading of the poetry. Separate from the questions of whether one individual is responsible for the complete works of Shakespeare, or whether that one individual was William Shakespeare, there are questions about that canon associated with its attributed greatness that are worth exploring using objective techniques. The question of whether the corpus of Shakespeare plays is homogeneous is really one about the probability that all of the works were authored by the same person. More finely grained questions can be posed with respect to characterization within the plays. For example, it may well be the case that the constraints of iambic pentameter impose constraints on sub-lexical features of the texts that render individual characterization impossible, bar use of proper nouns.

We explore characterization within plays that are confined to metric verse, (Jonson and Shakespeare) and those not in verse at all (Wilde and Shaw). Of course, in such a limited sample, any results that emerge might have to do with the issue of being verse or prose, time of writing, national heritage of the author, or other predictable or unpredicted confounding factors. Nonetheless, we think this is a useful starting point in a larger scale analysis of this sort. In particular, we are interested in applying the question of textual similarity and homogeneity to characters within plays. We quantify the extent to which, for example, the texts associated with Romeo are most like Romeo, as opposed to texts of other Shakespearean characters or characters of the other playwrights analyzed, most like *Romeo and Juliet* as opposed to the other plays considered, and most like the Shakespearean canon. We do so for each character, play and author.

The findings are that the characterization provided by George Bernard Shaw was significantly distinctive. The specific results depend on the number of files under consideration, as elaborated in the rest of the paper. For example, individuating files into unbroken word units of approximately 1,000 letters, spaces and punctuation marks, the most homogeneous character in the set of plays considered was Merc in *Cynthia's Revels*. The next most distinctive characters are: Tuc from Jonson's *Poetaster* (ironically enough); Octavius from Shaw's *Man and Superman*, Rufio from *Caesar and Cleopatra*, and Androcles from *Androcles and the Lion*; Shakespeare's King Henry from *Henry the VII, Part I*. If the files are individuated at twice the size, then some characters are removed from consideration (see "Methods" section) because there is insufficient associated text to have at least five files in that *a priori* category, and this has an impact on homogeneity of the remainder, yet Shaw's Rufio remains consistent. Jonson has the most distinctive character, and Shaw the greatest number of such characters.

If one were to apply an aesthetic judgment to the form of analysis constructed here it would be attached to the capacity of a writer to develop distinct homogeneous characters. On this analysis, the playwright is remarkable to the extent that the characters are distinct and more identifiable with the rest of the character's constructed speech than with their playwright. Identifiability of characters with their play, on the basis of textual similarity alone, is a measure of the individuality of that play within the writer's canon. That is, the background aesthetic considered here is that a combination of internal homogeneity within characterization and within-canon heterogeneity of texts jointly contribute to objectively measurable indices of a writer's control over language. In terms of methodology, the outcome is clear that the number of categories chosen from has an impact on the likelihood of homogeneous categories emerging, and correspondingly interacts with the method used for assessing homogeneity.

We briefly describe the background to the analytical tools we use, then give details on the exact method we used to individuate files and analyze them. The file sizes employed are small, in part because this is representative of the demands of attribution tasks in forensic linguistics; first we report on an experiment with files of about 1000 bytes per file, and five files per character, then a second set of experiments replicates the study with double the file size, and a third set of experiments limits the total number of available files (some sources are larger and have more possibilities from which to sample). We present the results in more detail, and then emphasize the main results. The methods do appear to reveal homogeneity in author style in that the plays are more distinctive of their authors, in general, than the characters are to their plays, in the small pool of literature considered here. Secondly, the precise findings per character, given their heterogeneity, is highly dependent on the sampling parameters, particularly the number of files to draw on to constitute an *a priori* category.[1]

2 Background

We assume a method for parsing plays into the contributions of their characters [15]. This method allows us to individuate characters of plays by their entire textual contribution, separated into files of balanced size. The text associated with characters in the plays is divided into units that we can sample arbitrarily. The analysis we employ is based on letter n-gram distributions. This follows from our exploration of suggestions in the literature that this level of tokenization is most efficacious for authorship attribution tasks in forensic linguistics, and because of replicability, fit for the Daubert test of expert evidence in a court of law [2]. The suite of programs we have developed allows tokenization by n-grams for arbitrary values of n at the level of letter, word, or part of speech tag (we use TreeTagger [21] and its English parameter file, in general; however, here we report only on letter unigram analysis). At first blush, comparison of letter

---

[1] For ease of expression, we refer to files of a character "finding their character", "finding their play" or "finding their author" among natural *a priori* classifications, and we also examine instances of maximal similarity to alternative categories (other characters, plays or authors) represented in the data set.

unigram distributions do not seem to offer great face validity as a procedure through which to measure textual similarity. However, an individual with a Latinate vocabulary may be more inclined to use the words "equestrian" or "aquifer" than "horse-riding" or "water-table", and will thus have a distinctive distribution of the letters Q and U, for example. Letter bigram analysis perhaps more directly approximates English morphology expressed orthographically; however, bigrams have unigrams as constituents, and not all morphemes are limited to two-letter sequences. This is not to say that bigram analysis is fruitless. On the contrary, we employ it regularly. For example, [7] uses an analysis quite like the one reported here, but addressed to documents rather than characters within documents, employing mainly letter bigrams in an analysis of a large diachronic corpus of Latin texts to date "The Donation of Constantine"; there the techniques evaluate favorably, corroborating philological theory dating from the 15th Century [4], placing the text as a relatively good 8th century forgery of a 4th century style. One could also use word level analysis (and words also have letters as constituents), but this introduces the problem of lemmatization of words, and other issues about how to individuate distinct types, issues that do not emerge at the level of letters. Part-of-speech analysis would also be possible, but reliable automatic tagging of Shakespearean text is not promising, and hand tagging is prohibitive. Independent evidence also exists for a relationship between part of speech distributions and letter sequence distributions, to the extent that orthography is representative of natural language phonology: recently it has been shown that nouns and verbs tend to cluster as grammatical categories on the basis of phonological properties of the words in those categories [5]. Thus, sublexical features are relevant to higher level linguistic categories in a number of respects. Whichever level of tokenization chosen, selecting larger values for n creates greater data sparseness problems. We have argued (and are not alone in arguing) for the merits of letters as an appropriate and efficacious level of tokenization, and within that we have worked with unigrams and bigrams extensively.[2] As the results have largely been consistent across choices of n for letter-tokenization, we have tended to report, as we do here, on representative results within a single choice for n. Here, it is letter unigram analysis.

The assessment of similarity among distributions of tokens in general is adopted from work using word frequency distributions [11,10]. The method [25] computes a χ^2 value (which thus relativizes to file size) that accumulates for each token compared between two files and in the end divides by the total number of comparisons. Suppose one has two files, 1 and 2, $| 1 |$ and $| 2 |$ denote the number of tokens in each file and $|| 1 ||$ and $|| 2 ||$ denote the total number of distinct tokens in each file (or in other words, the total number of token-types in each file; necessarily, $|| i || \leq | i |$ for any file i). The total number of token-types (TTT) between the two files is given in (1)

(1) $TTT \doteq || 1 || + || 2 ||$

If k token-type and i is a file, let $o(i, k)$ denote the number of observed instances of that type in file i. If two files come from the same population, then taking into account file size differences, the observed value for any token type should yield expected values

---

[2] Nonetheless, we also explore the other levels of tokenization and sequence length, but do not undertake each level of analysis for each study.

within a certain range. Let $e(i, k)$ be the expected number of observations of tokens of type k in file i. Thus (2) gives the expected number of occurences of an individual type in the first file, and (3) gives the method to calculate the expected values for the second file in the two files being compared.

(2) $e(1, k) \doteq (o(1, k) + o(2, k)) * \frac{|1|}{|1|+|2|}$

(3) $e(2, k) \doteq (o(1, k) + o(2, k)) * \frac{|2|}{|1|+|2|}$

So, suppose two files of different sizes—file 1 might have 100 instances of Q in its 1000 letters and 2 might have 12 instances of Q in its 4000 letters. The expected value of Q for 1 is 112 * 1000/5000, or about 22, while the expected value for file 2 is 112 * 4/5, or about 90. The actual χ^2 value pools expected and observed values across token types as in (4), to measure how far the distribution actually is from what it would be if the texts are drawn from the same population at random.

(4)

$$\sum_{k=1}^{TTT} \left(\frac{(o(1, k) - e(1, k))^2}{e(1, k)} + \frac{(o(2, k) - e(2, k))^2}{e(2, k)} \right)$$

The sum in (4), divided by the number of degrees of freedom, $(TTT - 1)$ gives a cumulative χ^2 value as a measure of similarity between the two files. When the value is less than the significance cut off point (3.86) normally used to assess whether two distributions are significantly different, one can infer that the two files are not significantly different in their distributions of the tokens.[3] The value is computed for all pairwise comparisons of files and can be used as a rank index of similarity of files within categories. Given a collection of files, the files have natural *a priori* categories (all speeches by the same politician [9], all segments of the same political party manifesto [23], all texts on a comparable legislative topic [16] all composed by the same writer, all comprising the text of one character's contribution, etc). This averaged χ^2 value provides an index that can be used to rank order the compatibility of each file with respect to its *a priori* category and alternatives. A file treated in this respect can have statistically significant compatibility (using the Mann-Whitney rank ordering test) with a number of categories. A separate test is conducted to quantify the significance of a subset of files from a category being classified in the same way. The common-sense method we use to assess category homogeneity, whether evaluation of an *a priori* category or to test the likelihood of objective clustering on the basis of mutual similarity using the χ^2 method with some other category, is in relation to the fairness of a c-sided coin (where c is the number of possible categories) in repeated experiments of n tosses (where n is the number of files in the category; and r is the number of times that the category comes

---

[3] It is an average χ^2 over each comparison of individual token-types and their frequencies in the two files. It is also possible to examine the specific points, the specific token types, at which the files differ significantly. But for this reasoning and rejecting the null hypothesis of similarity, the normal constraints on χ^2 hypothesis testing apply, like having a minimum of five observed values in both cells. This constraint does not apply when using the value as an index of similarity instead.

up as a best fit). The Bernoulli formula is given in (5), where the fairness/randomness hypothesis associated with the c-sided coin can be rejected when a category comes up often enough for the value of p such that $p \leq 0.05$. In practice, we actually simulate the experiments of tossing c-sided coins for the category size related number of tosses hundreds of times to establish the cut-off point to use in determining significance for some number of files to be classified within *a priori* or *a posteriori* categories [24].

$$(5) \quad p \doteq \frac{n!}{r!(n-r)!} \times \left(\frac{1}{c}\right)^r \times \left(1 - \frac{1}{c}\right)^{n-r}$$

We thus begin by individuating a corpus under scrutiny into individual files, and relevant categories. In the experiments here the files are of balanced size, and with an equal number of files in each category. In each case, the files are determined by arbitrary selection of contiguous subsets of a character's contributions to a play. We explore whether the files so constructed for a character are more like the other files of that character or some other character in the pool; whether the files of that character are more like those of the rest of the play the character appears in or the other plays; whether the files of character are more like those of the rest of the author of the character than those of the other authors under consideration.

3   Method

Project Gutenberg[4] provides the source of the plays considered here: *Androcles and the Lyon, Caesar and Cleopatra, Candida, Man and Superman* and *Pygmalion* (Shaw); *An Ideal Husband, The Importance of Being Earnest, Lady Windermere's Fan* and *A Woman of No Importance* (Wilde); *The Alchemist, Cynthia's Revels* and *Poetaster* (Jonson). We also include a gamut of Shakespeare's plays.[5] Selections were made to have three or four Shakespeare works at a time for some experiments, as described below. We did not control for type by selecting from among the histories only, or tragedies only, say. The plays were parsed into files of the consecutive lines of speech associated with individual characters [15]. Sampling from the characters was constrained to occur only when the character was represented by sufficient text for the experiment at hand. In the first instance, each character was represented by five thousand letters (including spaces and punctuation), divided into five files each.

A second range of experiments replicated this using double the file size. Similarly, we look at whether the characters' files find firstly their plays and secondly authors. To examine the role of sampling, we repeat the experiment with an alternative sampling from the same data set. Importantly, the sampling in each case is randomized, so the same segments of each character are not necessarily repeated in each experiment. This

---

[4] http://www.gutenberg.org/ – Last verified October 27, 2007.

[5] They were: *Anthony and Cleopatra, As You Like It, Comedy of Errors, Coriolanus, Cymbeline, Hamlet, Henry the 4th Part1, Henry the 4th Part2, Henry the 6th Part1, Henry the 6th Part2, Henry The Eighth, Henry The Fifth, Julius Caesar, King John, King Lear, Loves Labor Lost, Macbeth, Measure for Measure, Merchant of Venice, A Midsummernight's Dream, Much Ado about Nothing, Othello, Richard The Second, Richard The Third, Romeo and Juliet, Taming of the Shrew, The Tempest, Timon of Athens, Titus Andronicus, Twelfth Night, The Winter's Tale.*

is because if the character is homogeneous, for example, then homogeneity should be robust across samples. This sampling method resulted in a total of 1240 files used in the experiments in their entirety. In testing characters finding their authors, we first consider sampling from Shakespeare plays that balance samples against those available from other playwrights. We are interested in the best match and the most significant alternative match. As there were significantly more Shakespeare plays available via Project Gutenberg than those of the other writers, we constructed average comparisons using groups of four Shakespeare plays chosen arbitrarily in a series of 100 comparable experiments. Thus, the Shakespeare plays changed, while those of the other writers were held fixed.

The files are individuated as described above for all of the experiments. What varies is the sampling from them, and the relevant *a priori* category. In reporting results in the next section, it is sometimes helpful to present them using category cross-classification.

Experiment 1: Characters to themselves.

The *a priori* category assigned to sets of files is the name of the character speaking. This is repeated three times, each with five files per character and the number of characters per play depending on the availability of sufficient text. In the first test, the file sizes are 1KB and in the subsequent two independent samplings, the file sizes are balanced at 2KB. In this experiment, balancing by playwright is not performed. Thus, Shakespeare has many more characters under consideration. That should not impact a study of characters finding themselves (as opposed to characters finding their authors). While the same character or play may be represented in each of the three experiments, the same speech may well not, because of the balance in the size of the files sampled.

Experiment 2: Plays to their plays

The *a priori* category assigned to a file is the name of the play containing the speech. Thus, there are 42 categories. This is repeated three times exactly as above. We identify the play that is the overall significantly most similar in its constituent text (which is not necessarily the play itself), and the best matching alternative.

Experiment 3: Characters to their play.

The *a priori* category of a file is the name of the play the speech is part of. Sampling is based just on 2K file sizes. Of interest is which characters within plays are the strong ones: which characters' speeches are significantly identifiable with their play via overall textual similarity. Again, the "best match" alternative is noted.

Experiment 4: Characters to their author.

The *a priori* category is the author's name. Sampled files were 2K. We note which characters are significantly attributed to their author, and significant alternatives.

Experiment 5: Authors to themselves.

The *a priori* category is the author's name. Sampling is based just on 2K file sizes. We use 10 characters per playwright, 5 files to each character. Results shown average over 100 such samplings. Best alternatives are examined.

4   Results and Discussion

4.1   Experiment 1: Characters Find Themselves

Table 1 indicates the number of characters examined across the 42 plays addressed who turned up as distinctive. In this table, we consider by play, a number of characters from

Table 1. Number of Homogeneous Characters from Each Play ($\frac{\text{\# Homogeneous}}{\text{\# Considered}}$)

Play	1K	2K I	2K II
TheAlchemist	0/6	1/3	1/3
CynthiasRevels	3/10	3/5	2/5
Poetaster	4/10	1/4	1/4
Androcles	1/4	n/a	n/a
CaesarCleo	1/6	2/3	2/3
Candida	0/4	1/3	1/3
ManAndSuperman	6/13	4/7	4/7
Pygmalion	1/6	2/3	1/3
AWomanOfNoImportance	n/a	3/5	3/5
AnIdealHusband	2/7	1/4	2/4
Earnest	2/6	3/5	2/5
LadyWindermeresFan	0/5	1/4	2/4
AntCleo (WS)	0/4	1/4	2/4
AsYouLike	0/6	0/4	0/4
ComedyErrors	0/5	3/3	1/3
Coriolanus	1/7	3/6	0/6
Cymbeline	0/6	0/6	2/6
Hamlet	0/7	1/4	1/4
Henry4thPart1	0/5	2/4	1/4
Henry4thPart2	0/5	0/2	0/2
Henry6thPart1	3/5	0/2	0/1
Henry6thPart2	0/5	0/5	2/5

Play	1K	2K I	2K II
HenryTheEighth	1/5	0/3	1/3
HenryTheFifth	1/3	0/2	1/2
JuliusCaesar	1/4	0/3	0/3
KingJohn	1/3	2/3	0/3
KingLear	2/5	1/4	0/4
LovesLabor	1/8	0/4	0/4
Macbeth	0/3	0/2	0/2
Measures	0/4	0/4	0/4
MerchantVenice	2/6	0/3	0/3
MidSummerDream	1/6	0/1	n/a
MuchAdo	1/5	0/5	0/5
Othello	0/6	0/4	0/4
Richard2	0/7	0/3	0/3
RichardTheThird	1/8	0/5	0/5
RomeoJuliet	0/6	1/5	1/5
TameShrew	0/8	1/2	0/2
TheTempest	1/5	0/1	0/1
Timon	1/3	0/1	0/1
TitusAndronicus	1/6	0/4	1/4
TwelfthNight	1/6	1/5	1/5
WinterTale	0/8	2/5	2/5

the play with sufficient text to analyze. The entries indicate how many times the characters found themselves as their most similar category. Examining the results in terms of the plays they originate from provides a sense of the playwright's construction of strong characters across plays. The table's columns indicate results with file size selection at 1KB each, at twice that, and at twice that with a secondary arbitrary selection, as discussed above. The effect of doubling the selection size between the first column and the second two meant that some characters within plays did not supply sufficient text for the comparison. Where a play or characters from a play have been excluded on these grounds, because of insufficient data, the number of characters (indicated in the denominator in the ratios in the tabular entries) reduces from one column to the next. Results within a sampling size are stable. It is evident that few characters are particularly strong. A strikingly large number of Shaw's characters are self-homogeneous compared to other writers' characters and the total number of plays and characters considered. Jonson's are also strong.

The individual characters and their level of homogeneity are depicted in Table 2. In this table, just the results for the small file size is reported. The category sizes (five files per character) and total number of categories is such that homogeneity achieves significance in the c-sided fair coin tossing experiment described above for about one sixth of the characters considered. The first column of this table indicates the name of a character and the play from which the character originates. Only the significantly ($p < 0.05$) homogeneous characters are reported. There are 248 characters in total, so the changes of two files from its category out of the five, that each character is split into is already significant. Greater levels of consistent assignment (three, four or five of five) are very significant, and it is thus safe to reject the hypothesis that the files randomly fall into that character's category. This leaves the 41 characters reported in the table

Table 2. Files Assigned Correctly to Their Character

Character	Correct
AARONTitusAndronicus	2/5
AGUECHEEKTwelfthNight	2/5
APEMANTUSTimon	2/5
AUFIDIUSCoriolanus	2/5
BeatMuchAdo	2/5
CALIBANTheTempest	2/5
CONSTANCEKingJohn	2/5
OBERONMidSummerDream	2/5
PRINCESSOFFRANCELovesLabor	2/5
TALBOTHenry6thPart1	2/5
PUCELLEHenry6thPart1	2/5
KINGHENRYHenry6thPart1	4/5
PUCKMidSummerDream	2/5
QUEENELIZABETHRichardTheThird	2/5
PORTIAMerchantVenice	2/5
SHYLOCKMerchantVenice	2/5
ANTONYJuliusCaesar	3/5
BUCKINGHAMHenryTheEighth	3/5
CHORUSHenryTheFifth	3/5
LearKingLear	3/5
GlouKingLear	2/5

Character	Correct
AlbPoetaster	2/5
HorPoetaster	2/5
VirgPoetaster	2/5
TucPoetaster	4/5
ASOCynthiasRevels	2/5
CRICynthiasRevels	3/5
MERCynthiasRevels	5/5
ANDROCLESAndroclesLion	4/5
RUFIOCaesarCleo	4/5
ANAManAndSuperman	2/5
ANNManAndSuperman	3/5
DONJUANManAndSuperman	2/5
OCTAVIUSManAndSuperman	4/5
THESTATUEManAndSuperman	2/5
STRAKERManAndSuperman	2/5
MRSPEARCEPygmalion	2/5
LadyBracknellEarnest	2/5
GwendolenEarnest	3/5
MRSCHEVELEYAnIdealHusband	2/5
LADYCHILTERNAnIdealHusband	2/5

whose results were significant. What is interesting here is that most of the most famous Shakespearean characters do not make the list as self-homogeneous.

4.2 Experiment 2: Plays Find Their Play

Tables 3 shows the outcome for files finding their play. This is a measure of the distinctiveness of each play. All of the plays are listed, not just the ones that were significantly homogeneous. The results show that few plays are internally homogeneous: the play is not the thing. As an indication of how homogeneous an author's text is, it is useful to note the best match for false negatives (in this case, constituent files of a play assigned to some other play) with respect to the *a priori* category of play, happens to be to another play by the same author or another. Experiment 5 returns to this issue, but here it is clear that the Shakespeare plays find other Shakespeare plays, and Wilde plays find other Wildes, but Shaw's find Wilde about as much as Shaw, and Jonson finds mainly Shakespeare. This suggests heterogeneity in the text of Shaw, self-homogeneity for Shakespeare and Wilde, and homogeneity with respect to Shakespeare for Jonson. This is demonstrated in Table 4. Only the best alternative indicated—this is individuated as the most frequently nominated alternative category with highest rank ordering significance for each of the files not most similar to its *a priori* category. Consider *Hamlet*. Only eight of the 35 files in the 1K sample found the same play. Of the remaining 27, the most frequent alternative was *Cymbeline*. Both of the 2K samplings were such that none of the *Hamlet* files were most like other *Hamlet* files. In one, the best alternative for half was *Coriolanus* and in the other the best alternative was only one quarter of the files being most similar to *Cymbeline*. *Cymbeline* and *Coriolanus* were sampled

Table 3. Files of Plays Find Their Play ($\frac{\text{\# Correct}}{\text{\# Files}}$)

Play	1K	2K I	2K II
TheAlchemist	1/30	7/15	3/15
CynthiasRevels	16/50	8/25	11/25
Poetaster	4/50	1/20	3/20
AndroclesLion	3/20	Excl.	Excl.
CaesarCleo	16/30	8/15	9/15
Candida	4/20	3/15	3/15
ManAndSuperman	14/65	7/35	5/35
Pygmalion	9/30	3/15	1/15
WomanOfNoImportance	Excl.	17/25	17/25
AnIdealHusband	30/35	9/20	3/20
Earnest	4/30	3/25	6/25
LadyWinderemeresFan	5/25	2/20	2/20
AntCleo	4/20	16/20	19/20
AsYouLike	4/30	9/20	11/20
ComedyErrors	7/25	9/15	8/15
Coriolanus	16/35	15/30	15/30
Cymbeline	15/30	3/30	6/30
Hamlet	8/35	0/20	0/20
Henry4thPart1	0/25	4/20	5/20
Henry4thPart2	0/25	0/10	0/10
Henry6thPart1	16/25	1/10	4/10

Play	1K	2K I	2K II
Henry6thPart2	8/25	12/25	14/25
HenryTheEighth	2/30	5/15	1/15
HenryTheFifth	0/15	0/10	1/10
JuliusCaesar	2/20	7/15	7/15
KingJohn	0/15	0/15	1/15
KingLear	1/25	3/20	2/20
LovesLabor	1/40	1/20	1/20
Macbeth	1/15	1/10	0/10
Measures	0/20	3/20	0/20
MerchantVenice	4/30	0/15	0/15
MidSummerDream	2/30	0/5	Excl.
MuchAdo	6/25	13/25	11/25
Othello	3/30	1/20	2/20
Richard2	4/35	4/15	3/15
RichardTheThird	8/40	3/25	1/20
RomeoJuliet	1/30	0/25	2/25
TameShrew	3/40	1/10	0/10
TheTempest	1/25	0/5	0/5
Timon	3/15	0/5	0/5
TitusAndronicus	7/30	5/20	6/20
TwelfthNight	6/30	11/25	7/25
WinterTale	10/40	8/25	8/25

for all three of the experiments. Where the sampling results in variability in the results, in this construction, it suggests that the plays themselves are not homogeneous. It is consistent with the possiblity that variance depends on the presence of strong characters from a play in the samples. Recall from Experiment 1 that none of the characters of *Hamlet* were strong in the sense studied here. The variablity within the author's canon is also consistent with homogeneity of the canon, and correspondingly weak characterization.

4.3   Experiment 3: Characters Find Their Play

There are 42 categories (plays), with five files per character (2K each), three out of five matching a category (whether *a priori* or *a posteriori*) achieves significance ($p \leq 0.05$). The tables in (5)-(8) show the results for the characters considered which were significantly similar to their play (or to some other alternative play). It is evident that a few of the characters of Jonson and Shaw find their play, and that most of the strong characters in Shakespeare and Wilde are actually homogeneous with respect to some other play by the same author. In the tables here, ratios are bracketed in the "correct" column to show the level of significance for the *a priori* category when an alternative category showed actual significance. Also, "n/a" means that there was no significantly homogeneous alternative. In Table 5, where a cell contains "n/a" and an indication of a play in parentheses, then two out of the five files matched the play, but that is not statistically significant. The reason the play is listed is that certain plays are frequently best matches.

Table 4. Best Alternative Assignment of Files of Plays to Their Play

Play	Results for 1k	Results for 2k 1	Results for 2k 2
TheAlchemist	Henry6thPart1 7/29	Corio. 2/8	Henry6thPart2 5/1
CynthiasRevels	Henry6thPart1 7/34	Corio. 4/17	Poetaster 4/14
Poetaster	Henry6thPart1 12/46	Corio. 4/19	Henry6thPart2 4/17
AndroclesLion	Husband 7/17	Excl.	Excl.
CaesarCleo	Husband 6/14	Husband 5/7	Husband 5/6
Candida	Husband 8/16	CaesarCleo 3/12	CaesarCleo 3/12
ManAndSuperman	Husband 18/51	Husband 10/28	Husband 10/30
Pygmalion	Husband 8/21	Candida 3/12	Candida 3/14
Woman	Excl.	Husband 5/8	Husband 5/8
Husband	Earnest 2/5	Woman 9/11	Woman 16/17
Earnest	Husband 23/26	Husband 13/22	Husband 10/19
LadyWinderemeresFan	Husband 9/20	Woman 6/18	Woman 6/18
AntCleo	Cymbeline 6/16	Corio. 4/4	Cymbeline 1/1
AsYouLike	Cymbeline 8/26	Corio. 5/11	AntCleo 3/9
ComedyErrors	Cymbeline 5/18	AsYouLike 2/6	Henry6thPart2 3/7
Corio.	AntCleo 7/19	AntCleo 14/27	AntCleo 14/15
Cymbeline	Corio. 5/15	AntCleo 14/27	AntCleo 16/24
Hamlet	Cymbeline 11/27	Corio. 10/20	Cymbeline 5/20
Henry4thPart1	Henry6thPart1 10/25	Corio. 4/16	Cymbeline 6/15
Henry4thPart2	Henry6thPart1 10/25	Corio. 3/10	AntCleo 3/10
Henry6thPart1	Cymbeline 3/9	AntCleo 2/9	Cymbeline 3/6
Henry6thPart2	Henry6thPart1 8/17	Corio. 4/13	AntCleo 7/14
HenryTheEighth	Corio. 7/28	Corio. 6/10	AsYouLike 3/9
HenryTheFifth	Henry6thPart1 9/15	Henry6thPart2 5/10	AsYouLike 3/9
JuliusCaesar	Henry6thPart1 7/18	Corio. 4/8	AntCleo 3/8
KingJohn	Henry6thPart1 6/15	Corio. 7/15	Cymbeline 4/14
KingLear	Cymbeline 8/24	Corio. 6/17	AntCleo 9/18
LovesLabor	Cymbeline 7/39	Corio. 6/19	Henry6thPart2 4/19
Macbeth	Corio. 3/14	Corio. 6/9	Corio. 4/10
Measures	Corio. 4/20	Corio. 8/17	Henry6thPart2 5/20
MerchantVenice	Henry6thPart1 6/26	Corio. 5/15	Henry6thPart2 5/15
MidSummerDream	Henry6thPart1 7/28	HenryTheEighth 2/5	Excl.
MuchAdo	AsYouLike 4/19	Corio. 3/12	ComedyErrors 4/14
Othello	Henry6thPart1 6/27	MuchAdo 6/19	Cymbeline 6/18
Richard2	Henry6thPart1 11/31	Corio. 3/11	Cymbeline 5/12
RichardTheThird	Henry6thPart1 8/32	Corio. 8/22	Henry6thPart2 11/19
RomeoJuliet	Cymbeline 9/29	AntCleo 6/25	AntCleo 10/23
TameShrew	Henry6thPart1 12/37	Corio. 3/9	Henry6thPart2 5/10
TheTempest	Corio. 6/24	Corio. 3/5	Corio. 3/5
Timon	Cymbeline 5/12	HenryTheEighth 2/5	Cymbeline 2/5
TitusAndronicus	Corio. 6/23	Corio. 7/15	Henry6thPart2 7/14
TwelfthNight	Cymbeline 9/24	Cymbeline 4/14	Cymbeline 6/18
WinterTale	Cymbeline 10/30	Corio. 6/17	Cymbeline 8/17

4.4   Experiment 4: Characters Find Their Author

Given the results of Experiment 3, one expects (and finds) that characters do tend to find their author. Because there are only four categories, one for each of the playwrights, and five files per character, four out of five matches only approaches statistical significance ($p \leq 0.06$). Again, it is interesting to reflect on which characters find their author and which do not. In Tables 9 and 10, no column is provided for the best alternative, as none achieved statistical significance for either Jonson or Shakespeare. Reconsider the results of Experiment 1. Of the characters who were significantly homogeneous in their speech samples, with 248 categories in competition, only Shaw's Rufio and Don Juan and Wilde's Mrs. Cheveley and Lady Chiltern also found their play.

Table 5. Characters find their play: Results for Shakespeare

Character	Play	Correct	Alternative
Antony	AntCleo	3/5	n/a
Caesar	AntCleo	4/5	n/a
Cleopatra	AntCleo	5/5	n/a
Enobarbus	AntCleo	4/5	n/a
Orlando	AsYouLike	3/5	n/a
Touchstone	AsYouLike	3/5	n/a
Adriana	ComedyErr	3/5	n/a
Antipholos	ComedyErr	3/5	n/a
Dromi	ComedyErr	3/5	n/a
Aufidius	Coriolanus	(2/5)	AntCleo (3/5)
Cominius	Coriolanus	(2/5)	AntCleo (3/5)
Coriolanus	Coriolanus	3/5	n/a (AntCleo)
Menenius	Coriolanus	3/5	n/a (AntCleo)
Sicinius	Coriolanus	(2/5)	AntCleo (3/5)
Voluminia	Coriolanus	3/5	n/a (AntCleo)
Belarius	Cymbeline	(0/5)	AntCleo (3/5)
Cymbeline	Cymbeline	(0/5)	AntCleo (5/5)
Iachimo	Cymbeline	(0/5)	Coriolanus (4/5)
King	Hamlet	(0/5)	Coriolanus (5/5)
Polonius	Hamlet	(0/5)	Coriolanus (3/5)
King	Hen4p1	(0/5)	Coriolanus (3/5)
Prince	Hen4p1	3/5	n/a
King	Hen4p2	(0/5)	Coriolanus (3/5)
King	Hen6p2	4/5	n/a
King	Hen8	(1/5)	Coriolanus (3/5)
QueenKatherine	Hen8	3/5	n/a
KingHenry	Hen5	(0/5)	Hen6p2 (4/5)

Character	Play	Correct	Alternative
Cassius	Julius Caesar	3/5	n/a
Constance	KingJohn	(0/5)	Hen6p2 (3/5)
KingJohn	KingJohn	(0/5)	Coriolanus (4/5)
Edg	KingLear	(0/5)	AntCleo (3/5)
King	LovesLabor	(0/5)	Coriolanus (4/5)
LadyMacbeth	Macbeth	(0/5)	Coriolanus (4/5)
Angelo	Measures	(0/5)	Coriolanus (3/5)
Isabella	Measures	(0/5)	Coriolanus (3/5)
Bassani	MerchantVenice	(0/5)	Coriolanus (3/5)
Bene	MuchAdo	3/5	n/a
Leon	MuchAdo	3/5	n/a (Coriolanus)
Pedro	MuchAdo	3/5	n/a
Desdemona	Othello	(0/5)	MuchAdo (3/5)
Othello	Othello	(0/5)	Cymbeline (3/5)
KingRichard	Richard2	3/5	n/a
QueenMargaret	Richard3	(0/5)	Cymbeline (3/5)
Nurse	RomeoJuliet	(0/5)	KingLear (3/5)
Tranio	TameShrew	(0/5)	Coriolanus (3/5)
Prospero	Tempest	(0/5)	Coriolanus (3/5)
Marcus	TitusAndronicus	(0/5)	Coriolanus (4/5)
Clown	TwelfthNight	3/5	n/a
Malvolio	TwelfthNight	3/5	n/a
Autolycus	WinterTale	3/5	n/a
Leontes	WinterTale	(2/5)	AntCleo (3/5)
Paulina	WinterTale	(0/5)	AntCleo (3/5)

Table 6. Characters find their play: Results for Wilde

Character	Play	Correct Matches	Alternative
Gerald	WomanOfNoImportance	5/5	n/a
LadyHunt.	WomanOfNoImportance	4/5	n/a
LordDillingsworth	WomanOfNoImportance	(2/5)	IdealHusband (3/5)
MrsArbuthnot	WomanOfNoImportance	5/5	n/a
LadyChiltern	Ideal Husband	3/5	n/a
LordGoring	Ideal Husband	3/5	n/a
MrsCheveley	Ideal Husband	(2/5)	WNI (3/5)
SirRobert	Ideal Husband	(1/5)	WNI (3/5)
LordWindermere	Lady Wind.	(0/5)	WNI (3/5)
Algernon	Earnest	(0/5)	IdealHusband (3/5)
Gwendolen	Earnest	(0/5)	IdealHusband (4/5)
Jack	Earnest	(1/5)	IdealHusband (3/5)
LadyBracknell	Earnest	(1/5)	IdealHusband (1/5)

4.5   Experiment 5: Authors Find Themselves

In this experiment, we used four categories for the speeches and balanced the samples: 10 characters for each playwright, five files for each character (samples of 2K each); 20 out of 50 achieves significance ($p \leq 0.025$). We ran 100 such experiments and report below the average response. The column headed by "Average" in Table 13 shows each of the authors to be significantly self-similar in comparison with the others. Shaw is

Table 7. Characters find their play: Results for Shaw

Character	Play	Correct	Alternative
Caesar	Caesar and Cleopatra	3/5	n/a
Cleopatra	Caesar and Cleopatra	3/5	n/a
Rufio	Caesar and Cleopatra	4/5	n/a
DonJuan	Man and Superman	4/5	n/a
Octavius	Man and Superman	(0/5)	Candida (3/5)
Ramsden	Man and Superman	(0/5)	Ideal Husband (4/5)

Table 8. Characters find their play: Results for Jonson

Character	Play	Correct	Alternative
Amorphus	Cynthias Revels	4/5	n/a
Cupid	Cynthias Revels	3/5	n/a
Caesar	Poetaster	(0/5)	Coriolanus (3/5)
FACE	The Alchemist	4/5	n/a

Table 9. Jonson's characters find Jonson

Character	Play	Correct
Amorphus	Cynthias Revels	4/5
Asotus	Cynthias Revels	4/5
Crites	Cynthias Revels	4/5
Cupid	Cynthias Revels	5/5
Mercury	Cynthias Revels	5/5
Caesar	Poetaster	5/5
Crispinus	Poetaster	5/5
Horace	Poetaster	5/5
Tucca	Poetaster	5/5
FACE	The Alchemist	4/5
Mammon	The Alchemist	4/5
Subtle	The Alchemist	4/5

Table 10. Shakespeare's find Shakespeare

Character	Play	Correct
Camillo	A Winters Tale	4/5
Paulina	A Winters Tale	4/5
Polixenes	A Winters Tale	4/5
Hamlet	Hamlet	5/5
Horatio	Hamlet	5/5
King	Hamlet	4/5
Polonius	Hamlet	4/5
Helena	MidSummerDream	4/5
Cassio	Othello	5/5
Desdemona	Othello	5/5
Iago	Othello	5/5
Othello	Othello	5/5

Table 11. Shaw's characters find Shaw

Character	Play	Corr.	Alternative
Cleopatra	Caesar and Cleo	4/5	n/a
Rufio	Caesar and Cleo	4/5	n/a
Candida	Candida	4/5	n/a
Morell	Candida	4/5	n/a
Ann	Man and Sman	4/5	n/a
Ramsden	Man and Sman	(0/5)	Wilde(4/5)
Higgins	Pygmalion	3/5	Wilde(2/5)
Liza	Pygmalion	5/5	n/a

Table 12. Wilde's characters find Wilde

Character	Play	Corr.	Alternative
Algernon	Earnest	5/5	n/a
Cecily	Earnest	4/5	n/a
Gwendolen	Earnest	5/5	n/a
Jack	Earnest	4/5	n/a
L.Bracknell	Earnest	5/5	n/a
L.Chiltern	I. Husband	5/5	n/a
LordGor.	I. Husband	5/5	n/a
M.Cheveley	I. Husband	5/5	n/a
SirRobert	I. Husband	4/5	n/a
DuchessB.	Lady Wind.	4/5	n/a
LadyWind.	Lady Wind.	3/5	Shaw(2/5)
LordWind.	Lady Wind.	5/5	n/a

interestingly less homogeneous than the others considered here. The final four columns of Table 13 show the breakdown of the best match alternatives over the 100 samplings. Given constrained verse style, it perhaps is not surprising that Shakespeare and Jonson are each other's own best alternative. It is curious that Shakespeare is the best alternative for Shaw nearly twice as often as Wilde is; that the best alternative for Wilde is nearly evenly split between Shakespeare and Shaw; that Jonson is rarely the best alternative for either Wilde or Shaw.

Table 13. Playwright and best alternatives

	Average	Best Alternative			
Playwright		Jonson	Shakespeare	Shaw	Wilde
Jonson	44.8/50	n/a	100	0	0
Shakespeare	40.33/50	100	n/a	0	0
Shaw	30.03/50	2	68	n/a	30
Wilde	43.01/50	5	47	48	n/a

5   General Discussion

In this work we have constructed a set of experiments to establish baselines for the exploration of the issue of small sample sizes in computing similarity across texts in the larger context of stylistic analysis. Our task has been one of computational stylometry. We wanted to know if the effects of iambic pentameter in Shakespeare would constrain the language sufficiently to make the individual characters indiscriminable when using letter unigram distributions as the basis of similarity assessment. It has been noted [22, p. 268] that Milman Parry [20] argued of Homeric verse that it was susceptible to otherwise inappropriate descriptive epithets, evidently with preservation of meter being the best explanation of occurrence. Thus, we pool the characters of several Shakespearean plays with some of the verse plays of Jonson (a contemporary who is a contender in the literature as "the real Shakespeare", or the author of the works with primary attribution dispute [6]), and along with those non-contemporary prose plays. The metric of characterization that we wished to explore within the work is whether characterization is strong to the extent that characters find themselves, and to a lesser extent their plays, and that characterization is weak if the files of a character more easily find their author. By the results reported here, the works of Shaw analyzed herein reveal interesting clusters: some characters themselves cluster in themselves as homogeneous, but Shaw's files are the least likely to find their author of the writers considered (even though as an author, his files find him as author to a significant extent). Thus, the quantificational analysis we offer suggests that his control of character is markedly greater than that of the other writers considered. The suggestion is that in the alternative case, the author is less prone to separate the authorial voice from that of the created characters.

Table 14 pools results across experiments. The characters listed are those which were internally homogeneous, and the first column recapitulates the strength of homegeneity in that regard (Experiment 1). The second column indicates the strength of homogeneity of that character with respect to its play, and the third column indicates strength with respect to author in the weak sense of being significantly homogeneous with respect to another play by the same author (Experiment 3). The final column displays the characters homogeneity frequency using authorship as a category (Experiment 4). From this perspective, using the measure of strength outlined here, Jonson and Wilde are similar in that their strong characters find them as authors more reliably than those characters find their plays. Shakespeare's strong characters are more likely to find a play another Shakespeare play than the one in which they appear, if they find a play at all, but not their author. Shaw's strong characters (except Rufio) also do not find their author, but do find their play or another Shaw play. Using the aesthetic outlined at the outset, this

Table 14. Characters across experiments

Character	Self	Play	Author (another play)	Author (total corpus)
AARONTitusAndronicus	2/5	×	×	×
AGUECHEEKTwelfthNight	2/5	×	×	×
APEMANTUSTimon	2/5	×	×	×
AUFIDIUSCoriolanus	2/5	×	3/5	×
BeatMuchAdo	2/5	×	×	×
CALIBANTheTempest	2/5	×	×	×
CONSTANCEKingJohn	2/5	×	4/5	×
OBERONMidSummerDream	2/5	×	×	×
PRINCESSOFFRANCELovesLabor	2/5	×	×	×
TALBOTHenry6thPart1	2/5	×	×	×
PUCELLEHenry6thPart1	2/5	×	×	×
KINGHENRYHenry6thPart1	4/5	×	3/5	×
PUCKMidSummerDream	2/5	×	×	×
QUEENELIZABETHRichardTheThird	2/5	×	×	×
PORTIAMerchantVenice	2/5	×	×	×
SHYLOCKMerchantVenice	2/5	×	×	×
ANTONYJuliusCaesar	3/5	×	×	×
BUCKINGHAMHenryTheEighth	3/5	×	×	×
CHORUSHenryTheFifth	3/5	×	×	×
LearKingLear	3/5	×	×	×
GlouKingLear	2/5	×	×	×
AlbPoetaster	2/5	×	×	×
HorPoetaster	2/5	×	×	5/5
VirgPoetaster	2/5	×	×	×
TucPoetaster	4/5	×	×	5/5
ASOCynthiasRevels	2/5	×	×	4/5
CRICynthiasRevels	3/5	×	×	4/5
MERCynthiasRevels	5/5	×	×	5/5
ANDROCLESAndroclesLion	4/5	×	×	×
RUFIOCaesarCleo	4/5	4/5	×	4/5
ANAManAndSuperman	2/5	×	×	×
ANNManAndSuperman	3/5	×	×	×
DONJUANManAndSuperman	2/5	4/5	×	×
OCTAVIUSManAndSuperman	4/5	×	3/5	×
THESTATUEManAndSuperman	2/5	×	×	×
STRAKERManAndSuperman	2/5	×	×	×
MRSPEARCEPygmalion	2/5	×	×	×
LadyBracknellEarnest	2/5	×	×	5/5
GwendolenEarnest	3/5	×	4/5	5/5
MRSCHEVELEYAnIdealHusband	2/5	×	3/5	5/5
LADYCHILTERNAnIdealHusband	2/5	3/5	×	5/5

places Shakespeare and Shaw in the same pigeon-hole in having strong characters that do not find their author. But, it merits repeated emphasis that that the strong characters in this sense are not the famous ones. Recall that the ratios that count as significant depend on the parameters of the test. We have not presented in this table the characters which turned up as strong according to subsequent tests, but not with respect to character internal homogeneity.

6   Final Remarks

Note that this study depended solely on letter unigram analysis. The efficacy of letter unigram analysis within the forensic linguistics literature has been noted above. Additional arguments for the face validity of this level of tokenization were provided.

Further, it has proven robust in a range of other experiments as well ([9,19] supplement experiments cited earlier). It would be useful to replicate the experiments of this paper at other levels of token individuation. However, letter n-gram analysis does seem to be an apt level of objective sub-lexical tokenization of texts in order to assess stylistic properties of texts that associate to meter. Of course, this is not a definitive study on the topic. For example, it does not take into the temporal dislocation of the construction of the plays even within a single author's own canon. Yet, it is representative of the sort of analyses we intend to pursue within computational stylometry. Our immediate ongoing work here is a replication of this study in a context with a larger pool of plays and playwrights and characters to consider. In this paper, we controlled for drama composed as verse versus prose, and Elizabethan versus the modern era; however, in this experiment the categories overlapped in that the prose works were the modern ones and verse, Elizabethan. It is difficult to identify a data set in which those categories can be independently controlled for, but if the overall data set is expanded, it will be interesting to know if the few strong characters from this study will remain so.

This article has introduced a novel form of computational stylistic analysis, applying techniques for assessing homogeneity from corpus linguistics to evaluating the homogeneity of speeches of characters in plays, with respect to their character, their play and their author. The approach is consistent with prior quantitative analyses of style, for example it is an instance of local vs. pervasive characteristics in fiction as discussed by [14], which are there not individuated as measures of strength of characterization. Variations in style have been amply qualified and quantified in the past; [1] for example addresses register in non-fiction and types of communication, work that transfers partly to the present sort of study in that it is about communication at least one level closer to the intended audience. And, of course [18] provides a compact survey of the extent to which statistical methods have been applied to analyze style and authorship in literary analysis. We are not aware of other work which is more directly comparable in terms of trying to quantify the strength of characterization within an author's canon using these objective measures and for the set of authors we have addressed herein. Normally, the questions addressed computationally in this area are about global properties of a writer's corpus, perhaps by genre within the corpus—for example, linguistic complexity in general or changes in complexity over time—not features like distinctiveness of characterization. We apply our analysis to iconic characters of landmark playwrights to consider whether this allows an assessment of the extent to which a writer composes characters that are distinct from each other and from the writer's prose voice in general. In this small set of experiments we found that playwrights tend not to write distinctive characters. We noted Shaw and Jonson as exceptions within this study, in one sense, and Shakespeare and Shaw in another. In contrast, the texts of each of the four authors was significantly homogeneous as an individual corpus. These results suggest immediately replication of the experiments with a larger pool of works under consideration. Orthogonally, we need to discuss with literature experts whether the distinctions revealed here have any relevance to debate on interpretive approaches to the works considered. Separately, we need to extend the baselines provided here much further if they are to become useful in constructing metrics of independence of character voice from author voice in assessing the realism of avatar communications.

Acknowledgements. We are grateful to Science Foundation Ireland (RFP 05/RF/CMS002). This research has benefited from collaboration with Sofie Van Gijsel, Geraldine Herbert, Lucy Hogan, Jerom Janssen, Cormac O'Brien, Niamh McCombe, Julia Medori, Myriam Mencke and Mary Ronner. Suggestions from anonymous reviewers have been very helpful, and this paper has benefited from attempting to address them.

References

1. Biber, D.: Dimensions of Register Variation. Cambridge University Press, Cambridge (1995)
2. Chaski, C.: Who Wrote It? Steps Toward a Science of Authorship Identification. National Institute of Justice Journal 233, 15–22 (1997)
3. Chaski, C.: Empirical Evaluations of Language-based Author Identification Techniques. Forensic Linguistics 8(1), 1–65 (2001)
4. Coleman, C.: The Treatise Lorenzo Valla on the Donation of Constantine: Text and Translation. Russell & Russell, New York (1971); First published 1922
5. Farmer, T., Christiansen, M., Monaghan, P.: Phonological Typicality Influences On-line Sentence Comprehension. Proceedings of the National Academy of Sciences of the United States of America 103(32), 12203–12208 (2006)
6. Foster, D.: Author Unknown. On the Trail of Anonymous. Macmillan, London (2001)
7. Frontini, F., Lynch, G., Vogel, C.: Revisiting the Donation of Constantine. In: Kibble, R., Rauchas, S. (eds.) 2008 Artificial Intelligence and Simulation of Behavior – Symposium: Style in Text
8. Healey, P.G.T., Vogel, C., Eshghi, A.: Group Dialects in an Online Community. In: Arnstein, R., Vieu, L. (eds.) DECALOG 2007, The 10th Workshop on the Semantics and Pragmatics of Dialogue, Università di Trento (Italy), May 30 – June 1, 2007, pp. 141–147 (2007)
9. Hogan, L.: A Corpus Linguistic Analysis of American, British and Irish Political Speeches. Master's thesis, Centre for Language and Communication Studies, Trinity College, University of Dublin (2005)
10. Kilgarriff, A., Salkie, R.: Corpus Similarity and Homogeneity via Word Frequency. In: Proceedings of Euralex 1996 (1996)
11. Kilgarriff, A.: Comparing Corpora. International Journal of Corpus Linguistics 6(1), 97–133 (2001)
12. Laver, M. (ed.): Estimating the Policy Position of Political Actors. Routledge (2001)
13. Laver, M., Garry, J.: Estimating Policy Positions from Political Texts. American Journal of Political Science 44(3), 619–634 (2000)
14. Leech, G.N., Short, M.H.: Style in Fiction: A Linguistic Introduction to English Fictional Prose. Longman, London (1981)
15. Lynch, G., Vogel, C.: Automatic Character Assignation. In: Bramer, M. (ed.) AI-2007 Twenty-seventh SGAI International Conference on Artificial Intelligence, pp. 335–348. Springer, Heidelberg (2007)
16. Mencke, M.: Benchmarking a Text Classification Technique. Master's thesis, Computational Linguistics Group, Trinity College Dublin (2007)
17. Nijholt, A., Reidsma, D., Ruttkay, Z., van Welbergen, H., Bos, P.: Non-verbal and Bodily Interaction in Ambient Entertainment. In: Esposito, A., Keller, E., Marinaro, M., Bratanic, M. (eds.) The Fundamentals of Verbal and Non-Verbal Communication and the Biometrical Issue, pp. 343–348. IOS Press, Amsterdam (2007)
18. Oakes, M.P.: Statistics for Corpus Linguistics. Edinburgh Textbooks in Empirical Linguistics. Edinburgh University Press, Edinburgh (1998)

19. O'Brien, C., Vogel, C.: Spam Filters: Bayes vs. Chi-squared; Letters vs. Words. In: Alesky, M., et al. (ed.) Proceedings of the International Symposium on Information and Communication Technologies, pp. 298–303 (2003)
20. Parry, A.: The making of Homeric verse: the collected papers of Milman Parry. Oxford University Press, Oxford (1971) (Reprinted 1987)
21. Schmid, H.: Probabilistic Part-of-Speech Tagging using Decision Trees. In: International Conference on New Methods in Language Processing (1994)
22. Smith, J.D.: Winged Words Revisited: Diction and Meaning in Indian Epic. Bulletin of the School of Oriental and African Studies, University of London 62(2), 267–305 (1999)
23. Van Gijsel, S., Vogel, C.: Inducing a Cline from Corpora of Political Manifestos. In: Aleksy, M., et al. (eds.) Proceedings of the International Symposium on Information and Communication Technologies, pp. 304–310 (2003)
24. Vogel, C.: Corpus Homogeneity and Bernoulli Schema. In: Mining Massive Data Sets for Security. NATO Advanced Study Institute, pp. 93–94 (2007)
25. Vogel, C.: N-gram Distributions in Texts as Proxy for Textual Fingerprints. In: Esposito, A., Keller, E., Marinaro, M., Bratanic, M. (eds.) The Fundamentals of Verbal and Non-Verbal Communication and the Biometrical Issue, pp. 189–194. IOS Press, Amsterdam (2007)
26. Vogel, C., Brisset, S.: Hearing Voices in the Poetry of Brendan Kennelly. In: Varieties of Voice, 2006. 3rd international BAAHE conference. Leuven, Revised version Belgian Journal of English Language & Literature, December 7-9 (to appear, 2006)

The Acoustic Front-End in Scenarios of Interaction Research

Rüdiger Hoffmann[1], Lutz-Michael Alisch[2], Uwe Altmann[2], Thomas Fehér[1],
Rico Petrick[1], Sören Wittenberg[1], and Rico Hermkes[2]

[1] Technische Universität Dresden, Department of Electrical Engineering and
Information Technology, 01062 Dresden, Germany
[2] Technische Universität Dresden, Faculty of Education
01062 Dresden, Germany
{ruediger.hoffmann,thomas.feher,rico.petrick,
soeren.wittenberg}@ias.et.tu-dresden.de,
{lutz-michael.alisch,uwe.altmann,rico.hermkes}@mailbox.tu-dresden.de
http://www.ias.et.tu-dresden.de/sprache/,
http://tu-dresden.de/die_tu_dresden/fakultaeten/erzw/erzwiae/ewwm/

Abstract. The paper is concerning some problems which are posed by
the growing interest in social interaction research as far as they can
be solved by engineers in acoustics and speech technology. Firstly the
importance of nonverbal and paraverbal modalities in two prototypical scenarios are discussed: face-to-face interactions in psychotherapeutic consulting and side-by-side interactions of children cooperating in a
computer game. Some challenges in processing signals are stated with
respect to both scenarios. The following technologies of acoustic signal
processing are discussed: (a) analysis of the influence of the room impulse
response to the recognition rate, (b) adaptive two-channel microphone,
(c) localization and separation of sound sources in rooms, and (d) single-
channel noise suppression.

Keywords: Human-human interaction, multimodality, acoustic front-
end, acoustic signal processing.

1 Introduction

One goal of interaction research is to find rules of human-human interaction in
different scenarios. In the humanities and social sciences some specific interactions are studied which could be denoted as teleological interactions [1]. In this
case one person tries to modify the behaviour or the mental states of another
one, e.g. via therapist interventions or teacher instructions. Research in interaction could be helpful to improve the performance of psychotherapy, teaching etc.
In contrast to that, interaction research in the engineering sciences is motivated
e. g. by questions in the context of human-computer interfaces [29]. In order
to capture high quality acoustic data in such a context, an acoustic front-end
could be used which incorporates hardware and software components for audio

A. Esposito et al. (Eds.): HH and HM Interaction 2007, LNAI 5042, pp. 187–199, 2008.

recordings (e. g. microphone arrays), signal processing (e. g. denoising) and signal analysis (e. g. speech recognition). Interaction research is interested in an acoustic front-end for reasons of objective and reliable measurement of ongoing paraverbal behaviour [22], [27] and research economics. The latter means the transition from manual to automated data capture. The outcome is a reduction in time amount and personal costs for data capture. The former yields the measurement of physical variables (e. g. intensity of speech) with high resolution and low noise in contrast to manual codings like "the patient speaks angry". Such data could be used to study voice correlates of mental disorders and based on it the time course of the disorder [14], [25] or to predict the outcome of psychotherapy [8].

As early as in the seventies of the last century acoustic front-ends were used in interaction research. Cassotta et al. [12], for example, developed the AVTA-system for automated data capture of turn-taking patterns (on-off-patterns) in conversations. It has been used to study the interaction between the patient and therapist for example by Krause [18], [19], Brähler [6] and Brähler et al. [7]. At the time speech technologies are available to capture more than turn taking, such as speech quality or prosody which are closer to emotions and involvement and convey the internal states of speakers much better than turn taking [13], [15]. Furthermore, speech recognition systems could be used to get a transcription of the dialogue. In the following a content analysis is possible, which is frequently done in interaction research (see e.g. [10] for a computer based text analysis of manually transliterate psychotherapy session). To sum up, an acoustic front-end should be able to cover turn-taking and furthermore verbal and paraverbal communication behaviour.

Besides the communication behaviour under study, signal recording and signal processing play an important role. A perfect setting for an acoustic recording is present in the speech laboratory, e. g. the microphone could be placed close to the signal source. However, interactions occur oftenly in a more natural environment accompanied by suboptimal influences on the speech recording. Furthermore, the factors that have to be controlled are not time invariant and differ from scenario to scenario. For example, in psychotherapeutic consulting the use of head sets is out of place because a patient should communicate unembarrassed. But if children are engaged in a computer game like flight simulation, a head set makes the game more realistic.

In a certain sense a general solution for an acoustic front-end for all possible scenarios seems to be unreasonable. Therefore we only discuss two selected prototypical scenarios with respect to multimodality and the role of the acoustic channel in the scenarios: face-to-face interaction in psychotherapeutic consulting and side-by-side interaction of children while cooperatively playing a cooperative computer game (section 2). In the following section, we analyse the acoustic situation of the two scenarios with respect to the requirements of acoustic and speech technologies for the acoustic front-end. In section 4, selected technologies for acoustic signal processing are discussed, in detail: (a) analysis of the influence of the room impulse response to the recognition rate, (b) adaptive two-channel microphone, (c) localization and separation of sound sources in rooms, and (d) single-channel noise suppression.

The system UASR which was discussed in a paper for the Vietri COST 2102 workshop [17] serves as the baseline system for our investigations. Note, however, that an optimization of the acoustic frontend targets as yet to the maximization of the recognition rate. Improving the acoustic frontend for an optimal extraction of paralinguistic information is due to future challenges.

2   Two Prototypical Scenarios of Interaction Research

In this section we discuss two scenarios concerning dyadic interaction: face-to-face interaction in psychotherapeutic consulting and side-by-side interaction of children cooperatively playing a cooperative computer game. In the scenarios two persons do interact.

In the scenarios the interacting partners are sitting on chairs. Therefore the spatial loci of the interaction is predetermined (see Figure 1). As a result multimodal interaction is restricted. In face-to-face interactions information about the partner is accessible in the visual channel. Contrary to that the spatial configuration of the interactions partners in the side-by-side case necessitates the regulation of the interaction using other modalities. It may be expected that the paraverbal dimensions (e. g. prosodic features) are of greater importance.

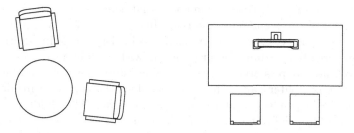

Fig. 1. Typical arrangement of seats in a psychotherapeutic setting (left) and in a computer game situation (right)

In the following, we discuss the scenarios both with respect to multimodality and the role that speaking and listening play in those scenarios.

2.1   Face-to-Face Interaction in Psychotherapeutic Consulting

In psychotherapeutic consulting the patient and therapist interact face-to-face. As a rule, the persons are sitting on armchairs with an orientation between 90 and 180 degrees (see Figure 1 left). The seat positions the predetermine orientations of the bodies resp. the focus of the visual perception. Furthermore, the regulation of the interpersonal distance is restricted: (i) the corresponding behaviour is reduced to leaning forward and backward. (ii) if the distance between the seats is not too close then violations of personal space may be expected seldom. At least, in face-to-face interactions one modality could be substituted, underlined or extenuated by other modalities.

Our concern with face-to-face-interactions in psychotherapeutic consulting focuses intrapersonal conflicts of social phobia patients and their expression through "emotional overinvolvement" (EOI) [2]. Typical symptoms of social phobia are intensive anxieties in social situations (e.g. speaking in public), low self-confidence and fear of criticism (see DSM IV, F40.1 [3]). EOI could be expected if the therapist addresses sensitive themes like social situations or biographical facts which are related to low self-confidence and fear of criticism on the patient's side.

Our decision to measure EOI via speech features is based on two reasons. (i) The emotional expression (measured by prosody and speech quality) and the affective reference object (the content, measured by speech recognition) are given simultaneously. It allows for some intonation analysis of important keywords like "my parents" or "criticism", and the comparison of the keyword intonations from the beginning of the therapy to its ending. (ii) We assume that the paraverbal expression of EOI in contrast to its facial expression allows for a measurement with greater subtleties.

2.2 Side-by-Side Interaction of Children Cooperating in a Computer Game

In side-by-side interactions the partners are sitting or standing parallel close to each other. Their body orientation and visual perception are focusing a third issue, e.g. a teacher or a computer interface. In education side-by-side interaction is a very typical one, e. g. seating arrangements in classrooms. In addition, some kinds of experiential learning require working with computers.

Our working group is studying side-by-side interactions of children playing a cooperative computer game. In order to reduce the degree of freedom some modalities are suspended. Visual contact is not given. The children could not communicate through facial expressions. Mutual glances are used to regulate the interaction. In realising eye-contact the children have to move their heads extensively. Those turns are simple to identify when video sequences are available. Gestures and touching are highly restricted because the children have to handle a game pad with both hands. As a result verbal and paraverbal communication are the dominant modalities in this interaction.

The pauses between the game levels are of particular interest. During the time intervals the visual fixation of the monitor is not necessary. The interaction changes from the verbal channel to multimodality.

We used a modified computer simulation referred in [2]. Tests showed that the free moving space in the flight simulation (first version) was too high. So players could solve the game levels under low cooperation conditions. To restrict the free moving space a new version of the game was developed by Biemer and Müller [4]. Now, the children have to navigate a submarine in a futuristic world with narrow tunnels and collect important items with a tractor beam (see Figure 2). The game ends in case of too many collisions or of a too small number of

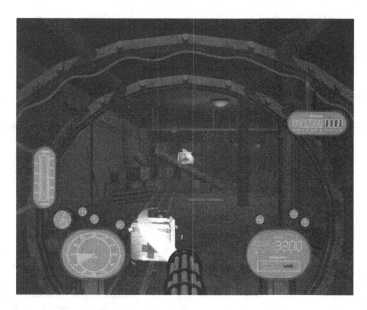

Fig. 2. Screenshot of the computer game

collections. In this game design makes an intensive cooperation of both players necessary to solve the game levels.

To increase the conflictuality in the interaction the computer displays the causer of miscues during the game. We expect that this evokes discussions about the failure of cooperation.

This game provides two interaction situations which are equal for all children under study: (i) playing time (mainly unimodal interaction sequences with lower interaction activities) in contrast to (ii) pauses (multimodal interaction sequences with intensive interaction activities). Both are comparable between pairs and within a pair (e. g. 1st pause versus 2nd pause).

3   Problems of Acoustic Signal Processing

In the two scenarios mentioned above verbal and paraverbal communication is of great importance. As a rule these interactions occur in natural environments suffering from suboptimal conditions for recordings. To capture some high quality acoustic data hardware and software components of an acoustic front-end should be coordinated with the acoustic situation. In the following, the acoustic situation of the two scenarios is analysed. It gives a foundation to deduce the required speech technologies.

3.1   Analysis of the Acoustic Situation

In the scenarios mentioned above dyadic interaction is under study (only two persons interact). The interaction is taking place in a separate room. Some features of the acoustic situations are listed in Table 1.

Table 1. Features of the two scenarios

	positive	negative
room	– known and well defined	– suboptimal with respect to acoustics (noise and reverberation) – positions of the microphones known but not regular
speakers	– constant number of speakers – known speakers – many sessions with the same pair	– moving speakers – eventually speakers are in greater distance to the microphones – high degree of affective speech (many barge in, inarticulate speaking etc.) – high number of non-verbal components

The choice of some optimal microphones is essential. In the computer game situation head sets could be used. It makes the game more realistic and the microphone is close to the signal source. The recording situation for the voice signals could be denoted as optimal. Contrary to that, in a psychotherapeutic session head sets are inadequate. Instead, in our research project wearable wireless microphones are used. Directional microphones on the table are suboptimal in this case. Perhaps the microphone is in the visual field of the patient at all times. This is counterproductive with respect to the ambition that the patient should forgot that he/she is under study. Furthermore the persons could get out of the sensitivity range of the microphones because of movement of torsos.

3.2 The Acoustic Front-End

The acoustic front-end could be described with the three main components: recording, acoustic signal processing, and speech analysis. Each component incorporates miscellaneous speech technologies which briefly are summarized in Figure 3.

The application of acoustic signal processing in the acoustic front-end is a part of the research field of *acoustic scene analysis* [5]. The application of microphone arrays [9] offers a high potential especially if it is combined with powerful signal processing [16]. However, practical situations like the interaction scenarios which

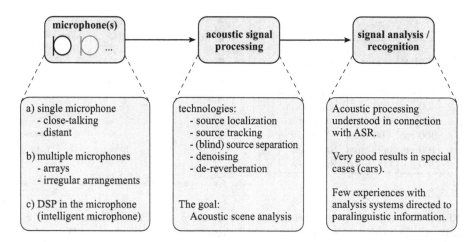

Fig. 3. Components of the acoustic front-end and related speech processing technologies

we are discussing here are characterized by a larger number of microphones which are *not* arranged in a regular way as microphone arrays.

4 Selected Experiments in Speech Technology for the Acoustic Front-End of the UASR System

In the last section, we have outlined features of the scenarios. It was shown which components of an acoustic front-end are necessary to handle the requirements. In the following sections, four experiments are presented which serve to improve the acoustic front-end of the UASR system [17].

4.1 Word Recognition with Distant Microphones

It is known that the recognition rate of a speech recognizer breaks down if the distance between the speaker and the microphone is increased. This problem is normally avoided by using head-sets which guarantee the required close-talking. As it was discussed above, this is not applicable in certain situations of interaction research like psychotherapy. The following experiments were performed to get some detailed information about the dependencies between the properties of the room and the recognition rate. We used a command recognizer basing on the UASR technology with the Apollo corpus as test material [21]. Figure 4a summarizes the experimental conditions. Figure 4b shows how the recognition rate drops off with growing speaker-microphone distance (SMD).

The influence of the room was evaluated by two other experiments. In the first one, the room impulse response was separated in early and late reflection at a variable cut-off time. In this way, the recognition experiments were repeated including either only the early reflections or only the late reflections. The results

No.	SMD	T60	Room
1	100 cm	400 ms	Living room
2	300 cm	400 ms	Living room
3	100 cm	700 ms	Office
4	300 cm	700 ms	Office
5	100 cm	3,000 ms	Staircase
6	300 cm	3,000 ms	Staircase

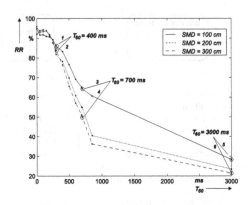

Fig. 4. Influence of the speaker-microphone distance (SMD) in different rooms [24]. Left (a): Experimental setup. Right (b): Recognition rate dependent on T60 and the SMD.

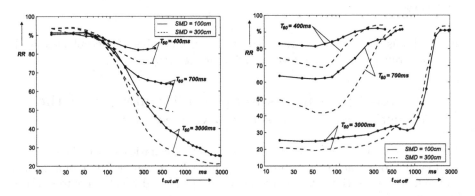

Fig. 5. Dependency of the recognition rate on early (left) and late (right) reflections [24]

are shown in Figure 5. Obviously, very early (< 70 ms) and very late ($> 2/3$ T60) reflections do not affect the performance of the recognizer. A dereverberation method should therefore focus at reflections between 70 and approx. 300 ms.

Another experiment was performed to investigate the influence of the highpass and lowpass components of the spectrum of the room impulse response. The recognition is disturbed mainly by low-frequent reverberations between 250 and 2,500 Hz. This is not surprizing because this range includes the most essential components of the speech signal.

4.2   Adaptive Two-Channel Microphone

The directivity of the microphones plays an important role in the layout of the acoustic front-end. Traditionally, directivity is achieved by geometries which are large compared to the wavelength (shotgun microphone, microphone arrays, microphones with parabolic mirror or acoustical lens). Small microphones can

Fig. 6. Arrangement of the capsules in the microphone UM930-twin (Microtech Gefell GmbH) [26]

be directional if they are able to measure both, the acoustic pressure and the particle velocity. Combining both signals allows to obtain directivity patterns like cardioid, super cardioid, and hyper cardioid.

The microphone shown in Figure 6 provides the output signals of two microphone capsules separately. Therefore it is possible to process these signals immediately by a digital signal processor (DSP) which offers the following possibilities of "intelligent processing" [26]:

– Continuous adjustment of the directivity pattern between ball, broad cardioid, cardioid, super and hyper cardioid, and figure eight,
– rotation of the zeroes of the directivity pattern towards unwanted noise sources,
– adaptation of the transfer function of the microphone,
– analysis of the direction of the sound source.

The adaptive algorithms can be applied either on-line or in a batch mode after recording both output signals. In this way, the adaptive microphone offers a number of interesting features which can be utilized for the acoustic scene analysis.

4.3 Localization and Separation of Sources in Rooms

A number of algorithms has been developed in the past for localizing, separating and tracking several sound sources in rooms. A comparative evaluation of the algorithms is useful for improving the performance of the front-end. Until now, we evaluated algorithms for the localization of sources [20] and for the multi-channel source separation [23].

Interesting improvements in multi-channel source separation can be obtained using the *Independent Component Analysis* (ICA). This is a group of algorithms, which try to separate signals on the basis of statistical or information theoretical

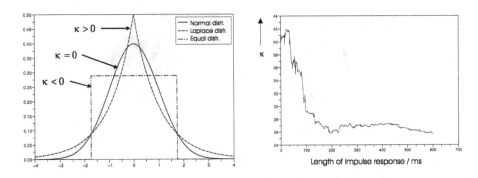

Fig. 7. Independent Component Analysis (ICA). Left (a): Probability density functions with different degrees of "non-Gaussianity" or kurtosis κ. Right (b): Dependency of the kurtosis of room impulse responses on their length.

properties. These algorithms can also be used to find a directivity pattern which reduces room reflections and interfering sources on the recorded signal optimally. Therefore it will be interesting to apply the ICA algorithms in the DSP of the intelligent microphone described above.

The independence of the signals is measured in this case by its Gaussianity. The ICA looks for the signal with the most non-Gaussian probability density function. The Gaussianity of the signal is measured by the fourth order cumulant, the kurtosis (see Figure 7a), which is defined by

$$\kappa = \mathbf{E}\{x^4\} - 3$$

for the simplified case of zero mean and unit variance.

Figure 7b shows an interesting property of the ICA if it is applied to room acoustics. It is an example plot of the measured kurtosis of a speech signal which was convolved with room impulse responses of different lengths. The longer the impulse response, the smaller is the kurtosis, this means the probability density function of the signal gets more Gaussian.

4.4 Single-Channel Noise Suppression

Single-channel noise suppression can be performed by spectral subtraction, if the speech and the noise signals are additively combined and uncorrelated. In a frame-wise processing mode (frame number i), the spectrum $M_{(i)}$ of the microphone signal m is reduced by the spectrum $N_{(i)}$ of the noise n to obtain the spectrum $S_{(i)}$ of the speech signal s (ν indicates the number of the spectrum line):

$$\underline{S}_{(i)}(\nu) = \underline{M}_{(i)}(\nu) - \underline{N}_{(i)}(\nu)$$

The noise spectrum $\underline{N}_{(i)}$ must be estimated in the speech pauses. The block diagram of the algorithm (Figure 8) includes therefore an voice activity detector (VAD).

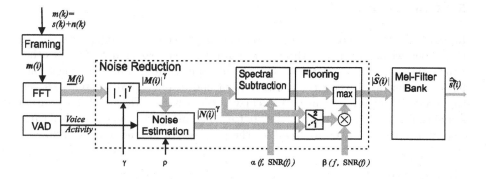

Fig. 8. Block diagram of the noise suppression algorithm [28]

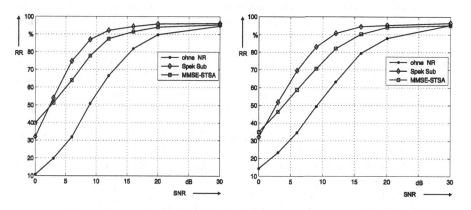

Fig. 9. Word recognition rate without and with noise reduction by spectral subtraction with dynamic adaptation of the flooring factor β [28]. The noise sources are a vacuum cleaner in the left and artificial white noise in the right diagram. For comparison, the results with the MMSE-STSA algorithm from Cappé [11] are included. UASR-based command recognizer, training with Verbmobil data, recognition experiments with 20 speakers from the Apollo database [21].

Experiments with this method have been performed combining the block diagram of Figure 8 and the UASR based command recognizer in client-server architecture which was presented already in [17, Fig. 6]. To avoid musical tones in the speech pauses, a residual noise must be maintained in the pauses, the level of which is expressed by the flooring factor β. The handling of this flooring factor proves to be essential for the result.

The result of the optimization depends on the criterium: If listeners have to judge the quality of the speech signal after the noise suppression at a MOS scale, a modified algorithm by Cappé (MMSE-STSA, [11]) is preferred. If the recognition rate has to be optimized, however, the simpler spectral subtraction with a dynamically adapted flooring factor β gives the better results. This is illustrated in Figure 9 for two different sources of noise.

5   Conclusions

Interaction research poses some requirements to the acoustic signal processing. In this paper, we demonstrated this by means of two specific scenarios. On the other hand, speech technology offers a number of sophisticated solutions which have been demonstrated using the acoustic front-end of our UASR system. As yet, these algorithms are optimized to achieve best results with speech recognition systems. It is the task of the near future to bring both parts together, this means, to optimize the acoustic front-end for the purposes of interaction research.

References

1. Alisch, L.-M.: Sprache im Kontext sozial- und humanwissenschaftlicher Forschung (Speech in the context of social and human sciences.). In: Hoffmann, R. (ed.) Elektronische Sprachsignalverarbeitung. Tagungsband der 17. Konferenz Elektronische Sprachsignalverarbeitung, Freiberg/Sachsen, August 28-30, 2006, pp. 9–10. TUDpress, Dresden (2006)
2. Altmann, U., Hermkes, R., Alisch, L.-M.: Analysis of nonverbal involvement. In: Esposito, A., Faundez-Zanuy, M., Keller, E., Marinaro, M. (eds.) COST Action 2102. LNCS (LNAI), vol. 4775, pp. 37–50. Springer, Heidelberg (2007)
3. American Psychiatric Association: Diagnostic and Statistical Manual of Mental Disorder (DSM VI). Washington D.C (1994)
4. Biemer, S., Müller, Ch.: Entwicklung eines Videospiels auf Basis von Open-Source-Bibliotheken für die Anwendung im Rahmen eines Experiments zur Untersuchung von dyadischen Interaktionsprozessen. Technische Universität Dresden, unpublished Diploma thesis (2008)
5. Blauert, J.: Analysis and synthesis of auditory scenes. In: Blauert, J. (ed.) Communication acoustics, pp. 1–25. Springer, Berlin (2005)
6. Brähler, E.: Die Erfassung des Interaktionsstiles von Therapeuten durch die automatische Sprachanalyse. Zeitschrift für Psychosomatische Medizin und Psychoanalyse 24, 156–168 (1978)
7. Brähler, E., Beckmann, D., Zenz, H.: Giessen-Test (GT) und Sprechverhalten bei neurotischen Patienten im Erstinterview. Medizinische Psychologie 1, 49–57 (1976)
8. Bos, E.H., Geerts, E., Bouhuys, A.L.: Nonverbal involvement as an indicator of prognosis in remitted depressed subjects. Psychiatry Research 113, 269–277 (2002)
9. Brandstein, M., Ward, D. (eds.): Microphone arrays. Signal processing techniques and applications. Springer, Berlin (2001)
10. Buchheim, A., Mergenthaler, E.: The relationship among attachment representation, emotion-abstraction patterns, and narrative style: A computer-based text analysis of the adult attachment interview. Psychotherapy Research 10(4), 390–407 (2000)
11. Cappé, O.: Elimination of the musical noise phenomenon with the Ephraim and Malah noise suppressor. IEEE Trans. on Speech and Audio Processing 2(2), 345–349 (1994)
12. Cassotta, L., Feldstein, S., Jaffe, J.: AVTA: A device for automatic vocal transaction analysis. Journal of Experimental Analysis of Behavior 7, 99–104 (1964)
13. Cowie, R., Douglas-Cowie, E., Tsapatsoulis, N., Votis, G., Kollias, S., Fellenz, W., Taylor, J.G.: Emotion recognition in human-computer interaction. IEEE Signal Processing Magazine 18(1), 32–80 (2001)

14. Ellgring, H.: Nonverbal communication in depression. Cambridge University Press, Cambridge (1989)
15. Gobl, C., Chasaide, A.N.: The role of voice quality in communicating emotion, mood and attitude. Speech Communication 40, 189–212 (2003)
16. Herbordt, W.: Sound capture for human/machine interfaces. Practical aspects of microphone array processing. LNCIS, vol. 315. Springer, Berlin (2005)
17. Hoffmann, R., Eichner, M., Wolff, M.: Analysis of verbal and nonverbal acoustic signals with the Dresden UASR system. In: Esposito, A., Faundez-Zanuy, M., Keller, E., Marinaro, M. (eds.) COST Action 2102. LNCS (LNAI), vol. 4775, pp. 200–218. Springer, Heidelberg (2007)
18. Krause, R.: Nonverbales interaktives Verhalten von Stotterern und ihren Gesprächspartnern. Schweizerische Zeitschrift für Psychologie 37, 177–201 (1978)
19. Krause, R.: Stuttering and nonverbal communication: Investigations about affect inhibition and stuttering. In: Giles, H., Robinson, W.P., Smith, P.M. (eds.) Language. Social psychological perspectives, pp. 261–266. Pergamon, Oxford (1982)
20. Lippmann, M.: Quellenortung in Räumen. Diploma thesis, TU Dresden (2007)
21. Maase, J., Hirschfeld, D., Koloska, U., Westfeld, T., Helbig, J.: Towards an evaluation standard for speech control concepts in real-worls scenarios. In: Proc. 8th European Conference on Speech Communication and Technology (EUROSPEECH), Geneva, September 1-4, 2003, pp. 1553–1556 (2003)
22. Maser, J.D. (ed.): Depression and expressive behaviour. Lawrence Erlbaum Associates, Hillsdale (NJ) (1987)
23. Näth, T.: Realisierung eines Algorithmus zur Quellentrennung auf Basis der Independent Component Analysis. Diploma thesis, TU Dresden (2007)
24. Petrick, R., Lohde, K., Wolff, M., Hoffmann, R.: The harming part of room acoustics in automatic speech recognition. In: Proc. Interspeech, Antwerpen, August 27-31, 2007, pp. 1094–1097 (2007)
25. Philippot, P., Feldman, R.S., Coats, E.J.: The Role of Nonverbal Behavior in Clinical Settings: Introduction and Overview. In: ibid. (ed.) Nonverbal Behavior in Clinical Settings, pp. 3–13. Oxford University Press, Oxford (2003)
26. Richter, D.: Richtmikrofon mit digitaler Signalverarbeitung. In: Fellbaum, K. (ed.) Elektronische Sprachsignalverarbeitung. Tagungsband der 18. Konferenz Elektronische Sprachsignalverarbeitung, Cottbus, September 10-12, 2007, pp. 143–148. TUDpress, Dresden (2007)
27. Scherer, K.R.: Foreword. In: Philippot, P., Feldman, R.S., Coats, E.J. (eds.) Nonverbal Behavior in Clinical Settings, pp. v–vi. Oxford University Press, Oxford (2003)
28. Wittenberg, S., Petrick, R., Wolff, M., Hoffmann, R.: Einkanalige Störgeräuschunterdrückung zur Steigerung der Worterkennungsrate eines Spracherkenners. In: Fellbaum, K. (ed.) Elektronische Sprachsignalverarbeitung. Tagungsband der 18. Konferenz Elektronische Sprachsignalverarbeitung, Cottbus, September 10-12, 2007, pp. 52–59. TUDpress, Dresden (2007)
29. Zue, V.: On Organic Interfaces. In: Proc. Interspeech, Antwerpen, August 27-31, 2007, pp. 1–8 (2007)

Application of Expressive Speech in TTS System with Cepstral Description

Jiří Přibil[1] and Anna Přibilová[2]

[1] Institute of Photonics and Electronics, Academy of Sciences CR, v.v.i.,
Chaberská 57, CZ-182 51 Prague 8, Czech Republic
Jiri.Pribil@savba.sk
[2] Slovak University of Technology, Faculty of Electrical Engineering & Information
Technology, Dept. of Radio Electronics, Ilkovičova 3, SK-812 19 Bratislava, Slovakia
Anna.Pribilova@stuba.sk

Abstract. Expressive speech synthesis representing different human emotions has been in the interests of researchers for a longer time. Recently, some experiments with storytelling speaking style have been performed. This particular speaking style is suitable for applications aimed at children as well as special applications aimed at blind people. Analyzing human storytellers' speech, we designed a set of prosodic parameters prototypes for converting speech produced by the text-to-speech (TTS) system into storytelling speech. In addition to suprasegmental characteristics (pitch, intensity, and duration) included in these speech prototypes, also information about significant frequencies of spectral envelope and spectral flatness determining degree of voicing was used.

Keywords: Speech analysis and synthesis, expressive speech, text-to-speech system.

1 Introduction

Naturalness of synthetic speech in the text-to-speech (TTS) system can be improved by its multi-voice realization (including male, female, and childish voices) [1], by expressing different emotions (sadness, anger, joy, etc.) [2], [3], [4], [5], speaking styles (formal/informal) and by other means. Storytelling speaking style may be used for child-directed speech synthesis [6] or in special software for blind people enabling them to read books. Prosody change from neutral speaking style to general storytelling speech style improves not only storytelling quality and expression of suspense, but naturalness as well [7]. However, the degree of prosody modification in the TTS system depends on the target group which it is designed to. Experiments described in [6] had shown that children prefer larger pitch manipulations for naturalness than adults. On the other hand, duration modification is considered by children to be less natural, but more funny than by adults. According to [7] higher degrees of prosody modification were perceived as unnatural. In spite of the fact that the same prosodic extremes naturally occur in human speech, they are less acceptable in the context of synthetic speech.

A. Esposito et al. (Eds.): HH and HM Interaction 2007, LNAI 5042, pp. 200–212, 2008.
© Springer-Verlag Berlin Heidelberg 2008

2 Description of Expressive Speech Conversion Method

Our new method of expressive speech synthesis combines our previous experiences in voice conversion [1] (for speaker characteristics modification), in modification of degree of voicing in voiced segments using the spectral flatness measure [8] (also characteristic for every speaker), and in prosodic parameters modification according to the prototype in a similar way as it has been used for emotional style conversion [5]. The developed expressive speech conversion technique is based on modification of the fundamental frequency, the energy, and the frame length (time duration) contours of the target (output) synthesized sentence by the parameters of the chosen prosodic prototype on the one hand, and on modification of voice properties (significant frequencies position and spectral flatness values) on the other hand. The prosodic prototype relative contours and parameters were created in dependence on the current frame voiceness – separate contours exist for voiced and unvoiced parts of a speech signal.

2.1 Overview of Used Cepstral Analysis and Synthesis Method

The cepstral speech model corresponds to the resynthesis of the speech spectrum comprising poles as well as zeros of the model transfer function and containing also information about the spectrum of the model excitation. The cepstral speech synthesis is performed by a digital filter implementing approximate inverse cepstral transformation. The system transfer function of this filter is given by an exponential relation, where the exponent is the Z-transform of the truncated speech cepstrum. To realize this system transfer function the approximation of the inverse cepstral transformation based on Padé approximation of the exponential function was applied. This approximation was realized by a cascade connection of a number of elementary filters using the cepstral coefficients representing the minimum phase approximation of the real cepstrum [9].

Phonetical research of Czech sounds had shown that some vowels and voiced consonants contain – besides the voiced excitation – also a high frequency noise component. A useful measure for distinguishing between voiced and unvoiced speech is a spectral flatness [10] successfully used also for empty speech pauses identification [11] or whispered speech recognition in noisy environment [12].

As follows from the experiments, the value of the spectral flatness measure S_F (calculated during the cepstral speech analysis [13]) also depends on a speaker [8]. Therefore we need to compute the S_F values of the input sentence generated by the TTS system and the S_F values of the target sentence pronounced in the expressive speech style and calculate ratio between these values.

The range of S_F values is theoretically $0 \div 1$. The value $S_F = 0$ represents totally voiced signal (for example a pure sinusoidal signal), $S_F = 1$ corresponds to totally unvoiced signal (for example a white noise signal). According to the statistical analysis of the Czech and Slovak words the ranges of $S_F = (0 \div 0.25)$ for voiced speech frames and $S_F = (0 \div 0.75)$ for unvoiced frames were evaluated [8].

To apply this voice adjustment approach to the cepstral speech synthesis, a modification of the excitation signal preparing phase must be executed. This modification has effect only for the synthesis of voiced frames. The high frequency noise component is added to the periodical signal from the impulse generator. It is produced by the basic random noise generator, which signal output is high-pass filtered and it is subsequently used for production of voiced frames. The mutual proportion between both generated signals is determined by the parameters $K_U = \sqrt{S_F} / \left(\sqrt{S_F} + \sqrt{1 - S_F} \right)$ and $K_V = 1 - K_U$. The excitation, in case of unvoiced frames, is produced by the basic random noise generator. Fig. 1 shows the structure of the cepstral speech synthetizer with mixed excitation.

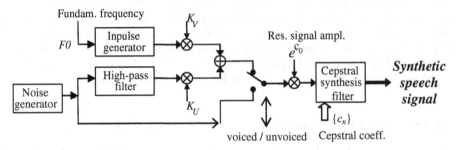

Fig. 1. Structure of the cepstral speech synthesizer with mixed excitation

2.2 Voice Properties Determination Technique

For voice properties determination the algorithm based on LPC modelling of the log speech spectrum envelope was designed. This algorithm for significant frequencies determination of the speech signal consists of four steps:

1. Creation of the spectral envelope from each frame of the speech signal.

2. Transformation of the log spectrum envelope to the time domain.

3. Computation of the LPC model parameters by autocorrelation method (gain G and LPC coefficients a_1 to a_{16} for $f_s = 16$ kHz).

4. Determination of significant frequencies from complex poles of the all-pole model (for further processing only first six significant frequencies $f_1 \div f_6$ are used, because we are interested in a perceptually relevant frequency interval <80 Hz, 5.5 kHz> [1]).

The spectral envelope is determined by spline interpolation using inverse B-spline filtering [1], [14] applied to local maxima at pitch harmonics of the log spectrum computed from the frame of pre-emphasized speech signal weighted by the Hamming window. The preemphasis filter of the form $H_p(z) = 1 - 0.9\, z^{-1}$ was used to suppress the so called glottal formant. However, for total elimination of its effect, more elaborate techniques are necessary [15].

Corresponding frequencies $f_1 \div f_6$ of all processed expressive voices were compared with the neutral voice of the text-to-speech (TTS) system and their ratio was computed. This analysis was performed on segments of five vowels ('a', 'e', 'i', 'o', 'u') in the same phonetic context comparing sentences spoken in expressive style and sentences generated by the TTS system. The significant frequencies ratios were averaged through all segments for each vowel, then through all vowels and at last the mean ratio for the first six frequencies was computed. This value corresponds to the overall significant frequencies modification factor as a ratio of the target speaker frequency and the source speaker frequency. Obtained mean ratio value γ is applied as the modification factor for calculation of the non-linear frequency scale mapping function used for spectral envelope transformation. For values $\gamma > 1$ the significant frequencies are shifted to the right, and for $\gamma < 1$ they are shifted to the left. The basic principle of the used non-linear method of mapping between the input frequency scale f and the output frequency scale $\eta(f)$ is described in more detail in [1], its graphical form is shown in Fig. 2, an example of application of this technique is shown in Fig. 3.

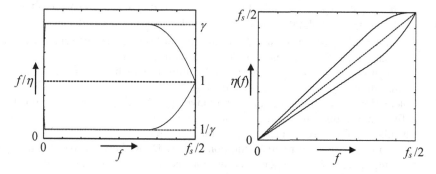

Fig. 2. Basic principle of non-linear method of mapping between the input frequency scale f and the output frequency scale $\eta(f)$: significant frequencies modification factor (left), derived frequency scale mapping function (right)

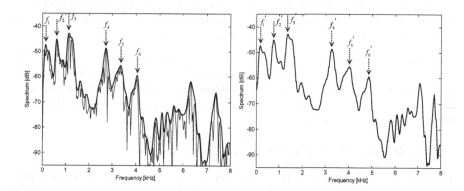

Fig. 3. Demonstration of non-linear frequency scale mapping: the original speech spectrum (stationary part of vowel 'a', male speaker, F0 $\cong$ 105 Hz, $f_s = 16$ kHz) and its envelope acquired by inverse B-spline filtering (left), non-linear modification (20% shift of significant frequencies f_1 to f_6 in a perceptually relevant frequency interval) of the speech spectrum envelope (right)

2.3 Building of the Prosodic Prototypes

The melody of speech utterances is given by the *fundamental frequency* (F0) contour. Together with the intensity and the speech unit duration it plays an essential role in transmission of prosodic information. The F0 contour is obtained during the utterance's analysis in the frames with the length of 10-30 ms, where speech can be supposed to be stationary[1]. According to the energy of the analyzed speech signal, several beginning and ending frames are not included in the F0 contour. As the basic F0 contour is not continuous curve, the *virtual contour* (VF0) must be obtained by linear, cubic, or another interpolation in the unvoiced parts of the speech. The problem with the different number of frames between the basic (generated by TTS) and the processed utterance can be solved by *linear time scale mapping* (LTSM) operation of the VF0, energy, and time duration contours.

The building process of prosodic prototypes of expressive speech style is similar to the emotional style prototype preparation [5], so it consists of following steps:

1. Cepstral analysis of the basic (TTS) and the target (expressive) sentences – determination of the fundamental frequency and energy contours.
2. Removal of the low energy starting and ending frames by the energy threshold, definition of prototype working length W_{LR}.
3. Calculation of virtual F0 contour for unvoiced frames by cubic interpolation, definition of minimum, maximum, and mean values.
4. Calculation of relative values of the virtual F0 contour.
5. Determination of time relative duration ratio (RDUR) between basic and target speaking style parts in dependence on voiceness – voiced/unvoiced; calculation of mean ratio values.
6. Calculation of virtual relative time duration contours (VRDUR) – by cubic interpolation separately for voiced and unvoiced frames.
7. Determination of the energy ratio (REn) – between basic and target speaking style speech parts in dependence on voiceness; calculation of mean ratio values.
8. Calculation of virtual relative energy contours (VREn) – by cubic interpolation separately for voiced and unvoiced frames.

For modelling of prosodic parameters every prototype record consists of five relative virtual contour files: VF0 contour, and separate files corresponding to voiced and unvoiced frames for VRDUR and VREn contours. It contains also information about the used frame length L_F in samples, working length WL_{LR}, energy threshold En_{min}, minimum, maximum, and mean values of F0.

2.4 Application of the Expressive Speech Conversion

The application of expressive speech parameters can be realized in the form of post-processing operation on the speech utterances produced by the TTS system, or by including new function blocks to the structure of the real-time TTS system [5]. In both cases it is supposed, that the initial two phases (voice frequency properties

---

[1] The frame length depends on the mean pitch period of the processed signal. We had chosen 24-ms frames for the male voice, 20-ms frames for the female voice, and 12-ms frames for the childish voice.

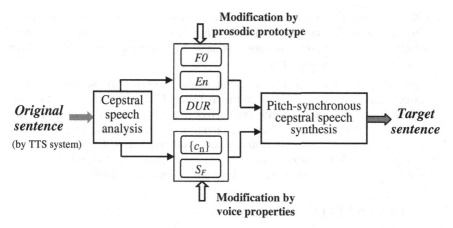

Fig. 4. Block diagram of post-processing application for expressive speech conversion

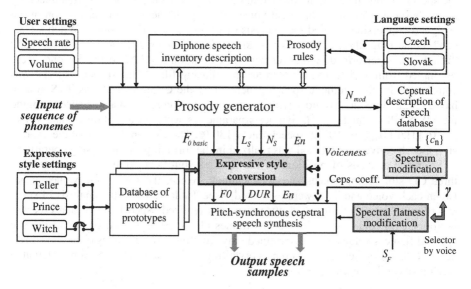

Fig. 5. Block diagram of the kernel of the Czech and Slovak TTS system with cepstral description together with applied new function blocks for expressive speech conversion

determination including the spectral flatness measure calculation and prosodic expressive style preparation) were passed.

In the case of post-processing realization, the developed expressive speech conversion method consists of following four steps (see block diagram in Fig. 4):

1. Cepstral analysis of source sentences generated by the TTS system with basic prosody by rules.
2. Linear time scale mapping of the prosodic prototype of the selected expressive voice to the processed sentence (compression or expansion of relative F0, energy, and time duration contours).

3. F0, energy, and time duration contours modification by the prosodic prototypes.
4. Resynthesis of the target sentences by the cepstral speech model (with transformed significant frequencies position, applied S_F values, and modified F0, energy, and time duration contours).

Instead of expressive speech conversion method realized in the form of postprocessing, new blocks can be added in the real-time TTS system (between the prosody generator and the output speech synthesizer – see Fig. 5). This approach leaves out the cepstral analysis steps, because parameters of cepstral description are available for each frame together with information about voiceness, frame length, pitch period, and energy. Application of the expressive style prototype consists in modification of prosody parameters used to control the output speech synthesis.

3 Material and Experiments

For our first experiments with the expressive speech conversion we had at disposal the speech corpus from the multi-medial CD with 10 stories in Slovak pronounced by the male speaker imitating different voices of story characters. For verification of the designed conversion method the analysis of 65 sentences of the story "Witch's Garden" containing three expressive – *storytelling voices* ("Teller", "Prince", and "Witch") was performed. Sentences with time duration from 2.2 to 15.5 seconds were resampled from 44.1 to 16 kHz with an anti-aliasing filter. This speech material was compared with the synthetic speech generated by the Czech and Slovak TTS system based on the diphone inventory with cepstral description realized as the speech engine for MS SAPI 5 standard [1]. Synthesis parameters were set as follows: male voice, $f_s = 16$ kHz, $F0_{basic} = 110$ Hz, speech rate = 130 %. The first application of the expressive speech conversion method was realized in the form of post-processing operation.

From the analysis of positions of the first six significant frequencies for each of three CD storytelling voices and TTS synthetic voice, the mean ratio values γ between each voice and TTS were evaluated – see Table 1. Then, the analysis of spectral flatness values of all tested utterances was realized. Speech signal analysis was performed for total number of 56 695 frames classified as voiced or unvoiced. The spectral flatness values were determined only from the voiced frames (totally 33 118), next the S_F ratios between different storytelling voices and the TTS were calculated (see results in Table 2).

Table 1. Summary results of mean significant frequencies ratios between different storytelling voices and the TTS (for all vowels)

	teller: TTS	prince: TTS	witch: TTS
mean ratio γ	1.0924	1.1146	1.2026

Table 2. Summary results of analysis of spectral flatness values (voiced frames only)

Type of voice	Number of frames	S_F mean [-]	S_F ratio [-] (X:TTS)
Basic (TTS)	17745	0.0232	1
Teller	12486	0.0379	1.6336
Prince	777	0.0431	1.8577
Witch	2110	0.0439	1.8922

A small database of prosodic prototypes in storytelling style was created. There are three prototypes for prosody parameters modification (F0, energy, and time duration) corresponding to each of three mentioned storytelling voices. Cepstral analysis of processed sentences was performed with segmentation in 24-ms frames[2] and the frame rate f_F = 83.3 Hz. Generally, the length (in frames) of calculated VF0 contour of prosodic prototypes is different from the processed sentence, which it is transposed to. The time modification factor Γ corresponds to the ratio of the number of frames of the prototype N_{prot} and the original N_{orig}. Values of $\Gamma > 1$ correspond to time compression, $\Gamma < 1$ corresponds to time expansion [5].

Practical realization of the storytelling speech conversion process is demonstrated on the sentence (from the Slovak story "Witch's Garden") *Majte so mnou zľutovanie* (Please, don't be angry with me). Progress of conversion to the "Witch" speech style and voice applied to this sentence is shown in Figures 6 to 13.

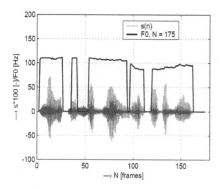 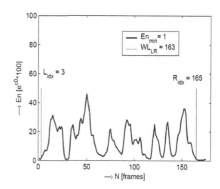

Fig. 6. Input speech signal of the sentence *Majte so mnou zľutovanie*, generated by the TTS system (f_s = 16 kHz, frame length = 24 ms) together with F0 contour (left), corresponding energy contour and definition of the working length W_{LR} by the energy threshold (right)

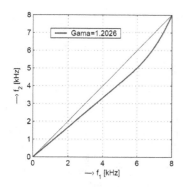 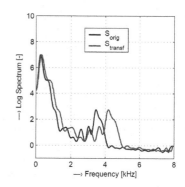

Fig. 7. Applied non-linear frequency scale mapping function for γ = 1.2026 (left), demonstration of corresponding spectral envelope transformation (right)

---

[2] It corresponds to choice of a male voice – the CD storytelling speech material was pronounced by the male professional actor, and the TTS system was set to produce the synthetic speech with male voice.

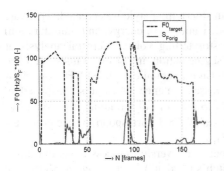
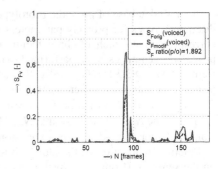

Fig. 8. Spectral flatness of the original sentence together with target F0 contour (left), application of S_F modification – for voiced frames only (right)

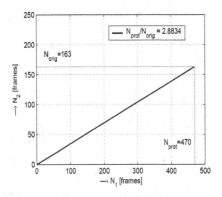
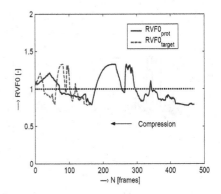

Fig. 9. Linear time scale mapping of the "Witch" storytelling style prototype to the length of processed sentence (left), compression of RVF0 prototype contour (right)

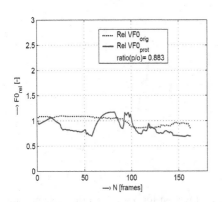
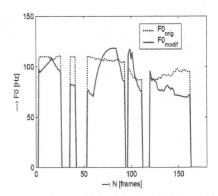

Fig. 10. Comparison of VF0 contours from original and "Witch" prototype (left), transposition of the target F0 contour derived from the prototype (right)

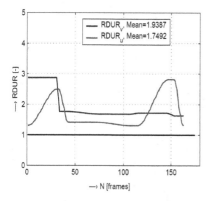
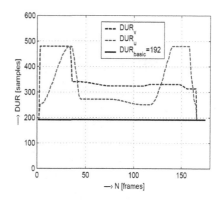

Fig. 11. Demonstration of time duration modification: prototype relative contours RDUR (left), modification of the synthesis absolute frame length in samples (right)

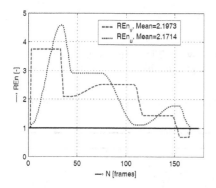
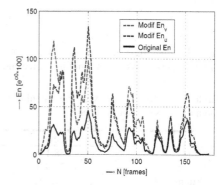

Fig. 12. Demonstration of energy modification: prototype relative contours REn in dependence on voiceness (left), modification of the synthesis energy (right)

3.1 Evaluation of Storytelling Speech Conversion

For evaluation of applied storytelling speech conversion the listening test called *Determination of storytelling speech type* has been processed. In this test, eighteen listeners (10 Slovaks and 8 Czechs, 13 men and 5 women) chose the storytelling speech type from "Teller", "Prince", "Witch", or "Cannot be recognized". Every listening test consists of ten evaluation sets randomly selected from the testing corpus. The testing corpus was created with the help of the above-mentioned Czech and Slovak TTS system. It consists of 150 sentences altogether in the Slovak language (with the average time duration of 3.5 seconds) – every evaluation set contains one basic sentence (for comparison with its sound before application of storytelling speech conversion) and three representative sentences for each of three storytelling speech types (it means nine sentences with converted storytelling speech).

For practical realization of listening test the internet version was used [16]. The listening test program and testing speech corpus are stored on the server PC, where the

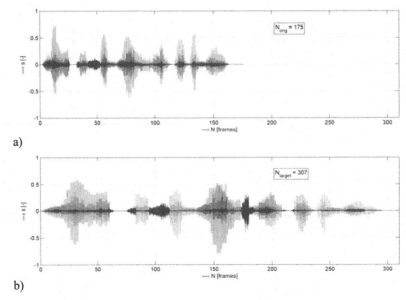

a)

b)

Fig. 13. Time signal of original sentence generated by the TTS system (a), after resynthesis with transposed "Witch" storytelling voice and style prototype (b)

Table 3. Confusion matrix of the listening test where columns contain true values and rows contain values chosen by listeners

	Teller	Prince	Witch
Teller	**58.1 %**	30.0 %	1.9 %
Prince	26.9 %	**55.0 %**	0 %
Witch	1.3 %	0.6 %	**96.9 %**
Not recognized	12.7 %	14.4 %	1.2 %

listening tests are also practically executed. The performance of current listening test is controlled from the user local computer. The testing program also automatically generates the text protocol about the currently running test. Continuously collected test output values are stored on the server, which can perform also statistical post-processing and evaluation of results. Obtained results of executed listening tests are shown in the confusion matrix in Table 3. The confusion rate of the original voices did not have to be calculated, because it was given by the semantic context of the story (it was evident what can/cannot say teller, prince, or witch).

4 Conclusion

Our first experiments with expressive speech conversion were realized in the form of post-processing operation on the speech utterances produced by the TTS system with neutral (flat) prosody. An advantage of the used method is that expressive − storytelling voice and style prototypes can be applied to the sentences regardless of their information content and lexical context.

The first listening test for evaluation of the applied storytelling speech was realized. From obtained results follows, that there always exist audible differences between the basic sentences generated by the TTS system and those modified by storytelling speech conversion. The best determination results are for "Witch" voice, because there were applied the greatest changes of frequency voice properties together with prosodic parameters (first of all, typically two to three times longer time duration). The "Prince" and "Teller" voices and styles were interchanged in a number of cases, because their frequency voice properties and prosodic parameters were similar.

At present, we work on the implementation of storytelling speech conversion directly into the real-time TTS system. In future, it would be necessary to build a large database of storytelling prosodic prototypes adding new voices from speech material of other Slovak and Czech stories (like "Princess", "Dwarf", "Soldier", etc.)

Acknowledgments. The paper was realized within the framework of the research project AVOZ 20670512 and has been supported by the Grant Agency of the Academy of Sciences of the Czech Republic (1QS108040569), and the Ministry of Education of the Slovak Republic (1/3107/06).

References

1. Přibilová, A., Přibil, J.: Non-linear Frequency Scale Mapping for Voice Conversion in Text-to-Speech System with Cepstral Description. Speech Communication 48, 1691–1703 (2006)
2. Iida, A., Campbell, N., Higuchi, F., Yasumura, M.: A Corpus-Based Speech Synthesis System with Emotion. Speech Communication 40, 161–187 (2003)
3. Navas, E., Hernáez, I., Luengo, I.: An Objective and Subjective Study of the Role of Semantics and Prosodic Features in Building Corpora for Emotional TTS. IEEE Transactions on Audio, Speech, and Language Processing 14, 1117–1127 (2006)
4. Tao, J., Kang, Y., Li, A.: Prosody Conversion from Neutral Speech to Emotional Speech. IEEE Transactions on Audio, Speech, and Language Processing 14, 1145–1154 (2006)
5. Přibil, J., Přibilová, A.: Emotional Style Conversion in the TTS System with Cepstral Description. In: Esposito, A., Faundez-Zanuy, M., Keller, E., Marinaro, M. (eds.) COST Action 2102. LNCS (LNAI), vol. 4775, pp. 65–73. Springer, Heidelberg (2007)
6. House, D., Bell, L., Gustafson, K., Johansson, L.: Child-Directed Speech Synthesis: Evaluation of Prosodic Variation for an Educational Computer Program. In: Proceedings of Eurospeech, Budapest, pp. 1843–1846 (1999)
7. Theune, M., Meijs, K., Heylen, D., Ordelman, R.: Generating Expressive Speech for Storytelling Applications. IEEE Transactions on Audio, Speech, and Language Processing 14, 1137–1144 (2006)
8. Přibil, J., Přibilová, A.: Voicing Transition Frequency Determination for Harmonic Speech Model. In: Proceedings of the 13th International Conference on Systems, Signals and Image Processing, Budapest, pp. 25–28 (2006)
9. Vích, R.: Cepstral Speech Model, Padé Approximation, Excitation, and Gain Matching in Cepstral Speech Synthesis. In: Proceedings of the 15th Biennial International EURASIP Conference Biosignal, Brno, pp. 77–82 (2000)

10. Gray, A.H., Markel, J.D.: A Spectral-Flatness Measure for Studying the Autocorrelation Method of Linear Prediction of Speech Analysis. IEEE Transactions on Acoustics, Speech, and Signal Processing ASSP-22, 207–217 (1974)
11. Esposito, A., Stejskal, V., Smékal, Z., Bourbakis, N.: The Significance of Empty Speech Pauses: Cognitive and Algorithmic Issues. In: Proceedings of the 2nd International Symposium on Brain Vision and Artificial Intelligence, Naples, pp. 542–554 (2007)
12. Ito, T., Takeda, K., Itakura, F.: Analysis and Recognition of Whispered Speech. Speech Communication 45, 139–152 (2005)
13. Přibil, J., Madlová, A.: Two Synthesis Methods Based on Cepstral Parameterization. Radioengineering 11(2), 35–39 (2002)
14. Unser, M.: Splines. A Perfect Fit for Signal and Image Processing. IEEE Signal Processing Magazine 16, 22–38 (1999)
15. Akande, O.O., Murphy, P.J.: Estimation of the Vocal Tract Transfer Function with Application to Glottal Wave Analysis. Speech Communication 46, 15–36 (2005)
16. Přibil, J., Přibilová, A.: Distributed Listening Test Program for Synthetic Speech Evaluation. In: Proceedings of the 34 Jahrestagung für Akustik DAGA 2008, Dresden (to be published, 2008)

Speech Emotion Perception by Human and Machine

Szabolcs Levente Tóth, David Sztahó, and Klára Vicsi

Laboratory of Speech Acoustics, Budapest University of Technology and Economics,
Department of Telecommunications and Media Informatics,
Stoczek u. 2, 1111 Budapest, Hungary
{toth.sz,vicsi,sztaho.david}@tmit.bme.hu

Abstract. The human speech contains and reflects information about the emotional state of the speaker. The importance of research of emotions is increasing in telematics, information technologies and even in health services. The research of the mean acoustical parameters of the emotions is a very complicated task. The emotions are mainly characterized by suprasegmental parameters, but other segmental factors can contribute to the perception of the emotions as well. These parameters are varying within one language, according to speakers etc. In the first part of our research work, human emotion perception was examined. Steps of creating an emotional speech database are presented. The database contains recordings of 3 Hungarian sentences with 8 basic emotions pronounced by nonprofessional speakers. Comparison of perception test results obtained with database recorded by nonprofessional speakers showed similar recognition results as an earlier perception test obtained with professional actors/actresses. It was also made clear, that a neutral sentence before listening to the expression of the emotion pronounced by the same speakers cannot help the perception of the emotion in a great extent. In the second part of our research work, an automatic emotion recognition system was developed. Statistical methods (HMM) were used to train different emotional models. The optimization of the recognition was done by changing the acoustic preprocessing parameters and the number of states of the Markov models.

Keywords: Emotion Recognition, Automatic Speech Recognition, Human Speech Perception, Speech Technology, Hidden Markov Models, MFCC.

1 Introduction

Linguistic and paralinguistic elements are both important parts of human-human communication. The additional meaning (emotions and attitude) represented in multimodal forms of communication helps to understand the contextual background. In human-machine communication the recognition and synthesis of emotions serves a various range of purposes: it helps to improve user acceptance level of communication applications (with special focus to the frustration emotion/attitude), it can support a parallel telecommunication channel (e.g. automatic generated emoticons in online text messaging), it helps to achieve more naturalistic virtual characters, it can even help researches in psychology. Multimodal emotion synthesis and recognition applications are widely used in user-orientated information technology.

A. Esposito et al. (Eds.): HH and HM Interaction 2007, LNAI 5042, pp. 213–224, 2008.
© Springer-Verlag Berlin Heidelberg 2008

Researchers of emotion perception and recognition use mostly acted (simulated) emotional databases (e.g. the Berlin database [14], the Groningen corpus [10]or the Danish emotional speech database [7]. Natural emotional reactions are much harder to inspire; the number of truly spontaneous databases is limited [9]. One way of obtaining spontaneous emotional data is to record radio or television talk shows (but here the aired shows are already strongly edited), data from call centers, therapy sessions, etc. [1, 2, 5, 9]. Ethical problems may also come up with designing emotionally triggered situations. The difference between the much less accessible spontaneous emotional expressions and the acted emotions is a matter of discussion [4, 6].

It is widely known that prosody contains at least part of the emotional information in speech. Prosody can be divided into three components: intonation, tempo, and loudness, represented as pitch, duration and energy features of the speech signal [11], and according to our opinion, the tonal information, represented as spectra. The question, which main features contribute the most to understanding emotion information, is yet to be answered.

In the first part of our research, human speech emotion perception was examined. Our first aim was to decide whether the emotional database built from nonprofessional speakers' recordings can compete with professional actor/actress databases. Our second aim was to find out how much an emotionally neutral sentence of the same speaker contributes to the recognition of a sentence with emotional content.

In the second part of our research, automatic speech emotion recognition tests were carried out using a greatly expanded database. We were looking for the most important features for the automatic speech emotion recognition.

2 Examination of Speech Emotion Perception

2.1 Creating the Emotional Database

International literature of emotion research uses a number of basic sets of emotions: from just three emotions (depression, neutrality, suicidal state [9]) up to thirteen different kinds of emotions (like the [3, 16]) or even more. One of the most common sets is fear, anger, sadness and happiness. This categorization reflects the theory that a few universal types underlie the whole emotional life [6]. Another possible categorization is the one commonly used in psychology, linguistics and speech technology, also described in the MPEG-4 standard [15]: happiness, sadness, anger, surprised, and scorn/disgusted. The emotions in MPEG-4 standard were originally created to describe facial animation parameters (FAPs) of virtual characters. Our final selection of emotions is based on the six emotions described above, together with the nervous/excited emotion (because of its obvious role in telecommunication situations), and the emotionally neutral state.

The emotions recorded in our database were acted, forced emotions. Spontaneous speech emotions would have been a better base for a perceptual investigation, but they are much harder to acquire; not to mention the ethical dilemma of forcing people to produce genuine emotions. In most social environment it is highly impolite for a grownup human being to express emotions aloud in most circumstances. This dilemma is a common problem in emotional database projects, although a number of researches [4, 6] showed that a well-designed acted emotional database can play a useful role, too.

Table 1. Range of emotions examined

1. happy
2. sad
3. angry
4. surprised
5. disgusted/scorn
6. afraid
7. nervous/excited
8. neutrality

Table 2. Hungarian sentences without emotional meaning

Sentence in Hungarian	Translation
Kovács Katival szeretnék beszélni!	I would like to speak with Kate Smith, please.
A falatozóban sört, bort, üdítőitalokat és finom malacsültet lehetett kapni.	In the restaurant, you can get beer, wine, beverages and delicious pork.
A jövő hétvégén megyek el.	I leave the next weekend.

Building an emotional database, one must make sure that the emotional information carried by the speech should not be affected with the possible emotional information of the semantic layer already present in the speech. Therefore we decided to record sentences with the least possible emotional meaning, each one of the sentences spoken with all kinds of emotions. Three Hungarian sentences were selected for the speech database created for the speech emotion perception tests (Table 2).

The recorded speakers had to pronounciate three sentences with each emotion. Repetitions were carried out, if it was necessary. The first sentence is a commonly used phrase in telecommunication dialogues. The second sentence is often used in Hungarian speech databases because of its phonetic richness. The third sentence is lacking high frequency components (fricatives), which can be useful for a later spectral domain investigation.

7 speakers (3 women and 4 men) were selected for the subjective tests, each one of them making 8-8 emotional recordings of the 3 sentences. These speakers were workers of the laboratory and associates. The records were made under the same conditions in the Laboratory of Speech Acoustics. The recording equipment we used was PC with soundcards (Creative Audigy), and condensate microphones (Monacor). All speech was recorded at 44100 Hz sample rate, 16 bits and mono sound. The recordings were amplitude-normalized.

2.2 Speech Emotion Perception Tests

The human speech emotion recognition tests were carried out using software we built, ran on both portable and desktop computers. 13 listeners were contributing to the research as subjects for the perception tests. The listeners had to listen to series of

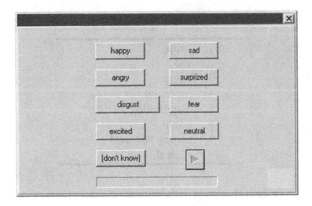

Fig. 1. User interface of the software used for subjective testing

emotional speech recordings through headphones, and after each emotional recording, they had to choose, which emotion they recognized. The speech recordings were played back using software developed for subjective testing purposes (Figure 1).

The software statistically mixed the playing order of the recordings. Because of that, subjects never listened to a recording of the same speaker successively, they could not get used to one or another person's individual way of expressing emotions. The perception tests began with instructions and a few samples of the emotional speech to make the subjects familiar with the test setup. In the first sequence, the test subjects listened to a sequence of emotional sentences alone. In the second sequence they listened to emotional sentences just after a neutral sentence of the same speaker and sentence type. In order to check the learning effect, a third sequence of shuffled recordings was also played (once more, without the reference sentences). The listening tests lasted about 30-40 minutes; therefore we enrolled two short brakes to avoid the effects of fatigue.

2.3 Discussion of the Perception Test Results

Perception test results are shown in Figures 2-4. During the emotion perception tests, one of our aims was to decide whether the emotionally neutral sentence before the emotional one helps the human emotion recognition. Figure 2 shows the emotional recognition of the previously described three test-phases. The light gray columns represent recognition results of the emotional sentences alone (first sequence of listening), the darker columns stand for results of emotional sentences after neutral ones (second turn), and the white bars represent the results of emotional sentences alone again (third listening). The average and standard deviation values presented in the legend of the figure were calculated according to the different speakers.

The test results show that the listeners can recognize all of the emotions better together with emotionally neutral sentences, but the order of magnitude of the standard deviations makes the improvements less significant. This result suggests that the emotional sentence alone may give almost all the information necessary for the recognition of its emotion. The learning effect does not influence the result, because results

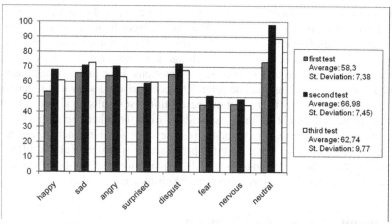

Fig. 2. Emotional perception test results; in percentage

of the third listening series do not differ from the first one in a big extent, considering the order of magnitude of the standard deviation.

The best recognized emotions were sad, disgust/scorn, and angry. These emotions are mostly categorized as strongly negative emotions [6], but so is fear, which was the least recognized emotion in our perception research. The next level below the best recognized three emotions includes surprised and happy. Fear and nervous were the least recognized emotions during the speech emotion perception tests. Altogether, it is clear, that at this rate of human speech emotion recognition (around 60%); it will be a hard task to create automatic speech emotion recognition system with much higher recognition results. It is also obvious from the results, how much the semantic information improves human emotion recognition.

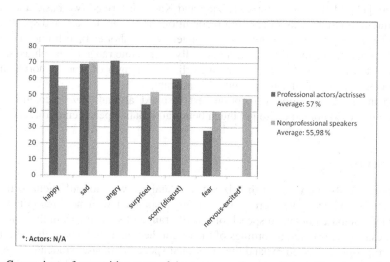

Fig. 3. Comparison of recognition rates of the corresponding emotions, with actors and nonprofessional speakers; in percentage

The results of our subjective listening tests were compared to a former Hungarian emotion perception research result [8]. The speech recordings of the former research were made with professional actors and actresses. The purpose of perception tests in that research was to help evaluation of a Hungarian emotional speech synthesis. Our research and [8] had a common set of seven emotions. Five different sentences were recorded from two actresses and one actor. The comparison is shown in Figure 3.

It was interesting for us to see that our perception test results obtained with nonprofessional speakers does not differ systematically from the other one with actors. Happiness and anger was recognizable better in case of professional actors, all the other emotions were recognized better with nonprofessional speakers, But the difference is not considerable. This knowledge is useful for planning new emotional databases in the future, for the expenses of the actors can be eliminated [8], [12].

3   Automatic Emotion Recognition

Discrete recognition in general means to estimate, which communicable, discrete symbol (in our case: emotion) the examined section of the signal (speech) contains. The estimation should be based on certain measurable properties of the infinitely diverse, continuous speech signal. In the automatic recognition task, the recognizable shape should first be characterized by measurable parameters. This step is often called feature extraction, because the preprocessing intends to create the most efficient parameters for the recognition. The aim of feature extraction is to select those features, which can be a base of a good classification. Unfortunately, currently, we do not know exactly, which speech parameters characterize the emotions. In general, fundamental frequency and energy (intensity) time courses are the most commonly used features in speech emotion research.

In the literature, there are detailed experiments looking for the most efficient parameters [11], [17]. For example, Hozjan and Kacic described two basic approaches in feature extraction tasks in emotion recognition. The time-domain and spectral features of the signal can be examined in a longer or in a shorter time frame. The long-term features' frame length is characteristically in the time range of the phrases, while the short-term frames are of smaller range, like the length of words, morphemes or phonemes, or even smaller-than-phoneme time range.

Human speech emotion perception test resulted around 60% recognition rate, Therefore, we do not expect to get much better automatic speech emotion recognition results.

3.1   Database

Preliminary tests showed that the size of the database was not sufficient to train an automatic recognizer; therefore it was greatly expanded with new recordings. The expanded database contained speech of a wider range of speakers as in the perception tests: besides the original recordings of the researchers and students of the laboratory, 30 more people joined to expand the emotional speech database: students from other faculties, e.g. physiologists, teachers, lawyers, musicians and many more were included. In view of the former subjective test results, the new recordings were elaborately selected by listening tests; thus the worst recognized recordings were not included in the final database. The listening tests were carried out by a small group of the researchers; altogether 133 recordings were excluded from the training and testing databases. The expanded database contained emotional speech recordings from 37 speakers. The new database contained altogether 888 recordings (37 speakers, 3 sentences, 8 emotions), from which 755 were selected to train the recognizer. In average, every sentence was recorded 31 times with each emotional state.

3.2 Recognition Experiment

The emotional recognizer was built using HTK [13] for training Hidden Markov Models. The feature extraction was done by the prosodic acoustic preprocessor unit of a segmentator and recognizer developed in our laboratory [19], computing the smoothed fundamental frequency and intensity values. The classification was prepared by the framework of HTK. The fundamental frequency and intensity values were calculated from the input speech signal with 10 ms frame rate, fundamental frequency with 75 ms, intensity with 150 ms window. Fundamental frequency values were corrected by median filtering. Delta and delta-delta parameters were obtained by derivating fundamental frequency and intensity; using both time and frequency domain derivating. The spectral vector-coefficients were obtained with the commonly used Bark-scale filtering.

The average length of the spoken sentences was 2 to 3 seconds; therefore the number of training vectors per recordings was about 200-300. The HMM tries to divide the frames (coming in every 10 ms) by 2 less than the number of states. Defining the number of states in the Markov-model is a basic question during optimization. Number of states set too low or too high has an influence on the basic functioning of the recognizer.

Numerous optimization experiments were done to obtain the best emotion recognition parameters. In the first experiments we looked for the optimal number of states of the HMM emotion models. In the second part, spectral domain features were added to the recognizer's input vectors. Trouble with spectral domain processing is, that phonetic variability in sentences causes a problem calculating the long-term spectrum of different sentences (especially the fricatives, because of their wide spread spectrum). In accordance with some sources, another problem is that, although the third and following formants may be defining the emotional content of speech, the higher second formant of certain phonemes (e.g. in the phoneme "i") can have a higher average frequency, then the third formant of other phonemes (e.g. "a"). Therefore, there is no way to differentiate by formant frequencies without segmenting and recognizing the corresponding segments. If the speech is unknown, with no fixed vocabulary, this information is hard to get and will cause another important source of error in the emotion recognition procedure.

3.3 Test Results and Evaluation

Four sets of training data were separated:

- all three sentences,
- the first sentence,
- the second sentence, and
- the third sentence.

32 recordings of each sentence, of the best 4 speaker (selected with subjective tests) served as testing data.

After the preliminary selection of recordings it turned out that the amount of training data was insufficient for training the third sentence alone with 8 emotions. Therefore training the recognizer with the third sentence type was not possible.

The results of our preliminary tests showed that the size of the training database was clearly insufficient. The further expansion of the database would probably lead to better recognition results, but for that we have not had the resources. Therefore, it was decided to carry on with the automatic speech emotion recognition experiments with the reduced set of the four best recognized emotions (Figure 4).

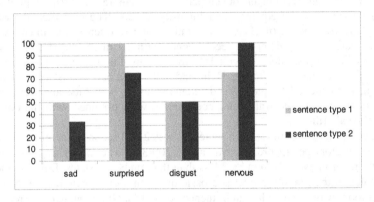

Fig. 4. Recognition of 4 emotions (surprised, disgust, nervous, sad), recognizer trained with two sentences separately (Kovács Katival szeretnék beszélni! – A falatozóban sört, bort, üdítőitalokat és finom malacsültet lehet kapni.). The input training vectors were composed of the values of fundamental frequency and energy, together with their first and second derivates.

Figure 4. shows that the results of the recognizer trained with the reduced set of emotions were in the same order of magnitude as the subjective (human) recognition results.

In the first optimization experiment fundamental frequency and intensity features together with their first and second derivates were extracted as acoustical preprocessing (14 dimensional vectors, 7 for intensity and 7 for fundamental frequency). The state numbers were changed from 3 up to 17. The best results were obtained when the state number was 13, that is the state number we used in the recognition experiments

In the second experiment we added spectral domain information to the training data. The spectral parameters were calculated with 25 ms window size, with an HTK implementation of discrete cosine-transformation of Mel-scale cepstral filter coefficients.

Comparison of the automatic speech emotion recognition results, recognizer trained with fundamental frequency, energy, and with or without spectral features is shown in Figure 5.

Adding spectral features to fundamental frequency and intensity clearly improved recognition rates.

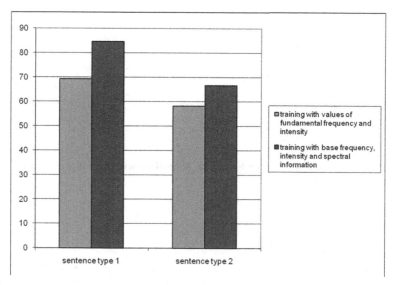

Fig. 5. Recognition of 4 emotions (surprised, disgust, nervous, sad), recognizer trained with the two sentences separately. Training data composed of fundamental frequency and energy (light grey bars) and fundamental frequency, energy and spectral values.

In these experiments, the recognizer was trained separately with two different types of sentences. We also trained the recognizer with the two different types of sentences together, but the recognition was much weaker. While the first sentence is a short stating sentence, the second one is a complex sentence with enumerations. The different grammatical structure probably forces the speaker to choose different supra-segmental expressions. The automatic recognizer performs better, when only separate grammatical type of sentence serves for training data. Multiple types of training sentences clearly prevent the recognizer from creating good classes. We suppose that this is the reason, why separate training resulted better recognition rates.

By a thorough examination of the vowel duration, fundamental frequency and energy time-courses of the speech signals, it was found that these three prosodic parameters depend on the linguistic type of the sentences in a big extent. Examples of vowel duration and fundamental frequency time-courses of sentence type 1. and 2. are shown in Figures 6-9.

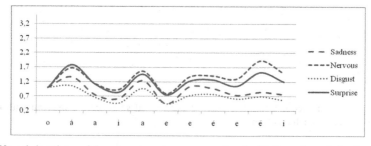

Fig. 6. Vowel durations of the second sentence, normalized with the value of the first vowel's duration, for each emotion

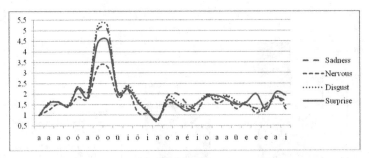

Fig. 7. Vowel durations of the second sentence, normalized with the value of the first vowel's duration, for each emotion

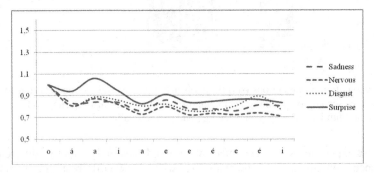

Fig. 8. Fundamental frequency time-course of the first sentence, normalized with the first frequency value, for each emotion

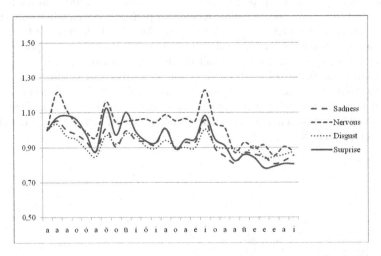

Fig. 9. Fundamental frequency time-course of the second sentence, normalized with the first frequency value, for each emotion

It was observed, that according to the emotions, the time courses of these prosodic parameters were changing in parallel for most part of the sentences. Special places were found, where theses parallelisms were mixed up, e.g. the second part of the second sentence. These places were found in different locations, according to the linguistic type of sentences [18]. The semantic meaning of all of the sentences were carefully selected not to affect the emotional meaning, therefore, we suppose that the basic grammatical structure of the sentences is involved with the location of the emotional expression.

4 Conclusions

The article shows early steps in development of an emotion recognition system capable of recognizing eight basic emotions. The number of these emotions was reduced during the development of the automatic recognizer to the four best recognized emotions: sad, surprised, disgusted/scorn and nervous/excited. The first aim of our research was to learn about the processes of human emotion recognition. Our second aim was to construct an emotion recognizer and optimize its important parameters.

In the human emotion perception experiment, we did not get significantly different results with emotional speech recordings of nonprofessional and professional speakers. The test results show that the listeners cannot recognize the sentences with emotional meaning better together with sentences without emotional meaning in a great extent. This result suggests that a sentence with emotional meaning alone may give all the information necessary for emotion recognition.

In general, fundamental frequencies and intensities time courses were the most commonly used features for the expression of emotions, both in the field of speech recognition and synthesis. In our automatic emotion recognition experiment, it was found, that adding spectral information greatly improves the recognition results.

On the other hand, it was also found, that recognition results with separately trained sentence-types are much better than training all sentence types together. Examination of certain features of the speech signal showed why the recognition result was improved.

In the future, increased training database is necessary to clear out the nature of speech emotions better, and to improve the results of the automatic recognition.

References

1. Amir, N., Ziv, S., Cohen, R.: Characteristics of authentic anger in Hebrew speech. In: Proceedings of Eurospeech 2003, Geneva, pp. 713–716 (2003)
2. Ang, J., Dhillon, R., Krupski, A., Shipberg, E., Stockle, A.: Prosody-based automatic detection of annoyance and frustration in human-computer dialog. In: Proceedings of ICLSP 2002, Denver, Colorado, pp. 2037–2040 (2002)
3. Banse, R., Scherer, K.: Acoustic profiles in vocal emotion expression. J. Pers. Social Psychol. 70(3), 614–636 (1996)
4. Bänziger, T., Scherer, K.R.: Using Actor Portrayals to Systematically Study Multimodal Emotion Expression: The GEMEP Corpus. In: Affective Computing and Intelligent Interaction, pp. 476–487. Springer, Berlin (2007)

5. Batliner, A., Fischer, K., Huber, R., Spilker, J., Noeth, E.: How to find trouble in communication. Speech Commun. 40, 117–143 (2003)
6. Douglas-Cowie, E., Campbell, N., Cowie, R., Roach, P.: Emotional speech: towards a new generation of databases. Speech Communication 40, 33–60 (2003)
7. Engberg, I.S., Hansen, A.V., Andersen, O., Dalsgaard, P.: Design, recording and verification of a Danish Emotional Speech Database. In: Proceedings of the Eurospeech 1997, Rhodes, Greece (1997)
8. Fék, M., Olaszy, G., Szabó, J., Németh, G., Gordos, G.: Érzelem kifejezése gépi beszéddel. Beszédkutatás 2005. MTA-NyTI, pp. 134–144 (2005)
9. France, D., Shiavi, R., Silverman, S., Silverman, M., Wilkes, D.: Acoustical properties of speech as indicators of depression and suicidal risk. IEEE Trans. Biomed. Engng. 47(7), 829–837 (2000)
10. Groningen corpus S0020 ELRA, http://www.icp.inpg.fr/ELRA
11. Hozjan, V., Kacic, Z.: A rule-based emotion-dependent feature extraction method for emotion analysis from speech. The Journal of the Acoustical Society of America 119(5), 3109–3120 (2006)
12. Hozjan, V., Kacic, Z.: Context-Independent Multilingual Emotion Recognition from Speech Signals. International Journal of Speech Technology 6, 311–320 (2003)
13. HTK: HMM Toolkit; Speech Recognition Toolkit,
    http://htk.eng.cam.ac.uk/docs/docs
14. Kienast, M., Sendlmeier, W.F.: Acoustical analysis of spectral and temporal changes in emotional speech. In: Proceedings of the ISCA ITRW on Speech and Emotion, Newcastle, September 5–7, pp. 92–97 (2000)
15. Mozziconacci, S.: Speech Variability and Emotion: Production and Perception. Technical University of Eindhoven, Proefschrift (1998)
16. MPEG-4: ISO/IEC 14496 standard (1999), http://www.iec.ch
17. Navas, E., Hernáez, I., Luengo, I.: An Objective and Subjective Study of the Role of Semantics and Prosodic Features in Building Corpora for Emotional TTS. IEEE transactions on audio, speech, and language processing 14(4) (July 2006)
18. Sztahó, D.: Emotion perception and automatic emotion recognition in Hungarian. In: Proceedings of Scientific Conference for Students, BME (2007),
    http://www.vik.bme.hu/tdk
19. Vicsi, K., Szaszák, G.: Automatic Segmentation for Continuous Speech on Word Level Based Suprasegmental Features. International Journal of Speech Technology (April 2006)

Expressive Speech Synthesis Using Emotion-Specific Speech Inventories

Csaba Zainkó, Márk Fék, and Géza Németh

Department of Telecommunications and Media Informatics,
Budapest University of Technology and Economics,
Magyar tudósok körútja 2., 1117 Budapest, Hungary
{zainko,fek,nemeth}@tmit.bme.hu

Abstract. In this paper we explore the use of emotion-specific speech invento-ries for expressive speech synthesis. We recorded a semantically neutral sen-tence and 26 logatoms containing all the diphones and CVC triphones necessary to synthesize the same sentence. The speech material was produced by a profes-sional actress expressing all logatoms and the sentence with the six basic emo-tions and in neutral tone. 7 emotion-dependent inventories were constructed from the logatoms. The 7 inventories paired with the prosody extracted from the 7 natural sentences were used to synthesize 49 sentences. 194 listeners evalu-ated the emotions expressed in the logatoms and in the natural and synthetic sentences. The intended emotion was recognized above chance level for 99% of the logatoms and for all natural sentences. Recognition rates significantly above chance level were obtained for each emotion. The recognition rate for some synthetic sentences exceeded that of natural ones.

Keywords: Expressive speech synthesis, basic emotions, diphone and triphone inventory, listening test, forced choice.

1 Introduction

The goal of expressive speech synthesis can be defined as expressing convincing and authentic emotions by good quality synthesized speech generated automatically from text. Currently no system known to the authors is capable to achieve this goal, even for a limited set of emotions.

It is known that emotions in speech are conveyed by both prosody and voice qual-ity [1]. Most state-of-the art concatenation based text-to-speech (TTS) systems allow some control over prosody parameters (F0, sound durations, and intensity). In turn, the voice quality of synthetic speech is intrinsically determined by the speech inven-tory from which the concatenated segments are chosen. Automatic voice quality con-version techniques are not yet able to generate good quality synthetic speech [2].

There have been previous experiments [3,4] for several languages to explore the use of emotion-specific speech inventories in unit selection based speech synthesis. Most of the generated synthetic samples conveyed the intended emotions, but their quality was far from satisfactory especially in case of happy speech. The authors of

A. Esposito et al. (Eds.): HH and HM Interaction 2007, LNAI 5042, pp. 225–234, 2008.

[3] and [4] speculated that the unit selection algorithm concatenated segments having differing voice quality which introduced audible distortion.

In this paper we explore the use of emotion-specific diphone and triphone inventories for expressive speech synthesis using a non-unit selection concatenative speech synthesis framework. Our underlying idea was that the recording of short logatoms for inventory building would result in a database having more homogenous voice quality than a unit selection database consisting of recorded sentences. The obtained results justify our assumption.

2 Related Work

In both of the experiments reported in [3] and [4] a speaker read some text in several versions conveying a set of previously specified emotions. The recorded speech was used to create emotion specific speech inventories. Unit selection TTS engines were used to synthesize semantically neutral sentences from the emotion-specific inventories. The prosody of the synthetic sentence was copied from natural target sentences conveying the specified emotion. Further in [3] (second experiment) the prosody was generated by the TTS engine. Listening tests were performed to evaluate the recognition rate of the intended emotions in the synthetic sentences. The main differences between the two experiments are summarized below.

Montero et al. [3] recorded semantically neutral text in Spanish produced by a professional actor simulating four emotions and neutral style. They achieved above chance level identification rates (neutral 76%, happiness 62%, surprise 91%, sadness 81%, cold anger 95%) using copy synthesized prosody from natural sentences in a 6-choice listening test (including a "non-identifiable" option). Similar results were obtained (except for surprise 53%) for automatically generated prosody trained on the emotion-specific recordings.

Bulut et al. [4] recorded short passages of text eliciting happiness, sadness, anger, and neutrality read by a semi-professional actress. All the emotions were identified above chance level (anger 86%, sadness 89%, happiness 44%, neutral 82%) in a forced 4-choice listening test.

Schröder and Grice [5] carried out different experiment. They recorded a complete German diphone inventory for three levels of vocal effort (soft, modal, and loud). The vocal effort corresponding to different muscle tensions is considered to play an important role in expressing emotions. The diphones were embedded in nonsense words (logatoms) and were uttered by a German male speaker instructed to maintain constant pitch. A concatenation based engine (without unit selection) was used to synthesize test sentences. Listening tests showed that vocal effort in the synthetic voice was perceived as intended. Their results indicate that the voice quality of logatoms was preserved in the concatenated speech.

Our experiment is similar to previous ones with the following main differences. We used a non unit selection based TTS engine and recorded nonsense logatoms similarly to [5], but the uttered logatoms conveyed the emotions directly, like the texts read for inventory construction in [3] and [4]. Our inventory contained both diphones and CVC triphones reducing the concatenation discontinuity compared to diphone only inventories. We verified the recognition rates for the logatoms during a listening test. Such formal verification of the source material was not carried out in previous works. Contrary to [5], the actress was free to vary her pitch that changed considerably both within and across logatoms, and within sentences. This can lead to large F0 differences during pitch modification introducing additional artifacts in the synthesized signal. Even unit selection engines are sensible to large F0 deviations present in emotional speech, especially when using small inventories as reported by [3] and [4]. Pitch modification artifacts probably influenced the outcome of the cited experiments, too. We examined more emotions than the cited authors which resulted in more choices for the listening test probably worsening the expected recognition rate. Our experiment was carried out in Hungarian, but, similarly to the previous experiments, the method can also be applied to other languages.

The scale of the experiment did not allow us to collect and examine data from several speakers. Nevertheless, in Section 6, we compare our results to those presented in [3] and [4]. The lack of contradictions may indicate some interpersonal and cross-cultural validity.

3 Speech Data Recording

The following semantically neutral Hungarian sentence was used in the experiment: "A menüben minden szükséges információ elhangzik" ("All necessary information is announced in the menu"). We determined the sequence of diphones and CVC triphones constituting the phonetic transcription of the sentence. 14 CVC triphones were used to cover all CVC segments while 12 diphones covered the remaining segments of which 3 were VV and 9 were CC diphones. The diphones and triphones were embedded in semantically nonsense words (logatoms) consisting of two syllables for CC diphones and three syllables for the other diphones and triphones.

We recorded the semantically neutral sentence and the 26 logatoms in seven versions expressing the six basic emotions (happiness, anger, surprise, disgust, sadness, fear) and neutral tone. The speech material was produced by a professional Hungarian actress (age 30) who had prior experience in TTS inventory recording and in producing expressive sentences for speech experiments. The actress was selected over two other professional candidates who produced less convincing initial samples.

No scripts were given to define eliciting situations for each emotion as we found them to be difficult to use in previous experiments. Instead, the actress was asked to recall emotional situations from her own personal experience. For each emotion, several (4-7) versions of the logatoms and sentences were produced in an iterative manner till the authors judged them appropriate. An informal listening test was conducted after the recording where two of the authors selected the emotionally most convincing logatoms and sentences. About 20% of the logatoms were found not to convey the appropriate emotion, and they were re-recorded in a second session. The most convincing samples from the first recording were played to the actress before we started recording an emotion. Several (4-6) versions were produced for each logatom and the best ones were selected by two of the authors.

The recordings were made in an anechoic chamber using an AKG C-414 B-ULS condenser microphone switched to cardioid pattern and with the 75 Hz low-pass filter turned on. A pop filter was mounted in front of the microphone. The sound was digitized on 44.1 kHz using 16 bits per sample.

4 Synthetic Stimuli Preparation

The seven emotion-specific inventories (built from the logatoms) and the seven natural sentences were paired up in all possible ways. For each of the 49 pairs, the prosody of the natural sentence was copied to a sentence synthesized from the emotion-specific inventory.

The synthesis and prosody transplantation were performed as follows. The sound boundaries were marked manually in the recorded logatoms and sentences. The F0 contours were detected using the autocorrelation based pitch detection implemented in Praat [6]. The target F0 curves contained one frequency value for each pitch period. The intensity was calculated in every 8 ms using a 32 ms wide window. The PSOLA based prosody modification implemented in Praat [6] was used to copy the target durations, F0, and intensity contours to each diphone and triphone.

It is important to note that the diphones spanned over the entire duration of two consecutive sounds and the triphones spanned over three consecutive sounds. As shown in Fig. 1, the modified diphones and triphones were concatenated using time domain cross-fade with 50% overlap between the last and first sounds of neighboring speech segments. The vertical continuous lines in the figure indicate sound boundaries, the vertical dotted lines indicate the overlap region. The upper two curves (a and b) represent the concatenated triphones with the linear cross-fade windows indicated. The bottom curve (c) shows the concatenated signal.

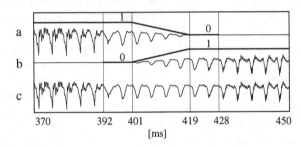

Fig. 1. Concatenation of neighboring triphone segments using time domain cross-fade (50% overlap)

5 Listening Test

A web based listening test was conducted to determine the perceived emotion expressed in the recorded logatoms and in the natural and synthetic sentences. 208 native speakers of Hungarian participated in the test. Most of the listeners were motivated undergraduate computer science students.

The results of 14 listeners were excluded from the evaluation because they either did not finish the test, or were found to respond randomly. Some of the excluded listeners reported playback difficulties. The remaining 194 listeners consisted of 159 male and 35 female testers having a mean age of 23 years. 83 listeners used head- or earphones while 111 testers listened to loud speakers.

The listening test took 18 minutes to complete, on average. The test consisted of six parts. The listeners evaluated the logatoms in the first part and the natural and synthetic sentences in the fourth part. The second and fifth parts were used for another unrelated study. The third and sixth parts were included to filter out randomly clicking testers. In these two parts, the listeners used a 5-point scale to grade the quality of a sentence in natural and three synthesized versions having obvious quality differences. Four listeners whose grading did not reflect the quality differences were excluded.

To lessen the load of the testers, a listener had to evaluate only a part of the logatoms and sentences. The 49 synthetic and 7 natural sentences were mixed together and were distributed in two groups each containing 28-28 randomly chosen sentences. 98 listeners evaluated only the first, while another 94 only the second group of sentences. Similarly, the logatoms corresponding to all emotions were distributed into seven groups containing equal number of randomly chosen logatoms. At least 23 listeners were assigned to each group.

The listeners had to evaluate the emotions expressed in the natural logatoms and in the natural and synthetic sentences in a forced 7-choice (six basic emotions and neutrality) listening test. The instructions at the beginning of the test were read by the same actress who gave her voice to the experiment. This allowed the listeners to familiarize themselves with the emotionally neutral speaking style of the actress. To avoid listeners skipping the introduction, they had to enter a randomly generated verification code announced at the end of the instructions. The test was self-paced. The listeners had the option to replay a stimulus as many times as they wished, but they were not allowed to go back to a preceding stimulus, once they rated it. The playback order was randomized individually for each listener.

The subjective quality of the synthetic samples was not judged by the listeners, but we report the important artifacts in the next section. Speech samples can be downloaded at the website of our laboratory: http://speechlab.tmit.bme.hu

6 Results

A binomial test ($p<0.05$) with unequal (1:7) proportions was used to determine if the recognition rates were significantly above the 14% chance level. Recognition rates above 30% were significantly above chance level for the logatom evaluation test (23 listeners). Recognition rates above 21% were significantly above chance level for the sentence evaluation test (94 listeners).

Fig. 2 shows the recognition rates of the intended emotion for the logatoms in each emotion-specific inventory. The bottom line in each figure indicates the lowest recognition rate that is significantly above chance level. The upper line indicates the mean recognition rate for the given inventory.

The intended emotion was recognized above chance level for 180 of the 182 logatoms. Anger was the best recognized emotion on average (86%), while disgust (60%) and fear (55%) were much less recognizable. There were several logatoms of disgust and fear scoring above 80% showing that listeners were able to recognize these emotions even from short samples. This may indicate that the low scores are due to the actress having difficulty in conveying these emotions consistently on all samples.

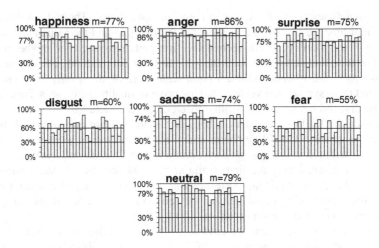

Fig. 2. Recognition rates of the intended emotion for the 26 logatoms

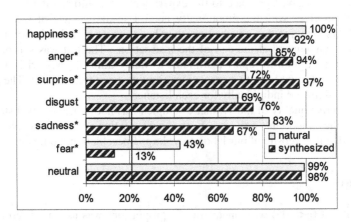

Fig. 3. Recognition rates of natural sentences and of synthetic sentences having matching prosody and inventory. The significant differences are marked by *.

Fig. 3 shows the recognition rates of the intended emotion for natural sentences and for synthetic sentences having matching prosody and inventory. Two sample t-tests ($p<0.05$) were performed to check whether recognition rates for natural and synthetic sentence pairs were significantly different.

The recognition rates higher than the vertical line are significantly above chance level. The best scoring natural sentence was the happy (100%) one. Anger (85%) was considered as neutrality by 9% of the listeners. Surprise (72%) was considered as happiness by 28 % of the listeners. This is because the actress ended the sentence smiling, probably to indicate positive surprise. The actress had difficulty in conveying disgust (69%) which was considered as happiness by 12% and as anger by 10% of the listeners. Sadness (83%) was considered as neutral by 11% of the listeners. The worst scoring fear (43%) was recognized as neutral by 30% and as sad by 22% of the listeners. The actress stopped producing pitch fluctuation at the second part of the sentence which can explain the high number of neutral responses. Moreover, the actress expressed the sentence in a soft tone which can explain its recognition as sad. The sentence scored even below the average score of fear logatoms indicating its unfortunate realization. The natural neutral sentence (99%) was identified easily.

Synthesized happiness (92%) was easily recognizable. The achieved score is largely superior to previous results reported in [3], and [4]. The authors of [3] supposed that a mixture of units from smiling and non-smiling speech decreased the happy quality of the synthesized voice. The authors of [4] attributed the relatively low-score of happiness (in part) to the less successfully conveyed intended emotion in the original target sentences and inventory. The high scores obtained for the natural happy sentence and for the happy logatoms indicate that none of these problems were present in our experiment. Synthesized anger (94%) was easy to recognize, too. Interestingly, the recognition rate of synthesized anger surpassed that of natural anger significantly. We found that the prosody modification algorithm introduced some additional harshness as an artifact which can explain the enhanced scores. This is consistent with the observation in [3]. Synthesized surprise (97%) was easily recognizable and, unlike natural surprise, was not mistaken for happiness. This can be explained by considering that the perceived timbre of the synthesized sentence, unlike that of the natural sentence, did not turn into smiling at the end. Synthesized disgust (76%) was mistaken for anger by 13% of the listeners. Furthermore, its recognition score exceeded that of natural disgust, although not significantly. Both observations might be explained by the more rough voice quality of the synthesized sentence. Synthesized sadness (67%) was mistaken for neutrality by 17% and for fear by 7% of the listeners. We observed that the synthetic sad sentence was more distorted than the ones obtained for other emotions. This can explain the relatively lower score. By examining the perceptually most distorted segments in the synthetic sad sentence, we found that they corresponded to irregular glottal excitation (glottalization) in the sad logatoms. Similar distortions were observed in all sentences produced with the sad inventory. Further we noticed that the natural sad sentence contained glottalization, too. The actress used glottalization possibly as a cue for sadness, but the irregular periods disturbed the pitch detection and prosody modification algorithms and led to additional distortion. Synthetic fear (13%) was recognized below chance level. It was mistaken for anger by 64%, for neutrality by 16%, and for disgust by 6% of the listeners. The low recognition rate can be explained in part by the low score obtained for the natural fear sentence. Synthesized neutrality (98%) scored nearly as well as the natural one.

Table 1 shows the result obtained for all inventory and prosody pairings. The seven shaded cells correspond to pairings that express a given emotion the best. For non matching inventory and prosody pairs, a vertical arrow indicates that the identified emotion matched the inventory. A horizontal arrow indicates that the identified emotion matched the prosody target. The recognized emotion is explicitly indicated if it neither matched the inventory nor the prosody target, and its score was significantly above chance level. Boldface numbers indicate the best recognized emotion for a given pairing.

The best recognition rate for a given emotion was obtained with matching inventory and prosody, except for fear and happiness. Fear scored only 13% for matching

Table 1. Recognition rates of synthetic sentences for all inventory and prosody pairings

↑inventory: ←prosody:	happiness	anger	surprise	disgust	sadness	fear	neutral
happiness	92%	←2% ↑74%	←35% ↑14% fear 33%	←2% ↑14% fear 37%	←3% ↑50% fear 29%	←11% ↑35% sadness 23%	←1% ↑50% sadness 23%
anger	←1% ↑93%	94%	←12% ↑12% fear 41%	←63% ↑22%	←3% ↑39% neutral 27% fear 26%	←60% ↑2%	←35% ↑39%
surprise	←68% ↑31%	←56% ↑41%	97%	←82% ↑5%	←75% ↑5%	←85% ↑1%	←87% ↑4%
disgust	←13%, ↑82%	←48% ↑49%	←23% ↑10% happiness 29%	76%	←14% ↑45%	←71% ↑2%	←68% ↑9%
sadness	←1%, ↑78%	←0% ↑33% neutral 34% disgust 30%	←11% ↑12% neutral 37%	←16% ↑43%	67%	←20%, ↑12% disgust 36% neutral 28%	←32%, ↑52%
fear	←3%, ↑74%	←1%, ↑87%	←60%, 11%	←6%, ↑22% anger 58%	←62% ↑18%	13% anger 64%	←9%, ↑77%
neutral	←22%, ↑75%	←33%, ↑54%	←79%, ↑9%	←80% ↑13%	←79% ↑13%	←85%, ↑0%	98%

inventory and prosody. Much better scores were obtained by copying the fear prosody of the natural fear sentence to a sentence synthesized from sad (62%) or surprise (60%) inventories.

These scores even exceeded the scores obtained for the natural fear sentence (43%). We observed that the logatoms of the fear inventories were produced with pressed voice, unlike the logatoms in the sad and surprise inventories. This can explain that the timbre of the latter two synthetic sentences was much softer than the timbre of the sentence synthesized from the fear inventory. According to Fig. 2, the pressed logatoms in the fear inventory conveyed more or less the intended emotion (mean=55%), but the additional harshness introduced by the prosody modification shifted the perception of the synthetic sentence towards anger (64%).

The happy inventory combined with angry prosody (93%) achieved a slightly better score than combined with happy prosody (92%). Moreover, happiness was in general insensitive to prosody, except for surprise. High identification rates were achieved for the combination of happy inventory and disgust (82%), sad (78%), fear

(74%), and neutral (75%) prosody. This indicates that happiness was mainly conveyed by voice quality.

By examining pairings with neutral target prosody in Table 1, we can see that the expression of synthetic anger (54%) and happiness (75%) depended more on the inventory. Pairings with neutral inventory indicate that synthetic surprise (87%) and disgust (68%) depended more on prosody. Similar findings were made in [3] and [4], with the exception of disgust (not included in previous experiments) and sadness which was found to depend on prosody in both papers. The possible explanation of the latter difference is that our actress relied on glottalization to express sadness. The used synthesis technique could not handle the irregular pitch periods which prevented the correct transplantation of sad prosody on a synthetic neutral sentence (13%). This is confirmed by the results obtained for pairings of sad inventory with happy (sad 50%), angry (sad 39%) and disgust (sad 45%) prosody. The prosody of these sentences was better transplanted and they were recognized as sadness in the first place.

7   Summary and Conclusions

The experiment proved that synthetic anger and happiness can be expressed in a convincing way using emotion-specific inventories. The happy inventory combined with any prosody (except surprise) achieved considerably high identification rates, while happy prosody combined with non-happy inventories achieved low scores. This indicates the importance of voice quality in expressing happiness.

Surprise and disgust can be expressed by prosody alone, but they can be further enhanced by using an appropriate inventory. The natural target sentences for disgust and fear were less convincingly realized than other emotions. This explains in part the less successful recognition of their synthetic versions. The prosody modification introduced an additional harshness to the pressed logatoms in the fear inventory. A less pressed inventory should be used to express fear under the given technical constraints.

The natural sad recordings contained irregular pitch periods which were not handled properly by the synthesis algorithm. The additional distortion introduced in the synthetic samples explains the less successful recognition of synthetic sadness. The synthesis of sad sentences might benefit from adding artificial glottalization, as an additional cue. However, glottalization should be avoided in the inventories because of the technical constraints.

Concatenative speech synthesis can be used to express convincing emotions, but it is demanding to control the expressiveness during inventory recording. Expressive voice quality probably remains more consistent in logatoms than in natural sentences. A voice conversion model trained on a relatively small but consistent logatom inventory could be used to make large unit selection inventories expressive.

Acknowledgments. The work was supported by the Hungarian National Office for Research and Technology (NKFP 2/034/2004).

References

1. Ladd, D.R., Silverman, K., Tolkmitt, F., Bergmann, G., Scherer, K.R.: Evidence for the independent function of intonation contour type, voice quality, and f0 range in signalling speaker affect. Journal of the Acoustic Society of America 78(2), 435–444 (1985)
2. Inanoglu, Z., Young, S.: A system for Transforming the Emotion in Speech: Combining Data-Driven Conversion Techniques for Prosody and Voice Quality. In: Interspeech (2007)
3. Montero, J.M., Arriola, G.J., Colas, J., Enriquez, E., Pardo, J.M.: Analysis and Modeling of Emotional Speech in Spanish. In: Proc. of ICPhS, pp. 957–960 (1999)
4. Bulut, M., Narayanan, S.S., Syrdal, A.K.: Expressive Speech Synthesis Using a Concatenative Synthesizer. In: ICSLP-2002, pp. 1265–1268 (2002)
5. Schröder, M., Grice, M.: Expressing Vocal Effort in Concatenative Synthesis. In: Proc. of ICPhS, Barcelona, Spain, pp. 2589–2592 (2003)
6. Boersma, P.: Praat, a system for doing phonetics by computer. Glot International 5(9/10), 341–345 (2001)

Study on Speaker-Independent Emotion Recognition from Speech on Real-World Data

Theodoros Kostoulas, Todor Ganchev, and Nikos Fakotakis

Artificial Intelligence Group, Wire Communications Laboratory,
Electrical and Computer Engineering Department,
University of Patras, 26500 Rion-Patras, Greece
{tkost,tganchev,fakotaki}@wcl.ee.upatras.gr

Abstract. In the present work we report results from on-going research activity in the area of speaker-independent emotion recognition. Experimentations are performed towards examining the behavior of a detector of negative emotional states over non-acted/acted speech. Furthermore, a score-level fusion of two classifiers on utterance level is applied, in attempt to improve the performance of the emotion recognizer. Experimental results demonstrate significant differences on recognizing emotions on acted/real-world speech.

Keywords: Emotion recognition, real-life data.

1 Introduction

The use of spoken dialogue systems has been increased over the last decades. Knowledge of the user's emotion can provide the means for successful human-machine interaction experiences. In various applications, such as: call routers, voice portals, smart-home systems, access-control applications, etc, which target on wide public, the user group is potentially unlimited. This imposes dealing with speaker-independent emotion recognition and, specifically, with the detection of negative emotions.

To this end, much work had been reported towards recognizing emotions from speech. In [1], Devillers and Vidrascu studied data collected from a medical emergency call center, using lexical and paralinguistic cues to perform emotion recognition. Robust fusion of prosodic and verbal cues, towards speaker independent emotion recognition, took place in [2]. The comparison of several concepts towards recognizing emotions led to average accuracy 71.6%. In [3] Lugger and Yang showed that intelligent combination of prosodic and voice quality features yields in improved speaker-independent emotion recognition. Lee and Narayanan [4] worked on data obtained from a call center, introducing the notion "emotional salience". For the corpus used, the results indicated that combination of acoustic and linguistic information enhances the system's performance.

In the present work, we report results from ongoing research activity in the area of speaker-independent emotion recognition. The great challenge when facing the emotion recognition problem is dealing with real-life data. Real-world speech data differ much from acted speech. In order to investigate this phenomenon we perform

A. Esposito et al. (Eds.): HH and HM Interaction 2007, LNAI 5042, pp. 235–242, 2008.

experimentations on acted speech databases and on real-world data, obtained from the interaction of naïve users with a smart-home dialogue system. The detector of negative emotional states consists of a conventional feature-set and a GMM-based classifier. Finally, a score-level fusion scheme between the baseline classifier and a second one fed with a feature-set estimated at utterance level is evaluated.

2 System Description

The block diagram of the detector of negative emotional states is illustrated in Fig. 1. Fig. 1(a) illustrates the training of the Gaussian Mixture Models and Fig. 1(b) the operational phase. Specifically, each speech recording is subject to preprocessing and feature extraction. The resulting feature vector consists of the first 12 MFCC coefficients (with the 0-th coefficient excluded), the fundamental frequency, frame energy and harmonics-to-noise ratio (harmonicity). Both the fundamental frequency and the harmonicity are computed using the Boersma's algorithm [5]. MFCCs are calculated according to the methodology of Davis and Mermelstein [6]. MFCCs and frame energy were calculated over time window 25 ms, with skip step 10 ms. For accurate estimation of the fundamental frequency and the harmonic-to-noise ratio we utilized frame size of 40 ms and 80 ms, respectively.

The 15-dimensional feature vector computed so far is used for silence/voiced/unvoiced speech separation. Our detector utilized only the voiced speech frames, since they contain the most of the emotional cues of speech.

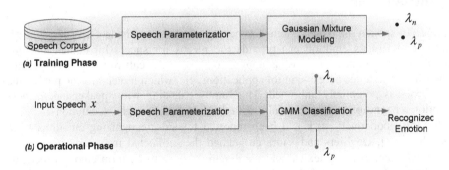

Fig. 1. Block diagram of the detector of negative emotional states

During the training phase, emotionally labeled speech utterances are utilized for creating the speaker-independent emotion models. Emotion modeling is performed via training diagonal covariance matrix Gaussian Mixture Models [7]. In the initialization step the k-means clustering algorithm is employed. Afterwards, a number of EM iterations [8] refine the model parameters. This number of training iterations depends on the underlying data distribution and a threshold that specifies the error decrease between two subsequent iterations.

The result of the aforementioned procedure is two emotion models: one representing the negative emotional state (λ_n), and another one modeling the non-negative emotions (λ_p).

The emotion models built during training are utilized in the operational phase for computing log-likelihoods for the input data. A decision about the emotional content of the input utterance x is made by applying a threshold on the log-likelihood ratio computed from the negative $p(x \mid \lambda_n)$ and non-negative models $p(x \mid \lambda_p)$.

3 Speech Corpora

Real-world data differ much from acted speech [9]. To investigate this phenomenon, we performed experimentations on well-known acted speech databases (LDC Emotional Prosody Speech and Transcripts [10], Berlin Database of Emotional Speech [11]), and on real-world data [12], [13].

The LDC Emotional Prosody Speech and Transcripts database consists of English language acted speech recordings. Eight actors (5 females and 3 males) were asked to utter four-syllable dates and numbers in 15 different emotional states. The following emotion categories were covered: {*neutral, hot anger, cold anger, happy, sadness, disgust, panic, anxiety, despair, elation, interest, shame, boredom, pride* and *contempt*}. For the purpose of our experimentations, all data were down-sampled to 8 kHz (single channel audio, 16 bit resolution).

The Berlin Database of Emotional Speech contains about 500 utterances spoken by 10 actors (5 males, 5 females) in the German language. The emotions covered are: *happy, angry, anxious, fearful, bored* and *disgusted* as well as *neutral*. The recordings were down-sampled to 8 kHz (single channel audio, 16 bit resolution).

The real-world data consists of Greek recordings obtained during the interaction of naïve users with a smart-home dialogue system. To this end, 42 people have participated, each recorded in one session with duration of 25 minutes. None of the participants was an actor or had any previous experience with a smart-home dialogue system. The participants were asked to enter a room, decorated in living room environment, where the spoken dialogue system was installed. Task-cards were provided to them, which constructed a real-world scenario and forced the participants to use several devices of the smart-home. The users had the ability to observe the dialogue flow through a simulator installed on a personal computer. To this end, 29 sessions (14 females, 15 males) had been annotated manually.

The annotation procedure consists of three stages. In the first stage, one annotator tags the participant's emotion, in each utterance segmented by the speech recognizer (sampling rate 8 kHz, single channel audio, 16 bit resolution), in one of the following emotional states: {*delighted, pleased, neutral, confused, angry* or *hot angry*}. Moreover, this annotator tags the command that the user issued to the spoken dialogue system. In the second step, six annotators are asked to tag the emotion of each utterance in one of the aforementioned categories, using their human intuition.

Based on the annotations from the seven annotators, a final decision for each utterance was made. For utterances where at least five annotators agree, the corresponding label was decided. However, for 1179 of the 3269 utterances there was significant disagreement among the annotators. Thus, in the third stage of annotation, a committee of three experts listened to these 1179 utterances and force-categorized them in one of the aforementioned six categories.

4 Experimental Setup and Results

In all experiments we target distinguishing between two emotion categories: negative vs. non-negative. In the first experiment we investigate the difference between detecting negative emotional states from acted vs. non-acted speech. For this purpose, experiments on three different databases were performed. In the experiments with the LDC corpus the utterances labeled {*neutral, hot anger*} were utilized. For the Berlin corpus {*neutral, anger*} categories were selected. In the real-world data, the negative class consisted of {*confused, anger, hot anger*}, and the non-negative one of those labeled as {*neutral, pleased, delighted*}.

In all experiments, GMMs with 16 mixture components were built for the negative and non-negative class. The number of mixture components was selected after extensive experimentation on the datasets, with respect to the system's performance. The maximum number of iterations was set to 1000 and the training was terminated when the error between two subsequent iterations of the EM algorithm decreased with less than 0.1. The leave-one-session-out technique had been used, for better utilization of the speech data available. In Fig. 2 the DET (Detection Error Trade-off) plots that correspond to the three experiments are illustrated.

As shown in Fig. 2, the detector of negative emotional states performs significantly better for the acted speech databases than for the real-life data. This observation is in harmony with previous research conducted on the relation between acted and non-acted speech [9]. However, it is interesting to note that there is significant difference even between the results for the two acted-speech databases. Specifically, we observed much lower error rates for the Berlin corpus when compared to those for the LDC corpus. We can explain this effect by the larger number of actors in the Berlin database, and the balanced gender distribution, which provide the means for better modeling of the speaker-independent emotion cues.

On the other hand, despite the balanced distribution over genders and the larger number of participants, the experimental results for real-world speech demonstrate significant increase of the EER, when compared to the acted speech. In our opinion, this is due to the different nature of real-world speech. The real-world data were recorded from moving speakers, who use spontaneous speech to interact with the smart-home assistant. Spontaneous speech grows the vocabulary of the dataset, where experimentations are performed. Moreover, each utterance segmented by the speech recognizer is assumed to belong in one of the aforementioned emotion classes. However, the dominant emotion revealed by one utterance is, often, not equally distributed over its whole duration. Additionally, the low performance of the detector of negative emotional states can be justified by the observation that humans, also, disagree, when trying to categorize a given utterance. (For about 1/3 of the real-world speech data more than three out of seven annotators disagreed).

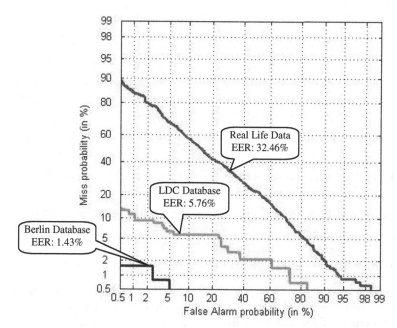

Fig. 2. Plot of DET curves for the evaluation of the detector of negative emotional states over the three emotional speech corpora

Improving the performance of our detector of negative emotional states is of interest, especially on real-world speech data. Aiming at better performance, we enriched the feature vector with sentence-level features. For each utterance we computed a 26 dimensional vector, which results from the computation of the mean values (μ_i) and the standard deviation (σ_i) of the baseline feature-set {12 MFCCs, harmonicity, Fundamental frequency, Energy}. Additionally, the {duration of voiced frames}/{duration of unvoiced frames} and the {duration of voiced frames}/{duration of the whole utterance} are computed. The feature vectors computed for the training data are utilized for creating the sentence-based speaker-independent emotion models λ_n^s and λ_p^s. The number of Gaussians was set to 4, since the number of available data is smaller when compared to the frame-level features. Specifically, a single feature vector with dimensionality 1×26 represents a whole utterance.

The score-level fusion between the two classifiers that utilize frame-level and utterance-level feature sets is illustrated in Fig. 3. For each input utterance, the GMM models λ_n, λ_p are utilized for computing the log-likelihoods $p(x|\lambda_n)$ and $p(x|\lambda_p)$, respectively. Correspondingly, the utterance-level speaker independent emotion models GMM, λ_n^s and λ_p^s are used to compute the log-likelihoods $p(x|\lambda_n^s)$ and $p(x|\lambda_p^s)$. The score-level fusion consists of linear combination of the outputs of the emotion models created using frame-level features, and of those trained with utterance-level features.

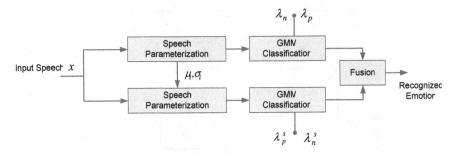

Fig. 3. Block diagram of the operational phase for the case of score-level fusion

The scores computed for a given input utterance x, for the negative s_n and non-negative s_p emotion models are:

$$s_n = (1-w)p(x\,|\,\lambda_n) + wp(x\,|\,\lambda_n^s) \quad \text{and} \quad s_p = (1-w)p(x\,|\,\lambda_p) + wp(x\,|\,\lambda_p^s),$$

respectively. To investigate the optimal weight for the fusion scheme, we varied the values of the weight w between 0 and 1, computing the EER for each case. It was found that the minimum EER is obtained for $w = 0.2$.

Fig. 4 presents the recognition performance for the baseline ($w = 0$) and for the fusion scheme. As the results show, no significant improvement is observed after fusion.

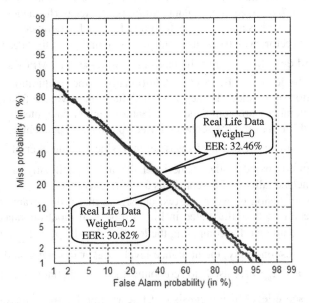

Fig. 4. DET curves for the real-world emotional speech corpus: with fusion ($w = 0.2$), and without fusion ($w = 0$)

We deem that this outcome is, primarily, due to the limited number of speakers available in the real-world corpus. As mentioned before, the number of available data is smaller when compared to the frame-level features, which leads to less accurate speaker-independent sentence-based emotion models.

The experimentations presented in this section indicated that the performance of our detector of negative emotional states is much higher when evaluating on acted speech corpora (1.43% EER for the Berlin corpus and 5.76% EER for the LDC corpus), when compared to the real-world corpus (32.46% EER). Using of additional classifier with utterance-level-based features resulted to minor improvement of 1.64% in terms of EER.

In summary, we consider that the results for real-world data are somehow promising. We believe that further reduction of the error rates is possible, when more advanced modeling techniques are developed, or when larger corpora with emotional speech become available.

5 Conclusion

We investigated speaker-independent detection of negative emotional states from acted and real-world speech. The experimentations demonstrated some important differences on recognizing acted vs. non-acted speech, which cause significant drop of performance, for the real-world data.

Score-level fusion of classifiers using the baseline frame-level features and utterance-level features did not lead to significant improvement of the recognition accuracy. We deem that this is, primarily, due to the limited number of speakers in the real-world data. We presume that large-scale emotional speech corpora would assist for proper modeling of emotional states in the speaker-independent emotion recognition tasks.

Acknowledgments. This work is partially supported by the PlayMancer project (FP7-ICT-215839-2007), which is funded by the European Commission.

References

1. Devillers, L., Vidrascu, L.: Real life emotions detection with lexical and paralinguistic cues on human-human call center dialogs. In: Proc. of the Interspeech 2006, pp. 801–804 (2006)
2. Schuller, B., Müller, R., Lang, M., Rigoll, G.: Speaker independent emotion recognition by early fusion of acoustic and linguistic features within ensembles. In: Proc. of the Interspeech 2005, pp. 805–808 (2005)
3. Lugger, M., Yang, B.: The relevance of voice quality features in speaker independent emotion recognition. In: Proc. of the ICASSP 2007, vol. IV, pp. 17–20 (2007)
4. Lee, C.M., Narayanan, S.S.: Towards detecting emotions in spoken dialogs. IEEE Transactions on Speech and Audio Processing 13(2), 293–303 (2005)
5. Boersma, P.: Accurate short-term analysis of the fundamental frequency and the harmonics-to-noise ratio of a sampled sound. In: Proc. of the 17 IFA 1993, pp. 97–110 (1993)

6. Davis, S.B., Mermelstein, P.: Comparison of parametric representations for monosyllabic word recognition in continuously spoken sentences. IEEE Transactions on ASSP 28, 357–366 (1980)
7. Reynolds, D.A., Rose, R.C.: Robust text-independent speaker identification using Gaussian mixture speaker models. IEEE Trans. Speech Audio Processing 3, 72–83 (1995)
8. Dempster, A.P., Laird, N.M., Rubin, D.B.: Maximum likelihood from incomplete data via the EM algorithm. J. Roy. Stat. Soc. 39, 1–38 (1977)
9. Wilting, J., Kramber, E., Swerts, M.: Real vs. acted emotional speech. In: Proc. of the Interspeech 2006, pp. 805–808 (2006)
10. University of Pennsylvania, Linguistic Data Consortium, Emotional Prosody Speech (2002),
    http://www.ldc.uppen.edu/Catalog/CatalogEntry.jsp?cataloId=LDC2002S28
11. Burkhardt, F., Paeschke, A., Rolfes, M., Sendlmeier, W., Weiss, B.: A Database of German Emotional Speech. In: Proc. of Interspeech 2005, pp. 1517–1520 (2005)
12. Artificial Intelligence Group, Wire Communication Laboratory, University of Patras,
    http://www.wcl.ee.upatras.gr/ai/Research/SEmo.htm
13. Kostoulas, T., Ganchev, T., Mporas, I., Fakotakis, N.: A real-world emotional speech corpus for modern Greek. In: Proc. of LREC 2008, Morocco (May 2008)

Exploiting a Vowel Based Approach for Acted Emotion Recognition

Fabien Ringeval and Mohamed Chetouani

Université Pierre et Marie Curie – Paris 6,
Institut des Systèmes Intelligents et de Robotique, 3 rue Galilée,
94200 Ivry sur Seine, France
Fabien.Ringeval@isir.fr, Mohamed.Chetouani@upmc.fr

Abstract. This paper is dedicated to the description and the study of a new feature extraction approach for emotion recognition. Our contribution is based on the extraction and the characterization of phonemic units such as vowels and consonants, which are provided by a pseudo-phonetic speech segmentation phase combined with a vowel detector. The segmentation algorithm is evaluated on both emotional (Berlin) and non-emotional (TIMIT, NTIMIT) databases. Concerning the emotion recognition task, we propose to extract MFCC acoustic features from these pseudo-phonetic segments (vowels, consonants) and we compare this approach with traditional voice and unvoiced segments. The classification is achieved by the well-known k-nn classifier (k nearest neighbors) on the Berlin corpus.

Keywords: Emotion recognition, automatic speech segmentation, vowel detection.

1 Introduction

The manifestation of emotions is a particularly complex field of the human being communication, and concerns pluridisciplinary research areas such as affective computing, psychology, cognitive science, sociology and philosophy [1,2,3]. This pluridisciplinarity is due to the high variability of the human behaviour, which involves multifaceted emotions for both production and perception process. Affect (feelings and the physical associated changes), cognition, personality, culture and ethics are the most important components described in the literature for the emotions [4]. Although that some studies list more than a hundred emotions terms [5], six primary emotions qualified as full-blown are widely accepted in the literature: fear, anger, joy, boredom, sadness and disgust. Plutchik [6] postulates that all other emotions are mixed or derivate states, and occur as combinations, mixtures, or compounds of the primary ones.

Emotion-oriented computing aims at the automatic recognition and synthesis of emotions in speech, facial expression, or any other biological communication channel [7]. Concerning emotional speech classifications, one of the main difficulties resides in the determination of both feature sets and classifiers [8]. Other difficulties appear among them the definition of emotions and their annotation [9]. The commonly used

A. Esposito et al. (Eds.): HH and HM Interaction 2007, LNAI 5042, pp. 243–254, 2008.

feature extraction schemes are based on both acoustic and prosodic features resulting in a very large feature vector. The most discriminant ones are commonly determined by features selection algorithms [10]. This procedure was successful in many studies [11, 12, 13]. The mainly used acoustic features are derived from speech processing (e.g. Mel Frequency Cepstrum Coding - MFCC), whereas the prosody is characterized by large statistics measures of pitch, energy and duration computed during the voiced segment. Since the manifestations of the emotions are particularly complex and concern different levels of communication, the identification and the extraction of optimally emotional speech descriptors are still open issues. The classification stage is usually based on machine learning methods such as distance based (k-nn), decision trees, Gaussian Mixture Models (GMM), Support Vector Machines and fusion of different methods [14].

In this paper we propose a new feature extraction scheme based on a pseudo-phonetic approach (figure 1). Prosodic features are usually extracted from the voiced segments even if some approaches use also unvoiced segments for specific situations [15]. The key idea of this work is to extract the features from different segments such as vowels and consonants. These segments are identified by a segmentation of stationary segments (Divergence Forward Backward algorithm - DFB) combined with a vowel detector. The segmentation process is language independent and does not aim at the exact identification of phonemes as it can be done by a phonetic alignment. As a result, the obtained segments are termed pseudo-phonetic units.

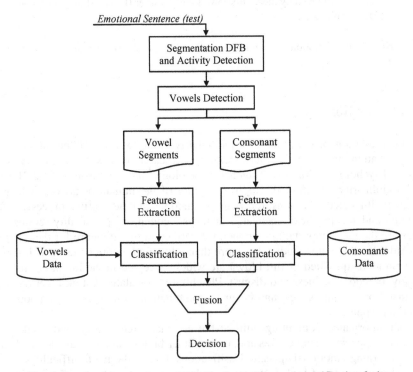

Fig. 1. Pseudo-phonetic approach: features extraction and classification fusion

The remainder of this paper is organized as follows: the segmentation DFB and the vowel detector are described and evaluated in section 2. Acoustic based emotion recognition results for both vowels-consonants units and voiced frames are presented in section 3.

2 Vowel-Based Approach

The following sections are dedicated to the study of the segmentation phase. For this purpose, we firstly present the used databases and secondly we give details about the segmentation algorithm. An evaluation of the vowel detection phase is also presented.

2.1 Description of the Databases

In order to evaluate our vowel based approach, we used three phonetically labelled databases: TIMIT [16], NTIMIT [17] and Berlin [18]. The TIMIT database contains 10 sentences pronounced by 630 speakers from 8 major dialect of American English. For each speaker, the sentences are grouped on three types. There are 5 phonetically-compact sentences (SX), 3 phonetically-diverse sentences (SI) and 2 dialect calibration sentences (SA). These sentences were labelled in a narrow transcription including word, orthographic, and phonetic time-alignment from a lexicon of 52 phonemes (20 vowels and 32 consonants). The NTIMIT database was created by transmitting all the 6.300 TIMIT recordings through a telephone handset and over both short and long-distance channels.

Concerning the Berlin corpus, it contains German emotional speech (six primary emotions plus the 'neutral' one) and is commonly used in the emotion recognition [19, 20, 21]. 10 utterances (five short and five long) which could be used in everyday communication have been emotionally coloured by ten gender equilibrated native German actors, with high quality recording equipment (anechoic chamber). 535 sentences marked as min. 60% natural and min. 80% recognisable by 20 listeners in a perception test have been kept and phonetically labelled in a narrow transcription similar to the TIMIT database, excepted special diacritics and stress markers related to both emotional and articulatory characteristics. The Berlin corpus has a lexicon of 59 phonemes (24 vowels and 35 consonants).

2.2 Pseudo-phonetic Units Extraction

This section is dedicated to the description of the pseudo-phonetic segmentation method. The segmentation process used in this paper is based on the Divergence Forward Backward (DFB) algorithm [22]. For the DFB segmentation, the speech signal is hypothetically described by a sequence of stationary and transitory zones, each ones characterized by a statistical auto-regressive (AR) model. The method is based on a change detection criterion using prediction errors computed on two analysis windows M_0 and M_1 (figure 2). M_0 is a long-term and length fixed window sliding along the time axis, while M_1 is growing inside the long-term analysis window (M_0). The distance from the two AR models is performed by the use of a mutual entropy computation (Kullback divergence). Three segments sorts are then identified: shorts or impulsive, transitory and quasi-stationary. Once the segmentation is processed, a variance threshold from the resulting ones enables speech activity detection from these segments.

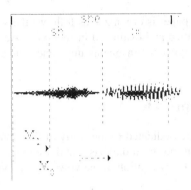

Fig. 2. Locations of the models in the DFB segmentation

2.3 Vowels Detection

According to the source-filter model of the vocal tract, the vowels are known to be characterized by a particular spectral envelope qualified as formantic. This spectral structure reveals the position of the formants (LPC model). The detection of vowel-like segments from the DFB ones is based on the characterization of the spectral envelope. To this purpose, Pellegrino et al. [23] proposed a spectral measure termed the 'Reduced Energy Cumulating' (REC) function (equation 1) for the vowel spectrum characterization. The key idea is to compare the energy computed from Mel bank filters. Firstly, the speech signal is segmented into overlapping frames. N energy values E_i are then extracted for each k frame, and those that are superior to their respective mean value $\bar{E}$ are cumulated and weighted by the energy ratio from low E_{LF} and total E_T frequency bands. The REC criterion is defined as follows:

$$\text{Rec}(k) = \frac{E_{LF}(k)}{E_T(k)} \sum_{i=1}^{N} \left(E_i(k) - \bar{E}(k) \right)^+ . \tag{1}$$

For a given sentence, peak detection on the REC curve allows vowel detection from the DFB segments. Speech segments that are not detected as vowels are classified as consonant segments. However these segments are not really consonants contrary to the vowels. This is mainly due to the fact that the DFB does not provide exact phonetic segments but rather stationary ones. Figure 3 presents results of both DFB segmentation and vowel detection.

2.4 Evaluation of the Vowel Detector

We compare our automatic vowel detector based on the DFB segments with the reference ones provided by the phonetic transcriptions. The vowel error rate (VER) is used to evaluate the detector. The VER has been employed in many studies that are referenced in [24], and is expressed as follows:

$$\text{VER} = 100. \left[\frac{N_{del} + N_{ins}}{N_{vow}} \right] \% . \tag{2}$$

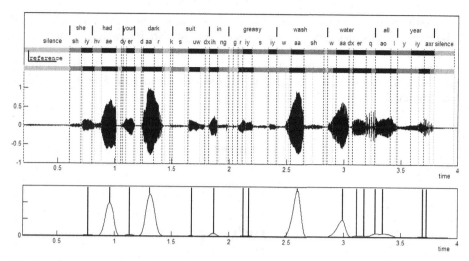

Fig. 3. (a) Comparison between the reference and the detected segments for the vowels (*black*) and the consonants (*dark gray*) from a TIMIT sentence. (b) Reduced Energy Cumulating (REC) function used for the vowels detection.

where N_{del} is the number of deletion (miss-detection), N_{ins} the number of insertion and N_{vow} the total number of vowels.

During the scoring process, a time-alignment between the detected vowels and the references ones is required to increment the number of detections, and one segment from our detector can not validate several reference ones. When no matching vowels from the N_{vow} references can be found, the number of insertions is then increased.

More than 120k vowels from the three databases are tested (table 1). In terms of VER, the best performances have been obtained on the TIMIT corpus 19.50%. This database contains read speech and due to the pronunciation, the detection is made easier. Though that NTIMIT is composed of the TIMIT data filtered at 8 kHz through real telephonic channel, implying an important and constraining spectral information reduction for vowels detection, the performances degradation are inferior to 5%. The vowels from the Berlin corpus are the best detected 90.06% as the most confused to 19.05%, producing the highest VER 29.08%. Berlin is an emotional database which contains full-blown acted emotions. Professional actors have therefore strongly emphasised their speech as the results show with high detection and insertion ratio from the vowel segments.

Table 1. Performances from the vowels detector on three speech corpus

Databases	Reference	Detection	Insertion	VER
Berlin	6437	5791 (89.96%)	1226 (19.05%)	29.08%
TIMIT	57501	50357 (87.56%)	4066 (7.07%)	19.50%
NTIMIT	57493	46601 (81.06%)	2948 (5.13%)	24.07%
All	121431	102755 (84.62%)	8240 (6.79%)	22.17%

Sensitivity to the duration from the vowel segments reference has been studied (figure 4). To this end, a percentage threshold on the duration ratio $d_{d.x}$ / $d_{r.x}$ from a detected vowel is introduced during the scoring computation.

Results show that more than 70% of the detected vowels from TIMIT and Berlin databases are included with a duration ratio superior than 50% from the reference ones (figure 5).

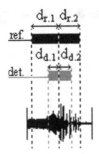

Fig. 4. Sensitivity to the duration from the detected vowel segments (*black*) according to the reference ones (*gray*)

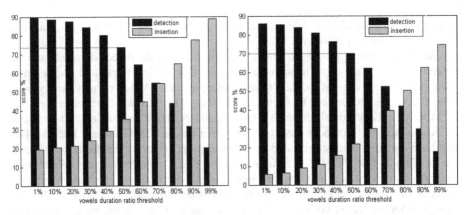

Fig. 5. Sensitivity of the detector to the duration from the vowel segments reference for Berlin and TIMIT databases respectively

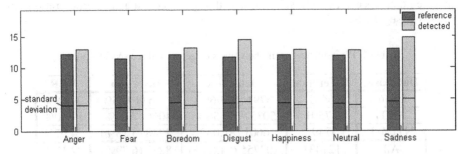

Fig. 6. Mean number of vowels per sentence (reference and detected) according to the seven emotions from Berlin

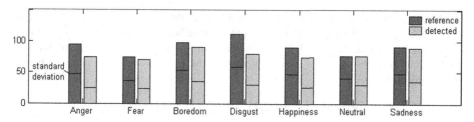

Fig. 7. Mean duration of vowels in *ms* (reference and detected) according to the seven emotions from Berlin

According to the seven emotions from Berlin, we extracted vowel characteristics such as mean number per sentence (ie. file) (figure 6) and mean duration (figure 7) from both reference and detected vowels. As the statistics show, the variability of the vowels number per sentence is better conserved than their mean values. On the whole, the detection is more less correctly done for all the emotion classes.

While three sorted groups can be defined from vowels duration statistics for both mean and standard-deviation: 1-Anger, Boredom and Disgust, 2-Happiness and Sadness and 3-Fear and Neutral with both lowest mean and distribution values. Since the neutral emotion is produced with no particular emphasis contrary to the others, few differences appear from reference and detected vowel characteristics.

Similar performance are obtained with a single configuration of the detector for the three databases (performance decrease only less than 4% for independent language detection), the employed approach seems therefore to be adequate for the vowels detection in speech.

3   Acoustic Based Emotion Recognition

This section presents methods and results for our acoustic-based emotion recognition approach for the Berlin corpus. Two approaches are studied: voiced and vowel based. Figure 1 illustrates the method employed for both features extraction and classification phases. During the voiced-based approach, speech is segmented by a sliding window of 32ms with a frame rate of 16ms. A voicing detector is then used to differentiate the voiced frames from the unvoiced ones. For the vowel-based approach, variable length segments according to the vowels and consonants segments are provided by the combination of both DFB segmentation and vowel detector as previously described (section 2). The feature extraction is performed by the computation of 24 MFCC parameters (Mel Frequency Cepstrum Coding). Concerning the classification phase, the MFCC features are labeled for each frame by a k-nn classifier (k nearest neighbors, k = 1), which returns emotion labels corresponding to the nearest MFCC emotions data from the learning phase. The scoring computation is based on a n-fold cross validation scheme where n is equal to 10.

3.1   Voiced Fusion

Two emotion labels vectors are obtained by the k-nn classification from voiced and unvoiced MFCC features. In order to fuse them, we firstly compute their conditional probabilities $p(C_i \mid V)$ and $p(C_i \mid UV)$ according to the seven emotions classes from Berlin (C_1 to C_7). Secondly, two different approaches are employed to fuse them: static and dynamic. The used fusion methods are a linear combination of the two conditional probabilities. For a given sentence, the emotion decision is taken by the following equation:

$$E = \mathrm{argmax}\left(\lambda_V * p(C_i \mid V) + \lambda_{UV} * p(C_i \mid UV)\right) . \tag{3}$$

The differentiation between static and dynamic fusion appears during the estimation of the weights from the voiced λ_V and unvoiced λ_{UV} classifiers. For the static fusion (equation 3), we estimate the optimal combination from the training data. Obtained values are then fixed for the all the test sentences. While the dynamic fusion is based on a voicing ratio computed for each test sentences. The voicing ratio r is defined as the proportion of voiced frames in speech. A power function is then applied to parameterize the decreasing velocity of the fusion weights: r^{α}.

$$E = \mathrm{argmax}\left(r^{\alpha} * p(C_i \mid V) + \left(1 - r^{\alpha}\right) * p(C_i \mid UV)\right) . \tag{4}$$

This method has been successfully used by Clavel [15] for 'fear' and 'neutral' emotions differentiation.

As we can expect, performances of the voiced frames classification from Berlin 74.91% are better than the unvoiced ones 45.66%, which is not a low score compared with a naïve classifier 27.37% (classifying all the test utterances as the most common

Table 2. Performances from voiced and unvoiced classifiers with two different fusion approaches: linear combination (static) and voicing ratio combination (dynamic)

Approach	Recognition rate
Voiced	74.91%
Unvoiced	45.66%
Static Fusion	75.66%
Dynamic Fusion	76.04%
Naïve	27.37%

Table 3. Confusion matrix of the dynamic fusion based emotions recognition

	A.	F.	B.	D.	H.	N.	S.	Recognition
Anger	130	0	0	0	0	0	0	100%
Fear	24	28	4	0	0	1	3	47%
Boredom	0	1	68	0	0	7	4	85%
Disgust	9	1	2	33	0	5	0	66%
Happiness	38	0	0	5	27	0	0	39%
Neutral	0	1	16	0	0	61	2	76%
Sadness	0	0	4	0	0	0	56	93%
Confusion	47%	91%	69%	90%	100%	79%	88%	**76.04%**

emotional class) (table 2). Static fusion from these two classifiers reaches a very high recognition rate of 75.66% with the following weights: $\lambda_V = 0.8$ and $\lambda_{UV} = 0.1$. The dynamic fusion achieves the best score 76.04% with $\alpha = 0.5$, revealing the interest of the voicing ratio normalization during this phase.

In the case of the dynamic fusion, and according to the literature [12,14], 'Anger' and 'Sadness' are the best detected emotions with 100% and 93.33%, and 'Fear' and 'Happiness' are the worst ones: 46.67% and 38.57% respectively. The confusion matrix of this fusion can be found in table 3.

3.2 Vowels and Consonants Fusion

Unlike to the voiced fusion process, two labels vectors are obtained from the detected emotions by the k-nn classifications from both vowels and consonants. Since the Berlin corpus provides a phonetic transcription from the emotional speech data, we therefore separately perform MFCC computations from the references and detected segments (section 2). Similar classification process than for the static voiced fusion is applied to the pseudo-phonetic segments:

$$E = \text{argmax}\left(\lambda_{Vow} * p\left(C_i \mid Vowels\right) + \lambda_{Csn} * p\left(C_i \mid Consonants\right)\right) . \tag{5}$$

Since the DFB segmentation trends to over-segment the speech signal for the consonant segment which are the most represented (detected consonant/vowel ratio is about 2.09 against 1.69 for the reference), dynamic fusion was not explored. Similar recognition rates are achieved for static fusion for both references and detected segments (table 4); the confusion matrices can be found in table 5. As the consonant segments are much more represented than the vowels, we can consider that the vowels MFCC features are more discriminant than the consonants ones in spite of a lower recognition rate: 46.42% (reference) and 52.56% (detected) against respectively 59.06% and 56.71% for the consonants. This consideration is agreed to the fact that among the speech structuring units, vocalic nucleus have been proved to be the most perceptive ones [25].

Table 4. Emotions recognition performances for the vowel-based approach

Approach	Reference	Detected
Vowels	46.42%	52.56%
Consonants	59.06%	56.71%
Fusion	60.57%	59.06%

Since a lot of information reduction takes place when only vowels and consonants segments are used for the emotions recognition, obtained performances are about 25% lower than the voiced-based fusion. During this approach, the speech is segmented by a sliding window with an overlap ratio of 50%, which involves numerous information extractions including some redundancy. Since a small quantity of information is provided by the MFCC extraction from the pseudo-phonetic approach unlike to the voice-based one, we can carefully suppose that the acoustic characteristics from the vowel segments are relevant for the emotion recognition.

Table 5. (a) Confusion matrix of the vowel-based emotions recognition (reference transcription). (b) Confusion matrix of the vowel-based emotions recognition (detected vowels).

(a)

	A.	F.	B.	D.	H.	N.	S.	Recognition
Anger	**126**	3	0	1	0	0	0	97%
Fear	26	22	5	0	1	2	4	37%
Boredom	8	5	**29**	0	1	18	19	36%
Disgust	18	0	4	**21**	2	2	3	66%
Happiness	39	3	2	0	19	6	1	42%
Neutral	3	3	10	0	2	**57**	5	71%
Sadness	0	0	5	0	0	8	**47**	78%
Confusion	57%	61%	53%	95%	76%	61%	59%	**60.57%**

(b)

	A.	F.	B.	D.	H.	N.	S.	Recognition
Anger	**130**	0	0	0	0	0	0	100%
Fear	36	12	3	1	1	4	3	20%
Boredom	7	3	**33**	0	1	20	16	41%
Disgust	18	3	1	**21**	1	3	3	42%
Happiness	35	0	0	4	14	12	5	20%
Neutral	5	0	9	0	0	**51**	15	64%
Sadness	3	0	2	1	0	2	**52**	87%
Confusion	52%	64%	68%	84%	60%	59%	53%	**59.06%**

4 Conclusion

A new features extraction scheme for the emotions recognition is presented in this paper: the vowel based approach. The automatic vowels detector is evaluated on three different databases with both language independent and noisy environment. Obtained mean VER score from these data is 22.17%. The best results are obtained on the read speech corpus 19.50% and the lowest on the emotional database 29.08%. The employed method seems therefore to be appropriate for vowel extraction. An emotion recognition system is processed on the Berlin corpus with two different approaches: voiced and the proposed pseudo-phonetic. The voiced-based approach reaches a very high recognition rate for dynamic fusion 76.04%, while the vowels and consonants fusion score is 60.57%. According to the important information reduction that takes place during the vowel-based approach, obtained results from the vowels segments can be carefully considered as relevant to the emotion recognition. Beyond the acoustic characterization of the pseudo-phonetic units, vowels and consonants segments may have a strong potential of interest in the emotion recognition as they convey a lot of prosodic information such as duration and rhythm. We therefore propose to integrate the vowels and consonants units presented in this paper into the emotions recognizer systems to improve their performances.

References

1. Athanaselis, T., Bakamidis, S., Dologlou, I., Cowie, R., Douglas-Cowie, E., Cox, C.: ASR for emotional speech: clarifying the issues and enhancing performance. Neural Networks 18, 437–444 (2005)
2. Plutchik, R.: The psychology and Biology of Emotion, Harper-Collins College, New York (1994)
3. Sherer, K., et al.: Acoustic correlates of task load and stress. In: Proceedings of ICSLP (2002)
4. Cowie, R.: Emotion-Oriented Computing: State of the Art and Key Challenges. Humaine Network of Excellence (2005)
5. Appendix, F.: Labels describing affective states in five major languages. In: Scherer, K. (ed.) Facets of emotion: Recent research, pp. 241–243. Lawrence Erlbaum, Hillsdale (1988) [Version revised by the members of the Geneva Emotion Research Group]
6. Plutchik, R.: A General Psychoevolutionary Theory of Emotion. In: Plutchik, R., Kellerman, H. (eds.) Emotion: theory, research, and experience, vol. 1, pp. 3–33. Academic press, New York (1980)
7. Picard, R.: Affective Computing. MIT Press, Cambridge (1997)
8. Ververidis, D., Kotropoulos, C.: Emotional Speech Recognition, Features and Method. Speech Communication 48(9), 1162–1181 (2006)
9. Devillers, L., Vidrascu, L., Lamel, L.: Challenges in Real-Life Emotion Annotation and Machine Learning Based Detection. Journal of Neural Networks 18(4), 407–422 (2005)
10. Spence, C., Sajda, P.: The Role of Feature Selection in Building Patterns Recognizers for Computer-Aided Diagnosis. In: Kenneth, M.H. (ed.) Proceedings of SPIE, vol. 3338, pp. 1434–1441. Springer, Heildberg (1998)
11. Oudeyer, P.-Y.: The Production and Recognition of Emotions in Speech: Features and Algorithm. International Journal of Human-Computer Studies, special issue on Affective Computing 59(1-2), 157–183 (2002)
12. Xiao, Z., et al.: Hierarchical Classification of Emotional Speech. IEEE Transactions on Multimedia (submitted to, 2007)
13. Vogt, T., André, E.: Comparing Feature Sets for Acted and Spontaneous Speech in view of Automatic Emotion Recognition, pp. 474–477. ICME (2005)
14. Shami, M., Verhelst, W.: An Evaluation of the Robustness of Existing Supervised Machine Learning Approaches to the Classification of Emotions in Speech. Speech Communications 48(9), 201–212 (2007)
15. Clavel, C., Vasilescu, I., Richard, G., Devillers, L.: Voiced and Unvoiced Content of Fear-type Emotions in the SAFE Corpus. In: Proc. of Speech Prosody (2006)
16. Garofolo, J.-S., et al.: DARPA TIMIT Acoustic-Phonetic Continuous Speech Corpus CDROM. In: NIST (1993)
17. Jankowski, C., et al.: NTIMIT: A Phonetically Balanced, Continuous Speech, Telephone Bandwidth Speech Database. ICASSP 1, 109–112 (1990)
18. Burkhardt, F., et al.: A Database of German Emotional Speech. In: Proc. of Interspeech (2005)
19. Truong, K., Van Leeuwen, D.: An open-set Detection Evaluation Methodology for Automatic Emotion Recognition in Speech. In: Workshop on Paralinguistic Speech - between models and data, pp. 5–10 (2007)
20. Vogt, T., André, E.: Improving Automatic Emotion Recognition from Speech via Gender Differentiation. In: Proc. of Language Resources and Evaluation Conference (2006)

21. Datcu, D., Rothkrantz, L., J.-M.: The Recognition of Emotions from Speech using GentleBoost Classifier. A Comparison Approach. CompSysTech Session V (2006)
22. André-Obrecht, R.: A New Statistical Approach for Automatic Speech Segmentation. IEEE Transaction on ASSP 36(1), 29–40 (1988)
23. Pellegrino, F., André-Obrecht, R.: Automatic Language Identification: an Alternative Approach to Phonetic Modelling. Signal Processing 80, 1231–1244 (2000)
24. Rouas, J.-L., Farinas, J., Pellegrino, F., André-Obrecht, R.: Rhythmic Unit Extraction and Modeling for Automatic Language Identification. Speech Communication 47(4), 436–456 (2005)
25. Pillot, C., Vaissière, J.: Vocal Effectiveness in Speech and Singing: Acoustical, Physiological and Perspective Aspects. Applications in Speech Therapy. Laryngol Otol Rhinol Journal 127(5), 293–298 (2006)

Towards Annotation of Nonverbal Vocal Gestures in Slovak

Milan Rusko[1] and Jozef Juhár[2]

[1] Institute of Informatics of the Slovak Academy of Sciences, Dubravska cesta 9, Bratislava
[2] Faculty of Electrotechnical Engineering, Letna 9,
Technical University Košice, Slovak Republic
milan.rusko@savba.sk, jozef.juhar@fei.tuke.sk

Abstract. The paper presents some of the problems of classification and annotation of speech sounds that have their own phonetic content, phonological function, and prosody, but they do not have an adequate linguistic (or text) representation. One of the most important facts about these "nonverbal vocal gestures" is that they often have a rich semantic content and they play an important role in expressive speech. The techniques that have been used in an effort to find an adequate classification system and annotation scheme for these gestures include prosody modeling and approaches comparing the nonverbal vocal gestures with their verbal (lexical) and body counterparts.

Keywords: Nonverbal vocal gestures, non lexical speech sounds, paralinguistic speech, grunts.

1 Introduction

Building of speech databases including TV debates recording, court proceedings, and dialogues have started in Slovakia recently. These databases will become parts of the Slovak National Corpus [1] that has only had a text part up till now. For a deeper study of expressive speech phenomena a sophisticated classification and description scheme of non-lexical speech sounds in Slovak is needed. This paper presents ideas and concepts that will hopefully give rise to a first version of such a classification scheme. As there was no expressive speech database available, the speech corpus based approach was not possible. Therefore we decided to take the advantage of existence of the Japanese-Chinese-American-Slovak Picture dictionary of gestures [2]. We tried to find out which of these gestures have their vocal counterpart or accompanying sound. This analysis made it possible to define first set of candidates for our list of "nonverbal vocal gestures". This was further enriched by candidates obtained from Slovak National Corpus and from tools for crossword solvers and scrabble players. Problems of description - orthographic representation, acoustics/phonetics, prosody, semantics and pragmatics of this special class of speech sounds are presented in this paper.

A. Esposito et al. (Eds.): HH and HM Interaction 2007, LNAI 5042, pp. 255–265, 2008.
© Springer-Verlag Berlin Heidelberg 2008

2 Nonverbal Information in the Speech Signal

The information communicated in spoken language can be categorized as linguistic, paralinguistic, and extra-linguistic [3]. The verbal content, the actual meaning of the words, is thought of as linguistic information. The extra-linguistic channel contains information about the speaker's basic state and culture. The paralinguistic channel carries information about momentary changes in the usual (extra-linguistic) baseline, such as expression of emotions etc.

In this study we will aim at nonverbal vocal gestures (NVG) that we define as speech sounds that have their own phonetic content, phonological function, and prosody, but they do not have an adequate linguistic (or text) representation. One of the most important facts about these non-lexical speech sounds [4] is that they often have a rich semantic content and they play an important role in expressive speech and human communication [5].

3 Method

In our work we want to utilize knowledge and methods used in verbal communication research: liguistics, orthography, orthoepy, phonetics, phonology, speech acoustics, pragmatics, nonverbal non-vocal gestures research, and know-how coming from speech synthesis and speech recognition research. The first draft annotation scheme will be used for test annotations and will then be modified according to their results. In the second round a bigger database will be annotated and an inter-annotator agreement will be tested. The resulting detailed annotation should enable clustering the whole space of nonverbal speech gestures into subspaces (groups) according to various features (e.g. similar acoustic structure, semantics etc.).

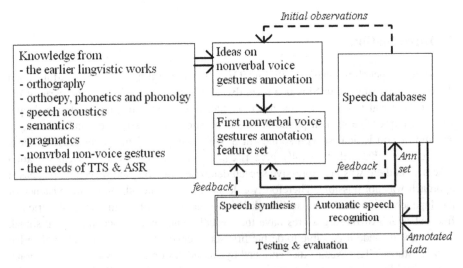

Fig. 1. Schematic diagram of our approach to nonverbal speech gestures classification scheme design and testing

The definitive version of the annotation scheme will be used to annotate training speech database and speech synthesis database and tested in automatic speech recognition and unit-selection speech synthesis. We will compare the scheme to the existing ones [6].

4   Gestures

A gesture is a form of non-verbal communication made with a part of the body, used instead of or in combination with verbal communication [7].

As we did not have any speech material, nor classification or description conventions available to start with in our research, we decided to take the advantage of existence of the Japanese-Chinese-American-Slovak Picture dictionary of gestures [2]. The material of the dictionary comprises four groups according to the generic meaning. Such division is directed by semantics. According to the author the gestures express physical body, initiative contact, emotional body or mental body. The optics of the dictionary is directed towards only one body at a time; both verbal and non-verbal communication is taken into account.

We checked the list (classification, pictures) of body gestures and tried to find those of the gestures which (according to our opinion) have a vocal counterpart.

Fig. 2. Several examples of the gestures from the Picture dictionary of Gestures [2], which have their vocal counterparts (published with courtesy of E. Ružičková)

Table 1. to Table 4. present a list of gestures scheduled in [2]. Slovak name of the semantic group is shown in first column, and English one in the second column. The characters in the third column represent different types of gestures belonging semantically to the same group. Gestures that have their vocal counterparts are in underlined and bold font.

Table 1.

Gestures manifesting physical body		
Veľkosť	*Bigness*	A,B
Chlad	*Coldness*	**A,B,C,D**,E
Hĺbka/ plytkosť	*Depth/ Shallowness*	A
Pitie	*Drink*	**A**,B
Plný nápoja	*Full of drink*	A
Jedenie	*Food*	A,B
Plný jedla	*Full of food*	**A**
Tučnota	*Fatness*	A,B
Horúčka/horúci	*Heat/hot*	**A,B**,C,**D**
Výška	*Height*	A
Dĺžka/Krátkosť/Šírka/ Úzkosť(miera)/Hrúbka/ Tenkosť	*Length/Shortness/Breadth/ Narrowness/Thickness/ Thinness*	A
Spanie	*Sleep*	**A,B**
Štíhlosť	*Slimness*	A,B
Vôňa	*Smell*	**A,B**
Unavenosť	*Tiredness*	A,**B,C**,D
Čo?	*What?*	A

Table 2.

Gestures manifesting initiative contact		
Pozornosť	*Attention*	**A**,B,**C**,D,E,**F,G,H,I**,J
Byť ticho	*Be quiet*	**A**,B,C,D,**E**
Prísť	*Come*	**A,B,C,D,E,F,G**
Smery	*Directions*	A,B,C,D,E,F
Pozdravy	*Greetings*	**A,B**,C,D,E,F
Zbohom	*Good-Bye*	**A**,B,C,D,E,F,G,H
Zhon, Rýchlo	*Haste/Quick*	**A,B**
Stop	*Hitchhiking*	**A,B**
Odísť	*Leave*	A,B,C,D
Peniaze	*Money*	A,B,C,D,E,F
Sľub(Prísaha)	*Oath*	A,B,C
Fotografovanie	*Photograph*	**A,B,C**
Obdržať	*Receive*	**A**,B
Opakovanie	*Repetition*	**A,B**
Požiadavky	*Requests*	A,**B,C**,D,**E,F**,G,**H**,I,J

Table 2. (*continued*)

Reštauračné gestá	*Restaurant gestures*	A,B,C,D,E,F,G,H,I,J,K,L
Sadnúť	*Sit*	A
Spomaliť	*Slow down*	A
SMS (Short Message Service)	*SMS*	A
Vstať	*Stand up*	A
Zastaviť	Stop	A,B,C,D
Telefonovať	*Telephone*	A,B
Čas	*Time*	A,B,C
Čakať	*Wait*	A,B
Varovanie	*Warning*	A,B,C

Table 3.

Gestures manifesting emotional body		
Hnev	*Anger*	A,B,C,D,E,F,G,H
Očakávanie	*Anticipation*	A,B,C
Ospravedlnenie	*Apology*	A,B,C,D,E,F,G,H
Odpor	*Aversion*	A,B
Odsúdenie(Zavrhnutie)	*Condemnation*	A
Sklamanie	*Disappointment*	A,B,C
Rozpaky	*Embarrassment*	A,B,C,D,E
Vzrušenie	*Excitement*	A,B,C,D
Faux pas	*Faux pas*	A,B,C,D,E,F
Strach	*Fear*	A
Sklamanie	*Frustration*	A,B,C
Vďačnosť	*Gratitude*	A,B,C
Šťastie	*Happiness*	A
Nenávisť	*Hatred*	A
Nedočkavosť	*Impatience*	A
Urážky (útoky)	*Insults*	A,B,C,D,E,F,G,H,I,J
Bozk	*Kiss*	A
Nervozita	*Nervousness*	A,B,C,D
Ľútosť	*Regret*	A,B,C,D
Pomsta	*Revenge*	A,B,C,D
Smútok	*Sadness*	A
Sexuálny	*Sexual*	A,B,C
Zahanbenosť	*Shame*	A
Prekvapenie	*Surprise*	A,B,C,D
Hrozba (vyhrážka)	*Threat*	A,B,C,D,E,F,G,H

Table 4.

Gestures manifesting mental body		
Súhlas(dohoda)	Agreement	**A,B**
Súhlas(uznanie)	Approval	**A,B,C,D,E,F,G,H**
Komplikácia	Complication	**A,B,C,D**
Odmietnutie(popretie)	Denial	**A,B,C,D**
Nesúhlas(nezhoda)	Disagreement	**A,B,C,D,E**
Neschválenie(nesúhlas)	Disapproval	**A**
Úspech	Good luck	**A,B,C,D,E,F**
Reči	Gossip	**A**
Inteligencia	Intelligence	**A**
Nedostatok inteligencie	Lack of intelligence	**A,B,C,D,E**
Viacmenej	More or less	**A,B**
Žiadna informácia	No information	**A**
Dokonalé	Perfect	**A,B,C**,D
Modlitba	Prayer	**A,B,**C,D
Hrdosť(pýcha)	Pride	**A,B,C,D,E,F**,G
Svätosť	Saintliness	**A,B**
Seba(Vlastný)	Self	**A,B**
Úspech	Success	A,**B,C,D,E,F,G,H,I,J**
Rozmýšľanie	Thinking	**A,B,C,D,E,F**
Víťazstvo	Victory	**A,B,C**

It can be seen from the tables, that nearly all gestures manifesting emotional and mental body have their vocal counterparts.

We are aware of the fact, that the vocal forms of the body gestures can confirm the identicalness of the use of the same body gesture for different meanings or on the contrary the same body gesture can have different accompanying vocal gestures that make its meaning different.

From dialogue research most of the vocal gestures are known as discourse markers and backchannels; in speech databases design they are generally classified as speaker noises, grunts, fillers or filled pauses. We also include laughing, crying, and yawning in the set of voice displays that are object to our research.

From the grammatical point of view most of them can be classified as particles or interjections.

5 Orthographic Transcription

A lot of effort has been done to find a set of words that would be able to represent or "encode" orthographically the non-lexical English speech sounds. The most sophisticated sets were designed for speech databases annotation in dialogue and generally speech communication research (e.g. [8], [13]).

The most comprehensive list of orthographic forms of the NVG in Slovak we have obtained from the tools for crossword puzzle solvers and scrabble players and this was enriched by the list of interjections and particles taken from the Slovak National Corpus. The result is a list of sveral hundreds of orthographic expressions, from which several tenths are candidates to represent speech gestures in our future scheme.

While Picture Dictonary of Gestures offers the picture of the gesture, the name of its class, generic meaning, description (of the body gesture), its specific message in four cultures, and a description of four categories of context (formality, gender, age, social status), the text sources provide us only with orthographic transcroption of the sound and in some cases with their linguistic context.

The list will be regularly updated by new gestures found during the database annotation (feedback).

6 Orthoepy – Phonetics

Ordinary phonetic transcriptions of NVGs reflect only the linguistically informative quality. Orthographic transcription is insufficient – it is highly ambiguous and reflects the phonetic content only to very limited extent. Therefore some kind of „phoneme transcription" is needed.

As the standard set of 54 Slovak phonemes and allophones is not sufficient to express the phonetic structure of NVGs, there is a need for new phonemes, e.g.:

Glottal stop /ʔ/ - which can be used to represent a **hard onset**
Neutral wovel (schwa) - /ə/ - (which does not belong to a Slovak phoneme set)
long neutral wovel (long schwa) - /ə:/
Inhaled phonemes – e.g. in the word /hi:/,
Inhaled "t,t,t..." (which is in fact not inhaled, because the air is not aspirated by lungs, but sucked in the mouth cavity by the piston function of the tongue.
Other inhaled phonemes – e.g. in inhaled "Aj, jaj, ja,ja, jaj..." or "Ej, jej, jéj, ..."
New nasal phonemes:
nasal murmured /h/ e.g. in the grunt "mhm" pronounced with closed mouth,
nasal schwa=long m - /m:/,
long n - / n:/
New phonemes (consonants) to create syllable nucleii (e.g. to use in the words imitating sounds: /ps:t/, /ne-ps:-kaj/ (= Don't make "pssst" sound!)):
/s: /, /š: /, /z: /, /ž: /, /x: /, /m: /, /n: /, /f: /, etc.
New quantity class should be added – extra long phonemes: e.g. "Ááááh" should be transcribed like /a:: h/.

7 Terminology ☺

The phonemes we are speaking about in fact do not follow exactly all aspects of the classical definition of a phoneme (distinctive function, etc.).

How about calling them:	NVG phonemes	→ nonemes	
The same holds with:	NVG syllables	→ nyllables	
	NVG words	→ nords	
Or even:	NVG phrase	→ nrase	...and
	NVG sentence	→ nentence	

8 Prosody

The research on prosody of nonverbal speech sounds is rather extensive [e.g. 7].
There is a deeper relatedness between the verbal and the non-verbal than is generally
understood. It seems probable that pre-verbal archetypes of vocal gestures exist, and
that the newer versions of gestures keep similar prosody to their ancient predecessors.
Note the similarity among the pitch contours in the interjection "íha" and its semantic
eqivalent "mm-hm" (Fig. 3a). The same phenomenon can be observed on the "čo?" –
"hm?" (= *what?*) pair and many others.

Also some syllabic/rythmic patterns seem to be adopted to lexical words from
their non-lexical counterparts. Slovak word "nie" (= *no*) is normally pronounced as
one syllable with a diphtong /ie/ in its nucleus. But in expressive speech with strong
emphasis on this word it would be often pronounced as "ni-je", broken into two syllables in the same way as its non-lexical counterpart "ə-ə" (= *no*) (Fig. 3b).

We are aware of complexity of these dependences and relations which can ilus-
trated on many examples that do not follow the mentioned principals (Fig 3c, showing
"áno" – "mhm" pair expressing positive answer (= *yes*), but having totally different
pitch contours).

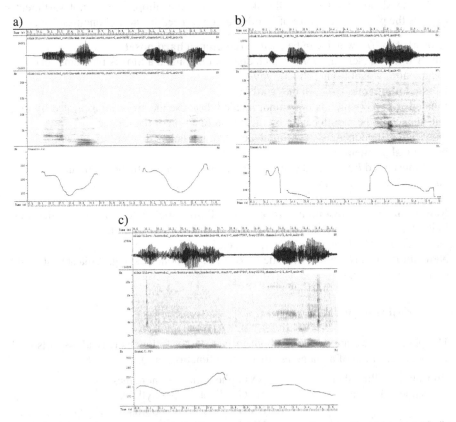

Fig. 3. Oscillograph, spectrograph and pith contour of the examples described higher a) "íha" -
"mm-hm", b) "nie" - "ə-ə", "áno" - "mhm"

9 Intonation Model

When thinking about an appropriate annotation of intonation we were inspired with such schemes as ToBI [10] or INTSINT [11].

The frequency range in expressive speech can be enlarged and 2-3 levels of tones high, (middle), low (H, (M,) L), generally used for standard speech may need to be expanded to 4-5 levels (HH, H, (M,) L, LL). For instance in the word „Really?" the pitch reaches L,H tones in neutral speech, LL,L when surprised&having doubt, H,HH when excited.

Moreover the pitch contour is often changing fluently (gliding) or in small steps. Therefore we think that basic set of tone symbols that would give a usable simplified representation of pitch contour of the NVGs can be:

T – very high tone (top)
H – high tone
L – low tone
B – very low tone (bottom)
D – small step downwards (e.g. "No, no, no, no, no, no, no! – T D D D D D D L)
U – small step upwards

And their "glided" combinations (excluding D and U) to express continual rise or fall: H+T, L+T, L+B, etc.

10 Voice Quality – Loudness – Timing

Voice quality is a very important feature in expressive speech and it carries a high amount of information. Some authors consider voice quality to be "the fourth prosodic parameter" [12].

Although can the voice quality reflected to a certain amount in the definition of the "noneme" set, it is better to use Laver's voice quality classification scheme to annotate strongly changed (non-standard) voice quality.

More complex NVGs seem to be organized in time in syllable-like segments. Sometimes they are shorter (in a *staccato* manner, filling only part of the "beat"), other time they are longer and not separated by any pauses (which reminds of notes played *tenuto*).

Therefore we would like to allow using terms/signs from Italian musical terminology (*pp, ff, stacc.,* etc.) to mark some phenomena of loudness and rhythm. These signs would serve only as a comment.

11 Semantics and Pragmatics

How is it possible, that a single vocal gesture is often able to bear the same information as the whole sentence? One of the possibilities is that the gesture occurs often in a fixed combination with certain type of semantic units (SU) with certain meaning. Then when the gesture occurs alone, it borrows the same meaning as the NSG-SU combination.

To be able to check hypotheses like this, we will need a kind of semantic annotation system.

Semantics represents the first level, significant meaning, i.e. what the gesture "says" in general. We are inspired by the semantic description and classification of the gestures in body gesture dictionaries (e.g. [2]), by classification schemes of particles and interjections, and by the different metadata annotation specifications (e.g. [13]).

Pragmatics represents the situational meaning - what does the speaker really mean/intend by his gesture shown to the particular interlocutor in the actual situation (second level meaning). Differences in pragmatic meaning are often achieved by adding ironical, satirical undertone e.t.c.

The communication follows certain rules based on conventions and it will be successful only if the receiver understands both meanings (the standard one, and the situational one). Therefore the gestures are culturally dependent and they can be exported / imported together with foreign culture (Yessss!, Wow!).

12   Conclusion

A preliminary stage of the research of the nonverbal speech gestures in Slovak is presented. The authors discuss their ideas of the development of a coding scheme which would make the annotation of nonverbal vocal gestures in Slovak possible.

Topics discussed in the paper include orthographic annotation, orthoepic representation using extended phoneme set, intonation coding scheme and the need for new terminology. Voice quality, loudness, timing, semantic and pragmatic content annotation, were also discussed.

Acknowledgments. This work was supported by the of the Ministry of Education of the Slovak Republic, Scientific Grant Agency project number 2/0138/08 Applied Research project number AV 4/0006/07 and by the European Education, Audiovisual and Culture Executive Agency LLP project EURONOUNCE.

Education and Culture DG

This project has been funded with support from the European Commission. This publication reflects the views only of the authors, and the Commission cannot be held responsible for any use which may be made of the information contained therein.

References

1. http://korpus.juls.savba.sk/ (December 2007)
2. Ružičková, E.: Picture dictionary of gestures (American, Slovak, Japanese, and Chinese). Comenius University Publishing House, Bratislava (2001) ISBN 80-223-1675-X

3. Eckert, H., Laver, J.: Menschen und Ihre Stimmen. Beltz Psychologie Verlags Union, Weinheim (1994)
4. Ward, N.: Non-Lexical Conversational Sounds in American English. Pragmatics and Cognition 14(1), 113–184 (2006)
5. Campbell, N.: On the Use of NonVerbal Speech Sounds in Human Communication. In: COST 2102 Workshop, pp. 117–128 (2007)
6. Annotation Schemes for Verbal and Non-Verbal Communication: Some General Issues. Niels Ole Bernsen and Laila Dybkjær COST 2102 Workshop 11-22 (2007)
7. http://en.wikipedia.org/wiki/Gesture (December 2007)
8. http://www.univie.ac.at/voice/documents/VOICE_spelling_conve ntions_v2-1.pdf (December 2007)
9. Benus, S., Gravano, A., Hirschberg, J.: Prosody of backchannels in American English. In: Proceedings of 16th International Coneference of Phonetic Sciences, Saarbrucken (2007)
10. Silverman, K., et al.: ToBI: a standard for labelling English prosody. In: Proceedings of the International Conference on Spoken Language Processing, Banff, Alberta, vol. 2, pp. 867–700 (1992)
11. Hirst, D.: Intonation models: towards a third generation. In: Actes du XIIeme Congres International des Sciences phonetiques, 19-24 aout 1991, pp. 305–310. Universite de Provence, Service des Publications, Aix-en-Povence (1991)
12. Campbell, N., Mokhtari, P.: Voice Quality; the 4th prosodic parameter. In: Proc 15th ICPhS, Barcelona, Spain (2003)
13. Linguistic Data Consortium (LDC) (December 2007), http://projects.ldc.upenn.edu/MDE/Guidelines/SimpleMDE_V6.2. pdf

The *CineLingua* Approach: Verbal and Non-verbal Features in Second Language Acquisition. Film Narrative to Anchor Comprehension and Production

Rosa Volpe

University of Perpignan Via Domitia
Department of Letters and Human Sciences and French as a Foreign Language
152 Paul Alduy, 66000 Perpignan
rosa.volpe@univ-perp.fr

Abstract. This study has as a central focus a foreign language classroom environment that makes daily use of multimedia film lessons in the target language. More specifically this study explores whether first-semester, first-year college students of Italian will understand film narrative, and how, the comprehension of the film narrative will affect their written production. Eighty-one first year college students participated in this study. The results suggest that the Anchored Learning Group performed better than the Basic-Skills Learning Group in the comprehension tasks of the two film segments. The second experimental probe, consisting in a production task, shows that compared to the Basic-Skills Learning Group, the written productions of the Anchored Learning Group reflect far better the structure of the narrative discourse participants have been exposed to. On the occasion of this production task, students were required to write their essay using at least ten Italian verbs.

Keywords: Verbal and non-verbal, information, second language acquisition, anchored instruction, multimedia film narrative, linguistic analysis.

1 Introduction

The claim that meaning, and not only linguistic knowledge is essential to language development is widely spread within the various fields that have language learning as a focus. According to linguists, meaning is drawn from semantics and depends on the organization of discourse, which provides contextual structures [1]. For the sociolinguists, meaning also derives from social interaction. For the psycholinguists, it originates mainly from perception and from schemata, tacit and explicit knowledge of the world. Consequently, it is argued that language development depends on extra-linguistic non-verbal cues, as much as it depends on linguistic, verbal ones [2]. It is a widely held belief, in fact, that natural language development relies on pre-linguistic, *non-verbal* knowledge even before the coming into play of language. Moreover, due to the complexity of the mental activity in which language processing is engaged and considering that problem solving capabilities are also implied in the language faculty, such notion of pre-linguistic, *non-verbal* knowledge has been referred to in terms of pre-linguistic cognitive structures. These structures are said to trigger production [3], [4].

A. Esposito et al. (Eds.): HH and HM Interaction 2007, LNAI 5042, pp. 266–279, 2008.

1.1   Verbal and Non-verbal Information in Language Development

Language production has also been defined as a projection of internal language [5]. As a matter of fact, the relationship between perception, meaning and language structures have been studied in particular to show that what we see is translated into what we say [6]. Namely, Jackendoff [6] has posited the need for a set of *correspondence rules* according to which we would first translate acoustic and visual information into meanings in order to gain language understanding. Later on, we would translate these pre-structured meanings into messages by making use of the vocal tract thus producing speech. These rules would allow to explain the way in which the mind reconstructs "what is out there in the world," thus translating visual information (*non-verbal* meanings) into linguistic expressions (verbal meanings). With this respect, Schlesinger [7] described production as a cognitive process that derives the meanings of sentences from the level of cognitive structures. According to him these structures contain information that is much more dense and detailed than what appears from their actual production in utterances. Moreover, they are actualized at a non-linguistic, *non-verbal* level. These pre-linguistic structures are fundamentally important in the comprehension and production of sentence meaning in natural language [8].

1.2   The *CineLingua* Approach to Develop Linguistic Awareness

In this article, we specifically set out to study the role of extra-linguistic knowledge on the development of a second language, namely Italian, with the intention of exploring the validity of the above mentioned assumptions within the context of second language development, namely written production skills. To reach this goal, findings from film theory, linguistic theory, and cognitive science are brought into play in an attempt to understand how to make use of learners' general and tacit knowledge in order to enhance the development of more specific second language abilities as well as general knowledge about the structure of the target language [9]. In particular, this study emphasizes the role that the development of non-verbal, and extra-linguistic knowledge plays upon learners' abilities in the development of second language skills and meta-linguistic awareness from being exposed to original film segments in Italian with no subtitles. Mutlimedia lessons were designed to lead students from comprehension to production. The *CineLingua* CDROM used for this experiment contains lessons that were developed from film segments drawn from Ettore Scola's masterpiece *We all loved each other so much* (See Appendix).

2   Theoretical Background and Experimental Design

By broadening our model of language instruction to include film discourse at the onset of language learning, the interactions among perception, meaning, memory, and thinking, together with those related to the development of social capabilities become important [10]. Compared to written language with its more restricted register consisting only of graphemes, filmic discourse has the potential of representing these interactions within the classroom environment as it displays language in use through conversations and dialogues that are visually supported. In addition, it is a perceptual peculiarity of cinema that it takes the spectator into the world of the imaginary allowing him or her to identify with the new culture and social context to improve understanding [11]. Understanding then becomes possible even at beginning levels of language learning because students can experience the use of language within social interactions. Their witnessing of such interactions brings into play previous and general knowledge of the world together with schemata through the formation of mental anchors made possible by film [12].

2.1 Film Theory and Language Learning

For this study, the movie *C'eravamo tanto amati* (We all loved each other so much) was chosen because it portrays simple life situations that have the potential to trigger previously acquired knowledge for which no unusual specific linguistic knowledge would be required to understand the main ideas of the film's plot. Thus, within the *Cinema Situation* created in the classroom, students become aware that their individuality can come into play and that more specific acquisition of the structure of the target language will be drawn from a more general knowledge about the world already available to them. Such knowledge originates from mental activities such as making inferences, generalizations, and analogies. Real experiences are also part of this shared knowledge or schemata. In *Il Cinema di poesia* Pasolini challenged the common belief that language, rather than images, is the foundation of communication [11]. The difference between the reader and a movie-goer in understanding meaning stands, according to Pasolini in the fact that the movie-goer has developed the habit of *visually reading* reality. In fact, by simply walking down the street, one experiences the environment through its images: such as people's presence, expressions, gestures, actions, silence, and much more. In other words, there is a whole world within mankind that mostly expresses itself through meaningful images. He called these meaningful images *im-segni*. This is, according to Pasolini, the world of memory and dreams. Thus, images provide mankind with an alternative way of communicating, and film in particular exploits this universal language.

Compared to the traditional medium of written communication, representing on the contrary a well established and sophisticated language system, visual and *non-verbal* communication through images appears to be unorganized, inelegant, and wild. To access meaning through language, one has to develop specific language skills, while to access meaning through images, previous experience with the external world is enough. Convinced as we are that these ideas would benefit second language acquisition, we set out to apply them within the context of foreign language learning, especially at the early levels of instruction given that, to access the *non-verbal* information from film *im-segni*, students will not need to rely on the development of specific language knowledge. Providing visual language through the medium of cinema instead of specific language rules about the target language would make it possible then to trigger learning in a more universal fashion [9].

The question then presents itself: would it be possible to shift instruction from a more constrained medium such as linguistic information, to non-verbal filmic language representing a system of communication universally accessible where the *im-segni* are not organized into a dictionary nor they have a grammar, hence anyone can understand them? Film language being as valid a means of communication as written language is, with the difference that it is more easily accessible because it does not require a specific linguistics knowledge in order to seize meaning, why not train our students to understand filmic *im-segni* instead of vocabulary items of a specific target language, at least during the first phase of instruction? Starting with the understanding of meaning through images being only a first step to the development of foreign language skills, production being the last one.

2.2 Predicate Argument Structures: Linking Verbal and Non-verbal Cues

This study is aimed at the development of written production at the level of predicate-argument structures. These structures, serving a linguistic function while organizing visually derived information, put the emphasis on the role of language and vision to semantics. Therefore, in addition to portraying the organization of lexical semantic representation, predicate argument structures (PAS) serve as a point of connection between linguistic and non-linguistic information, and verbal and non-verbal cues [13]. Canseco-Gonzales [14] elaborated on Badecker's position by claiming that PAS have the function of linguistically representing nonlinguistic modes in which information is organized. Thus, they operate as a translation device across cognitive domains. Results from research on anchored instruction suggest that enriching classroom environments with video materials is bound to affect students' learning experience [15].

When it comes to foreign and second language learning one could expect that, by providing *anchored* and *situational* target language input, visually supported input could play a major role in allowing learners actively to participate in the construction of knowledge by shifting their involvement from passive language assimilators to gradually becoming active language generators. The notion of *anchored* and *situational* instruction refers to the *macro-context* of learning environments. These environments are characterized by the complexity of the situations that are involved within them. Compared to conventional classroom learning environments, that represent instances of micro-contexts, and that are characterized by the alternation of disconnected micro-contexts, these situations are said to motivate students to solve first smaller scale problems that are connected to the main ones [15].

The table below (Table 1) illustrates the characteristics of the different learning environments of this study.

2.3 The Subjects of the Experiment

Eighty-one first-semester first year college students participated in this study as part of their regular class. The course was taught 5 days a week. None of them had been exposed to the Italian language before, and they were all undergraduate students enrolled in the *Humanities* program. Twenty students attended the Anchored session of Italian 101. The remaining students attended the three Basic-skill sessions of the same offering. The author of this research was also the instructor within the Anchored Learning session.

2.4 The Treatment

The Anchored Learning Group was exposed to film narrative from the beginning of the semester. Instruction was anchored by the multimedia *CineLingua* CDROM lessons aiming at leading students to developing production skills from the

Table 1. Basic-Skills and Anchored Instruction learning environments

Learning Environments		
	Basic-skills	*Anchored Instruction*
Written Materials	Grammar Textbook Reading book	Written Script of the Film Reading Book Grammar Textbook
Technology	Instructional Video *Buongiorno Italia* Watched Every Two Weeks for 25 minutes Language Lab Weekly Attendance	Film Narrative. Original Version. No English subtitles. Watched Three Times Weekly for 15 minutes The *CineLingua* Software. Steps: *Seguire* (attending to visual sense) (film segment with Italian subtitles) *Capire* (building up meaning) (integrating narration with graphics) *Imparare* (anchored learning) (from discourse to sentence structure) *Pronuncia* Practice (learning pronunciation) Vocabulary Learning Discourse Analysis Glossary *Pronuncia* Program (pronunciation program)
Teaching Approach	Morphology Grammar Rules	Discourse analysis Predicate Argument Structures Phrase Structure Rules Applied Morphology
Criterial Tasks	Homework Assignments Fill-in the Blank Others . . .	Create Your Own Scripts Create Your Own Exercises Practice Asking Questions Practice Answering Questions

development of comprehension skills in the first place. Training to linguistic analysis at the level of discourse was also provided during classroom time from the written script of the film narrative.

The Basic-Skill Learning Group was exposed to instructional video materials once every two weeks. The video activity simply consisted in watching the selected segment for the duration of about half an hour with no interaction among students and teacher. Classroom instruction was based on the classical approach of grammar explanation from the course textbook followed by exercises to practice the implementation of the previously explained grammar rules.

2.5 First Assessment Probe: Developing Comprehension Skills

The main research question with respect to the development of comprehension skills consisted in finding out whether beginning foreign language learners could develop comprehension skills from exposure to natural discourse that was visually supported, for example: film narrative in the original version, compared to simple aural exposure to the same film segment, provided in terms of previously recorded sound-track only.

Materials
Two different film segments (FS1, FS2) from two different movies were shown one at the time. The sound-track of both film segments previously recorded on a separate cassette tape were also used to test students' understanding from aural exposure only. With respect to the visually supported film segments, no English subtitles were provided. Students were instructed to rely on the visual input without worrying about understanding the words.

Experimental Treatment
Students watched the FS1 and answered, in English, a set of questions written in Italian. They did the same for FS2. Then they listened to the sound-track version of both FS1 and FS2 and answered in English a set of questions written in Italian.

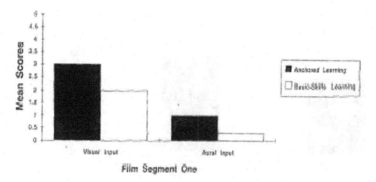

Fig. 1. Comprehension Test: visual and /or aural performance on the first film segment

Dependent variable
With respect to this specific task: answering questions, students' answers were evaluated as being either right or wrong.

Results
The data collected on the occasion of the first experimental treatment have shown that compared to the Basic-Skills group, the Anchored learning group were able to produce better results for both experimental tasks, FS1 and FS2 (See Figures 1, 2, 3).

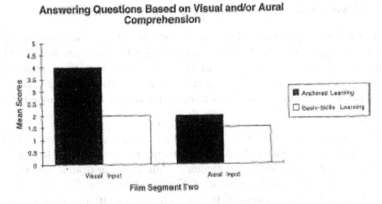

Fig. 2. Comprehension Test: visual and/or aural performance on the second film segment

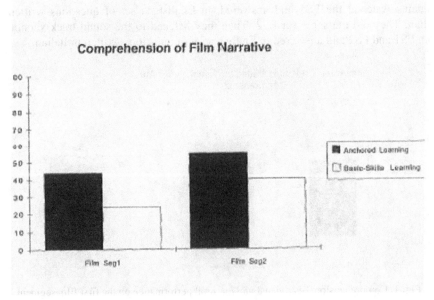

Fig. 3. Comprehension Test: visual and /or aural performance for film segment one and two

2.6 Second Assessment Probe: Developing Production Skills

If it becomes possible, as the results on the development of comprehension skills have shown, to develop overall understanding from exposure to film narrative at the beginning level of instruction, the next question is: how does the development of comprehension skills affect the development of written production of beginning foreign language students?

Materials
Using film narrative as the point of departure of language learning also made available the written version of the film script, which was used to enhance language instruction during class time. Carrying out the analysis of the structure of discourse leading to the discovery of grammar rules in context became than natural. In the same way, aiming at the development of learners' cognitive flexibility leading to production in the target language from the visual anchor provided by watching the film became also attainable. To carry out this experimental task a handout providing instructions on how to write a short essay in Italian was given to the students.

Experimental Treatment
Students were asked to make a list of ten Italian verbs they were familiar with and to build around them their accounts, in Italian, about the film narrative.

Dependent Variables
<u>Morphology of the Verb</u>: only the Italian verbs conjugated correctly were counted.

<u>Syntax of the Phrase</u>: only those sentences that included the correct use of a direct and indirect object pronouns in Italian were counted.

<u>Structure of the Discourse</u>: only those correct sentences containing subordinate clauses and conjunctions were counted.

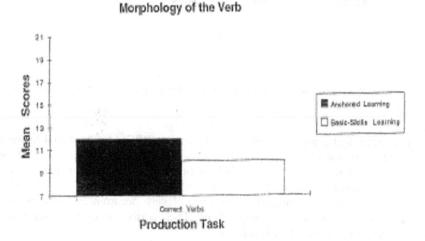

Fig. 4. Production Test. Accuracy of verb conjugation at the level of morphology.

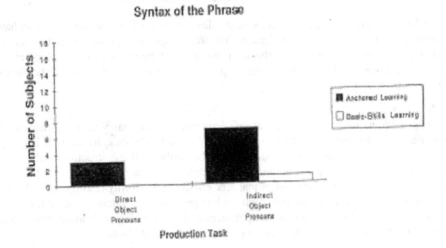

Fig. 5. Production Test. Occurrences of the complement of the verb by the use of preposition.

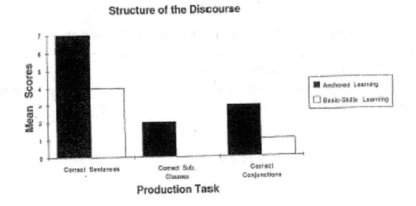

Fig. 6. Production Test. Sentence accuracy in subordinate clauses by use of conjunctions.

Results
Results indicate that compared to Basic-Skills Group (BSG), the Anchored Learning Group (ALG) performed better with respect to the three major categories. More specifically, with respect to the Morphology of the Verb, in spite of the fact that students were required to base their essay on the use of at least ten verbs, beginning students within the ALG outgrew the number of verb occurrences. This tendency suggests students' motivation to keep writing. Their performance was better also in terms of accuracy in terms of verb conjugation.

When looking at the results with respect to the Syntax of the Phrase, these show that the experimental group (ALG) attempted and succeeded to use more Direct Object Pronouns (DOP) and Indirect Object Pronouns (IOP) correctly. The occurrence of DOP and IOP within such a short essay can be interpreted as a sign of flexibility that students are starting having in manipulating the target language input originated from the film narrative. As a matter of fact, unless specifically required to do so, beginning foreign language learners seem to somehow resist understanding the use of DOP and IOP. Finally, as far as the Structure of the Discourse is concerned, students within the ALG outperformed the students within the BSG with respect to the total number of sentences making up the whole essay. Significant results also marked the occurrence of subordinate sentences, and as a consequence, the occurrence of the use of conjunctions (See Fig. 4, 5, 6).

3   General Discussion

The results suggest that the Anchored Learning Group performed better than the Basic-Skills Learning Group in the comprehension of the two film segments. The second experimental probe consisted in a production task and shows that compared to the Basic-Skills Learning Group, the written production of the Anchored Learning Group reflects far better the structure of the narrative discourse they have been exposed to. In the occasion of this production task, students were required to write their essay using at least 10 Italian verbs they were familiar with. The performance of the Anchored Group was different from the performance of the Basic-Skills Group in quantity and quality. Compared to the Basic-Skills group, the Anchored Group performed better in terms of verb conjugation, and production of more correct sentences. Moreover the structure of their written discourse was closer to the structure of the discourse of the target language narrative.

Generally speaking these results from students' productions suggest that it was beneficial for beginning students of Italian to be exposed to film narrative from the beginning of the semester not only because it enhanced the building up of comprehension skills based on natural use of the target language, but also because it affected the development of their flexibility in terms of production of the target language. With respect to the impact that viewing film segments in the target language has had on the development of comprehension skills in particular, we would like to refer to what Colin calls the *spectator work* [16]. According to Colin writing a movie as well as *reading* it implies the sharing of common knowledge. Such knowledge originates from mental activities such as making inferences, generalizations and analogies, real and personal experiences being also part of such shared knowledge structure, or schemata. With his work, Colin intended to show that film structure is homologous to language structure. According to him such correspondance between language structure and film structure should explain, he states, the process of film comprehension.

By analyzing the relationship between linguistic and non-linguistic information in the development of comprehension and production skills in second language learning, this research intended to emphasize the importance of anchoring the learning of linguistic information with non-linguistic non-verbal and visual input instead, especially in consideration of the findings exploring the role that predicate argument structure play in linking verbal and non-verbal cues. With this respect these structures are said to serve a linguistic function while organizing visually derived information [17].

Acknowledgments. Particular thanks to Prof. Diane Schallert at the *University of Texas at Austin* for her strong belief in this research; the *McDonnell Foundation* for the financial support provided allowing turning theory into practice; the *Cognition and Technology Group*, namely Dr. John Bransford, at Vanderbilt at the *Learning Technology Center* at Peabody College, for providing the perfect working environment to carry out such vision; Michael McCrickard for introducing me to the challenges of getting involved with *Information Technology*, David Law for helping with statistic analysis.

References

1. Zacks, J.M., Speer, N.K., Swallow, K.M., Braver, T.S., Reynolds, J.R.: Event Perception: A Mind-Brain Perspective. Psychological Bulletin 133(2), 273–293 (2007)
2. Lakoff, G.: Women, Fire and Dangerous Things. The University of Chicago Press (1987)
3. Shridar, S.N.: Cognition and Sentence Production. A Cross Linguistic Study. Springer, New York (1985)
4. Osgood, E.C., et Bock, K.J.: Salience and Sentencing: Some Production Principles. In Sentence Production. Developments in Research and Theory. Sheldon Rosenberg. Lawrence Erlbaum Associates Publishers, Hillsdale (1977)
5. Waltz, D.L.: On the Interdependence of Language and Perception. In: Theoretical Issues in Natural Language Processing 2. University of Illinois at Urbana-Champaign. July 25-27 (1978)
6. Jackendoff, R.: An Argument on the Composition of Conceptual Structures. In: Theoretical Issues in Natural Language Processing 2, July 25-27, 1978, University of Illinois at Urbana-Champaign (1978)
7. Schlesinger, I.M.: Production and Comprehension of Utterances. Erlbaum, Hillsdale (1977)
8. Osgood, E.C.: Lectures on Language Performance. Springer, New York (1980)
9. Ferretti, T.R., McRae, K., Hatherell, A.: Integrating Verbs, Situation Schemas, and Thematic Role Concepts. Journal of Memory and Language 44, 516–547 (2001)
10. Parisi, D.: Elementi di Grammatica. Editore Boringhieri, Torino (1973)
11. Pasolini, P.P.: Empirismo Eretico. Saggi Edn. Garzanti (1972)
12. Underwood, G., Jebbett, L., Roberts, K.: Inspecting pictures for information to verify a sentence: Eye movements in general encoding and in focus search. The Quarterly Journal of Experimental Psychology 57A(1), 165–182 (2004)
13. Badecker, W.: On Some Proposals Concerning the Status of Predicate Argument Structure Representations. Brain and Language 40, 373–383 (1991)
14. Canseco-Gonzales, E.: Predicate-Argument Structure as a Link between Linguistic and Non Linguistic Representations. Brain and Language 39, 391–404 (1990)
15. Cognition and Technology Group at Vanderbilt, The Jasper Series as an Example of Anchored Instruction: Theory, Program, Description, and Assessment Data. Educational Psychologist 27(3), 291–315 (1992)
16. Colin, M.: Structures Syntaxiques du Message Filmique. Documents de Travail. Centro Internazionale di Semiotica e di Linguistica. Univesità di Urbino. Settembre-Ottobre (1983,1985)
17. Cordier, F., Pariollaud, F.: From the choice of the patients for a transitive verb to its polysemy. Current Psychology Letters 21(1) (2007)

Appendix

The *CineLingua* CDROM from *We all loved each other so much* by Ettore Scola.
Students watched first the original version with no subtitles of the film segment, then they carried out independent study tasks following the steps on the CDROM. The structure of the multimedia CDROM is shown in Figure 7. The steps to the development of comprehension and production are described here below.

First Step. *Narration Integration. CAPIRE*/Comprehension Skills.
The narration integration includes a string of individual sentences, previously recorded at the pace of normal *teacher's speed*, introducing each film segment by the means of a *narration*. This strategy *situates* the learner without overwhelming her. Additional graphics are provided to accompany the story plot building up comprehension skills. The purpose of this narration is to introduce the new vocabulary by providing additional visual input helping learners better understand the dialogue (See *Capire*/Understanding, Fig. 7).

Second Step. IMPARARE/Learning about discourse and sentence structure.

I. ASCOLTA/LISTENING TO. Developing listening comprehension skills by associating words to visual input.

Level 1 *Ascolta/Listening to.* Each previously selected film segment runs one more time in the narration phase. Aural input is provided. The complete sentence appears on the screen. The film segment matches the narration of the sentence (See Fig. 8).

Level 2 *Stills.* At the end of the playing of each film segment a film-still related to the interaction of the film segment remains on the screen. This screen matches with the verb of the sentence as it appears on the screen (See Fig. 8).

Level 3 *Click.* Each word on the sentence is made *clickable* allowing access to additional graphics, visual input and stills for the acquisition of vocabulary.

II. STRUTTURA/DISCOURSE STRUCTURE. Developing linguistic awareness at the level of the structure of discourse.

Level 1. *Struttura/Discourse structure.* Visual icons appear on the screen representing the structure of each sentence students have already heard. Each icon has a different color to allow for visual association with each sentence topic (agent, predicate, patient) to happen by asking questions of the type: who/what? Does what? How? Why? (See Fig. 9).

Level 2. *Click to hear it.* Each icon releases its "element" (call it topic, predicate, argument, etc) when clicked. The Italian word appears on the screen while it is pronounced one more time.

Level 3. *Click on each sentence element.* Each word in the sentence gives access, when clicked, to a glossary.

Level 4. *Glossary*. This glossary includes: *Noun Phrases*. All the nouns that learners have encountered appear in this list. The goal of this list is to give more specific information about the type of the noun phrase the learner is working with from the specific sentence structure, thus allowing her to become aware of the distinction between agent/patient, subject/object/prepositional phrases without the intervention of metalanguage.

Verbal Phrases. All the verbs that learners have encountered appear in this list. The goal of this list is to give more specific information about the type of verb phrase the learner is working with from the specific structure of the sentence.

Fig. 7. Structure of the *CineLingua* CDROM illustrating Step One and Step Two

Fig. 8. *Illustrated* sentence from the narration integration CAPIRE step

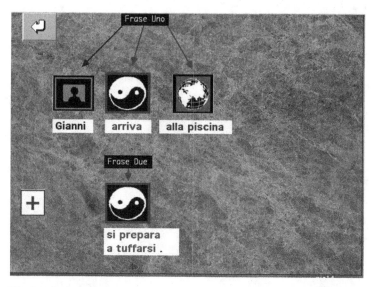

Fig. 9. Who? Does? What? Discourse structure during the IMPARARE step

Author Index